Rehabilitation
Institute of
Chicago

PSYCHOLOGICAL
ASPECTS OF
GERIATRIC
REHABILITATION

AN ASPEN PUBLICATION®
Aspen Publishers, Inc.
Gaithersburg, Maryland
1991

THE REHABILITATION INSTITUTE OF CHICAGO
PUBLICATION SERIES
Don A. Olson, Ph.D., Series Coordinator

Rehabilitation
Institute of
Chicago

PSYCHOLOGICAL ASPECTS OF GERIATRIC REHABILITATION

Edited by
Robert J. Hartke, PhD
Senior Psychologist
Rehabilitation Institute of Chicago
Clinical Associate
Departments of Psychiatry & Behavioral Sciences and
Physical Medicine and Rehabilitation
Northwestern University Medical School
Chicago, Illinois

AN ASPEN PUBLICATION®
Aspen Publishers, Inc.
Gaithersburg, Maryland
1991

Library of Congress Cataloging-in-Publication Data

Psychological aspects of geriatric rehabilitation /
edited by Robert J. Hartke.
p. cm. — (The Rehabilitation Institute of Chicago publication)
(Rehabilitation Institute of Chicago procedure manual) Includes
bibliographical references and index.
ISBN: 0-8342-0211-5
1. Aged—Mental health. 2. Aged—Rehabilitation. I. Hartke, Robert J.
II. Series. III. Series: Rehabilitation Institute of Chicago procedure
manual. [DNLM: 1. Aged—psychology. 2. Rehabilitation—in old age.
3. Rehabilitation—psychology. WB 320 P9735]
RC451.4.A5P7773 1990
618.97'03'019—dc20
DNLM/DLC
for Library of Congress
90-14530
CIP

Editorial Services: Ruth Bloom

Library of Congress Catalog Card Number: 90-14530
ISBN: 0-8342-0211-5

Printed in the United States of America

1 2 3 4 5

What it is like, this growing old—
When your joints start to ache
And you feel the cold
A lot more than you did
In years gone by
And your gait's not so steady
But still you try
'Cause it feels so good
To be alive—
You might even hang together
'Till you reach ——— 95?

A. Isabella Clarke
age 95

Table of Contents

Rebecca Brashler, MSW, ACSW
Social Work Supervisor
Rehabilitation Institute of Chicago
Chicago, Illinois

Robert J. Hartke, PhD
Senior Psychologist
Rehabilitation Institute of Chicago
Clinical Associate
Departments of Psychiatry & Behavioral
    Sciences and
Physical Medicine & Rehabilitation
Northwestern University Medical School
Chicago, Illinois

Michael Horowitz, PhD
Core Faculty
Illinois School of Professional Psychology
Clinical Associate
Department of Psychiatry & Behavioral
    Sciences
Northwestern University Medical School
Chicago, Illinois

Dorene M. Rentz, PsyD
Staff Neuropsychologist
Lecturer on Neurology
Division of Neuroscience and Behavioral
    Neurology
Beth Israel Hospital
    and
Department of Neurology
Harvard Medical School
Boston, Massachusetts

Elliot J. Roth, MD
Assistant Professor of Rehabilitation Medicine
Northwestern University Medical School
Director of Stroke Rehabilitation Program
Rehabilitation Institute of Chicago
Chicago, Illinois

Richard R. Trezona, Jr., PhD
Staff Psychologist
Rehabilitation Institute of Chicago
Clinical Associate
Department of Psychiatry & Behavioral
    Sciences
Northwestern University Medical School
Chicago, Illinois

Series Foreword

In the early 1980s, it became apparent that the future held increasing numbers of older citizens. Since then, many programs have been developed to improve the quality of life for our aging population. However, an important key to the success of these programs frequently has been neglected or totally overlooked. Few of these programs look at the *total* needs of the growing aging population. Rehabilitation as a discipline offers such a model. It is a comprehensive and holistic approach that provides the most effective method of managing the special health care needs of the older population.

I recently visited a friend in the hospital who had sustained a stroke 20 years ago and was now being treated for lung cancer. My friend needed acute medical care that placed her cancer treatment within the context of her prior stroke. Unfortunately, it seemed that only her cancer diagnosis was being considered in her treatment. Little thought was being given to her prior stroke and the limitations it continued to impose upon her in later life. The staff were only minimally accounting for my friend's mobility restrictions, and she was becoming labeled as agitated and resistant. Her caregivers were not attending to her age and her total medical condition. In a similar situation, I recall an older stroke patient who was being evaluated for decreasing strength and fatigue. She was left alone in an examining room without her walking cane, totally immobilizing her for an extended time period. These anecdotes highlight how professional staff can become restricted in their view of older patients and inadvertently mismanage their care. Geriatric health care requires a different approach.

The rehabilitation model views the older person as important; it identifies that person's needs, and provides him or her with opportunity, protection, and encouragement. An older adult's quality of life can be greatly enhanced by timely and appropriate rehabilitation intervention. More and more older people have said to me, "I'm not afraid of dying; I'm afraid of living!" reflecting their fear of surviving, but with an unacceptable quality of life. Such a statement is indeed thought provoking for any health care professional working with older disabled patients. Living can be fraught with difficulty for frail older adults, and unfortunately, it is made even more complicated by the lack of programs available. To successfully treat geriatric patients, we must pay special attention to their unique needs and gain the special knowledge required to help them.

In this book, Dr. Hartke and his colleagues contribute to a better understanding of the psychology of the aging process as it relates to physical disability. Their practical yet scholarly approach will assist all health care professionals treating older adults (physicians, psychologists, social workers, nurses, as well as other allied health professionals) in better understanding their aging patient and delivering effective rehabilitation health care to them. The book uniquely combines an overview of the aging process, a positive approach to adjustment to disability by the older person, and specific recommendations for managing psychological problems in the older disabled patient. This information will enable professionals to facilitate a more stimulating, fruitful, and satisfying life for this patient population.

Psychological Aspects of Geriatric Rehabilitation will challenge you, the reader, to view your older patients as functioning, contributing members of society, and to enter their psychological world to gain insight and sensitivity to the problems confronting them as disabled adults. I feel it is an important addition to the library of any health care professional interested in the geriatric patient.

Don A. Olson, PhD
Director
Education and Training Center
Rehabilitation Institute of Chicago
Associate Professor
Departments of Physical Medicine and
Rehabilitation and Neurology
Northwestern University Medical School
Chicago, Illinois

Preface

Psychological Aspects of Geriatric Rehabilitation is a valuable resource for clinicians with concerns about the mental health of their older patients. The number of older adults utilizing rehabilitation services is rapidly growing and an understanding of the psychology of aging is imperative for their effective treatment. This book is unique in its specific, sole focus on psychological issues in geriatric rehabilitation, permitting more in-depth exploration of this vital topic. In addition, it strives to intermingle concepts and practice in a thought provoking and useful manner. Comprehensive literature reviews are provided with suggested areas for further research, as well as guidelines for clinical practice with illustrative case examples. Topics covered include normative changes associated with aging, the cognitive and emotional components of rehabilitation potential, and the assessment and treatment of psychological problems unique to older adults and their caregivers as they face physical disability. All professions associated with geriatric rehabilitation will find this information helpful to their understanding of the experience of the disabled older adult; treatment disciplines primarily concerned with the mental health of older patients will find the text particularly useful.

This book is guided by the overriding philosophy that later life with a disability need not be simply the end of life. Older adults, formerly dismissed as incapable of intensive rehabilitation, can enhance their quality of life through their own efforts and those of a team of rehabilitation professionals. The present and future challenge in rehabilitation is to meet this need effectively. This text focuses on the psychological issues in that challenge.

Robert J. Hartke
April 1991

Acknowledgments

The editor and contributing authors have many people to thank for their assistance in this project. We extend a note of thanks to Dr. Henry Betts, Chief Executive Officer, and Dr. Don Olson, Director of Education and Training, for their support of such publication efforts at the Rehabilitation Institute of Chicago. We are also grateful to the staff at Aspen Press, Inc. for their professional approach and technical assistance. A special note of thanks to Dr. Yvonne Shade-Zeldow, Director of the Psychology Department, for her encouragement of the project from its very beginnings, thoughtful influence on administrative matters, and review of the text. The authors also acknowledge the generosity of several colleagues who informally reviewed selected chapters of the text: Gloria Tarvin, Marlene Morgan, and Drs. Rosemary King, Meyer Gunther, and Mark Moulthrop. We also thank the several library assistants who worked with us throughout the project including Deirdre Dennehy-Basile, Susan Needham, and Miriam Riggle, as well as Karen Kaluzsa for her technical assistance in literature searches. A project of this longevity and magnitude does not proceed in a vacuum. We are grateful for the cooperation and support of our colleagues in bringing this text to publication.

Chapter 1

Introduction

Robert J. Hartke

WHAT IS *OLD?*

The concept of old is enigmatic. It seems at once simple, yet its meaning is elusive and perplexing. Attempts have been made to define it in an objective as well as a subjective way when, in fact, old may be most accurately conceived as relative.

The objective, statistical approach appears to provide a clear-cut definition of what is old. We are said to be living in an aging society. In the United States, people aged 65 years and older numbered 29.8 million in 1987. This represented 12.3 percent of the population, a figure that has tripled since the turn of the century. People are living longer, and the older population itself is getting even older. The 85 years and older age group, with a 23-fold increase since 1900, is the fastest growing subgroup of older persons (Fowles 1988). Such differential rates of change have prompted analysts to refine age grades of later life development into the young-old (age 65 to 74), the middle-old (age 75 to 84), and the old-old (age 85 or over) (Atchley 1987). Projections for the future indicate a continuation of these societal aging trends. Current predictions suggest that the age group likely to experience the greatest growth into the twenty-first century will be that of those past age 55. With the aging of the baby boom generation, those over 65 years of age will comprise 21.8 percent of the population by the year 2030 (Fowles 1988). These statistics imply the relativity of the concept of old. As the human life span extends and developmental milestones are possibly redelineated, the notion of what is old could clearly change, attesting to the arbitrariness of designating age 65 as the entrance into old age.

Alternatively, the concept of old can also be viewed subjectively as a state of mind, following the adage, "you're only as old as you feel." Such perceptions are influenced by sociocultural trends and the well-documented physical health changes that are an inevitable part of aging. A plethora of positive and negative

1

images of aging have been propagated through the years. At one extreme, older age has been feared as a time of unavoidable dependency and burden on children, disengagement, loss, and regression. At the other extreme, it has been touted as a time of golden prosperity and ultimate wisdom. The major fallacy of such images is the overgeneralization of emotionally charged features purely on the basis of one factor—chronological age. Individuality in personal make-up, most salient in older people by virtue of their lengthy life experience, is summarily discounted.

The term *older* is far more useful in describing later life than is old. It underscores the fact that aging is a dynamic, individualized process, rather than a static state. It also clarifies aging as development, placing it in the broader perspective of the life span and providing the reminder that the 3 year old is aging just as surely as the 83 year old.

GERIATRIC REHABILITATION

Modern rehabilitation medicine in the United States was, as Rusk (1969, 463) said, " . . . conceived in adversity and born of necessity" through the two world wars earlier in the twentieth century. Treatments to ameliorate war injuries, along with the need for vocational training of disabled veterans, were supported by federal legislation and funding. These efforts were born of the desire to return formally robust people to a productive role in society, giving them a fair chance for a satisfying life. Later, the field of rehabilitation concerned itself with polio disabilities, injuries from traumatic accidents in the population at large, and developmental disabilities (Brody and Ruff 1986). From this heritage comes the broad definition of rehabilitation as the process of restoring an individual to his or her former level of physical, mental, and vocational functioning, to the extent possible. As such, it has historically been an enterprise of and for youth (Becker and Kaufman 1988).

With increasing longevity and chronic disease states causing disability, rehabilitation medicine is faced with a growing new group of consumers—older adults. Most older people have at least one chronic condition and many have multiple problems (Fowles 1988). Forty percent of all disabled people are over the age of 65 (Wedgewood 1985). The older segment of the population also uses a disproportionately large amount of medical services. In 1987, older people accounted for 31 percent of all hospital stays and 42 percent of all days of care in hospitals. In 1984, the 65 and older age group was projected to account for 31 percent of total personal health care expenditures in the United States (Fowles 1988).

Recent admissions data at the Rehabilitation Institute of Chicago provide evidence of the growing use of rehabilitation services by older adults (Cichowski

1990). From 1985 to 1989, the percent of admitted patients aged 65 and older has steadily grown from 25 percent to 38 percent. During this five year period, 11.4 percent of admissions in the 65 and older age group were in the 85 to 94 year age range (i.e., the old-old). In contrast, the length of stay in acute rehabilitation has steadily decreased for those 65 years or older from an average of 37 days in 1985 to 27 days in 1989. It is likely that this represents both the national trend toward containment of health care costs and the growing admission of older adults who are good candidates for a short course of rehabilitation (e.g., after orthopedic surgery). Finally, this five year data base shows 68.6 percent of patients 65 years and older being discharged to a home environment versus 18.9 percent transitioning to some form of extended care facility. In sum, these statistics represent the growing use of inpatient rehabilitation services by older adults, especially the old-old; the expectation that they will quickly engage in therapy and benefit in a short time; and the continuing involvement of families in the rehabilitative care of elders. These national and local data confirm Brody and Ruff's (1986, xiv) comment that " . . . rehabilitation has come of and to age."

Geriatric rehabilitation requires notable shifts in the thinking of rehabilitation professionals, at both practical and conceptual levels. Rehabilitation with the older adult remains a process of restoring functional capacity, but not usually for the purpose of resuming gainful employment or monetary societal contribution. Geriatric rehabilitation sets as its goals the return of older adults to optimal function (including independence, *where possible,* or assisted independence) and, overall, the maintenance of a satisfying quality of life (Hyde and Tynan 1990). Ideally, this is accomplished by providing comprehensive functional evaluation and treatment service to the elder and his/her support system by way of an interdisciplinary treatment team.

The practice of geriatric rehabilitation involves several treatment distinctions as outlined by Brummel-Smith (1990). Older adults usually present with more than one primary medical problem and have age-appropriate biologic and psychologic changes which must be considered in treatment planning and goal setting. They require close primary medical supervision throughout the rehabilitation process, pacing of physically and cognitively demanding treatments, and routine cognitive/emotional evaluation, especially for underlying dementia and depression. Older rehabilitation patients are more susceptible to secondary complications which can become intermingled and deadly; they are more sensitive to the complexities of their environment, functionally and emotionally. Their caregiving systems, both formal and informal, tend to be more elaborate and, many times, over-stressed, requiring the attention of the rehabilitation treatment team. Finally, older patients face the double prejudice, held by themselves, by health care providers, and by society at large, against being old *and* disabled.

The philosophy of geriatric rehabilitation also involves a fundamental conceptual shift. Whereas earlier definitions of rehabilitation with younger patient

groups stress goals of independence and vocational reintegration, geriatric rehabilitation sets goals of restoration, where possible, and enhanced quality of life.
These are less "bankable" achievements. Historically, the expense of rehabilitation has been justified on the basis of returning people with disabilities to a productive, tax-paying status in society. Similarly, the rehabilitation of older adults
is sometimes justified as being less expensive than the cost of long-term custodial care of the nonrehabilitated (Binstock 1986). However, enhanced quality of
life, a major goal of geriatric rehabilitation, has no clear monetary translation.
This goal requires rethinking the intrinsic value of older adults in modern society and moving away from "work-oriented" rehabilitation to "caring-oriented"
rehabilitation (Eisdorfer 1986, 360).

PSYCHOLOGY AND GERIATRIC REHABILITATION

As a behavioral science, psychology has much to contribute to the work of
geriatric rehabilitation. Psychology involves the study of all facets of human behavior—development, cognition, motivation and emotion, personality and adjustment. These are all critical aspects of the older physically disabled person,
perhaps even more than in youth, as physical and mental systems become more
interdependent and reactive to each other with increasing age. An understanding
of the psychology of aging assists clinicians in distinguishing normal from
pathological changes in older adults, and physical from emotional problems. It
helps with understanding the dynamics of relationships between the older patient
and a youthful treatment team, as well as between the elder and a caregiving
family. Along with other social sciences, psychology conceptualizes the larger
picture of social systems, including their support and prejudices, in which the
older adult functions.

Psychologists, as members of rehabilitation treatment teams, can offer vital
services of emotional and cognitive assessment, psychotherapy, consultation,
and research. They can collaborate with other disciplines represented on the
treatment team to understand and manage the behavior of a poorly coping elder,
his/her adjustment to disability, the rehabilitation environment, and caregiving
systems. However, whether these functions are performed by a psychologist, as
the team's mental health professional, may be less important than recognition of
the need for all members of a geriatric rehabilitation team to develop an appreciation for the psychology of aging and incorporate it into their treatment planning. It has been the goal of this book to focus on various aspects of the psychology of aging, particularly as they relate to physical disability and rehabilitation.
It strives to inform rehabilitation professionals interested in geriatrics at both a
conceptual and clinical level.

OVERVIEW AND RATIONALE OF THE TEXT

This text was conceived as a hybrid of sorts—including scholarly, academic issues, as well as practical, clinical applications. It was felt that a clinical work would be incomplete without theoretical and research foundations. To this end, the initial two chapters beyond the introduction are heavily documented and are intended as references for the reader desiring an overview of aging processes. Later chapters provide theoretical formulations and supporting research where appropriate but have a primary intention of assisting the reader clinically. The book is derived from experience in acute inpatient rehabilitation with older adults and largely focuses on this setting. Certainly, the future will demand increasing variation in the settings for geriatric rehabilitation, including home therapy programming, outpatient and day hospital treatments, as well as less intense rehabilitation in extended care facilities. The psychological principles discussed herein will have application in these settings but may require some mental transpositions to make them applicable. Finally, the text assumes a basic level of understanding about the practice of physical rehabilitation in order to concentrate specifically on psychological issues in older adults. The philosophy of rehabilitation is discussed only to the degree that it may require reconceptualization in the case of geriatrics. The value of comprehensive functional evaluation and treatment and an understanding of the operation of an interdisciplinary treatment team are also assumed.

The inherent tension of the work of an interdisciplinary treatment team, requiring collaboration at many levels, also reflects the dilemma of addressing such a diverse audience in this book without territorializing or inadvertently offending a certain segment of readers. The readership is intended to be professionals from all disciplines of rehabilitation, but, admittedly, those who are more exclusively concerned with the psychological welfare of their older patients will find the majority of the text most relevant. Readers from less related disciplines will find selected chapters of greatest interest, and the book has been designed so that chapters are sufficiently independent of one another to be easily read separately.

In order to provide a common foundation, Chapter 2, The Aging Process: Physiological Changes, and Chapter 3, The Aging Process: Cognition, Personality, and Coping, review normative somatic and psychological changes associated with the aging process. These chapters are intended to heighten the reader's awareness of the complex background of normative physical changes against which an older adult experiences a disability, as well as to clarify possible misconceptions about usual changes with age in psychological functioning. Chapter 4, The Older Adult's Adjustment to the Rehabilitation Setting, focuses on how the older patient interacts with the rehabilitation environment to arrive at a functional hospital adjustment. Drawing upon theories of the ecology of aging, it describes the experience of hospitalization and strategies to facilitate acclimation. Chapter 5, The Assessment of Rehabilitation Potential: Cognitive Factors, and Chapter 6, The Assessment of Rehabilitation Potential: Emotional Factors, address a different issue of growing importance: identifying and assessing the psychological factors essential to reasonable rehabilitation potential in the older adult. These two chapters provide a review of pertinent outcome literature, speculate on cognitive and emotional factors essential to successful performance in geriatric rehabilitation, and suggest ways of assessing them. Chapter 5 particularly questions the belief that cognitively compromised older adults have no rehabilitation potential. Chapter 7, The Neuropsychological Assessment of Dementia in a Rehabilitation Setting, and Chapter 8, Management of the Cognitively Impaired Older Patient, also concentrate on the cognitively impaired older rehabilitation patient. The prevalence of dementia as a primary or coexisting disabling condition increases in significance with older patients, making this an essential area of concern for the professional in geriatric rehabilitation. Chapter 7 provides a comprehensive description of the dementia syndromes prevalent in an older rehabilitation patient population and the neuropsychological instruments relevant to their assessment. Chapter 8 discusses the management of such patients with an emphasis on behavioral prosthetics to compensate for incompetencies and avert catastrophic reactions. Chapter 9, Assessment and Treatment of Depression in the Older Rehabilitation Patient, deals with the problem of depression in older adulthood, specifically as it relates to physical disability. Differential diagnosis, alternative conceptualizations of the disorder, assessment instruments, and treatment approaches are reviewed and applied to rehabilitation. Chapter 10, Transference and Countertransference in the Therapeutic Relationship with the Older Adult, broadens the focus of the psychology of geriatric rehabilitation to consider the dynamics of the patient and therapist interaction. Drawing upon the psychoanalytic concepts of transference and countertransference, this chapter examines how patients' and staff's projection of values, conflicts, and suppositions about aging can facilitate or inhibit any therapeutic relationship in the rehabilitation setting. Chapter 11, Psychotherapy with the Older Rehabilitation Patient, discusses the unique aspects of conducting psychotherapy in a rehabilitation setting with older adults. An array of individual and group intervention formats are described, as are special issues frequently arising in psychotherapy with older adults. Finally, Chapter 12, The Caregiving Family for the Disabled Older Adult, shifts the focus to the role of significant others in caring for disabled elders. The chapter covers issues of identification and types of caregivers, assisting them in discharge planning, stress management, and the legal/ethical implications of surrogate decision making.

Aging and the risk of disability are both realities of life. Aging is inevitable; disability is possible and appears to be more probable with increasing age. As the natural life span continues to increase, some form of chronic illness and disability may become a normative developmental challenge in later life. The overriding philosophy of this text has been to validate a positive approach to aging, providing opportunities for maintenance, adaptation, and growth instead of automatic psychological regression or pathology. Physical disabilities are viewed as a health crisis confronting older people. Inherent in their longevity is a richness of life experience which can be tapped to elucidate strengths, define and compensate for weaknesses, and, hopefully, sustain satisfactory life quality through rehabilitation efforts.

Finally, this text advances the idea that chronological age is a simplistic, ill-informed criterion for judging the likelihood that an older patient will draw benefit from rehabilitation efforts. Older adults are viable candidates for rehabilitation; the question is whether rehabilitation can mature to serve the needs of the elder population. The unique features of older adulthood and the complications they impose are not the problem. Rather, they are the issues or the data with which one must deal. The challenge becomes to manipulate the vast array of existing health care policies, rehabilitation settings and approaches to meet the needs of the older health care consumer. It is hoped that this book will support current and future efforts toward that goal.

REFERENCES

Atchley, R.C. 1987. Age grading and grouping. In *The Encyclopedia of Aging,* edited by G.L. Maddox, 15. New York: Springer Publishing Company.

Becker, G., and S. Kaufman. 1988. Old age, rehabilitation, and research: A review of the issues. *The Gerontologist* 28: 459–68.

Binstock, R.H. 1986. Aging and rehabilitation: The birth of a social movement. In *Aging and Rehabilitation: Advances in the State of the Art,* edited by S.J. Brody and G.E. Ruff, 349–56. New York: Springer Publishing Company.

Brody, S.J., and G.E. Ruff. 1986. Preface. In *Aging and Rehabilitation: Advances in the State of the Art,* edited by S.J. Brody and G.E. Ruff, xiii–xviii. New York: Springer Publishing Company.

Brummel-Smith, K. 1990. Introduction. In *Geriatric Rehabilitation,* edited by B. Kemp, K. Brummel-Smith, and J.W. Ramsdell, 3–21. Boston: Little, Brown and Company.

Cichowski, K. 1990. *Program Evaluation and Follow-up Data System.* Chicago: Rehabilitation Institute of Chicago.

Eisdorfer, C. 1986. Aging and rehabilitation: Summary of meeting. In *Aging and Rehabilitation: Advances in the State of the Art,* edited by S.J. Brody and G.E. Ruff, 357–64. New York: Springer Publishing Company.

Fowles, D.G. 1988. *A Profile of Older Americans: 1988.* Washington, D.C.: American Association of Retired Persons.

Hyde, J.C., and M. Tynan. 1990. Geriatric rehabilitation: A policy definition. *Geriatric Rehabilitation Preview* 2, no. 2: 2. California: Rehabilitation Research and Training Center on Aging, Rancho Los Amigos Medical Center.

Rusk, H.A. 1969. The growth and development of rehabilitation medicine. *Archives of Physical Medicine and Rehabilitation* 50: 463–66.

Wedgewood, J. 1985. The place of rehabilitation in geriatric medicine: An overview. *International Rehabilitation Medicine* 7: 107.

Chapter 2

The Aging Process: Physiological Changes

Elliot J. Roth

THE AGING PROCESS IN PERSPECTIVE

Aging is a process and not a disease. There are numerous aspects of the aging process and consequently many different definitions and ways of conceptualizing the physiological changes of aging. Biologists note that aging is associated with a variety of biological changes. These alterations may include reductions in the integrity and functional viability of specific anatomic structures and physiologic processes and increases in the vulnerability of the individual to the adverse effects of various internal or external perturbations (Comfort 1979). Many of the processes of aging are characterized by a progressive decline in the ability of the body's organ systems to maintain homeostasis under conditions of physiological stress (Williams 1984). This gradual loss of function may ultimately progress to partial or total organ system failure or, alternatively, may remain subclinical, exerting no impact on the clinical state.

Aging involves a variety of continuously active processes such as maturation of some organ systems, steady erosion of the reserves of other systems, altered efficiency of homeostatic controls, and modified susceptibility to the effects of certain widely prevalent diseases of aging (Costa and Andres 1986). Clearly, these changes may have a profound impact on the processes of recovery and adaptation from acute illnesses or chronic conditions. Initiation of rehabilitation may be delayed, participation in an exercise program may be compromised, rehabilitation treatment planning and goal setting may be revised, and the process of psychological adaptation may be altered as a result of these changes. As a consequence, all members of the rehabilitation management team must work together to optimize medical management, maximize physical function, facilitate emotional adaptation, and recruit social resources of the older patient.

Biological problems of aging generally can be grouped into two broad but distinct categories: (1) gradual progressive physiological changes in various organ systems, and (2) specific diseases which tend to be more common in older individuals. It is important to note, however, that the progressive changes related to age and the discrete disease entities seen in older individuals are related to each other in subtle and complex ways (Williams 1984).

The majority of older individuals (four of every five) have at least one chronic condition and most have multiple medical problems (Kovar 1977). Conditions commonly found among older persons include arthritis (53 percent), hypertension (42 percent), hearing impairment (40 percent), heart disease (34 percent), cataracts (23 percent), orthopedic impairments (19 percent), visual impairments (14 percent), cerebrovascular disease (10 percent), and diabetes (10 percent). As a consequence, older people require and consume a sizable portion of health care resources (Fowles 1986).

Numerous biopsychosocial factors interact to determine the actual format and outcome of the aging process for any given individual (Costa and Andres 1986). As a consequence of the multiplicity of determinant factors, aging occurs at different rates and with different patterns for different individuals. Even within an individual person, different biological processes and organ systems demonstrate different rates and patterns of aging (Berman et al. 1979; Williams 1984).

This profound variability in the nature and magnitude of the effects of aging on the person is one of the most important concepts in geriatric care (Berman et al. 1979; Rowe 1977; Shock 1967; Williams 1984). Some individuals, and some systems within individuals, have enormous compensatory capabilities. Other individuals and systems have extensive reserves or a large "safety margin." This means that some degree of function may be diminished over time without affecting the overall homeostatic balance of the system (Kenney 1989; Rowe and Kahn 1987; Shock 1983).

This variability not only makes the establishment of a single definition or a broad overview statement on aging virtually impossible, but also poses an important challenge to clinicians involved with geriatric care. The presence of these intra- and inter-individual differences mandates that highly specific diagnostic assessment considerations and extensive individualization of therapeutic management approaches be provided for these patients. Practically speaking, this variability means that a large number of older people enjoy good health even into their later years, while others suffer the adverse effects of what may otherwise be relatively minor clinical problems. Most patients fall somewhere in between these two extremes (Kenney 1989; Rowe and Kahn 1987; Shock 1983), but it is the unpredictable nature of the aging process that is important in practical clinical care.

Despite the wide range of types of clinical manifestations of aging, certain common themes emerge during the biological process of aging and maturation. The complexities and intricacies of these specific biological functions, together with the large and growing size and significance of the aging population in our society, underscore the importance of understanding specific fundamental and applied concepts of the biological aspects of the aging process. Knowledge of these changes helps to focus management. Understanding the types or patterns of the alterations which may take place in these physiologic processes provides the rehabilitation professional with a perspective on the variety of physical challenges facing the aging individual. It also gives the clinician an insight into the nature of and the quality of life which older people experience.

This chapter provides a detailed description of the usual biological changes which occur as various bodily systems age. It also discusses special physical issues pertinent to geriatric rehabilitation and concludes with comments on health promotion and prevention for use with older adults. Any detailed description of physical aging unavoidably creates a negative impression of inevitable depletion and loss of resiliency. While there is a certain degree of reality to such an impression, it is important to remember that it is the variability in aging patterns that matters most. The human body is endowed with elaborate systems for compensation and a vast amount of reserve function despite the changes that aging can bring. In addition, advances in medical science continue to provide mechanisms for revision or remediation of losses. These facts allow the majority of older adults to function quite adequately even with some form of chronic illness. It is the balance or harmony of their bodily systems which becomes more delicately poised and creates the need for special medical and rehabilitative considerations when they are faced with a major disability. This chapter is intended as a reference resource for the allied health professional in geriatric rehabilitation. It will hopefully provide an appreciation for the variety of changes to physical systems that evolve with the passage of a lifetime and how they will affect the course of an older adult's rehabilitation.

PHYSIOLOGICAL CHANGES WITH AGING

The Skin

Obvious changes in skin structures include dryness, wrinkling, laxity, and pigment changes. Microscopically, there is a reduction in the degree of contiguity between the superficial epidermis layer and the deeper dermis layer. This results in functional declines in the communication between layers, lack of adequate nutrition of the superficial structures, and a decline in the ability to resist infection and trauma. A twenty percent loss of thickness of the dermis layer, immediately beneath the surface of the skin, accounts for the "thinning" quality of the skin in older adults. The portion of the skin layer that remains has limited vascularity, which may account for the gradual atrophy and scarring often seen in the other skin layers, hair follicles, sweat glands, and sebaceous glands

(Gilchrest 1982, 1986; Gomez and Berman 1985; Kenney 1989; MacMillan 1985; Shuster et al. 1975). Clinically, wound healing may be delayed or slowed somewhat, or the patient may be more prone to pressure sores (Kenney 1989).

Age-related loss of the functional barrier of the skin results in easier entry into and more extensive spread of irritants and toxins throughout the system. Loss of this barrier also contributes to impaired thermoregulation. Other common changes with aging include increased vulnerability to injury, poor wound healing, and weakened scarring. Finally, because the skin is a major component of the body's mechanism for the production and handling of Vitamin D, which is important in calcium absorption and utilization, age-related skin changes may decrease the calcium content of bones and indirectly increase the risk of fractures (Gilchrest 1982, 1986; Kenney 1989).

As can occur in other organ systems, some individuals have skin which has remarkable resilience to the effects of aging, with no alteration in its protective function and a minimum of thinning and wrinkling.

Body Composition

Changes in fluid volumes, electrolyte concentrations, body composition, and tissue structure are frequent but not universal findings among older people. There is a slight loss of height (Miall et al. 1967), weight (Forbes 1976; Master et al. 1960), and total body surface area, and a significant loss of active cell mass, most of which comes from muscle. From ages 25 to 75 years, the proportion of fat content increases by a factor of two (from 14 to 30 percent) (Durnin and Womersley 1974; Goldman 1970; Williams 1984) while both the total body water content and muscle mass decrease (Goldman 1970; Kenney 1989; Lye 1985).

At age 25, total body water represents 60 percent of total body mass for men and 52 percent of total body mass for women. By age 75, the proportions of total body water are 54 percent for men and 46 percent for women. Moreover, at age 25, that water volume is divided into 40 percent intracellular fluid and 20 percent extracellular fluid. By age 75, only 30 percent is intracellular and 24 percent is extracellular. This means that there is cellular *dehydration*. Generally, concentrations of electrolytes in the blood remain unchanged in the normal process of aging. Total blood volume quantities also remain unaffected by aging, as does functioning of the mechanoreceptors in the blood vessel walls which respond to blood volume (Kenney 1989). Clinically, it is common for older patients to readily become dehydrated or to have electrolyte abnormalities, especially when certain pathological or disease stressors are superimposed on the system (Leaf 1984; Phillips et al. 1984). Impaired thirst mechanisms contribute to this problem (Miller et al. 1982; Phillips et al. 1984).

Collagen, an important supporting protein found in numerous structures dispersed throughout the body, shows many changes with aging (Kenney 1989). These changes consist of decreased distensibility, increased rigidity, and decreased strength of the collagen. This means that tissues in which collagen is found, such as the skin and blood vessel walls, are weaker and have less deformability in shape in older persons than they do in younger individuals. As a consequence, the strength of the skin, ligaments, and other supporting structures is markedly reduced with age (MacMillan 1985).

The Endrocrine System

Except in the thyroid, which demonstrates gradual involution, age-related changes in the endrocrine system and its hormones generally are considered relatively minor. However, perturbations or "challenges" to the system may unmask what otherwise may be latent problems (Dolocek 1985; Noth and Mazzaferri 1985).

Pituitary

Changes in many of the pituitary hormone concentrations, including growth hormone, prolactin, thyrotropin, and corticotropin (ACTH), are minimal, as they are in the structure of the pituitary itself (Kenney 1989). Exceptions include follicle stimulating and lutenizing hormones (involved in reproductive organ supply) and antidiuretic hormone (also known as vasopressin, involved with maintenance of fluid volume and blood pressure), which show increases (Kenney 1989).

Thyroid

The thyroid gland undergoes a slow, insidious deterioration with age, resulting in a decrease in the secretion of thyroid hormones (Crantz and Crantz 1983; Hodkinson and Irvine 1985). This trend is thought to result from an autoimmune process. It often, but not always, continues to the point of nearly complete and clinically apparent thyroid failure late in its course. Because the thyroid gland and its hormones are actively involved in the processes of regulating enzyme levels and carrying out metabolic processes, these negative changes in thyroid function with aging result in a reduction in the basal metabolic rate.

Abnormalities in the heart, peripheral nerve and muscle function, and the body's handling of fluids, electrolytes, and metabolic processes are common problems resulting from thyroid dysfunction. Hypothyroidism may also contribute to depression and to the onset of dementia. Because the changes of hypothyroidism are potentially reversible with management, evaluation of thyroid function in older patients, especially in those with dementia, is critical.

"Biochemical" hypothyroidism, in which the patient has asymptomatic reductions in circulating thyroid hormone levels, has been found in 13 percent of apparently healthy subjects over 60 years of age (Rosenthal et al. 1987; Sawin et al. 1983; Sawin et al. 1985; Sawin et al. 1989). Because signs and symptoms of hypothyroidism are often atypical or completely absent in older individuals, routine screening of thyroid hormone levels in older people is recommended (Bahemuka and Hodkinson 1975).

Variability of responses to aging is a hallmark of the thyroid, as it is in many other systems. Many people suffer no clinical effects of thyroid changes, while others may demonstrate symptoms such as depression, weight loss, weakness, and cardiac dysfunction. For many of the patients, the course is a slow, insidious one that often is not recognized until late in the course of the disease.

Adrenal Cortex

Aldosterone secretion by the adrenal gland also has been found to decline with advancing age (Hegsted et al. 1983; Noth et al. 1977; Zadik and Kowarski 1980). Both the urinary excretion rate and the plasma concentration of aldosterone are lower in older individuals than in younger people. Plasma renin activity also decreases with age, probably as a secondary consequence of the reduction in aldosterone (Hegsted et al. 1983; Noth et al. 1977). Both of these changes affect the body's response to fluid, salt, and postural alterations. Thus, reductions of aldosterone and renin may ultimately predispose older adults to hypotension and electrolyte abnormalities. Glucocorticoids (steroids), which represent one component of the body's response to physiological stress, do not change significantly in their concentrations (Kenney 1989).

Pancreas

Insulin concentrations remain stable, but there is a deterioration in glucose tolerance with aging (FitzGerald and Kilvert 1985; Kenney 1989). This means that there are changes in the functional properties of insulin as the individual grows older. Some patients develop diabetes in later life. This syndrome is known as *maturity-onset* diabetes, and is a separate entity from the age-related changes in insulin and sugar handling (FitzGerald and Kilvert 1985).

Immune Response

Changes in immune function with age were first studied systematically more than 30 years ago when Makinodian and Walford (Walford 1969) established the field of *immunogerontology*. Characteristic features of immune senescence have been well described by many authors since that time (Fox 1985; Weksler 1983, 1986). The body's immune response can be classified into two categories—antibody-mediated and cell-mediated. Both are impaired in older people (Fox 1985; Mackay 1972; Weksler 1986).

The concentrations of the antibodies that fight infection tend not to change significantly with age, but their functional capabilities appear to be altered (Fox 1985; Pahwa et al. 1981; Patel 1981). Likewise, the bone marrow, which is the ultimate site of origin of these antibodies, has cells which are normal in appearance, but which are immature in function.

Age-related involution of the thymus gland, the structure that is involved in the production of immunologically active T-lymphocyte cells, is a universal finding in all individuals as they age, and occurs to such an extent in older individuals that the gland is reduced to 5 to 10 percent of its original mass (Boyd 1932; Lewis et al. 1978; Singh and Singh 1979; Weksler 1986). Again, while the absolute number of these lymphocytes does not change, the functional capacities of the cells are diminished (Fox 1985; Moody et al. 1981). Clearly, there are qualitative changes which adversely affect the efficiency and effectiveness of the immune system.

Clinically, these age-related changes in the immune system greatly increase the susceptibility of older people to a variety of viral and bacterial infectious diseases (Fox 1985; Weksler 1986). Immune senescence also tends to increase the severity and persistence of these conditions when they do occur. In addition, with increasing age there are increased chances of silent or unusual presentations of infection, unfavorable outcomes, and altered responses to antibiotic treatment. There also may be reactivation of latent infections with age. An example of a reactivated latent infection is herpes zoster virus re-infection, also known as shingles, which is a *reexpression* on the nerves and skin of the virus that caused chicken pox in earlier life (Hope-Simpson 1965; Weksler 1986). The relative suppression of the immune system in older persons is the major reason that shingles is five times more common in this age group than in younger individuals (Berger et al. 1981; Hope-Simpson 1965).

The frequencies of tuberculosis, influenza, septicemia, gastrointestinal salmonella infection, urinary tract infection, pneumonia, and bronchitis also increase in older adults because of the decline in immune function (Fox 1985; Haley et al. 1981; Stamm 1978). A number of other changes predispose the older individual to infection. These factors include prolonged immobility, chronic debilitation, dehydration and malnutrition, impaired physical capabilities, and morphological alterations in the lungs, gastrointestinal tract, and urinary tract (Fox 1985). Addressing each of these factors may help to limit the adverse impact on the course and outcome of infections in older adults. This is especially important in view of the mortality and medical morbidity associated with these infectious processes.

Rehabilitation professionals should be aware of the clinical implications of these factors, and of the positive impact which they may effect on them during the course of treatment. It is the responsibility of the treatment team to minimize the duration of bedrest and to remobilize the patient as early as possible. It is also critical that members of the treatment team attend to the nutritional and hydration needs of their patients. Early recognition of signs of infection, even if subtle, and prompt institution of appropriate physical and pharmacological therapy may help to ameliorate the effects of intercurrent illness on the course of recovery.

The Respiratory System

Respiratory function generally decreases with advancing age, as a result of anatomical and physiological changes which occur in the lungs and surrounding chest wall (Anderson et al. 1986; Cander and Moyer 1965; Pierce and Elbert 1958; Pump 1971). The alveolar sacs, which hold air and allow its diffusion to and from the bloodstream, enlarge progressively with age and join together with adjacent alveoli. This process of coalescence and dilatation ruptures alveolar walls, decreasing the surface area available for passage of air between the surrounding atmosphere and the blood. There is also a decrease in the supporting connective tissue of the lung, a loss of elastic recoil (reducing airway diameter), and a consequent increase in resistance of the airway to airflow. Progressive cartilage calcification and especially kyphoscoliosis may reduce the degree of contraction of the chest wall muscles, thereby decreasing the extent to which the chest may expand to draw in air (Anderson et al. 1986).

There is also diminished ciliary clearance and cough, increasing the risk of retained secretions and pneumonia with aging. In addition, there is a change in the central control of ventilation, resulting in a reduction of the respiratory response to a low blood oxygen level. In normal older adults, the response of the lungs to an imposed decline in the oxygen level of the blood is only 50 percent of the level it would be in normal young subjects (Berger et al. 1977; Peterson et al. 1981).

As a result of these morphological and regulatory changes, clinical pulmonary function testing, performed using a spirometer, shows reductions in both vital capacity (the degree of chest expansion during inspiration) and forced expiratory volume in one second (FEV_1—the rate at which air is exhaled) by 20 to 30 cc per year (Morris et al. 1971; Niewoehner and Kleinerman 1974; Schmidt et al. 1975). The work of breathing is 20 percent greater at age sixty than at age twenty, and the loss of the alveolar wall surface area results in a progressive drop in the arterial oxygen tension with age. Notably, the maximum possible oxygen consumption rate which can occur with exercise or stress declines.

Probably the most significant clinical implication of these respiratory changes results from the reduced bronchial elimination ability and impaired cough mechanism. These physiological alterations result in retention of bronchial secretions and pneumonia. As a consequence, pneumonias are extremely common in geriatric patients, and, when they occur, tend to be more severe in nature and difficult to treat. Indeed, pneumonia is the major cause of death in the old-old age group (Fox 1985).

Despite these changes, it has been noted that if cardiovascular and neuromuscular systems are relatively free of disease, then the progressive changes in pulmonary status will consist primarily of a loss of reserve capacity without obvious functional limitations (Keltz 1984; Larson and Bruce 1987; Naughton 1982). Regular exercise may actually improve cardiopulmonary fitness at any age. Training will increase oxygen consumption, enhance efficiency, decrease oxygen cost of effort, improve cardiopulmonary reserves, and reduce vulnerability to future stresses (Keltz 1984; Larson and Bruce 1987; Naughton 1982).

The Cardiovascular System

Heart

In the heart, aging is accompanied not only by several progressive pathologic and functional changes, but also by an increased incidence of some cardiac diseases (Fleg 1988; Kenney 1989; Kotler et al. 1986; Rodstein 1982; Verghese and Smith 1986; Weisfeldt 1980). Anatomic changes may be seen in the cardiac muscle, in the electrical pacemaker and conduction system, and in the supporting connective tissue structures (Kitzman et al. 1988; Lie and Hammond 1988; Roberts 1988; Scholz et al. 1988; Waller 1988). Functionally, there are decreases in the resting heart rate, in the myocardial contractility (the strength and force of each cardiac contraction), in the stroke volume (the volume of blood pumped during each contraction), and, consequently, in the cardiac output (the overall amount of blood pumped by the heart to the rest of the body each minute) (Brandfonbrenner et al. 1955; Kenney 1989).

Under ordinary conditions of rest and health, these changes may have no or minimal clinical significance. The normal aging heart is capable of generating adequate cardiac output to provide necessary blood and nutrients to the body. However, under conditions of physiological stress, exercise, or disease, the pumping ability of the aging heart often is unable to meet the needs of the peripheral tissues, especially the muscles. This may manifest itself acutely as fatigue, overwork of the heart, angina pectoris, congestive heart failure, arrhythmias, or other clinical problems. More typically, cardiac changes with advancing age present chronically or insidiously with gradually reduced exercise tolerance, limited endurance, easy and early fatigability, and a compromised ability to maintain prolonged sustained activity. Exercise tolerance level demonstrates a clear age-dependent decline.

It is important to note, however, that these age-related changes in cardiac output at rest and with exercise may be variable; advanced age need not necessarily result in a decline in exercise tolerance. Further, there is considerable evidence that conditioning exercises may actually improve functional capacity, or at least forestall the development of age-related changes in older adults (Larson and Bruce 1987; Morley and Reese 1989; Posner et al. 1986; Renlund and Gerstenblith 1987).

Most of the common cardiac disorders, such as coronary heart disease (CHD), congestive heart failure, and arrhythmias, are seen predominantly in old age. Despite the 37 percent decline in mortality from coronary heart disease over the past 20 years, CHD still accounts for approximately one-half of all deaths in older people (Caird et al. 1985). Even when nonfatal, CHD causes serious medical morbidity, with prolonged or complicated hospitalizations and additional limitations in functional capabilities. About two-thirds or more of all older people demonstrate a significant degree of coronary stenosis at autopsy. Clinically, CHD may present asymptomatically or with angina pectoris, myocardial infarction, arrhythmias, or abnormal electrocardiograms.

These findings suggest that significant coronary occlusion may occur in a large proportion of older people, and that clinical manifestations of CHD may be variable. Roth and associates (1988), for example, found that 34 percent of patients with stroke experienced cardiovascular complications during their hospitalization for comprehensive inpatient rehabilitation. These facts warrant careful assessment and application of appropriate precautions before and during physical activity (Smith 1988; Wenger et al. 1988). Roth and associates used a simple noninvasive monitoring system for assessing the cardiovascular response to physical therapy exercise in patients with stroke (Roth et al. 1986) and in those with amputation (Roth et al. 1990) who underwent rehabilitation.

Vascular System

Two structural changes within the peripheral arterial system are most prominent with age (Caird et al. 1985; Haimovici 1986; Kenney 1989). First, elasticity of the arterial wall is diminished, resulting in "stiff" arteries. This can result in an elevation in systolic blood pressure, a common finding in older adults.

Second, atherosclerotic plaque development, consisting of fatty material, calcium deposits, clotting factors, platelets, and other cells and cellular components, is common in and adjacent to the arterial wall. Atherosclerosis is virtually ubiquitous in the aging population, although the pattern, degree, distribution, and clinical manifestations of these changes may vary. Atherosclerotic changes result in a narrowing or stenosis of the arteries, reduced blood flow and a tendency toward arterial occlusion. Ischemia of end organs results in peripheral vascular disease of the trunk and extremities, cerebrovascular disease in the brain, and coronary heart disease in the heart.

The Genitourinary System

Kidneys

The size and weight of the kidneys decrease with age. These changes result from several processes, including a progressive decrease in the number of glomeruli (the microscopic functional units of the kidney) to about one-third to one-half of its baseline number by age 70 (Anderson and Brenner 1986). Other age-related alterations include biochemical and morphological changes in the supporting structures within the kidney tissue, progressive fibrosis, narrowing of the renal arteries, and changes in the tubules which allow passage of fluid through the kidneys (Feinstein 1985).

The remaining functioning glomeruli and tubules initially show compensatory hypertrophy, and for considerable time are able to maintain homeostasis of fluids and electrolytes. However, for some patients, this compensatory mechanism is insufficient to slow the progressive decline in function with age. Thus, the rate at which the glomeruli filter toxins from the blood progressively falls as the kidneys age. For example, clearance by the kidneys of urea progressively drops from a mean of 82 cc/min for younger subjects to a mean of 62 cc/min for subjects aged 60 years or more. However, serum creatinine levels, which signify renal function, often rise only slightly with aging, from under 1.0 mg/dl in the young to a maximum of 1.5 mg/dl in the older group; higher creatinine levels are due to intercurrent disease, and not to aging alone (Feinstein 1985). As in other physiological functions, focus on mean changes in renal parameters tends to hide the remarkable individual variation that is present in the kidneys of older adults. The number of "extra" or reserve glomeruli, and the degree to which these remaining functioning kidney units are able to compensate show profound variability. This is evidenced by the finding that up to one-third of all older adults demonstrate no change in clearance capabilities of the kidneys (Lonergan 1988).

For those patients in whom renal function does decline, decreased excretion of drugs and the body's metabolites may result from these impaired clearance mechanisms. This is one reason that older individuals experience medication effects for longer durations. There is also a risk of volume overload in which the vasculature has too much fluid, causing diffusion or seepage of fluid into the interstitial supporting tissues and generalized edema. Overt chronic renal failure may occur from the aging process alone, but the more common presentation is that of reduced renal function reserve. Thus, the typical problem among older adults is one of an increased susceptibility to renal failure induced by toxins (often medications) or other disease processes.

Bladder

Urinary incontinence is one of the most common and troubling of the clinical consequences of the aging process (Brocklehurst 1985a; Dontas et al. 1981; Hadley 1986; Hu et al. 1989; Nicolle et al. 1983; Nordenstam et al. 1986; Office of Medical Applications of Research—National Institutes of Health 1989; Resnick and Yalla 1985; Resnick and Yalla 1987; Sier et al. 1987; Williams and Pannill 1982). Its prevalence among older people ranges between 13 percent and 89 percent, depending on the definition of incontinence and on the group studied. Widely accepted prevalence figures approximate 15 percent of older adults in community settings and 50 percent in extended care facilities. Incontinence tends to affect women more than men, and its medical and social implications are extensive. The pathogenesis of urinary incontinence is multifactorial, and may include urinary tract infection, vaginitis, pelvic floor muscle weakness, neurologic dysfunction (neurogenic bladder from neuropathy, stroke, or other neurologic disorder), acute confusional state or dementia, prostate enlargement, or other factors. Many of these factors are potentially reversible, or are well managed with medical, surgical, or behavioral interventions. Thorough, conscientious evaluation and institution of appropriate treatment are critical to the remediation of incontinence and its consequences.

Genital System

In the male, changes begin to occur in the prostate gland after forty years of age. These changes consist of progressive fibrosis and connective tissue accumulation and are known collectively as benign prostatic hypertrophy. This syndrome, which is virtually ubiquitous in men as they age, can present with urinary hesitancy, incontinence, frequency, or urgency and is usually amenable to treatment by some form of prostatectomy. Prostatic cancer accounts for increasing proportions of cancer mortality in men. Prostate carcinoma may be present in 10 to 20 percent of men in their sixties and in 20 to 40 percent of men over seventy years old. Testicular cells show some fibrosis and involution. The production of sperm may be reduced by 30 to 50 percent in later years but does continue into advanced age for most men (Blacklock 1985).

Female sex hormone levels decline with age. As a consequence, the supportive connective tissue of the uterus, vagina, and fallopian tubes diminishes, and the organs decrease in size and in function. Loss of supporting structures also occurs in the breasts with advancing age (Brown 1985; Kenney 1989).

Sexual response times may be slower in older adults, and the quality of the libido, erection, ejaculation, or vaginal lubrication may be altered. However, these anatomical and physiological changes belie an important clinical observation: Full, normal, enjoyable sexual activity and relationships may continue well into later life, provided that general health is preserved (Post 1985). Specific approaches may be used to address sexual problems among older people, when they occur.

The Gastrointestinal Tract

Structural and functional changes occur at all levels of the gastrointestinal tract with aging. Most of these changes are characterized by loss of motility and of secretory function. In addition, certain discrete disease processes may be superimposed on these gradually progressive changes.

Mouth

Changes in the teeth and gums of older adults are generally more a reflection of dental hygiene than of aging alone (Kenney 1989). Loss of teeth, especially in the upper jaw, occurs because of changes in the enamel, dental pulp, supporting cement substance, gums (gingiva), and bone. While prosthetic teeth replacements may reduce taste and texture sensation, they are extremely useful to achieve and maintain a normal nutritional state. Frequently, a relatively simple dental intervention can help to both resolve major medical problems posed by malnutrition and improve self-esteem by restoring normal appearance.

Esophagus

Degenerative changes of the muscle in the wall of the esophagus result in alterations of esophageal motility, known as presbyesophagus (Brandt 1986a; Dymock 1985; Kenney 1989; Khan et al. 1977; Soergel et al. 1964). Esophageal peristalsis contractions are weaker and slower in older individuals, resulting in more frequent dysphagia (swallowing dysfunction) and delayed emptying of food into the stomach (Khan et al. 1977). Esophageal spasm, reflux esophagitis (heartburn), hiatal hernias, and other structural changes (such as lower esophageal "rings" and diverticuli) are common in older people. Hiatal hernias, for example, have a progressive increase in incidence from 10 percent in individuals under 40 years of age to 40 percent in 50 to 70 year olds and 70 percent in those older than seventy years (Brandt 1986a; Brick and Amory 1950). Esophageal cancer, a particularly virulent malignancy that accounts for 2 percent of all cancers, occurs most frequently between 50 and 70 years of age (Brandt 1986a; Langman 1971; Miller 1962).

Stomach

In the stomach, there is a diminution of gastric acid secretory function both at rest and in response to a meal (Andrews et al. 1967; Baron 1963; Bockus et al. 1932; Brandt 1986a; Dymock 1985; Palmer 1954). The condition known as atrophic gastritis is common among older adults, and is characterized by a reduction in the number of cells in the stomach lining, with an accompanying reduction in the volume of gastric acid secreted (Bock et al. 1963; Joske et al. 1955; Strickland and Mackay 1973). There is a reduced intensity and frequency of peristaltic movement of the stomach and a significant increase in gastric emptying time. Pernicious anemia is a disease involving the specific stomach lining cells which are indirectly involved with the absorption of Vitamin B_{12}. This disorder is also common with aging, and can have an insidious onset, either asymptomatically or with symptoms of weakness, sore tongue, and paresthesias (Brandt 1986a).

Peptic ulcer disease, both in the stomach and in the duodenum, is also common in the older age group (McKeown 1965; Mulsow 1941). For unknown reasons, the incidence of this disease is increasing (Brandt 1986a). With advancing age, ulcers often run a more virulent course (Narayanan and Steinheber 1976), with more acute presentations and more frequent complications of extensive bleeding, perforation, obstruction, intractability, and death. This complication rate rises progressively from 31 percent in patients aged 60 to 64 years old to 76 percent in those 75 to 7⁰ years old (Brandt 1986a; Brooks and Eralklis 1964; Leverat et al. 1966; Stafford et al. 1956). The course can be an indolent one, however, with chronic weight loss, malnutrition, chronic fatigue or weakness, and poor health as the only symptoms of ulcer disease in some older individuals (Brandt 1986a).

Stomach cancer, usually incurable at the time of diagnosis, is decreasing in frequency among older adults and increasing in frequency among younger people, for unknown reasons. Its presentation is similar to that of ulcer disease, causing diagnostic difficulties at times. However, these symptoms are often not produced until late in the course of the disease, reducing the likelihood of favorable responses to combined surgical, chemotherapeutic, and radiation treatments (Brandt 1986a).

Small Intestine

Duodenal ulcers are the most common problem in the small intestine (Brandt 1986a; Leverat et al. 1966), as noted above. In addition, progressive changes occur in the structure of the intestinal wall. The weight of the small bowel decreases after the fifth decade; the cells which line the intestine are shorter and wider, and there is a slowing of the turnover and production rates of new cells

(Brandt 1986a). As a consequence, the functional capacity of the intestines decreases with age. This results in vitamin deficiencies, reduced absorption of fats and carbohydrates (Feibusch and Holt 1982), electrolyte changes, and weight loss. Certain other conditions, such as celiac sprue, bacterial overgrowth syndrome, intestinal obstruction, fistulas, and cancer of the small bowel occur with some frequency in older age (Brandt 1986a) and present with various combinations of symptoms, including reduced appetite, nausea, emesis, diarrhea, weight loss, and cramping abdominal pain (Brandt 1986a). These conditions often are amenable to treatment if recognized early.

Large Intestine

As seen in the upper gastrointestinal system, the most significant changes seen in the large bowel with aging are decreased secretory functions and decreased motility (Brocklehurst 1985b). Morphological changes include atrophy of bowel cells, fibrosis of the bowel wall, and abnormalities of its secretory glands and of its muscle layer. There is a prolonged transit time through the bowel, and retention of fecal material (Brocklehurst and Khan 1960).

Clinically, the most common problem is constipation, which occurs in one-third or more of older adults (Brandt 1986b; Brocklehurst 1985b; Connel et al. 1965; Hinton and Lennard-Jones 1968; Milne and Williamson 1972). In addition to the age-related microscopic changes in the bowel, other factors contributing to constipation include depression, immobility, dehydration, neurological dysfunction, metabolic disorders, and endocrine diseases. Usually an increase in dietary fiber intake, increased fluid intake, and adjustments in personal habits are sufficient to correct the problem. Periodically, stool softeners, laxatives, enemas, or other interventions are required (Brocklehurst 1985b).

Other problems, including diverticulosis (outpouchings of the bowel wall), ischemic colitis (from atherosclerosis of the intestinal vessels), antibiotic-associated colitis (from Clostridium difficile bacterial overgrowth), and carcinoma of the colon and rectum (with an incidence rate of 80 per 100,000 at age 65 and a rate of 220 per 100,000 at age 85) are common and clinically significant problems for older adults (Brandt 1986b; Brocklehurst 1985b; Calabrese et al. 1973; Slater et al. 1982).

Liver

The liver loses weight with age as the number of functioning liver cells declines (Boyd 1933). There are also reductions in liver blood flow, metabolic capability of individual liver cells, and regenerative ability (Brandt 1986c). These changes result in a reduced overall capacity for drug and body chemical metabolism.

The Musculoskeletal System

Bones and Joints

Loss of skeletal mass is a normal, and at times disabling, consequence of aging. Osteoporosis is defined as a reduction in the amount of bone in the skeleton (Exton-Smith 1985). In women, bone quantity declines at a rate of about 0.5 percent per year after the fourth decade of life and about 2 percent per year during the fifth decade of life. The strength of the skeleton and the ability of bone to withstand trauma are dependent upon bone mass. In addition to a steady loss of bone mass, which may amount to 15 to 20 percent loss in the spine and 10 to 15 percent loss in the long bones, there is a large increase in the risk of bony fractures (Exton-Smith 1985, Kenney 1989). The large majority of these fractures occur in the neck of the femur, located at the hip. However, vertebrae, pelvis, and distal forearm (*Colles' fracture*) also are common locations for fractures in older adults. Estrogen replacement therapy, supplemental oral calcium, fluoride supplementation, exercise, and activity are extremely important measures to prevent and treat osteoporotic changes and their consequent fractures (Grisso and Attie 1989).

As age advances, the cartilage tissues that line the joints decline in cell number, metabolic activity, and function. They become dehydrated, more fibrous, and show signs of degeneration. There is often proliferation of bony spurs, known as osteophytes, in those areas. As a result of their development, degenerative arthritis, called osteoarthritis, occurs in and around many joints of the body. It may result in pain, deformity, limitations in range of motion, and progressive disability (Gardner and O'Connor 1985).

Degenerative disease of the intervertebral discs and vertebrae, known as spondylosis or spinal stenosis, also may result in pain and stiffness, located in the neck or back. In this condition, the proximity of the affected bony structures to the spinal cord and peripheral nerves may predispose the patient to additional disability resulting from neurologic dysfunction (myelopathy or radiculopathy), superimposed on the arthritis.

Muscles

Age-related muscle atrophy is a universal finding, and results from diminutions in both the number of muscle fibers and the size of each motor unit. About 30 percent of muscle mass in the body is lost between 30 and 80 years of age (Grimby et al. 1982; Grimby and Saltin 1983; Kenney 1989; Young et al. 1985). There are microscopic ultrastructural changes in the muscle cells as well. Muscle wasting occurs first and most noticeably in the small muscles of the hand, resulting in both an atrophic appearing hand and a loss of grip strength. Changes have also been found in leg muscles. Interestingly, there is considerable recent evidence that many of these changes may be prevented by exercise. A series of studies have demonstrated the value of a structured exercise program in retarding the physical losses in older adulthood (Grimby 1988; Grimby 1990; Larson and Bruce 1987). One recent study (Fiatarone et al. 1990) indicated that high-intensity weight training led to significant improvements in muscle strength, size, and functional mobility in frail persons who reside in nursing homes, even up to age 96.

Certain diseases of muscle, such as polymiositis and polymyalgia rheumatica, occur predominantly in older individuals.

The Nervous System

Brain

The general aging pattern of slow continuous decline in function seen in other organ systems occurs in some areas of neurologic functioning but spares others. Various anatomic and physiologic changes may be found in the aging brain.

There may be a decrease in cerebral blood flow (Fazekas et al. 1952; Katzman and Terry 1983), reflecting the metabolic needs of the brain, as measured by radioisotopic nuclear medicine studies. In addition, electroencephalographic changes, consisting of diffuse slowing of alpha wave frequency and other findings, are not uncommon (Davis 1941; Drechsler 1978; Hubbard et al. 1976; Katzman and Terry 1983; Otomo 1966). Computed tomography of the head in older adults often reveals both cerebral atrophy and ventricular enlargement (Jacoby et al. 1980; Katzman and Terry 1983; Roberts and Caird 1976; Yamamura et al. 1980).

Microscopically, the brains of older individuals reveal generalized neuronal atrophy, with reductions in each cell type by about 25 percent at age 65 (Brody 1955; Tomlinson 1977). Certain parts of the brain, especially the frontal and temporal lobes and the basal ganglia, demonstrate cell loss more than other areas (Bugiani et al. 1978). Within the nerve cells, there may be a dramatic reduction in the complexity of the cell structure. This results from a marked loss in the number, density, and length of dendrites, and some shrinkage and distortion of the cell body (Scheibel and Scheibel 1975). The dendrites are responsible for the synapses, or connections, with other nerve cells; their loss represents significant changes in clinical neurological functioning. Other common microscopic changes in the aging brain include the presence of lipofuscin, neurofibrillary tangles, and neuritic plaques (Dayan 1970; Katzman and Terry 1983; Mann and Sinclair 1978). Concentrations of some of the neurotransmitters may also be reduced (Katzman and Terry 1983; McGeer and McGeer 1976).

The specific pattern, distribution, and locations of these age-related morphological and biochemical changes give rise to the specific pattern of neurologic function or dysfunction seen clinically. There is no direct correlation between these structural changes and cognitive function, however. Chapter 3 of this text provides detailed information on normal age-related changes in cognitive functioning, and Chapter 7 discusses the changes associated with dementia.

Somatosensory System

Aging is almost universally accompanied by a gradual deterioration of sensory modalities, including declines in sensitivity to light touch, pinprick sensation, deep pain perception, position sense, and especially vibratory sensation. These clinical manifestations are uniquely and almost uniformly found in the distal lower extremities. Microscopically, a loss of the number and integrity of the peripheral receptors accounts for these alterations. These changes raise the sensitivity thresholds for pain, temperature, and perceived movement, and increase the risk of thermal and mechanical injury (Kenney 1989; Schaumburg et al. 1983).

Visual System

Deterioration of vision is a frequently recognized change with age and occurs because of several progressive, degenerative changes in the eyes (Kini et al. 1978; Wright and Henkind 1983). The prevalence of visual impairment is 6 percent in individuals under 65 years and 46 percent in those over 85 years. The most common visual manifestations of the aging process are cataracts, glaucoma, and macular degeneration. Known as presbyopia, the major age-related change in vision consists of a gradual loss of the ability of the lens to change its thickness and its curvature to focus on near objects. In addition to a marked decline in near vision, there may also be reductions in depth perception, sensitivity to glare, and color discrimination (Kenney 1989; Wright and Henkind 1983).

As the lens of the eye continues to evolve throughout life, old and drying lens fibers are compressed into the center of the lens. These fibers undergo sclerosis, producing an opacity in the center of the lens, which progressively increases in size. This opacity, called a cataract, is a common physiologic concomitant of the aging process and is one of the most important causes of loss of vision in the aged. Cataracts make near vision progressively more difficult over time. Some degree of lens opacification is present in 95 percent of the population over 65 years of age. Therapeutic intervention, in which the cataract is extracted from the eye, is considered when the impaired vision interferes with the individual's ability to function (Kenney 1989; Kini et al. 1978; McGuinness 1978; Sperduto and Seigel 1980; Wright and Henkind 1983). This safe and relatively simple procedure may greatly improve vision and thereby significantly enhance function.

Glaucoma is a condition of increased pressure inside the eye causing structural damage and functional loss of vision. This can be manifested as visual field defects. Reduction of intraocular pressure and prevention of blindness can be achieved with medical or surgical intervention. This is important, as glaucoma is one of the most common causes of blindness in later life (Kenney 1989; Kini et al. 1978; Wright and Henkind 1983).

Macular degeneration is defined as a progressive loss of the posterior portion of the eye, which contains the retina and photoreceptor cells responsible for reading and transmitting visual stimuli. With advancing age, there appears to be a gradual breakdown in the metabolic processes of these receptor cells, and eventual functional loss. As a consequence, damage to central vision may be profound. Unfortunately, no therapeutic intervention can correct this process, which is thought to be the leading cause of irremediable vision disturbance in older adults (Kenney 1989; Kini et al. 1978; Sarks 1976; Wright and Henkind 1983).

Auditory System

Major hearing impairment affects more than 25 percent of older people (Ruben and Kruger 1983). The prevalence rate increases steadily with advancing age from 6.5 percent for ages 45 to 64 to 48 percent for people between 75 and 79 years old. Hearing impairments in older adults may be classified as *conductive,* in which problems in the external or middle ear result in impaired sound sensitivity, or as *sensorineural,* in which a dysfunctional cochlea, auditory nerve, or central nervous system distorts the perception of sound. Clinically, there is a shrinkage of the frequency range, loss of auditory acuity, decline in the sensitivity for higher frequencies, and possibly, tinnitus (ringing of the ears) (Kenney 1989; Ruben and Kruger 1983).

The hearing loss of aging, known as presbycusis, occurs for unknown reasons but is usually secondary to loss of hair cells in the cochlea of the inner ear or changes of other sound receptor organ structures. Other causes of hearing loss may occur in older adults as well, including outer ear wax (cerumen) obstruction, middle ear infections (otitis media), and tumors such as acoustic neuromas. Early identification of these problems is important for several reasons. Many of these conditions may be reversible and amenable to treatment. Moreover, if aural rehabilitation and hearing aid use are instituted in a timely fashion, it is possible to avoid the additional functional decline, cognitive impairment, and social isolation, which often accompany the progressive hearing loss of aging (American Academy of Otolaryngology 1979). Frequently, the older patient is reluctant to accept the hearing aid because of the social stigma associated with its use. Overcoming this reluctance is an important step in the hearing rehabilitation process.

Balance and Equilibrium

The vestibular apparatus of older adults demonstrates a loss of receptor organs and their supporting structures. Consequently, the precision with which the motor system can maintain a stable posture is reduced. There may be unsteadiness in the standing or walking positions, postural sway, and wide-based gait. The complications of impaired equilibrium sense are compounded by reductions in position sense and central processing ability. These problems all contribute to the high frequency of falls documented in older adults (Kenney 1989).

SPECIAL CONSIDERATIONS IN GERIATRIC REHABILITATION

Altered Clinical Presentation of Disease

Frequently, common medical problems are manifested in unusual ways in older adults. For example, older patients with infections such as pneumonia or urinary tract infection may present only with symptoms of mental confusion; patients with acute heart disease may present asymptomatically with only laboratory investigation abnormality; patients with subdural hematoma may demonstrate only slow and mild deterioration in cognition or gait; and patients with ulcer disease may present with chronic weight loss (Burston and Moore-Smith 1970; Fox 1985; O'Dell 1988; Osmer and Cole 1966).

Three factors are thought to have an impact on the altered presentation of illness in an older person (Williams 1984). The first is an underreporting of illness, which may result from personal attitudes, social isolation, a perception of an unresponsive system of medical care, depression, denial, or economic fears. Altered patterns or distributions of illness make up the second factor adversely affecting the presentation of disease in older individuals. The accumulation of multiple chronic disorders is a feature of illness presentation in this age group. Finally, older adults have altered responses to illness. Manifestations of clinically important diseases are often attenuated, and serious diseases may remain latent for prolonged periods. At times, symptoms in one organ system may reflect abnormalities in another (Williams 1984).

The clinical implications of knowledge of these altered presentations are clear; medical management of the older person requires: first, a high index of suspicion for a variety of clinical conditions; second, conscientious assessment of every symptom, sign, and laboratory abnormality in an older person; and third, rapid identification of problems and institution of appropriate treatment when they do occur.

Altered Response to Drugs

Older adults are especially sensitive to the effects of drugs, including not only their intended pharmacologic effects, but also their untoward or adverse effects (German and Burton 1989; Ouslander 1981). This is an important clinical point because medications are used frequently by older adults. About one of every four prescription medications are taken by those over 65 years of age (Everitt and Avorn 1986; Vestal 1984). Because of interactions between various drugs, the altered response to medications is complicated by the *polypharmacy* phenomenon frequently seen in older people. The average older adult takes twice as many prescription medications as the average younger person. One study found that older women took an average of 5.7 prescription medications and 3.2 over-the-counter medications concurrently (Vestal 1984). Naturally, combining drugs may predispose the patient to more adverse effects.

A variety of additional factors contribute to altered drug reactions seen with advanced age (Greenblatt et al. 1982; Montamat et al. 1989; Ouslander 1981). These include variable compliance and physiologic changes due to aging or intercurrent disease, resulting in altered absorption, distribution, metabolism, and excretion of the drug (Greenblatt et al. 1982; Montamat et al. 1989; Ouslander 1981). As a consequence of these physiologic changes, the incidence of adverse side effects increases with age and with the number of drugs taken. The overall incidence of adverse reactions in older adults is 10 to 20 percent, which is about two to three times that found in young adults (Gardner and Cluff 1970).

Factors that may interfere with successful drug therapy have been identified and include failure to recognize symptoms of disease or adverse effects, altered reporting and presentation of illness and abnormality, multiplicity and complexity of illnesses, diminished sensation or cognition, and age-related changes in the body's handling and metabolism of the drug (Greenblatt et al. 1982; Kramer 1987; Ouslander 1981; Williamson 1985).

Physiologic changes which alter the way in which medications are handled by the body may occur in the absorption, distribution, metabolism, or excretion of the drug. Each of these changes may influence the effects of the drug on the system, by prolonging or shortening the duration of its activity, or by changing the qualitative nature of its effects (Greenblatt et al. 1982; Ouslander 1981; Williamson 1985). Extensive reviews of specific changes for a myriad of medications, including analgesics, laxatives, cardiovascular drugs, antibiotics, psychotropic medications, and others have been done (O'Malley et al. 1980; Ouslander 1981; Richey and Bender 1977; Vestal 1984).

Psychoactive agents are frequently prescribed for older adults to manage depression, confusion, agitation, anxiety, and insomnia. Unfortunately, the physiologic effects of aging often combine with the effects of the medications to induce more confusion, depression, or lethargy. For this reason, it is generally recommended that psychotropic medications be prescribed for older adults in doses 30 to 50 percent as large as those for younger people, if at all (Allen 1986; Jenike 1988; Larson et al. 1987; Thompson et al. 1983a, 1983b).

It is critical that the number of all medications used for any patient be minimized and that the dosages of medications be titrated. It is incumbent upon the clinician to reassess each medication, its indications, and its effects frequently and carefully for each patient, and to review its benefits and risks repeatedly.

Twelve general recommendations for prescribing for geriatric patients were enumerated by Ouslander (1981), and are listed in Exhibit 2-1. The two goals of insuring safety while enhancing effectiveness of drug therapy can be achieved by careful consideration of all aspects of the patient's clinical status, meticulous attention to the potential changes of aging, knowledge of drug effects and interactions, and a high degree of caution before and during medication use.

Altered Balance and Gait: Falls

About one of every three persons over the age of 65 years living in the community suffers a fall (Campbell et al. 1981; Tinetti and Speechley 1989). In institutions, falls occur at a rate of approximately 1,600 per 1,000 patients per

---

Exhibit 2-1 Guidelines for Medication Use in Older Adults

1. Evaluate carefully for previously undetected conditions that may affect drug therapy;
2. Manage medical problems without drugs when possible;
3. Avoid interactions between newly prescribed drugs, currently used drugs, and underlying conditions;
4. Start with small doses and increase gradually;
5. Adjust dosages according to age-related declines in renal function;
6. Adjust dosages for changes in liver metabolic function;
7. Measure drug concentration in the blood, when available;
8. Individualize and simplify the drug regimen as much as possible;
9. Consider altered memory, vision, and hearing when providing medication instructions;
10. Insure compliance by asking about availability of a pharmacy, ability to afford medications, and ability to open containers;
11. Use family and visiting health professionals to insure compliance;
12. Monitor the patient frequently for compliance, drug effects, and toxicity.

Source: Reprinted with permission from *Annals of Internal Medicine*, Vol. 95, p. 719, © 1981.

year. Injury is the sixth leading cause of death in this age group, causing about 9,500 deaths each year (Baker and Harvey 1985). About 5 percent of falls result in a bony fracture, 5 to 10 percent result in other serious injuries, many more result in serious soft tissue injuries, and a few result in devastating injuries such as subdural hematoma or cervical fracture (Tinetti and Speechley 1989).

Falls are an important clinical problem, not only because of their frequency, but also because of their physical, psychological, and social consequences. In addition, a fall may be an indicator of an occult medical problem and may suggest the need for comprehensive medical or neurologic evaluation.

Risk factors for falling include advancing age, cognitive impairment, gait and balance problems, diminished hearing and vision, musculoskeletal or neurologic disorders, decreased functional status, medication use (especially psychotropic medications), and postural blood pressure decline (Grisso and Attie 1989; Morris et al. 1987; Prudham and Evans 1981; Tinetti and Speechley 1989; Wild et al. 1980). Tinetti and associates (1986) have developed a Fall Risk Index, based on the older patient's number of chronic disabilities, which may be helpful for the clinician in identifying and managing this problem in older adults.

Prevention of falls relies on careful clinical assessment and on the institution of common sense environmental modifications such as adequate lighting, use of nonskid floors, availability of grab bars, and use of firm, low heel shoes (Daleiden 1990; Grisso and Attie 1989; Tideiksaar 1989; Tinetti and Speechley 1989).

PREVENTIVE MANAGEMENT OF OLDER ADULTS

Preventive geriatrics is not an oxymoron. Although the concept of health promotion and prevention in older adults may seem contradictory, practicing preventive medicine and maintenance are probably the keys to successful aging. Most prevention programs employ life style changes, medical screening, frequent assessments, close monitoring, and regular follow-up (Lavizzo-Mourey and Diserens 1989; Williamson 1985).

Disease Prevention

About 5 percent of older individuals have severe visual impairment and about 25 percent have hearing impairments (Koopman 1982; Padula 1982). Detection of sensory loss and its restoration or compensation may eradicate the confusion, depression, and isolation that accompany these disabilities and may enhance physical functioning.

Injuries are the fifth leading cause of death in persons older than 65 years; about five million persons over 65 sustain nonfatal injuries each year (Rubenstein 1983). Early recognition of somatosensory and equilibrium disorders, accurate assessment of level of functional independence in personal care, mobility, and homemaking, and timely institution of training to prevent injury are important. These measures may help to enhance or restore function, develop compensatory strategies, and prevent additional functional decline.

Medications are used widely by older adults, and about one-third of them report adverse reactions to these drugs (Klein et al. 1984; Seidel et al. 1966). Increased awareness of the potential for drug interactions and of the age-related changes in the way the body handles drugs may help to minimize the clinical impact of these problems. Medications should be used judiciously, and clinicians should be careful to review medications and their effects, especially with older patients.

Vaccines against the influenza virus and the pneumococcal bacteria are profoundly underutilized with older adults. Such available preventive measures have the potential for sharply reducing the morbidity and mortality of infections caused by these organisms (Sims 1989; Stultz 1984).

Certain specific diseases are particularly common among older adults. These include heart disease, hypertension, cancer, stroke, and arthritis. Careful and thorough assessment, close and frequent monitoring, and attention to details in the patient's presentation of signs, symptoms, and laboratory test results may allow both early identification and effective treatment. Examples of such assessment techniques include blood pressure checks, breast and rectal examinations, and testing for occult rectal blood. Specific screening criteria and frequencies have been developed (Day 1989a, 1989b).

Health Promotion

Maintenance of adequate nutrition is extremely important. Training of older adults in methods of proper nutritional maintenance is often taken for granted. Dietary assessment and management should not be neglected, as an estimated one-third of older individuals have dietary deficiencies. Despite this finding, approximately one-half of physicians fail to recognize malnutrition. Awareness and remediation of these problems can help to alleviate the incidence of infection, debility, dehydration, and metabolic disorders (Lavizzo-Mourey and Diserens 1989).

Unfortunately, older people often become unnecessarily sedentary. Only 36 percent of those over 65 years of age reported taking walks in a 1975 study (Lavizzo-Mourey and Diserens 1989). However, there is considerable scientific evidence that exercise programs can result in improved fitness, with increased aerobic capacity, muscle strength, flexibility, coordination, and range of motion (Council on Scientific Affairs—American Medical Association 1984; Fuller 1982; Valbona and Baker 1984). Because much of the functional decline seen in old age is a result of generalized deconditioning and associated loss of endurance, it is possible that the institution of an exercise program may increase levels of independence in self-care and mobility skill performance.

It is estimated that 15 percent of older adults smoke and 10 percent of older adults abuse alcohol (Remington et al. 1985; Stultz 1984). These behaviors serve to both accentuate the physiologic effects of aging and contribute to the occurrence of disease on their own. Their effects are often reversible, even in older people, if exposure to the inciting agent is stopped.

Fortunately, older adults are usually a receptive audience to proposed health practice and behavior changes (Lavizzo-Mourey and Diserens 1989). A 1979 National Center for Health Statistics study found that the prevalence of favorable health practices increases with age. A 1986 Harris Poll study found that those over 65 years of age had the best prevention scores on a survey of 21 health-seeking behaviors and had more interest in receiving guidance in health-promotion techniques from professionals than any other age group studied. However, only 30 percent of the older adults indicated that they had been counseled on disease prevention in the previous five years. Other studies have verified these findings (Huag 1981; Leventhal and Prohaska 1986; Prohaska et al. 1985). Clearly, clinicians can and should incorporate more health-promotion activities into their geriatric practices.

CONCLUSION: GERIATRIC REHABILITATION—A NEW LOOK

Recognizing the multiple physiologic problems of aging and understanding methods of prevention and remediation are critical for effective medical and rehabilitation management strategies. No single guideline or unique solution exists to address the issues facing the older adult. The expression of the aging process is too variable in quality, type, pattern, and timing. However, eight general clinical characteristics which distinguish geriatric patients from their younger counterparts have been enumerated and are listed in Exhibit 2-2. Often, these changes necessitate the restructuring of goals of medical, rehabilitative, and therapeutic management.

While designing a therapeutic program for the older adult and during active rehabilitation, it is important to remember that older adults often require more time to accomplish their tasks, have multiple medical problems, and frequently have a disability superimposed on a number of age-related physiologic disturb-

Exhibit 2-2 Common Clinical Features of Older Adults

---

1. Multiplicity and complexity of diseases;
2. Altered functional response of many organ systems;
3. Chronicity of disease or disability;
4. Greater severity of acute illness with slower, more protracted recovery;
5. Impairments in functional abilities;
6. Fragility of response to illness, stress, or intervention;
7. Instability of economic and social supports;
8. Limitations in reversibility of impairments.

Source: Reprinted with permission from *Annals of Internal Medicine,* Vol. 95, p. 372, © 1981.

---

ances. The deconditioning that is associated with aging may further impair functional ability, although this is an avoidable phenomenon.

It is also important to remember that there is profound variability in the pattern of aging from person to person. Compensation, hypertrophy, extra functional reserves, and reversability are characteristic of some of the body's systems. Therefore, the functional impact of a particular anatomical or physiological change may be minimal. On the other hand, many individuals experience rapidly progressive and significant losses.

Many psychological barriers interfere with maintaining or improving functional abilities in the older adult. Apathy, depression, ignorance, and especially attitudinal stumbling blocks, on the part of both patients and professionals, may significantly impair function and outcome (Hesse et al. 1984; Kemp 1986). Successful aging (Rowe and Kahn 1987) and successful restoration and maintenance of function rely in part on awareness of the influence of these important psychosocial factors on physical function, and also on anticipation, prevention, and appropriate intervention for these factors.

A favorable rehabilitation outcome depends upon conscientious information gathering, and realistic goals aimed at maximizing function and minimizing morbidity and mortality. Given the complex interrelationships of medical problems in older adults, comprehensive assessment and treatment planning is essential and should include medical, psychosocial, and functional considerations.

The goals of geriatric rehabilitative treatment must be kept realistic and mutually acceptable to patient and professional alike. They should be supported with sufficient time, resources, and opportunity for their achievement. Reliance on a team of experienced professionals who are sensitive to the problems of older adults and knowledgeable of the resources available for them improves the likelihood of achieving these goals and discharging the patient to continue a productive life.

REFERENCES

Allen, R.M. 1986. Tranquilizers and sedative/hypnotics: Appropriate use in the elderly. *Geriatrics* 41: 75–88.

American Academy of Otolaryngology. 1979. Guide for the evaluation of hearing handicaps. *Journal of the American Medical Association* 241: 2055.

Anderson, S., and B.M. Brenner. 1986. Effects of aging on the renal glomerulus. *American Journal of Medicine* 80: 435–42.

Anderson, W.M., G.G. Ryerson, and J.W. Wynne. 1986. Pulmonary disease in the elderly. In *Clinical Geriatrics*, 3d ed., edited by I. Rossman, 230–59. Philadelphia: J.B. Lippincott.

Andrews, G.R., B. Haneman, and B.J. Arnold. 1967. Atrophic gastritis in the aged. *Australian Annals of Medicine* 16: 230–5.

Bahemuka, M., and H.M. Hodkinson. 1975. Screening for hypothyroidism in elderly inpatients. *British Medical Journal* 2: 601–3.

Baker, S.P., and A.H. Harvey. 1985. Fall injuries in the elderly. *Clinics in Geriatric Medicine* 1: 501–12.

Baron, J.H. 1963. Studies of basal and peak acid output with an augmented histamine test. *Gut* 4: 136–44.

Berger, R., G. Florent, and M. Just. 1981. Decrease of the lymphoproliferative response to varicella-zoster virus antigen in the aged. *Infection and Immunity* 32: 34.

Berger, A.J., R.A. Mitchell, and J.W. Severinghaus. 1977. Regulation of respiration. *New England Journal of Medicine* 297: 92, 138, 194.

Berman, R., E. Corwin, M.B. Davidson, P.K. Hench, J.P. Murphy, T.R. Reiff, and A.J.J. Wood. 1979. Update on the basic science of aging. *Patient Care* 13: 24–67.

Blacklock, N.J. 1985. The genitourinary system—the prostate. In *Textbook of Geriatric Medicine and Gerontology*, 3d ed., edited by J.C. Brocklehurst, 648–58. Edinburgh: Churchill-Livingstone.

Bock, O.A.A., W.C.D. Richards, and L.J. Witts. 1963. The relationship between acid secretion after augmented histaminic stimulation and the histology of the gastric mucosa. *Gut* 4: 112–14.

Bockus, H.L., J. Bank, and J.H. Willard. 1932. Achlorhydria with a review of 210 cases in patients with gastrointestinal complaints. *American Journal of the Medical Sciences* 184: 185–200.

Boyd, E. 1932. The weight of the thymus gland in health and in disease. *American Journal of Diseases in Children* 43: 1162.

Boyd, E. 1933. Normal variability in weight of the adult human liver and spleen. *Archives of Pathology* 16: 350–72.

Brandfonbrenner, M., M. Landowne, and N.W. Shock. 1955. Changes in cardiac output with age. *Circulation* 12: 447.

Brandt, L.J. 1986a. Gastrointestinal disorders in the elderly. In *Clinical Geriatrics*, 3d ed., edited by I. Rossman, 260–77. Philadelphia: J.B. Lippincott.

Brandt, L.J. 1986b. The colon and retroperitoneum. In *Clinical Geriatrics*, 3d ed., edited by I. Rossman, 278–301. Philadelphia: J.B. Lippincott.

Brandt, L.J. 1986c. Pancreas, liver, and gall bladder. In *Clinical Geriatrics*, 3d ed., edited by I. Rossman, 302–25. Philadelphia: J.B. Lippincott.

Brick, I.B., and H.I. Amory. 1950. Incidence of hiatus hernia in patients without symptoms. *Archives of Surgery* 60: 1045–50.

Brocklehurst, J.C. 1985a. The genitourinary system—the bladder. In *Textbook of Geriatric Medicine and Gerontology*, 3d ed., edited by J.C. Brocklehurst, 626–47. Edinburgh: Churchill-Livingstone.

Brocklehurst, J.C. 1985b. The gastrointestinal system—the large bowel. In *Textbook of Geriatric Medicine and Gerontology*, 3d ed., edited by J.C. Brocklehurst, 534–56. Edinburgh: Churchill-Livingstone.

Brocklehurst, J.C., and Y. Khan. 1960. A study of fecal stasis in old age and use of Dorbanex in its prevention. *Gerontologia Clinica* 11: 293–300.

Brody, H. 1955. Organization of the cerebral cortex. III. A study of aging in the human cerebral cortex. *Journal of Comparative Neurology* 102: 511.

Brooks, J.R., and A.J. Eralklis. 1964. Factors affecting the mortality from peptic ulcer: The bleeding ulcer and ulcer in the aged. *New England Journal of Medicine* 271: 803–9.

Brown, A.D.G. 1985. The genitourinary system—gynecological disorders in the elderly. In *Textbook of Geriatric Medicine and Gerontology*, 3d ed., edited by J.C. Brocklehurst, 659–70. Edinburgh: Churchill-Livingstone.

Bugiani, O., S. Salvarani, F. Perdelli, G.L. Mancardi, and A. Leonardi. 1978. Nerve cell loss with aging in the putamen. *European Neurology* 17: 286.

Burston, G.R., and B. Moore-Smith. 1970. Occult surgical emergencies in the elderly. *British Journal of Clinical Practice* 24: 239–43.

Caird, F.I., J.L.C. Dall, and B.O. Williams. 1985. The cardiovascular system. In *Textbook of Geriatric Medicine and Gerontology*, 3d ed., edited by J.C. Brocklehurst, 230–67. Edinburgh: Churchill-Livingstone.

Calabrese, C.T., Y.G. Adam, and H. Volk. 1973. Geriatric colon cancer. *American Journal of Surgery* 125: 181–5.

Campbell, A., J. Reinken, B. Alan, and G.S. Martinez. 1981. Falls in older age: A study of frequency and related clinical factors. *Age and Aging* 10: 264–70.

Cander, L., and J.H. Moyer, eds. 1965. *Aging of the Lung: Perspectives*. New York: Grune and Stratton.

Comfort, A. 1979. *The Biology of Senescence*, 3d ed. New York: Elsevier.

Connel, A.M., C. Hilton, G. Irvine, J.E. Leonard-Jones, and J.J. Misiewicz. 1965. Variations in bowel habit in two population samples. *British Medical Journal* ii: 1095–99.

Costa, P.T., and R. Andres. 1986. Patterns of age changes. In *Clinical Geriatrics*, 3d ed., edited by I. Rossman, 23–30. Philadelphia: J.B. Lippincott.

Council on Scientific Affairs—American Medical Association. 1984. Exercise programs for the elderly. *Journal of the American Medical Association* 252: 544–46.

Crantz, J.G., and F.R. Crantz. 1983. Thyroid disease in the elderly. *Practical Gastroenterology* 7: 41–5.

Daleiden, S. 1990. Prevention of falling: Rehabilitative or compensatory interventions? *Topics in Geriatric Rehabilitation* 5: 44–53.

Davis, P.A. 1941. The electroencephalogram in old age. *Diseases of the Nervous System* 2: 77.

Day, S.C. 1989a. Principles of screening. In *Practicing Prevention in the Elderly*, edited by R. Lavizzo-Mourey, S.C. Day, D. Diserens, and J.A. Grisso, 11–22. Philadelphia: Hanley and Belfus.

Day, S.C. 1989b. Screening for cancer in the elderly. In *Practicing Prevention in the Elderly*, edited by R. Lavizzo-Mourey, S.C. Day, D. Diserens, and J.A. Grisso, 23–36. Philadelphia: Hanley and Belfus.

Dayan, A.D. 1970. Quantitative histologic studies on the aged human brain. *Acta Neuropathology* 16: 95.

Dolocek, R. 1985. Endocrine changes in the elderly. *Triangle* 24: 17–33.

Dontas, A.S., P.K. Charvati, P.C. Papanayiotou, and S.G. Marketos. 1981. Bacteriuria and survival in old age. *New England Journal of Medicine* 304: 939–43.

Drechsler, F. 1978. Quantitative analysis of neurophysiological processes of the aging CNS. *Journal of Neurology* 218: 197.

Durnin, J.V.G.A., and J. Womersley. 1974. Body fat assessed from total body density and its estimation from skin fold thickness: Measurement on 481 men and women aged from 16 to 72 years. *British Journal of Nutrition* 32: 77–9.

Dymock, I.W. 1985. The gastrointestinal system—the upper gastrointestinal tract. In *Textbook of Geriatric Medicine and Gerontology*, 3d ed., edited by J.C. Brocklehurst, 508–21. Edinburgh: Churchill-Livingstone.

Everitt, D.E., and J. Avorn. 1986. Drug prescribing for the elderly. *Archives of Internal Medicine* 146: 2393–6.

Exton-Smith, A.N. 1985. The musculoskeletal system—bone aging and metabolic bone disease. In *Textbook of Geriatric Medicine and Gerontology*, 3d ed., edited by J.C. Brocklehurst, 758–75. Edinburgh: Churchill-Livingstone.

Fazekas, J.F., R.W. Alman, and A.N. Bessman. 1952. Cerebral physiology of the aged. *American Journal of Medical Science* 223: 245.

Federated Council for Internal Medicine. 1981. Geriatric medicine: A statement from the Federated Council for Internal Medicine. *Annals of Internal Medicine* 95: 372–6.

Feibusch, J.M., and P.R. Holt. 1982. Impaired absorptive capacity for carbohydrate in the aging human. *Digestive Diseases Science* 27: 1095–1100.

Feinstein, E.I. 1985. Renal disease in the elderly. In *Clinical Geriatrics*, 3d ed., edited by I. Rossman, 215–29. Philadelphia: J.B. Lippincott.

Fiatarone, M.A., E.C. Marks, N.D. Ryan, C.N. Meredith, L.A. Lipsitz, and W.J. Evans. 1990. High-intensity strength training in nonagenarians—Effects on skeletal muscle. *Journal of the American Medical Association* 263: 3029–34.

FitzGerald, M.G., and A. Kilvert. 1985. The endocrine system—diabetes. In *Textbook of Geriatric Medicine and Gerontology*, 3d ed., edited by J.C. Brocklehurst, 715–30. Edinburgh: Churchill-Livingstone.

Fleg, J.L. 1988. Ventricular arrhythmias in the elderly: Prevalence, mechanisms, and therapeutic implications. *Geriatrics* 43: 23–9.

Forbes, G.B. 1976. The adult decline in lean body mass. *Human Biology* 48: 161.

Fowles, D.G. 1986. *A Profile of Older Americans: 1986*. Washington, D.C.: American Association of Retired Persons.

Fox, R.A. 1985. Immunology of aging. In *Textbook of Geriatric Medicine and Gerontology*, 3d ed., edited by J.C. Brocklehurst, 82–104. Edinburgh: Churchill-Livingstone.

Fuller, E. 1982. Exercise: Getting the elderly going. *Patient Care* 16: 67–114.

Gardner, D.L., and P. O'Connor. 1985. The musculoskeletal system—aging of articular cartilage. In *Textbook of Geriatric Medicine and Gerontology*, 3d ed., edited by J.C. Brocklehurst, 776–84. Edinburgh: Churchill-Livingstone.

Gardner, P., and L.E. Cluff. 1970. The epidemiology of adverse drug reactions. Preview and perspective. *Johns Hopkins Medical Journal* 126: 77–87.

German, P.S., and L.C. Burton. 1989. Medication and the elderly: Issues of prescription and use. *Journal of Aging and Health* 1: 4–34.

Gilchrest, B.A. 1986. Dermatologic disorders in the elderly. In *Clinical Geriatrics*, 3d ed., edited by I. Rossman, 375–87. Philadelphia: J.B. Lippincott.

Gilchrest, B.A. 1982. Age-associated changes in the skin: Overview and clinical relevance. *Journal of the American Geriatric Society* 30: 129–43.

Goldman, R. 1970. Speculation on vascular changes with age. *Journal of the American Geriatric Society* 18: 765–79.

Gomez, E.C., and B. Berman. 1985. The aging skin. *Clinics in Geriatric Medicine* 1: 285–305.

Greenblatt, D.J., E.M. Sellers, and R.I. Shader. 1982. Drug disposition in old age. *New England Journal of Medicine* 306: 1081–8.

Grimby, G. 1988. Physical activity and effects of muscle training in the elderly. *Annals of Clinical Research* 20: 62–6.

Grimby, G. 1990. Muscle changes and trainability in the elderly. *Topics in Geriatric Rehabilitation* 5: 54–62.

Grimby, G., B. Danneskiold-Samose, K. Hvid, and B. Saltin. 1982. Morphology and enzymatic capacity in arm and leg muscles in 78–81 year old men and women. *Acta Physiologica Scandinavia* 115: 125–34.

Grimby, G., and B. Saltin. 1983. The aging muscle. *Clinical Physiology* 3: 209–18.

Grisso, J.A., and M. Attie. 1989. Prevention of osteoporotic fractures. In *Practicing Prevention in the Elderly*, edited by R. Lavizzo-Mourey, S.C. Day, D. Diserens, and J.A. Grisso, 107–24. Philadelphia: Hanley and Belfus.

Hadley, E.C. 1986. Bladder training and related therapies for urinary incontinence in older people. *Journal of the American Medical Association* 256: 372–80.

Haimovici, H. 1986. The peripheral vascular system. In *Clinical Geriatrics*, 3d ed., edited by I. Rossman, 197–214. Philadelphia: J.B. Lippincott.

Haley, R.W., T.M. Hooton, D.H. Culver, R.C. Stanley, T.G. Emori, C.D. Hardison, D. Quade, R.H. Schachtman, D.R. Schakera, B.V. Shah, and G.D. Schatz. 1981. Nosocomial infection in U.S. hospitals, 1975–1976. Estimated frequency by selected characteristics of patients. *American Journal of Medicine* 70: 947–59.

Hegsted, R., R.D. Brown, N. Jiang, P. Kao, R.M. Weinshilboum, C. Strong, and M. Wisgerhof. 1983. Aging and aldosterone. *American Journal of Medicine* 74: 442–8.

Hesse, K.A., E.W. Campion, and N. Karamouz. 1984. Attitudinal stumbling blocks to geriatric rehabilitation. *Journal of the American Geriatric Society* 32: 747–50.

Hinton, J.M., and J.E. Lennard-Jones. 1968. Constipation: Definition and classification. *Postgraduate Medical Journal* 44: 720–3.

Hodkinson, H.M., and R.E. Irvine. 1985. The endocrine system—thyroid disease in the elderly. In *Textbook of Geriatric Medicine and Gerontology*, 3d ed., edited by J.C. Brocklehurst, 686–714. Edinburgh: Churchill-Livingstone.

Hope-Simpson, R.E. 1965. The nature of herpes zoster: A long-term study and a new hypothesis. *Proceedings of the Royal Society of Medicine* 58: 9.

Hu, T., J.F. Igou, and D.L. Kaltreider. 1989. A clinical trial of a behavioral therapy to reduce urinary incontinence in nursing homes: Outcome and implications. *Journal of the American Medical Association* 261: 2656–62.

Huag, M. 1981. Age and medical care utilization patterns. *Journal of Gerontology* 36: 103.

Hubbard, O., D. Sunde, and E.S. Goldensohn. 1976. The EEG in centenarians. *Electroencephalography and Clinical Neurophysiology* 40: 407.

Jacoby, R.J., R. Levy, and J.M. Dawson. 1980. Computed tomography in the elderly: I. The normal population. *British Journal of Psychiatry* 136: 249.

Jenike, M.A. 1988. Psychoactive drugs in the elderly: Antipsychotics and anxiolytics. *Geriatrics* 43: 53–65.

Joske, R.A., E.S. Finckch, and I.J. Wood. 1955. Gastric biopsy: A study of 1,000 consecutive successful gastric biopsies. *Quarterly Journal of Medicine* 24: 269–94.

Katzman, R., and R. Terry. 1983. Normal aging of the nervous system. In *The Neurology of Aging*, edited by R. Katzman, and R. Terry, 15–50. Philadelphia: F.A. Davis Co.

Keltz, H. 1984. Pulmonary function and disease in aging. In *Rehabilitation in the Aging*, edited by T.F. Williams, 13–220. New York: Raven Press.

Kemp, B. 1986. Psychosocial and mental health issues in rehabilitation of older persons. In *Aging and Rehabilitation: Advances in the State of the Art*, edited by S.J. Brody, and G.E. Ruff, 122–58. New York: Springer Publishing Co.

Kenney, R.A. 1989. *Physiology of Aging—A Synopsis*, 2d ed. Chicago: Year Book Medical Publishers.

Khan, T.A., B.W. Shragge, J.S. Crispin, and J.F. Lind. 1977. Oesophageal motility in the elderly. *American Journal of Digestive Diseases* 22: 1049–54.

Kini, M.M., H.M. Leibowitz, T. Colton, R.J. Nickerson, J. Ganley, and T.R. Dauber. 1978. Prevalence of senile cataract, diabetic retinopathy, senile macular degeneration, and open-angle glaucoma in the Framingham Eye Study. *American Journal of Ophthalmology* 85: 28.

Kitzman, D.L., D.G. Scholz, P.T. Hagen, D.M. Ilstrup, and W.D. Edwards. 1988. Age-related changes in normal human hearts during the first 10 decades of life. Part II (Maturity): A quantitative anatomic study of 765 specimens from subjects 20 to 99 years old. *Mayo Clinic Proceedings* 63: 137–46.

Klein, L., P.S. German, D.M. Levine, E.R. Ferdi, and J. Ardeny. 1984. Medication problems among outpatients. *Archives of Internal Medicine* 144: 1185–8.

Koopman, C., ed. 1982. Symposium of Geriatric Otolaryngology. *Otolaryngology Clinics of North America* 15, no. 2: 257–463.

Kotler, M.N., A.P. Goldman, and W.R. Parry. 1986. Geriatric cardiology: Managing the most common nonischemic disorders. *Geriatrics* 41: 45–53.

Kovar, M. 1977. Health of the elderly and use of health services. *Public Health Reports* 92: 9–19.

Kramer, P.A. 1987. Influence of aging on drug disposition and response. *Topics in Geriatric Rehabilitation* 2: 12–22.

Langman, M.J.S. 1971. Epidemiology of cancer of the oesophagus and stomach. *British Journal of Surgery* 58: 792–3.

Larson, E.B., and R.A. Bruce. 1987. Health benefits of exercise in an aging society. *Archives of Internal Medicine* 147: 353–6.

Larson, E.B., W.A. Kukull, D. Buchner, and B.V. Reifler. 1987. Adverse drug reactions associated with global cognitive impairment in elderly persons. *Annals of Internal Medicine* 107: 169–73.

Lavizzo-Mourey, R., and D. Diserens. 1989. Preventive care for the elderly. In *Practicing Prevention for the Elderly*, edited by R. Lavizzo-Mourey, S.C. Day, D. Diserens, and J.A. Grisso, 1–10. Philadelphia: Hanley and Belfus.

Leaf, A. 1984. Dehydration in the elderly. *New England Journal of Medicine* 311: 791–2.

Leventhal, E., and T.R. Prohaska. 1986. Age, symptom interpretation and health behavior. *Journal of the American Geriatric Society* 34: 185–91.

Leverat, M., J. Pasquier, R. Lambert, and A. Tissot. 1966. Peptic ulcer in patients over 60. Experience in 287 cases. *American Journal of Digestive Diseases* 11: 279–85.

Lewis, V.W., J.J. Twomey, P. Bealmear, G. Goldstein, and R.A. Good. 1978. Age, thymic involution and circulating thymic hormone activity. *Journal of Clinical Endocrinology and Metabolism* 47: 145.

Lie, J.T., and P.I. Hammond. 1988. Pathology of the senescent heart: Anatomic observations on 237 autopsy studies of patients 90 to 105 years old. *Mayo Clinic Proceedings* 63: 552–64.

Lonergan, E.T. 1988. Aging and the kidney: Adjusting treatment to physiologic change. *Geriatrics* 43(3): 27–33.

Lye, M.D.W. 1985. The milieu interieur and aging. In *Textbook of Geriatric Medicine and Gerontology*, 3d ed., edited by J.C. Brocklehurst, 201–29. Edinburgh: Churchill-Livingstone.

Mackay, I. 1972. Aging and immunological function in man. *Gerontogia* 18: 285.

MacMillan, A.L. 1985. Aging and the skin. In *Textbook of Geriatric Medicine and Gerontology*, 3d ed., edited by J.C. Brocklehurst, 915–34. Edinburgh: Churchill-Livingstone.

Mann, D.M.A., and K.G.A. Sinclair. 1978. The quantitative assessment of lipofuscin pigment, cytoplasmic RNA, and nucleolar volume in senile dementia. *Neuropathology and Applied Neurobiology* 4: 129.

Master, A.N., R.P. Lasser, and G. Beckman. 1960. Tables of average weight and height of Americans, aged 65 to 94 years, etc. *Journal of the American Medical Association* 172: 658.

McGeer, P.L., and E.G. McGeer. 1976. Enzymes associated with the metabolism of catecholamines, acetylcholine, and GABA in human controls and patients with Parkinson's disease and Huntington's chorea. *Journal of Neurochemistry* 26: 65.

McGuinness, R. 1978. The Framingham eye study. *American Journal of Ophthalmology* 86: 852.

McKeown, F. 1965. *Pathology of the Aged*. London: Butterworths.

Miall, W.E., M.T. Ashcroft, H.G. Lovell, and F. Moore. 1967. A longitudinal study of the decline of adult height with age in two Welsh communities. *Human Biology* 39: 445–54.

Miller, C. 1962. Carcinoma of thoracic oesophagus and cardia. A review of 405 cases. *British Journal of Surgery* 49: 507–22.

Miller, P.D., R.A. Krebs, B.J. Neal, and D.O. McIntyre. 1982. Hypodipsia in geriatric patients. *American Journal of Medicine* 73: 354–6.

Milne, J.S., and J. Williamson. 1972. Bowel habit in older people. *Gerontological Clinics* 14: 56–60.

Montamat, S.C., B.J. Cusack, and R.E. Vestal. 1989. Management of drug therapy in the elderly. *New England Journal of Medicine* 321: 303–9.

Moody, C.E., J.B. Innes, L. Staiano-Coico, G.S. Incefy, H.T. Thaler, and M.E. Weksler. 1981. Lymphocyte transformation induced by autologous cells: XI. The effect of age on the autologous mixed lymphocyte reaction. *Immunology* 44: 431–38.

Morley, J.E., and S.S. Reese. 1989. Clinical implications of the aging heart. *American Journal of Medicine* 86: 77–86.

Morris, J.F., A. Koski, and L.C.T. Johnson. 1971. Spirometric standards for healthy nonsmoking adults. *American Review of Respiratory Diseases* 103: 57.

Morris, R., E.H. Runbin, E.J. Morris, and S.A. Mandel. 1987. Senile dementia of the Alzheimer's type: An important risk factor for serious falls. *Journal of Gerontology* 42: 412–17.

Mulsow, F.W. 1941. Peptic ulcer in the aged. *American Review of Digestive Diseases* 8: 112.

Narayanan, M., and F.U. Steinheber. 1976. The changing face of peptic ulcer in the elderly. *Medical Clinics of North America* 60: 1159–72.

Naughton, J. 1982. Physical activity and aging. *Primary Care* 9: 231–8.

Nicolle, L.E., J. Bjornson, G.K.M. Harding, and J.A. MacDonell. 1983. Bacteriuria in elderly institutionalized men. *New England Journal of Medicine* 309: 1420–4.

Niewoehner, D.E., and J. Kleinerman. 1974. Morphologic basis of pulmonary resistance in the human lung and effects of aging. *Journal of Applied Physiology* 36: 412.

Nordenstam, G.R., C.A. Brandberg, A.S. Oden, C.M. Svanborg Eden, and A. Svanborg. 1986. Bacteriuria and mortality in an elderly population. *New England Journal of Medicine* 314: 1152–6.

Noth, R.H., M.N. Lassman, S.Y. Tan, A. Fernando-Cruz, and P.J. Mulrow. 1977. Age and the renin-aldosterone system. *Archives of Internal Medicine* 137: 1414–17.

Noth, R.H., and E.L. Mazzaferri. 1985. Age and the endocrine system. *Clinics of Geriatric Medicine* 1: 223–250.

O'Dell, C. 1988. Atypical presentations of neurological illness in the elderly. *Geriatrics* 43: 35–7.

Office of Medical Applications of Research—National Institutes of Health. 1989. Urinary incontinence in adults. *Journal of the American Medical Association* 261: 2685–90.

O'Malley, K., M. Laher, B. Cusack, and J.G. Kelly. 1980. Clinical pharmacology and the elderly patient. In *The Treatment of Medical Problems in the Elderly,* edited by M.J. Denham, 7–9. Baltimore: University Park Press.

Osmer, J.C., and B.K. Cole. 1966. The stethoscope and roentgenogram in acute pneumonia. *Southern Medical Journal* 59: 75.

Otomo, E. 1966. Electroencephalography in old age: Dominant alpha pattern. *Electroencephalography and Clinical Neurophysiology* 21: 489.

Ouslander, J.G. 1981. Drug therapy in the elderly: Diagnosis and treatment. *Annals of Internal Medicine* 95: 711–22.

Padula, W.V. 1982. Low vision related to fundamental service delivery for the elderly. In *Aging and Human Visual Function,* edited by R. Sekular, D. Kline, and K. Dismukes, 315–23. New York: Alan R. Liss.

Pahwa, S.G., R. Pahwa, and R.A. Good. 1981. Decreased in vitro humoral immune responses in aged humans. *Journal of Clinical Investigation* 67: 1094.

Palmer, E.D. 1954. The state of the gastric mucosa of elderly persons without upper gastrointestinal symptoms. *Journal of the American Geriatrics Society* 2: 171–3.

Patel, P.J. 1981. Aging and antimicrobial immunity. *Journal of Experimental Medicine* 154: 821.

Peterson, D.D., A.I. Pack, D.A. Silage, and A.P. Fishman. 1981. Effects of aging on ventilatory and occlusion pressure responses to hypoxia and hypercapnia. *American Review of Respiratory Diseases* 124: 387.

Phillips, P.A., B.J. Rolls, J.G.G. Ledingham, M.L. Forsling, J.J. Morton, M.J. Crowe, and L. Wollner. 1984. Reduced thirst after water deprivation in healthy elderly men. *New England Journal of Medicine* 311: 753–9.

Pierce, J.A., and R.V. Elbert. 1958. The barrel deformity of the chest, the senile lung and obstructive pulmonary emphysema. *American Journal of Medicine* 25: 13.

Posner, J.D., K.M. Gorman, H.S. Klein, and A. Woldow. 1986. Exercise capacity in the elderly. *American Journal of Cardiology* 57: 52C–8C.

Post, F. 1985. The central nervous system—the emotional disorders. In *Textbook of Geriatric Medicine and Gerontology,* 3d ed., edited by J.C. Brocklehurst, 328–41. Edinburgh: Churchill-Livingstone.

Prohaska, T.R., E.A. Leventhal, H. Leventhal, and M.L. Keller. 1985. Health practices and illness cognition in young, middle-aged and elderly adults. *Journal of Gerontology* 40: 569–78.

Prudham, D., and J. Evans. 1981. Factors associated with falls in the elderly: A community study. *Age and Aging* 10: 141–6.

Pump, K.K. 1971. The aged lung. *Chest* 60: 571.

Remington, P.L., M.R. Forman, E.M. Gentry, J.S. Marks, G.C. Hogelin, and F.L. Towbridge. 1985. Current smoking trends in the United States. *Journal of the American Medical Association* 253: 2975–8.

Renlund, D.G., and G. Gerstenblith. 1987. Exercise and the aging heart. *Cardiology Clinics* 5: 331–6.

Resnick, N.M., and S.V. Yalla. 1985. Management of urinary incontinence in the elderly. *New England Journal of Medicine* 313: 800–4.

Resnick, N.M., and S.V. Yalla. 1987. Detrusor hyperactivity with impaired contractile function: An unrecognized but common cause of incontinence in elderly patients. *Journal of the American Medical Association* 257: 3076–81.

Richey, D.P., and A.D. Bender. 1977. Pharmacokinetic consequences of aging. *Annual Review of Pharmacology and Toxicology* 17: 49–65.

Roberts, W.C. 1988. The aging heart. *Mayo Clinic Proceedings* 63: 205–6.

Roberts, M.A., and F.I. Caird. 1976. Computerized tomography and intellectual impairment in the elderly. *Journal of Neurology, Neurosurgery, and Psychiatry* 39: 986.

Rodstein, M. 1982. Heart disease in the elderly. *Primary Cardiology* 8: 159–91.

Rosenthal, M.J., W.C. Hunt, P.J. Garry, and J.S. Goodwin. 1987. Thyroid failure in the elderly: Microsomal antibodies as discriminant for therapy. *Journal of the American Medical Association* 258: 209–12.

Roth, E.J., K. Mueller, and D. Green. 1988. Stroke rehabilitation outcome—impact of coronary artery disease. *Stroke* 19: 42–7.

Roth, E.J., K. Mueller, and D. Green. 1986. Cardiovascular monitoring of stroke patients undergoing physical therapy. *Archives of Physical Medicine and Rehabilitation* 67: 643.

Roth, E.J., S. Wiesner, D. Green, and Y. Wu. 1990. Dysvascular amputee rehabilitation: The role of continuous noninvasive cardiovascular monitoring during physical therapy. *American Journal of Physical Medicine and Rehabilitation* 69: 16–22.

Rowe, J.W. 1977. Clinical research on aging. *New England Journal of Medicine* 297: 1331–6.

Rowe, J.W., and R.L. Kahn. 1987. Human aging—usual and successful. *Science* 237: 143–9.

Ruben, R.J., and B. Kruger. 1983. Hearing loss in the elderly. In *The Neurology of Aging*, edited by R. Katzman, and R. Terry, 123–48. Philadelphia: F.A. Davis Co.

Rubenstein, L.Z. 1983. Falls in the elderly: A clinical approach. *Western Journal of Medicine* 138: 273–5.

Sarks, S.H. 1976. Aging and degeneration in the macular region: A clinicopathological study. *British Journal of Ophthalmology* 60: 324.

Sawin, C.T., S.T. Bigos, S. Land, and P. Bacharach. 1985. The aging thyroid: Relationship between elevated serum thyrotropin level and thyroid antibodies in elderly patients. *American Journal of Medicine* 79: 591–4.

Sawin, C.T., A. Geller, J.M. Hershman, W. Castelli, and P. Bacharach. 1989. The aging thyroid: The use of thyroid hormone in older persons. *Journal of the American Medical Association* 261: 2653–4.

Sawin, C.T., T. Herman, M.E. Molitch, et al. 1983. Aging and the thyroid: Decreased requirement for thyroid hormone in older hypothyroid patients. *American Journal of Medicine* 75: 206–8.

Schaumburg, H.H., P.S. Spencer, and J. Ochoa. 1983. The aging human peripheral nervous system. In *The Neurology of Aging*, edited by R. Katzman, and R. Terry, 111–22. Philadelphia: F.A. Davis Co.

Scheibel, M.E., and A.B. Scheibel. 1975. Structural changes in the aging brain. In *Clinical, Morphologic, and Neurochemical Aspects in the Aging Central Nervous System,* edited by H. Brody, D. Harman, and J.M. Ordy, 11. New York: Raven Press.

Schmidt, C.D., M.L. Dickman, R.M. Gardner, and F.K. Brough. 1975. Spirometric standards for healthy elderly men and women. *American Review of Respiratory Diseases* 108: 933–9.

Scholz, D.G., D.W. Kitzman, P.T. Hagen, D.M. Ilstrup, and W.D. Edwards. 1988. Age-related changes in normal human hearts during the first 10 decades of life. Part I (Growth): A quantitative anatomic study of 200 specimens from subjects from birth to 19 years old. *Mayo Clinic Proceedings* 63: 126–36.

Seidel, L.G., G.F. Thornton, J.W. Smith, and L.E. Cluff. 1966. Studies on the epidemiology of adverse drug reactions. III: Reactions in patients on a general medical service. *Bulletin of Johns Hopkins Hospital* 119: 299–315.

Shock, N.W. 1967. Current trends in research on the physiological aspects of aging. *Journal of the American Geriatric Society* 15: 995–1000.

Shock, N.W. 1983. Aging of regulatory systems. In *Fundamentals of Geriatric Medicine,* edited by R.D.T. Cape, R.M. Coe, and I. Rossman, 51–62. New York: Raven Press.

Shuster, S., M.M. Black, and E. McVitie. 1975. Influence of age and sex on skin thickness, skin collagen and density. *British Journal of Dermatology* 93: 639–43.

Sier, H., J. Ouslander, and S. Orzeck. 1987. Urinary incontinence among geriatric patients in an acute-care hospital. *Journal of the American Medical Association* 257: 1767–70.

Sims, R.V. 1989. Immunization in the elderly. In *Practicing Prevention in the Elderly,* edited by R. Lavizzo-Mourey, S.C. Day, D. Diserens, and J.A. Grisso, 37–46. Philadelphia: Hanley and Belfus.

Singh, J., and A.K. Singh. 1979. Age-related changes in human thymus. *Clinical and Experimental Immunology* 37: 507.

Slater, G., A.E. Papatestas, P.I. Tartter, M. Mulvihill, and A.W. Aufses. 1982. Age distribution of right- and left-sided colorectal cancers. *American Journal of Gastroenterology* 77: 63–6.

Smith, L.K. 1988. Cardiac disorders: A guide to assessing risk in the elderly. *Geriatrics* 43: 33–8.

Soergel, K.H., F.F. Zboralske, and J.R. Amberg. 1964. Presbyesophagus: Esophageal motility in nonagenarians. *Journal of Clinical Investigation* 43: 1472–9.

Sperduto, R.D., and D. Seigel. 1980. Senile lens and senile macular changes in a population-based sample. *American Journal of Ophthalmology* 90: 86.

Stafford, C.E., E.J. Joergenson, and G.C. Murray. 1956. Complications of peptic ulcer in the aged. *California Medicine* 84: 92–4.

Stamm, W.E. 1978. Infections related to medical devices. *Annals of Internal Medicine* 89: 764–9.

Strickland, R.G., and I.R. Mackay. 1973. A reappraisal of the nature of chronic atrophic gastritis. *Digestive Diseases Science* 18: 426–40.

Stultz, B.M. 1984. Preventive care for the elderly. *Western Medical Journal* 141: 832–45.

Thompson, T.L., M.G. Moran, and A.S. Nies. 1983a. Psychotropic drug use in the elderly, Part 1. *New England Journal of Medicine* 308: 134–8.

Thompson, T.L., M.G. Moran, and A.S. Nies. 1983b. Psychotropic drug use in the elderly, Part 2. *New England Journal of Medicine* 308: 194–200.

Tideiksaar, R. 1989. Geriatric falls: Assessing the cause, preventing recurrence. *Geriatrics* 44: 57–64.

Tinetti, M.E., and M. Speechley. 1989. Prevention of falls among the elderly. *New England Journal of Medicine* 320: 1055–9.

Tinetti, M.E., T.F. Williams, and R. Mayewski. 1986. Fall risk index for elderly patients based on number of chronic disabilities. *American Journal of Medicine* 80: 429–34.

Tomlinson, B.E. 1977. Morphological changes and dementia in old age. In *Aging and Dementia,* edited by W.L. Smith, and M. Kinsbourne, 25–56. New York: Spectrum Publications.

Valbona, C., and S.B. Baker. 1984. Physical fitness prospects in the elderly. *Archives of Physical Medicine and Rehabilitation* 65: 194–200.

Verghese, A., and B. Smith. 1986. Early diagnosis of the older cardiac patient with multiple disorders. *Geriatrics* 41: 39–46.

Vestal, R.E. 1984. Drug use in the elderly: A review of special problems and special considerations. *Drugs* 16: 358–82.

Walford, R. 1969. *The Immunologic Theory of Aging.* Copenhagen: Munksgaard.

Waller, B.F. 1988. Hearts of the "oldest old." *Mayo Clinic Proceedings* 63: 625–9.

Weisfeldt, M.L. 1980. Aging of the cardiovascular system. *New England Journal of Medicine* 303: 1172–4.

Weksler, M.E. 1983. Senescence of the immune system. *Medical Clinics of North America* 67: 263.

Weksler, M.E. 1986. Biologic basis and clinical significance of immune senescence. In *Clinical Geriatrics,* 3d ed., edited by I. Rossman, 57–67. Philadelphia: J.B. Lippincott.

Wenger, N.K., R.A. O'Rourke, and F.I. Marcus. 1988. The care of elderly patients with cardiovascular disease. *Annals of Internal Medicine* 109: 425–8.

Wild, D., U.S.L. Nayak, and B. Isaacs. 1980. Characteristics of old people who fell at home. *Journal of Experimental Gerontology* 2: 271–87.

Williams, M.E. 1984. Clinical implications of aging physiology. *American Journal of Medicine* 76: 1049–54.

Williams, M.E., and F.C. Pannill. 1982. Urinary incontinence in the elderly: Physiology, pathophysiology, diagnosis, and treatment. *Annals of Internal Medicine* 97: 895–907.

Williamson, J. 1985. Preventive medicine and old age. In *Textbook of Geriatric Medicine and Gerontology,* 3d ed., edited by J.C. Brocklehurst, 1011–20. Edinburgh: Churchill-Livingstone.

Wright, B.E., and P. Henkind. 1983. Aging changes and the eye. In *The Neurology of Aging,* edited by R. Katzman, and R. Terry, 149–66. Philadelphia: F.A. Davis Co.

Yamamura, H., M. Ito, K. Kubota, and T. Matsuzawa. 1980. Brain atrophy during aging: A quantitative study with computed tomography. *Journal of Gerontology* 35: 492.

Young, A., M. Stokes, and M. Crowe. 1985. The size and strength of the quadriceps muscles of old and young men. *Clinical Physiology* 5: 145–54.

Zadik, Z., and A.A. Kowarski. 1980. Normal integrated concentration of aldosterone and plasma renin activity: Effect of age. *Journal of Clinical Endocrinology and Metabolism* 50: 867–9.

Chapter 3

The Aging Process: Cognition, Personality, and Coping

Robert J. Hartke

There are a variety of conceptions and misconceptions that have accumulated over time about the changes that occur with age in mental ability, personality, and coping. Most prominent and disputed are conceptualizations of decline: that people lose mental prowess, develop troublesome personality traits, and cope poorly with advancing years. However, there are also idealized views of older adulthood as a time of wisdom, integration, and acceptance. This chapter provides an overview of ideas and research on the changes in psyche associated with the aging process. It is designed as an abbreviated reference on the psychology of aging with a summary of the aging mind, personality, and coping processes, as well as an extensive bibliography for further reference. The chapter has few direct clinical applications, focusing instead on distinguishing normal psychological changes that accompany aging. Such distinction is critical for the clinician working in geriatrics where there is a risk of interpreting normal change or difference as psychopathology. The chapter is also intended to provide background for the subsequent concerns addressed in this text, as well as to raise broad, thought-provoking questions pertaining to geriatric rehabilitation.

AGING AND COGNITIVE CHANGES

Numerous approaches to the question of cognitive changes with age have led to several different answers. Neurophysiologists can readily point to changes in the structure and chemistry of the brain and state that subsequent functional changes are inescapable. Brain weight peaks at approximately 20 years of age and demonstrates a 10 percent loss by the eighties. Selective neuronal and synaptic loss, brain atrophy, depletion of neurotransmitters, and altered circulatory capacity and metabolism have also been demonstrated. Physically, there is thought to be decreased reserve, increased delicacy of balance, and heightened vulnerability in the brain with age (Cohen 1988).

Neuropsychologists and cognitive psychologists break mental functioning down into discrete abilities and demonstrate a timetable of changes with age on psychometric tests. Albert (1988, 48) provides a succinct summary:

> Cross-sectional studies indicate that the earliest change that occurs is in secondary memory function, the ability to retain relatively large amounts of information over long periods of time. Subjects in their mid-50s are significantly different from younger individuals. Proficiency at constructional tasks and divided attention capabilities show alterations in the mid-60s. Abstraction and naming ability are significantly different when subjects are in their 70s. Longitudinal findings are comparable, although . . . declines occur slightly later in the lifespan.

Psychologists and sociologists also focus upon factors extrinsic to the older person in explaining cognitive change with age. They emphasize the role of context (i.e., the environment and culture) in order to explain the impact of cognitive change on function (e.g., Labouvie-Vief et al. 1974).

Taken together, each of these approaches contributes to, yet simultaneously complicates, attempts to fully understand the cognitive life of older adults. They reflect varying underlying hypotheses regarding the etiology of cognitive change with age (Salthouse 1989). The following discussion of cognition and aging addresses major areas of mental ability relevant to the older adult within the context of rehabilitation. Comprehensive reviews of these topics are available in Birren and Schaie (1977, 1985, 1990).

Speed of Processing

The observation of slowed rate of information processing with increasing age has received considerable attention as a possible underlying cause for all age-related reductions in cognition (e.g., see Poon 1980). This speed hypothesis focuses on the influence of age-related slowing of peripheral and central nervous system processes. Salthouse (1985) and Salthouse and Kail (1983) observe that the general slowing of behavior has been shown to reliably correlate with age. Speed of behavior is shown to increase until about 20 years of age; steady, gradual decline occurs thereafter through the adult years. Drawing an analogy between the brain and a computer, they propose that neurophysiological or "computer hardware" changes slow the cycle time per mental operation. Cerella (1990) extends this thesis by viewing aging as resulting in defects distributed throughout a neural network (i.e., the brain). All cognition becomes slowed as signal pathways deteriorate with age. This type of explanation has a certain appeal due to its more basic, concrete level. It avoids the complications and conflicting research results of such cognitive and psychological concepts as attention, memory, or even more abstract ones such as motivation, intelligence, and problem solving. Nevertheless, translating changes in specific ability to changes in functional competence (Salthouse 1990) is difficult and unavoidably complicated. Experts in the field are far from explaining the discrepancy between studies showing decline in certain mental abilities in older adults and the daily successful functioning of these same people. In the absence of a more parsimonious explanation, placing chronological age in perspective with the interaction of multiple factors such as experience, health, and a variety of individual differences may remain most reasonable.

Intelligence

Botwinick (1977) concludes that intellectual functioning, as measured by standardized intelligence tests, shows decline with age. However, the amount is relatively small, occurs late in life, and varies by mental function. Both Schaie (1990) and Botwinick (1977) attempt to place the role of age in proper perspective with the many other variables that at least covary with intellectual function, if not directly influence it. These include health status, speed of performance, personality variables, and a variety of social/demographic factors. Botwinick notes that age only accounts for 20 percent of score variance on intelligence tests.

Experimental design plays a role in how intellectual changes with age are reported. Cross-sectional designs tend to magnify intellectual decline and demonstrate earlier onset, usually by the sixties. In contrast, longitudinal studies tend to minimize intellectual decline and show later onset, perhaps not until the late sixties to seventies (Albert and Heaton 1988). The Seattle Longitudinal Study serves as a good example of the general age trends found in research on general intelligence. On the average, the study shows gains until the late thirties to early forties, with stability until the mid-fifties to early sixties (Schaie 1990). On the basis of this data, Hertzog and Schaie (1988) suggest the range of 55 to 70 years of age to be, on the average, a transition time from a pattern of stability to one of decline in general intelligence.

Despite these variances in onset and amount, there is such striking consistency observed in the configuration of decline in abilities that it is commonly referred to as the *classic aging pattern*. This frequently confirmed finding refers to the early decline of nonverbal, perceptual skill during the fifties, while verbal skill remains stable well into the seventies. This difference cannot be fully explained by slowed speed of performance with age. It is not until later old age (seventies and beyond) that this more differentiated pattern gives way to overall decline in functioning. Such a pattern is corroborated by the relatively late and modest decline of language ability. In the seventies and beyond, decrements in comprehension, word retrieval, and verbal fluency are discernible, although they are sometimes construed as secondary effects of changes in other areas such as memory, processing time, hearing, and vision (Albert 1988; Bayles and Kaszniak 1987).

The classic aging pattern has been explained as a decline in ability to learn and integrate unfamiliar material, with the relative preservation of familiar, overlearned material. Horn and Cattell (1967) have described these subdivisions of intelligence as *fluid* versus *crystallized*. They postulate fluid intelligence to be more heavily dependent upon the integrity of the central nervous system and, thus, vulnerable to decline with the physical insults of aging; crystallized intelligence consists of a knowledge base acquired early in life which then remains stable for decades.

Now that longitudinal studies have yielded data sufficient to chart the general course of intellectual change in later life, the focus of research has shifted to discerning more individual patterns of change, identifying variables aside from age that can account for individual differences, and determining the efficacy of remediation (Schaie 1990). Labouvie-Vief (1985) discusses the need to view intellectual functioning as having greater breadth and complexity and being embedded in the context of the social/cultural and life-stage demands of older adulthood. She argues against automatically assuming youth-based standards and concluding regression in the intellectual life of elders. As such, cognitive maturity and adaptation may be more relevant conceptualizations than cognitive status, and intellectual *difference* instead of *deficit* may be a more apt descriptor in older adulthood.

Problem Solving

Intelligence tests are purported to measure abilities and skill, but problem solving implies more practical utilization of knowledge. While markers of intellectual change can be described psychometrically, it is far more difficult to discuss their real life implications for older adults. Schaie (1990) describes the burgeoning field of *practical intelligence* and aging, although results are still preliminary and inconclusive (e.g., Cornelius and Caspi 1987; Schaie 1990). Rabbitt (1977) and Reese and Rodeheaver (1985) provide reviews of literature on aging and problem solving, and point out the difficulties in drawing cogent conclusions in a field with no unifying theory and easily confused concepts. Both cite literature documenting older adults as less efficient, less flexible, and more cautious and primitive in their problem-solving strategies. Older adults commit more errors and are less successful at achieving solutions. They are also often described as regressive in their cognitive operations on Piagetian tasks (e.g., Papalia and Bielby 1974). However, Reese and Rodeheaver (1985) qualify these observations as differences rather than necessarily reductions in problem solving. Such differences in older adults may actually reflect decrements in more basic, underlying cognitive operations (such as memory, processing speed, and perception), instead of the loss of more integrated problem-solving skill. In real life circumstances, older adults are more competent than their performance on such tests would suggest (see Salthouse 1990). It may be necessary to pose the question, "What is appropriate problem solving for an older adult?" (Rodeheaver 1987). Older adults may in fact reframe a situation or choose a resolution to a problem more in tune with their needs and age-appropriate abilities.

Memory

Perhaps the most commonly noted cognitive change with aging is seen in memory. Older adults speak of memory diminution as common with increasing years, sometimes using it to rationalize more pathological cognitive impairment or inappropriately fearing it as a sign of dementia. Years of research now substantiate some forms of age-related memory decrement, although their mechanisms have yet to be fully explained. Craik (1977), Hultsch and Dixon (1990), Kausler (1982, 1987), and Poon (1985) provide comprehensive reviews of memory and aging. The current discussion provides a brief overview of these findings.

The term *sensory memory* is used to describe an initial, momentary registration mechanism. Modest age-related differences have been documented in this phase of memory, but they are considered to be of little practical consequence. Similarly, *primary* or *short-term memory,* the next brief repository for limited bits of information, is also relatively unaffected by aging. Older adults are noted to have minimal difficulty at this phase unless information must be rapidly manipulated or heavy demands are made on attentional capacity.

It is at the level of *secondary* or *long-term memory* that significant age-related decrements have been consistently documented. Secondary memory provides for long-term retention of unlimited amounts of information requiring analysis and organization for storage and effective retrieval at some later time. Older adults are found to be less proficient at free recall and, to a lesser degree, at cued recall and recognition. There are no specific age markers given for the onset of decline. It appears that the reduction in effectiveness is gradual, with the 50 to 70 year range being a point of transition to most notable decline. A host of mechanisms have been proposed to account for this reduction in memory ranging from biological to more broad contextual hypotheses. Processing effectiveness has received the most attention in the literature, specifically, alteration in the encoding and retrieval of information. Older adults are said to use fewer and less effective strategies to spontaneously organize material and, thus, process data less "deeply" (Craik 1977), making retrieval more difficult. The fact that older adults improve their recall when assisted with cues and strategies is cited in support of this hypothesis. Admittedly, the reasons that older adults perform poorly at this level of memory are complicated and multifactorial; many intervening variables having been discussed, such as verbal ability and speed, content familiarity, and incidental versus intentional acquisition.

Finally, at the level of *tertiary* or *remote memory,* older adults also demonstrate modest decrements (although there has been less research in this area and the research that has been done is marked by methodological problems). This finding contradicts the time-worn maxim that older adults are superior in recalling the past, while forgetting details in the present. Such anecdotal phenomena are more often a product of repetitious, well encoded reminiscence. They are also difficult to fully validate.

Most authorities in the area of memory and aging warn against the oversimplification of the memory process and the search for discrete explanations for age-related phenomena. More complex, interactive conceptualizations, in which the individuals, their environment, and the memory task are considered together, are advocated. Such broader conceptualizations encourage the inclusion of more qualitative, but perhaps no less important, variables in the process of memory. Motivation, personality, and sociocultural factors have received less attention than warranted; these factors focus away from deficit-related hypotheses to explain the variability in the memory performance of older adults. For example, within the concept of *metamemory* (i.e., how an individual understands his/her memory system), the manner in which memory skill is evaluated has shown significant age-related differences. Older adults tend to view themselves as less effective and having less control in cognitive areas. They more often make inappropriate attributions about their cognitive performance. Such factors illustrate the potential for self-fulfilling prophecies to work to the detriment of memory functioning in older adults.

Learning

Age-related changes in memory imply similar changes in learning as well. However, the multifactorial, complex nature of human learning also overpowers chronological age as a single critical factor in comprehending this process in later life. Specific age markers for performance decrements are, again, rarely delineated. The nature of the decline is often described as gradual and cumulative, still appearing most significant in the sixties and beyond. Older adults have been shown to be less effective in the mechanics of learning tasks compared to themselves at a younger age or to younger cohorts (Arenberg and Robertson-Tchabo 1977). Differences in pacing, encoding, and retrieval are also implicated in age-related changes in learning. Studies indicate that older adults require increased response time to demonstrate effective learning and are also hindered by lack or inefficient use of strategies to facilitate the process, such as organizational hierarchies, verbal mediators, and mnemonics. Cautiousness and performance anxiety have also been discussed as relevant to these differences. Research suggests that elders are more prone to the interference effects of prior learned material (*proactive interference*). They may resort to more time-worn learning approaches when contemporary instructional sets are confusing or misconstrued. Finally, age differences in learning have been corroborated by more controlled animal studies involving complex maze learning, discrimination, and avoidance tasks (Woodruff-Pak 1990).

Despite these discrete laboratory findings, there is also ample evidence of preserved learning capacity in older adults. Willis (1985) noted that, on the average, individuals in their early eighties are still cognitively functioning at 75 to 80 percent of the performance level of a 25-year-old counterpart. Baltes and Lindenberger (1988) provide evidence of the existence and range of *cognitive plasticity* in old age. They demonstrate that healthy older adults have sufficient cognitive reserve (i.e., ability to learn new material as well as refine and elaborate existing knowledge) to use self-directed and guided coaching to improve their performance on standard measures of fluid cognition. With age, this reserve or plasticity is proven, however, to be more limited in scope, speed, and maximum level. They conclude that the intact cognitive reserve of older adults can be exploited for optimal or successful cognitive aging.

With the demonstration of continued learning capacity in older adulthood, studies appropriately shift to understanding parameters for facilitating continued learning at this stage of life. For example, Gounard and Hulicka (1977) provide informative, concrete guidelines for maximizing learning efficiency in late adulthood, including pacing, cuing, verbal mediation, and overall style. Willis (1985) addresses the older adult as learner, viewing learning as a life-long process with goals of continued socialization and adaptation. She discusses the double jeopardy older adults face in new learning situations: less elaborated learning skill due to the limited formal educational experience of their generation, as well as decreased skill due to normal aging. These disadvantages are particularly relevant when elders are dealing with unfamiliar technical information, such as that found in medical settings. Willis further highlights less obvious, but no less important, broad motivations for learning in later adulthood—learning as a forum for socialization, to experience self-improvement, or make a contribution to society.

Aging, Health, and Cognition

There is an increasing foundation of literature investigating the relationship between cognition and health/illness in older adulthood. Such exploration seems to be a logical extension of the neurophysiological bases postulated for cognitive changes with aging and may become a viable hypothesis to explain cognitive decline with age (Salthouse 1989). Health status has been related to the rate of intellectual aging, as in the descriptive contrast between normal (healthy) versus pathological (disease-related) aging (Schaie 1990), or primary versus secondary aging (Busse 1969). The basic premise of this correlation is that healthy older adults remain more cognitively intact, while those with chronic disease processes show earlier decline. Research (including limited longitudinal results) tends to support this rationale, particularly in reference to such chronic processes as hypertension, cardiovascular disease, and diabetes (Elias et al. 1990; Schaie 1990; Siegler and Costa 1985). Health is often considered a more operative variable in cognitive decline than chronological age.

The concepts of terminal drop and critical loss (Botwinick 1977; Jarvik 1988; Steuer et al. 1981) address the relationship between intellectual function and mortality. Terminal drop refers to the observation of more significant decline on measures of intelligence in older adults in the years preceding death (Kleemeier 1962). As Steuer and associates (1981, 211) note, "According to the theory of terminal decline or drop, decrease in cognitive functioning is related to distance from death rather than chronological age." Similarly, critical loss (Jarvik 1962) refers to the observation of a greater rate of annual decline on selected cognitive measures as predictive of imminent death. In either instance, cognitive power is linked with the older individual's deteriorating physical state in the final years of life. Such a relationship has important implications for rehabilitation, given the preponderance of disabling residuals from chronic disease in older age. The subset of elders found in the rehabilitation setting may in fact have more than the usual amount of age-related cognitive change, although the areas most affected by poor health are not fully delineated.

The counterpart to the thesis of illness and accelerated decline with age is the preservation of cognitive skill with the maintenance of health. Healthy living has long been associated with activity or exercise—mental and physical. This also has relevance for the process of rehabilitation with older adults. For example, there is preliminary evidence that a more stimulating, enriched environment may be beneficial to cognitive status and actually stimulate neurological changes (increased neuronal synapses) in the brains of older organisms (Moss and Albert 1988; Restak 1988). Also, physical exercise has been found to bear some relationship to maintenance and improvement of cognition in older adulthood. Circulatory changes, causing increased blood and oxygen transport to the brain, are often given as the explanation for this phenomenon, with increased arousal as a mediating variable. However, metabolic, neural, hormonal, and psychological factors may also play a part. In distinguishing between elders who exercise and those who are sedentary, it has been found that active older adults perform better on a variety of cognitive measures (Clarkson-Smith and Hartley 1989; Stones and Kozma 1989). In addition, cognitive improvement has been demonstrated to be an acute effect of a single period of light aerobic and strengthening exercise (Molloy et al. 1988a). However, intervention studies designed to investigate the beneficial effect of an exercise program on cognition in older adults have yielded mixed results. Positive effect has been demonstrated with healthy, although sometimes sedentary, elders (Barry et al. 1966; Dustman et al. 1984; Elsayed et al. 1980), but many studies show no differences (Blumenthal and Madden 1988; Emery and Gatz 1990; Madden et al. 1989; Molloy et al. 1988b). Such factors as the type of exercise, its intensity, and the length of the program, as well as the areas of cognition being tapped and the timing of their measurement, have been implicated in explaining the variable results.

While research on the effect of mental and physical exercise on cognitive status is preliminary, implications for the rehabilitation setting are readily apparent. The rehabilitation setting may also be a natural milieu for further investigation. The rehabilitation process naturally treats physical and cognitive recovery simultaneously. The hypothesis that the typical level of mental and physical activity involved in rehabilitation therapies may also be beneficial to cognitive status for the older patient is appealing and appears straightforward, yet is likely quite complicated. Should the beneficial, acute effect of physical exercise on cognition prove to be a robust finding, it might also be considered in the timing and pacing of therapies (e.g., sequencing cognitively demanding activities subsequent to physically demanding ones).

In sum, specific cognitive changes with aging have been quantitatively demonstrated time and again in the voluminous literature in this area. The actual difference such changes make in the lives of older adults is varied and subject to interpretation. Compensatory mechanisms operate both among the older individual's various cognitive abilities and in the demands imposed by the stage of later life. Health status may influence the range of compensation available to the older adult. Illness may narrow compensatory cognitive options available as well as change the external demands (such as increasing dependency and hospitalization) confronting the older adult.

AGING AND PERSONALITY CHANGES

The search for definitive answers to the question of personality change and aging has spawned extensive theoretical and research literature. Despite this great amount of study, the existence and nature of personality change in later adulthood has not been conclusively established. Results are heavily influenced by the research methodology employed and the theoretical viewpoint taken (Bengtson et al. 1985; Costa and McCrae 1980; Neugarten 1977).

The literature on aging and personality does, however, negate the myths propagated about the aged personality profile. Descriptions of older adults as universally more rigid, overly cautious, more passive, and less hopeful, are at best simplistic and generally invalid. As is often the case in the study of socially stigmatized groups, these negative stereotypes are more likely the result of studying psychopathology in older adults instead of normal aging. For example, contrary to the bias that self-esteem is lowered in old age due to loss and inevitable depression, the literature on aging shows that self-esteem is maintained or even higher in the older generations studied (Bengtson et al. 1985). Other factors (such as social, situational, and personal life changes that occur in aging) are at least as important in determining self-esteem as age itself (McCrae and Costa 1988). The individual's attitudes toward growing older may also be of particular significance in maintaining self-esteem in older age (Ward 1977). The assumption that positive body image spontaneously declines in later years has been another stereotype propagated about growing older. In actuality, studies generally support stability in this area, contradicting the self-view of old as ugly. Conclusions, however, are limited by research design and the sampling largely of physically well older adults (Berscheid et al. 1973; Plutchik et al. 1971; Plutchik et al. 1973).

Finally, broad characterizations of regressive personality change or intensification of established traits with aging have not found substantial support (Cohen 1988). There is at least an equal amount of attention given to a growth model of personality and aging. This viewpoint states that positive change continues to occur in older adulthood as personality becomes more differentiated or individualized with time and an increasing variety of life experiences (e.g., Haan and Day 1974).

Assuming that the stereotypes of the aging personality have been laid to rest, the following discussion highlights important literature addressing the question of personality change from developmental and trait theoretical perspectives.

Developmental Theory

Developmental theorists emphasize the evolution of personality through the life span in a variety of forms (e.g., life stages, tasks, transitions, etc.). While theorists, such as Freud, placed greatest emphasis on early development, Carl Jung and Erik Erikson are both noted for focusing attention on later life as well. Jung described development as an individuation process with the ultimate goal of differentiation and balanced blending of the various facets of personality. He described later life as a period of turning energies inward with an emphasis on wisdom and spiritualism (Hall and Lindzey 1970). Erikson (1950), in defining his eight stages of ego crisis, described the last task of life as one of resolving the conflict of ego integrity versus despair. Achieving integrity involves accepting the personal inevitability of one's life as it has been lived, resulting in a wisdom of age and a heightened sense of kinship with mankind. More recent research that is specifically focused on intrapsychic change in personality and aging is based upon these theoretical foundations of Jung and Erikson. In the Kansas City Studies of Adult Life, Neugarten (1968, 1973, 1977) and her associates substantiate a shift toward introversion or growing interiority in the second half of life. This is described as a greater emotional preoccupation with one's own inner life, rather than emotional attachment to people and objects outside of oneself. Interiority does not necessarily imply social introversion, but reflects a growing attention to the control and satisfaction of personal needs and a lessened sensitivity to the external environment and reactions of others.

Neugarten and Gutmann (1968) also provide evidence of incorporation of traditionally defined opposite sex characteristics into self-conceptions with age. Men and women may be said to move to a more androgynous balance with age, predominately expressed in covert, indirect ways rather than through marked behavioral change. While each sex maintains its own dominant identified role, men in later life come to integrate a greater sense of nurturance, tenderness, and dependency or affiliation in their self-views. In contrast, women come to accept their more autonomous, aggressive, or dominating impulses. Costa and McCrae (1978) have also provided support for this shift in a longitudinal study of personality in males.

Gutmann (1977) has provided cross-cultural evidence for this phenomenon and further elaborates differences in his conclusion that men move from a more active to passive mode of mastery with age, while women develop in the reverse. In youth and middle years, men are socialized toward competitiveness and instrumentality, but later life brings a more passive expression of personal competence in the form of focus on family and religion. Gutmann also indicates that aging may bring a type of magical mastery in which a more primitive, reality-distorting aspect of personality emerges in reconciling the older man to the demands of his environment. In contrast to men, women are described as taking a position of passive mastery earlier in life, trading submission for security, and gravitating toward more active mastery in later years. Troll and Parron (1981) state qualified support for the thesis of sex role change and flexibility and further promote its adaptational value as increasing age brings diminishing resources. They review a variety of possible reasons for this shift, including biological changes, major life events, and socialization processes. The latter category highlights the puzzle of both generational and cultural shifts in understanding sex role changes in age, especially in contemporary American society where the changing role of women is evident and fluidity in sex roles is espoused (Erdwins et al. 1983).

Trait Theory

Traits may be defined as characteristic ways of thinking, feeling, and acting (Costa and McCrae 1989). Trait theorists take a more empirical, experimentally rigorous approach to personality by identifying it as a hierarchical aggregation of traits. They attempt to identify and analyze personality through varying levels of traits using more objective design, measurement, and analysis. Theorists such as Cattell, Eysenck, and Guilford have attempted to identify core personality traits that can be reliably conceived and measured across individuals. For example, Eysenck (1953, 1981) has analyzed personality along the three broad dimensions of neuroticism, extraversion-introversion, and psychoticism. He proposes that an individual's traits and characteristic responses flow from these overriding factors.

Investigators in this area have largely concluded that consistency in personality is more the rule than change in personality as one ages. Costa and McCrae (1980, 1989) are prominent researchers in this area. In their work with subjects in the Baltimore Longitudinal Study of Aging, they have repeatedly demonstrated the stability of essential personality traits in structure, consistency, and mean level. Costa and McCrae originally conceptualized personality in the form of three core factors—neuroticism, extraversion, and openness to experience. More recently, they expanded their concept to include two additional factors, agreeableness and conscientiousness (McCrae and Costa 1987; Costa and McCrae 1988). Employing large samples of primarily well-educated men, as well as variable measures and designs for data collection to illustrate convergent/discriminant validity, they have concluded that personality continues to change in the twenties (often considered the first decade of adulthood) but is largely stable after 30 years of age. Conley (1985) corroborates the stability of traits of neuroticism, social extraversion, and impulse control longitudinally over a 19 year period as well as providing limited supplementary evidence of the stability of neuroticism and social extraversion for up to 45 years. His study is distinguished by its elaborate design allowing for a multitrait-multimethod-multioccasion analysis of data.

The Question of Change

Despite the evidence for and against stability of personality, one cannot ignore the compelling fact that individuals perceive their personality to change as they age. In their review, Bengtson and associates (1985) provide evidence that individuals are prone to subjectively perceive change in their personality with age. Woodruff and Birren (1972), in a longitudinal study tracking subjects from adolescence to middle age, found subjects to retrospectively perceive greater change in their personality than could be objectively demonstrated. Ryff (1982), in a study of self-perceived change in personality in the middle- to old-age transition, also demonstrated patterns of subjective change when personality factors were selected on the basis of developmental theory. She argued that the discrepancy between the findings of objective and subjective personality change with age is significantly influenced by the extent to which developmental theory guides research and the measures selected to investigate personality. McCrae and Costa (1988) more recently illustrated this conclusion by finding only minimal evidence of age differences in a subjective measure of self-concept when the data were analyzed according to their less developmentally-based five factor model of personality. They concluded that self-perceived changes in personality with age are largely misperceptions (Costa and McCrae 1989).

Thus, the interaction of personality and aging remains an area of enigma in which clinical impression does not always match research, and varying theoretical positions lead to equally differing conclusions. Throughout the prolific literature on the topic (see Kogan 1990 for a recent updated review), however, most theorists are open to the possibility of both consistency and change in personality during the life span. While the weight of evidence suggests that personality structure or temperament (i.e., personality style) remains notably stable in maturity, Costa and McCrae (1980) suggest variation in the *expression* of traits with age. Similarly, Bengtson and associates (1985) distinguish between process-oriented (structural) dimensions of personality, which remain stable with time, and content-oriented dimensions (interests, role-related behaviors, attitudes), which are more susceptible to change with maturation. Trait theorists (Costa and McCrae 1980) acknowledge that their research does not exhaust the number of ways (traits) in which personality may vary with age. Ryff (1982) highlights the fact that choice of traits to be measured will also influence the answer to the question of personality change with age. Thus, it is possible that there are some aspects of personality more likely to continue to develop in later years, while other areas remain highly stable.

Consistency in personality through the years should not be confused with diminished individual differences. All researchers in this area promote a sense of respect for the continuing individuality of people as they age. In the words of McCrae and Costa, "People stay much the same in their basic dispositions, and these enduring traits lead them to particular and ever-changing lives" (1984, 2).

Aging, Illness, and Personality

The evidence of specific personality change in later years with the onset of illness has also been relatively inconclusive. It is obvious that personality influences one's reaction to illness, but whether illness interacts with the aging process to produce universal personality changes is less well understood. Research in this area is notably limited.

Proposals of less differentiated self-concept and increased introversion in older adults who are ill have met with very limited support and are often confounded by the depersonalizing effects of institutionalization, degree of physical impairment, and other age changes (e.g., Kahana and Coe 1969). Schwartz and Kleemeier (1965) suggested that aging and illness have similar effects upon certain aspects of personality (namely, self-concept and ego defenses) resulting in a cumulative, interactive influence. They proposed that the ill elder would be more introversive and passive, as well as have lower self-esteem and more intropunitive defenses. Results of their study provided very limited support for this hypothesis, but the experience of illness appeared to have a greater impact on personality than the aging process.

The notion of increased hypochondriasis with age and illness has also been suggested but has received only inconsistent support. Leon and associates (1979) presented longitudinal data on a group of high functioning males from repeated assessment with the Minnesota Multiphasic Personality Inventory over a 30 year period (from middle to old age). They found increases over time in scales measuring hypochondriasis, depression, and denial, confirming the results of earlier studies. All three of these scales are heavily weighted with items addressing physical symptomatology and modest elevations are often found in ill, hospitalized samples (Duckworth 1979). Their sample was biased by attrition due to death and only 39 percent of the final group reported chronic illness. In discussing the apparent increase in bodily concern, the authors are quick to point out the influence of realistic physical changes with age on the responses in later test administrations. It is also notable that scores on only two of the three scales (depression and denial) approached clinical significance.

In discussing hypochondriasis, neuroticism and aging, Costa and McCrae (1985) argue against indiscriminate increase in bodily preoccupation with age. They related hypochondriasis to neuroticism and propose that it varies by individual according to personality and not according to age. They further suggest that physical health does not significantly impact upon enduring personality traits as much as it influences affective states (such as depression and anxiety). The authors support this thesis with data on health care utilization among older adults and longitudinal patterns of symptom reporting with age. They conclude, "We cannot claim that there are no hypochondriacs among the elderly, but we do argue that hypochondriasis is no more prevalent in older age groups than in any other age groups" (1985, 26).

Control attribution is another facet of personality that has received some attention in relating aging, illness, and personality change. The widely researched concept of locus of control (Rotter 1966) refers to how individuals perceive influences in their lives, as being within their power (internal) to control or in the hands of outside agents (external), such as fate, chance, or powerful others. The literature on change with age in one's characteristic perception of locus of control is ambiguous. While it is often held that locus of control remains stable into older adulthood (e.g., Gatz et al. 1986; Kausler 1982; Kogan 1990; Ryckman and Malikiosi 1975), there has been limited evidence of increased externality in older adults (e.g., Bradley and Webb 1976; Lachman 1983; Pitcher et al 1987), as well as evidence of increased internality (e.g., Staats 1974; Wolk and Kurtz 1975). These conflicting results may not only be a product of research inconsistencies, but also of a failure to consider the multidimensionality of the control concept and its variation depending upon the context or domain being examined (Lachman 1986a, 1986b). Increased belief in external forces of control with age may occur in age-sensitive areas such as physical health and stamina. Thus, control attribution may be a facet of personality positioned for change in interaction with illness and aging. Lachman (1986a) found older adults to be more external than college students when specifically addressing areas of intelligence and health. Similarly, Bradley and Webb (1976) distinguished between a generalized locus of control trait and circumstance-specific reality orientations about control and found older subjects to be more externally oriented in social and physical areas. These studies promote the notion of differentiation in control attribution with increasing age and life experiences and support the possibility of a shift in this aspect of personality as older individuals begin to experience physical disability. Although internality is often viewed as critical to mental health and adjustment (Brown and Granick 1983; Linn and Hunter 1979; Wolk and Kurtz 1975), such personality change to selectively greater externality in older age may represent an adaptive refinement in coping, as discussed in the next section of this chapter.

In summary, the evidence for specific personality change related to the experience of illness in later years of life is slim. However, given the greater incidence of chronic disease and disability with increasing age, change in control attribution appears possible and warrants further study. Research in the area of illness, aging, and personality change frequently employs relatively healthy samples of older adults. So the interaction of more severe disability with age and personality is also yet to be fully explored. Speculations as to personality change in the severely ill older adult run the gamut. At one extreme, minimal effect is hypothesized; at the other extreme, radical personality change could occur with illness/disability that closely predates death. This could take the form of personality regression similar to the terminal drop hypothesis of cognition and aging.

AGING AND COPING CHANGES

Coping with stress is a complex, multifaceted process which is highly individualized. Isolating the effects of any single factor, such as age, is not only difficult but also of questionable utility. Age may be a factor involved in how people cope, but it has not proven to be a universally powerful one. In discussing age and coping, Lazarus and DeLongis state, "Obscuring any age effects are the ubiquitous individual and group differences in the way people manage their lives within any age span" (1983, 252).

Conceptualizations of Coping

Age-related changes in coping have been conceptualized from developmental, situational, and interactive (or transitional) viewpoints. Developmental interpretations focus upon the individual and largely support the idea of change in coping with age. The developmental view can be subdivided into opposing positions of regression and growth. The regression hypothesis (e.g., Pfeiffer 1977) states that in later life coping becomes more primitive, with increasing use of distortion and denial. The growth hypothesis proposes the evolution of more mature, adaptive coping behaviors in adulthood which are maintained or further refined in late life (e.g., Valliant 1977). The regression hypothesis has received minimal research support and is essentially based upon a model of psychopathology in later life. Some support for the growth hypothesis is evident in several studies demonstrating the use of less defensive, theoretically immature coping strategies in middle to late adulthood in comparison to adolescence and young adulthood (Irion and Blanchard-Fields 1987; McCrae 1982).

More recent research (Labouvie-Vief et al. 1987; Blanchard-Fields and Irion 1988a) provides a variation on the growth hypothesis by focusing on the concept of maturity as distinct from chronological age. Development of cognitive and ego complexity is stipulated as critical to more adaptive coping that is found with age. Increasing age and life experience may be necessary but not sufficient for growth in coping and successful adaptation in later life. This refined idea of maturity (versus simply growing older) supports the self-evident conclusion that people who have had a history of poor coping ability in life will most likely continue to have difficulty with increasing age.

Situational interpretations of coping and aging emphasize the importance of the type of stress experienced. Age differences in coping are viewed as largely a function of the changes in types of stressors facing the individual at different life stages (McCrae 1982, 1984). Research in this area focuses on the specific content and attributes of stressors as critical in determining coping. While older adults are said to experience fewer daily stresses and life transitions than their younger counterparts (Lazarus and DeLongis 1983), those experienced may be more frequently serious and uncontrollable. McCrae (1982) notes that more stressors are perceived as challenges in youth, while stressors in later life are often perceived as threats and losses. Health concerns (possibly perceived as threats or losses) tend to be prominent stressors for older adults (e.g., Folkman et al. 1987; Folkman and Lazarus 1980; Koenig et al. 1988).

Returning to the literature of life span/developmental theorists provides a means of understanding the stresses accompanying late adulthood. Several theorists have proposed developmental steps of late life in the form of tasks (Havighurst 1974), transitions (Levinson 1978), or crises (Erikson 1950; Peck 1968). In synthesizing their respective views, the following broad categories of stressors emerge: (1) dealing with multiple losses in such areas as health and vigor; social, work, and economic status; and significant others; (2) redirection of energies and formation of new identities (e.g., examining how one spends time; how one views youth and age, work and play); (3) re-examination of values including the importance placed upon physical strength, oneself and one's life, as well as one's place in society; and (4) review of life, establishing its meaningfulness, and preparation for death.

Consideration of these proposed developmental issues provides a means of describing and categorizing the kinds of stressors found in late life, as well as understanding some of the components of successful maturation in later years. Means of adaptation which are frequently associated with old age, such as the role of reminiscence (Butler 1963; Coleman 1986), disengagement (Cumming and Henry 1961), and re-engagement (Lazarus and DeLongis 1983), can be seen as relevant, broad coping strategies within the context of these developmental issues.

The interactive or transactional interpretation illustrates the complexity of coping (e.g., Folkman and Lazarus 1980). Both the attributes of the individual and the situation are considered in a dynamic, transactional process, making coping more complicated and individualized. Age becomes only one of many potentially relevant variables that influence coping. This comprehensive conceptualization permits consideration of mediating, buffering factors and acknowledges individual variation in process and outcome. Specifically, it allows for questioning how an individual of a given makeup and life position will cope over time in a specific stressful situation. Research in this area has demonstrated various coping patterns by age, situation, and other personality variables (Blanchard-Fields and Irion 1988b; Fiefel and Strack 1989; Feifel et al. 1987). If age is but one variable of potential importance in coping, then the interactive approach may help in discerning when it is of greater relevance than other variables. An area that has received substantial attention in this regard is that of coping, control, and aging.

Coping, Control, and Aging

Perceived control has long been viewed as a critical factor in the type of coping strategy employed and its success. Rodin (1986) and Rodin and associates

(1982) essentially equate coping with establishment of some form of control, whether it be actual or simply perceived. They view older adults as particularly vulnerable to loss of control in life and consequently increasingly susceptible to illness. Thus, they see the relationship between control (as coping) and health growing stronger with age. They intervened with a nursing home population to facilitate choice and personal responsibility and were able to demonstrate positive outcomes, including improved health.

Folkman and Lazarus (1980) propose differential use of coping strategies based upon stress appraisal. Thus, when a situation is perceived as controllable, more action-oriented, instrumental coping strategies are likely to be successfully employed. In contrast, in less controllable situations (such as many health related stressors), strategies to manage emotions predominate. This proposition has been used as the basis for considering older adults to be more likely to use emotion-focused coping in the face of the increasing number of uncontrollable stressors which they experience. This hypothesis may risk overgeneralization and has received only mixed support in the literature (Folkman et al. 1987; Koenig et al. 1988).

There is also evidence of greater differentiation in perceptions of control with age in the observation that middle-aged and older adults show a greater ability to accurately appraise stressors and thus choose a more adaptive coping strategy. Research specifically focused on controllability and coping (Blanchard-Fields and Robinson 1987; Blanchard-Fields and Irion 1988a, 1988b; Lachman 1986a) suggests that older adults may be more discriminating in their perception of control in specific situations and may expect there to be multiple sources of control. For example, Blanchard-Fields and Robinson (1987) report older adults to be more externally oriented regarding the cause of a stressor, but to express no less responsibility than younger subjects for coping with it. For the older adult, the selection of a coping strategy may flow from this more differentiated viewpoint and confound more general hypotheses about the relationship between controllability, coping, and aging.

Health Related Stressors and Aging

Coping with health stressors grows increasingly significant with age. A deterioration in health is most often perceived as less controllable (a threat or loss, according to McCrae 1984), and it is hypothesized that such stress would prompt more emotion-focused coping (Folkman and Lazarus 1980). However, research specifically focused on health related stressors has not conclusively supported this rationale. Studies in coping with illness show adult subjects coping in predominately active, problem-solving ways just as frequently as in emotionally-focused, palliative ways. In addition, there is limited support for the beneficial effects of active, instrumental coping over more passive, emotion-focused coping (Felton and Revenson 1984). Although the research is far from clear, it further shows that, overall, older adults faced with illness use active and passive coping strategies as much as their younger counterparts in similar situations (Folkman et al. 1987; Keyes et al. 1987; Koenig et al. 1988).

How health is appraised as a stressor with increasing age may be just as important in determining how older adults cope with illness and disability. Such factors as illness severity and the expectations regarding health that come with age appear relevant. Prohaska and associates (1987) found older subjects to exhibit a modest trend toward attribution of symptoms to the aging process, thus becoming more passive in their coping. While aging attribution was most operable in instances of mild symptoms, in some cases aging attribution undercut active coping with more severely labeled illness as well. Felton and Revenson (1987) studied six coping strategies in a group of chronically ill adults, controlling for illness severity and controllability. They concluded that age becomes more important in coping as the characteristics of the stressor (in this case, health) become more highly specified and relevant to the aging process.

In general, the literature continues to suggest that people are apt to use a range of coping strategies in very individualized combinations. Variability appears to be the norm, particularly in health related circumstances and perhaps with increasing age as well. In describing attributes of effective coping, Pearlin and Schooler (1978) propose that a wider repertoire of responses, higher socioeconomic status, higher inner resources of mastery and self-esteem, and lower self-denigration predict better coping across all ages. In view of inconclusive research results and the virtue of a varied range of responses, classifying either active or passive health related coping responses as more adaptive or more characteristic of older adults appears less useful than acknowledging the advantage of a combination of both.

Research suggests that encouraging control and an active role can be important for the coping of the chronically ill older adult (Rodin 1986; Rodin et al. 1982). Environmental manipulation and individual intervention to emphasize realistic choice and personal responsibility for health have been shown to be effective coping enhancers, and coaching in these areas may be needed for older adults. Active seeking of information and assistance as a coping strategy may also need to be encouraged as cohort differences and erroneous aging attributions may subvert these more active, adaptive coping strategies in older adults. Elders may inappropriately delay seeking treatment, view therapy as not viable for them, or tolerate correctable problems, all in the name of normal aging. However, the risk of ageism and erroneous age attributions may be equally pertinent to the professional. If subsequent research confirms the notion of older adults as having a more differentiated sense of controllability, then the older patient may at times be the better judge of what is personally possible than the usually younger professional advocating a particular goal or health-related activity.

Emphasis on maturity rather than chronological age (Labouvie-Vief et al. 1987) appears important to understanding coping in later life. Increasing cognitive complexity and ego integration, supporting more unique, elaborated inner standards and more mature emotional defenses, may mediate relationships between age and coping. This may be particularly important in coping with stressors where little direct control can be exercised (such as health and illness). While older adults may have developed these attributes by virtue of their more extensive experience with developmental tasks, age is no guarantee of complete, flawless development. Interventions to facilitate coping with illness in the older adult may need to capitalize upon these strengths when they exist and assist their development when they do not.

In sum, coping appears to evolve with age, but probably in a highly individualized manner. When addressing coping in a broad sense, stability throughout age groups is consistently shown; when specific stressors are highlighted, age may show a modest effect. Deterioration of coping ability with age has not proven to be true, but the concept of maturity highlights the fact that the older adult with a flawed developmental history will have fewer internal resources to cope with the threats and losses (including health) of late life. Age may be modestly related to coping with health related stressors, especially as seriousness of the illness increases. However, the relationships between intervening factors in this association are not yet clear. Health expectations and aging attributions, as well as cohort differences have been shown to play a role in how older adults cope with health stressors. Given the complex, multifactorial nature of coping, respecting individual differences in stress appraisal and strategy is essential, and it is incumbent upon the clinician to investigate the origins of individual coping behavior, especially in older adults, prior to judging its adequacy.

CONCLUSION

In this chapter, cognitive, personality, and coping changes with age have been reviewed along with discussion of how illness interacts with these aspects of the older individual. The concepts and research which are summarized here provide a background for understanding the psychology of the older adult and also have implications for the practice of geriatric rehabilitation.

Decline in specific areas of cognition have been demonstrated in older adulthood, but their functional implications are quite varied. Cognitive plasticity or reserve for new learning remains intact in later years, although its capacity may be diminished, particularly under the stress of chronic illness. Rehabilitation, as a learning experience, may require some special considerations for older adults (e.g., pacing and deliberately teaching learning and memory strategies). In developing treatment goals and facilitating learning and compliance, rehabilitation specialists may be helped by working in the context of teaching/learning; that is, the interaction of the older adult, the hospital environment, and specific therapy tasks. This approach raises important, complex questions, such as how older adults view physical disability and rehabilitation, what motivates them to learn in rehabilitation, and how much their apparent learning deficit is actually a knowledge deficit regarding contemporary medical technology.

Universal changes in personality with age are not clearly substantiated and depend upon the theoretical position one espouses. Developmental theorists propose evolution of personality with age and changing stages of life, citing increasing interiority and flexibility of sex roles in later years. Trait theorists provide evidence of the stability of core personality factors throughout adult life. Whichever position one favors, it is clear that aged personality stereotypes are unfounded and that individuality is preserved (and perhaps elaborated) in older adulthood. Most attempts at delineating personality changes with illness in later life have failed to produce significant distinguishing features, although control attribution may prove to be an exception. Investigation of personality change in later life in the context of severe illness/debilitation has yet to be fully addressed. In view of these findings, it is imperative that rehabilitation professionals avoid subordinating the older patient's individuality to a predominating disability. Older patients require as much investigation of their individuality as younger patients in order to discern who they are and how they will respond to treatment. Their extensive history will reveal a unique personality.

Coping is a very individualized, complex process and there are no clear-cut changes in how one copes with increasing years of life. Older individuals do not uniformly cope in more passive ways as compared to younger adults. It appears most adaptive to possess a wider range of coping strategies and the flexibility to use them to meet the stresses of life. Further, chronological age is independent of emotional maturity, and poor coping ability in youth will likely presage poor coping ability in age. Age may play a more significant role in determining coping if a stressor is particularly relevant to the aging process, such as health/illness. The perception of the severity and controllability of illness, as well as expectations for health, are influenced by age attributions and are important to understanding coping in the older adult. Rehabilitation professionals should assess maturity level and perceptions of disability, health, and aging when addressing how their older patients cope. Promoting patient involvement, enhancing a sense of realistic control/mastery, and addressing age misattributions are important to facilitate coping and adaptation in the older adult. Finally, the rehabilitation clinician must learn to respect the coping of the mature, self-aware elder and make provisions for psychotherapy in the case of the poorly adjusted elder where coping is underdeveloped.

REFERENCES

Albert, M.S. 1988. Cognitive function. In *Geriatric Neuropsychology*, edited by M.S. Albert and M.B. Moss, 33–56. New York: Guilford Press.

Albert, M.S., and R.K. Heaton. 1988. Intelligence testing. In *Geriatric Neuropsychology*, edited by M.S. Albert and M.B. Moss, 13–32. New York: Guilford Press.

Arenberg, D., and E.A. Robertson-Tchabo. 1977. Learning and aging. In *Handbook of the Psychology of Aging*, edited by J.E. Birren and K.W. Schaie, 421–49. New York: Van Nostrand Reinhold Co.

Baltes, P.B., and U. Lindenberger. 1988. On the range of cognitive plasticity in old age as a function of experience: 15 years of intervention research. *Behavior Therapy* 19: 283–300.

Barry, A.J., J.R. Steinmetz, H.G. Page, et al. 1966. The effects of physical conditioning on older individuals. II. Motor performance and cognitive function. *Journal of Gerontology* 21: 192–9.

Bayles, K.A., and A.W. Kaszniak. 1987. *Communication and Cognition in Normal Aging and Dementia*. Boston: Little, Brown and Co.

Bengtson, V.L., M.N. Reedy, and C. Gordon. 1985. Aging and self-conceptions: Personality processes and social contexts. In *The Handbook of the Psychology of Aging*, 2d ed., edited by J.E. Birren and K.W. Schaie, 544–93. New York: Van Nostrand Reinhold Co.

Berscheid, E., E. Walster, and G. Bohrnstedt. 1973. Body image. The happy American body: A survey report. *Psychology Today* 7(6): 119–131.

Birren, J.E., and K.W. Schaie. 1977. *Handbook of the Psychology of Aging*. New York: Van Nostrand Reinhold Co.

Birren, J.E., and K.W. Schaie. 1985. *Handbook of the Psychology of Aging*, 2d ed. New York: Van Nostrand Reinhold Co.

Birren, J.E., and K.W. Schaie. 1990. *Handbook of the Psychology of Aging*, 3d ed. New York: Academic Press, Inc.

Blanchard-Fields, F., and J.C. Irion. 1988a. Coping strategies from the perspective of two developmental markers: Age and social reasoning. *Journal of Genetic Psychology* 149: 141–51.

Blanchard-Fields, F., and J.C. Irion. 1988b. The relation between locus of control and coping in two contexts: Age as a moderator variable. *Psychology and Aging* 3: 197–203.

Blanchard-Fields, F., and S.L. Robinson. 1987. Age differences in the relation between controllability and coping. *Journal of Gerontology* 42: 497–501.

Blumenthal, J.A., and D.J. Madden. 1988. Effects of aerobic exercise training, age, and physical fitness on memory-search performance. *Psychology and Aging* 3: 280–5.

Botwinick, J. 1977. Intellectual abilities. In *Handbook of the Psychology of Aging*, edited by J.E. Birren and K.W. Schaie, 580–605. New York: Van Nostrand Reinhold Co.

Bradley, R.H., and R. Webb. 1976. Age-related differences in locus of control orientation in three behavior domains. *Human Development* 19: 49–55.

Brown, B.R., and S. Granick. 1983. Cognitive and psychosocial differences between I and E locus of control in aged persons. *Experimental Aging Research* 9: 107–10.

Busse, E.W. 1969. Theories of aging. In *Behavior and Adaptation in Later Life*, edited by E.W. Busse and E. Pfeiffer, 11–32. Boston: Little, Brown and Co.

Butler, R.N. 1963. The life review: An interpretation of reminiscence in the aged. *Psychiatry* 26: 65–76.

Cerella, J. 1990. Aging and information-processing rate. In *Handbook of the Psychology of Aging*, 3d ed., edited by J.E. Birren and K.W. Schaie, 201–21. New York: Academic Press, Inc.

Clarkson-Smith, L., and A.A. Hartley. 1989. Relationships between physical exercise and cognitive abilities in older adults. *Psychology and Aging* 4: 183–9.

Cohen, G.D. 1988. *The Brain in Human Aging.* New York: Springer Publishing Co.

Coleman, P.G. 1986. *Aging and Reminiscence Processes.* New York: John Wiley and Sons.

Conley, J.J. 1985. Longitudinal stability of personality traits: A multitrait-multimethod-multioccasion analysis. *Journal of Personality and Social Psychology* 49: 1266–82.

Cornelius, S.W., and A. Caspi. 1987. Everyday problem solving in adulthood and old age. *Psychology and Aging* 2: 144–53.

Costa, P.T., and R.R. McCrae. 1978. Age differences in personality structure revisited: Studies in validity, stability, and change. *International Journal of Aging and Human Development* 8: 295–309.

Costa, P.T., and R.R. McCrae. 1980. Still stable after all these years: Personality as a key to some issues in adulthood and old age. In *Life-Span Development and Behavior,* Vol. 3, edited by P.B. Baltes and O.G. Brim, Jr., 65–102. New York: Academic Press.

Costa, P.T., and R.R. McCrae. 1985. Hypochrondriasis, neuroticism, and aging. *American Psychologist* 40: 19–28.

Costa, P.T., and R.R. McCrae. 1988. Personality in adulthood: A six-year longitudinal study of self-reports and spouse ratings on the NEO personality inventory. *Personality and Social Psychology* 54: 853–63.

Costa, P.T., and R.R. McCrae. 1989. Personality continuity and the changes of adult life. In *The Adult Years: Continuity and Change,* edited by M. Storandt and G.R. VandenBos, 41–77. Washington, D.C.: American Psychological Association.

Craik, F.I.M. 1977. Age differences in human memory. In *Handbook of the Psychology of Aging,* edited by J.E. Birren and K.W Schaie, 384–420. New York: Van Nostrand Reinhold Co.

Cumming, E., and E.W. Henry. 1961. *Growing Old: The Process of Disengagement.* New York: Basic Books.

Duckworth, J.C. 1979. *MMPI: Interpretation Manual for Counselors and Clinicians,* 2d ed. Muncie, Ind.: Accelerated Development, Inc.

Dustman, R.E., R.O. Ruhling, E.M. Russell, et al. 1984. Aerobic exercise training and improved neuropsychological function of older individuals. *Neurobiology of Aging* 5: 35–42.

Elias, M.F., J.W. Elias, and P.K. Elias. 1990. Biological and health influences on behavior. In *Handbook of the Psychology of Aging,* 3d ed., edited by J.E. Birren and K.W. Schaie, 80–102. New York: Academic Press.

Elsayed, M., A.H. Ismail, and R.J. Young. 1980. Intellectual differences of adult men related to age and physical fitness before and after an exercise program. *Journal of Gerontology* 35: 383–7.

Emery, C.F., and M. Gatz. 1990. Psychological and cognitive effects of an exercise program for community-residing older adults. *The Gerontologist* 30: 184–8.

Erdwins, C.J., Z.E. Tyer, and J.C. Mellinger. 1983. A comparison of sex role and related personality traits in young, middle-aged, and older women. *International Journal of Aging and Human Development* 17: 141–52.

Erikson, E. 1950. *Childhood and Society.* New York: W.W. Norton and Co., Inc.

Eysenck, H.J. 1953. *The Structure of Human Personality.* New York: John Wiley & Sons.

Eysenck, H.J., ed. 1981. *A Model of Personality.* New York: Springer-Verlag.

Feifel, H., and S. Strack. 1989. Coping with conflict situations: Middle-aged and elderly men. *Psychology and Aging* 4: 26–33.

Feifel, H., S. Strack, and V.T. Nagy. 1987. Degree of life-threat and differential use of coping modes. *Journal of Psychosomatic Research* 31: 91–9.

Felton, B.J., and T.A. Revenson. 1984. Coping with chronic illness: A study of illness controllability and the influence of coping strategies on psychological adjustment. *Journal of Consulting and Clinical Psychology* 52: 343–53.

Felton, B.J., and T.A. Revenson. 1987. Age differences in coping with chronic illness. *Psychology and Aging* 2: 164–70.

Folkman, S., and R.S. Lazarus. 1980. An analysis of coping in a middle-aged community sample. *Journal of Health and Social Behavior* 21: 219–39.

Folkman, S., R.S. Lazarus, S. Pimley, et al. 1987. Age differences in stress and coping processes. *Psychology and Aging* 2: 171–84.

Gatz, M., I.C. Siegler, L.K. George, et al. 1986. Attributional components of locus of control: Longitudinal, retrospective, and contemporaneous analyses. In *The Psychology of Control and Aging,* edited by M.M. Baltes and P.B. Baltes, 237–63. Hillsdale, N.J.: Lawrence Erlbaum Associates.

Gounard, B.R., and I.M. Hulicka. 1977. Maximizing learning efficiency in later adulthood: A cognitive problem-solving approach. *Educational Gerontology: An International Quarterly* 2: 417–27.

Gutmann, D. 1977. The cross-cultural perspective: Notes toward a comparative psychology of aging. In *The Handbook of the Psychology of Aging,* edited by J.E. Birren and K.W. Schaie, 302–26. New York: Van Nostrand Reinhold Co.

Haan, N., and D. Day. 1974. A longitudinal study of change and sameness in personality development: Adolescence to later adulthood. *International Journal of Aging and Human Development* 5: 11–39.

Hall, C.S., and G. Lindzey. 1970. *Theories of Personality.* New York: John Wiley and Sons.

Havighurst, R.J. 1974. *Developmental Tasks and Education* 3d ed. New York: David McKay Co.

Hertzog, C., and K.W. Schaie. 1988. Stability and change in adult intelligence: 2. Simultaneous analysis of longitudinal means and covariance structures. *Psychology and Aging* 3: 122–30.

Horn, J.L., and R.B. Cattell. 1967. Age differences in fluid and crystallized intelligence. *Acta Psychologica* 26: 107–29.

Hultsch, D.R., and R.A. Dixon. 1990. Learning and memory in aging. In *Handbook of the Psychology of Aging,* 3d ed., edited by J.E. Birren and K.W. Schaie, 259–74. New York: Academic Press.

Irion, J.C., and F. Blanchard-Fields. 1987. A cross-sectional comparison of adaptive coping in adulthood. *Journal of Gerontology* 42: 502–4.

Jarvik, L.F. 1962. Biological differences in intellectual functioning. *Vita Humana* 5: 195–203.

Jarvik, L.F. 1988. Aging of the brain: How can we prevent it? *The Gerontologist* 28: 739–47.

Kahana, E., and R.M. Coe. 1969. Self and staff conceptions of institutionalized aged. *The Gerontologist* 9: 264–7.

Kausler, D.H. 1982. *Experimental Psychology and Human Aging.* New York: John Wiley.

Kausler, D.H. 1987. Memory and memory therapy. In *The Encyclopedia of Aging,* edited by G.L. Maddox, 429–32. New York: Springer Publishing Co.

Keyes, K., B. Bisno, J. Richardson, et al. 1987. Age differences in coping, behavioral dysfunction and depression following colostomy surgery. *The Gerontologist* 27: 182–4.

Kleemeier, R.W. 1962. Intellectual change in the senium. *Proceedings of the Social Statistics Section of the American Statistical Association* 1: 290–95.

Koenig, H.G., L.K. George, and I.C. Siegler. 1988. The use of religion and other emotion-regulating coping strategies among older adults. *The Gerontologist* 28: 303–10.

Kogan, N. 1990. Personality and aging. In *Handbook of the Psychology of Aging,* 3d ed., edited by J.E. Birren and K.W. Schaie, 330–46. New York: Academic Press.

Labouvie-Vief, G. 1985. Intelligence and cognition. In *Handbook of the Psychology of Aging,* 2d ed., edited by J.E. Birren and K.W. Schaie, 500–30. New York: Van Nostrand Reinhold Co.

Labouvie-Vief, G., J. Hakim-Larson, and C.J. Hobart. 1987. Age, ego level, and the life-span development of coping and defense processes. *Psychology and Aging* 2: 286–293.

Labouvie-Vief, G., W.J. Hoyer, M.M. Baltes, et al. 1974. Operant analysis of intellectual behavior in old age. *Human Development* 17: 259–72.

Lachman, M.E. 1983. Perceptions of intellectual aging: Antecedent or consequence of intellectual functioning? *Developmental Psychology* 19: 482–98.

Lachman, M.E. 1986a. Locus of control in aging research: A case for multidimensional and domain-specific assessment. *Journal of Psychology and Aging* 1: 34–40.

Lachman, M.E. 1986b. Personal control in later life: Stability, change, and cognitive correlates. In *The Psychology of Control and Aging,* edited by M.M. Baltes and P.B. Baltes, 207–36. Hillsdale, N.J.: Lawrence Erlbaum Associates.

Lazarus, R.S., and A. DeLongis. 1983. Psychological stress and coping in aging. *American Psychologist* 38: 245–54.

Leon, G.R., B. Gillum, R. Gillum, et al. 1979. Personality stability and change over a 30-year period—middle age to old age. *Journal of Consulting and Clinical Psychology* 47: 517–24.

Levinson, D.J. 1978. *The Seasons of a Man's Life.* New York: Ballantine Books.

Linn, M.W., and K. Hunter. 1979. Perception of age in the elderly. *Journal of Gerontology* 34: 46–52.

Madden, D.J., J.A. Blumenthal, P.A. Allen, et al. 1989. Improving aerobic capacity in healthy older adults does not necessarily lead to improved cognitive performance. *Psychology and Aging* 4: 307–20.

McCrae, R.R. 1982. Age differences in the use of coping mechanisms. *Journal of Gerontology* 37: 454–60.

McCrae, R.R. 1984. Situational determinants of coping responses: Loss, threat, and challenge. *Journal of Personality and Social Psychology* 46: 919–28.

McCrae, R.R., and P.T. Costa. 1984. *Emerging Lives, Enduring Dispositions: Personality in Adulthood.* Boston: Little, Brown and Co.

McCrae, R.R., and P.T. Costa. 1987. Validation of the five-factor model of personality across instruments and observers. *Journal of Personality and Social Psychology* 52: 81–90.

McCrae, R.R., and P.T. Costa. 1988. Age, personality, and the spontaneous self-concept. *Journal of Gerontology* 43: S177–85.

Molloy, D.W., D.A. Beerschoten, M.J. Borrie, et al. 1988a. Acute effects of exercise on neuropsychological function in elderly subjects. *Journal of the American Geriatrics Society* 36: 29–33.

Molloy, D.W., L.D. Richardson, and R.G. Crilly. 1988b. The effects of a three-month exercise programme on neuropsychological function in elderly institutionalized women: A randomized controlled trial. *Age and Aging* 17: 303–10.

Moss, M.B., and M.S. Albert. 1988. Future directions in the study of aging. In *Geriatric Neuropsychology,* edited by M.S. Albert and M.B. Moss, 293–303. New York: Guilford Press.

Neugarten, B.L. 1968. Developmental perspectives. *Psychiatric Research Reports—American Psychiatric Association* 23: 42–8.

Neugarten, B.L. 1973. Personality change in late life: A developmental perspective. In *The Psychology of Adult Development and Aging,* edited by C. Eisdorfer and M.P. Lawton, 311–35. Washington, D.C.: American Psychological Association.

Neugarten, B.L. 1977. Personality and aging. In *The Handbook of the Psychology of Aging,* edited by J.E. Birren and K.W. Schaie, 626–49. New York: Van Nostrand Reinhold Co.

Neugarten, B.L. and D.L. Gutmann. 1968. Age-sex roles and personality in middle age: A thematic apperception study. In *Middle Age and Aging: A Reader in Social Psychology,* edited by B.L. Neugarten, 58–71. Chicago: University of Chicago Press.

Papalia, D.E., and D.D.V. Bielby. 1974. Cognitive functioning in middle and old age adults: A review of research based on Piaget's theory. *Human Development* 17: 424–43.

Pearlin, L.I., and C. Schooler. 1978. The structure of coping. *Journal of Health and Social Behavior* 19: 2–21.

Peck, R.C. 1968. Psychological developments in the second half of life. In *Middle Age and Aging: A Reader in Social Psychology,* edited by B.L. Neugarten, 88–92. Chicago: University of Chicago Press.

Pfeiffer, E. 1977. Psychopathology and social pathology. In *Handbook of the Psychology of Aging,* edited by J.E. Birren and K.W. Schaie, 650–71. New York: Van Nostrand Reinhold Co.

Pitcher, B.L., B.R. Spykerman, and M. Gazi-Tabatabaie. 1987. Stability of perceived personal control for older black and white men. *Research on Aging* 9: 200–25.

Plutchik, R., H. Conte, and M.B. Weiner. 1973. Studies of body image. II: Dollar values of body parts. *Journal of Gerontology* 28: 89–91.

Plutchik, R., M.B. Weiner, and H. Conte. 1971. Studies of body image. I: Body worries and body discomforts. *Journal of Gerontology* 26: 344–50.

Poon, L.W., ed. 1980. *Aging in the 1980's.* Washington, D.C.: American Psychological Association.

Poon, L.W. 1985. Differences in human memory with aging: Nature, causes, and clinical implications. In *Handbook of the Psychology of Aging,* 2d ed., edited by J.E. Birren and K.W. Schaie, 427–62. New York: Van Nostrand Reinhold Co.

Prohaska, T.R., M.L. Keller, E.A. Leventhal, et al. 1987. Impact of symptoms and aging attribution on emotions and coping. *Health Psychology* 6: 495–514.

Rabbitt, P. 1977. Changes in problem solving ability in old age. In *Handbook of the Psychology of Aging,* edited by J.E. Birren and K.W. Schaie, 606–25. New York: Van Nostrand Reinhold Co.

Reese, H.W., and D. Rodeheaver. 1985. Problem solving and complex decision making. In *Handbook of the Psychology of Aging,* edited by J.E. Birren and K.W. Schaie, 474–99. New York: Van Nostrand Reinhold Co.

Restak, R.M. 1988. *The Mind.* New York: Bantam Books.

Rodeheaver, D. 1987. Problem-solving. In *The Encyclopedia of Aging,* edited by G.L. Maddox, 537–9. New York: Springer Publishing Co.

Rodin, J. 1986. Heath, control, and aging. In *The Psychology of Control and Aging,* edited by M.M. Baltes and P.B. Baltes, 139–65. Hillsdale: Lawrence Erlbaum Associates.

Rodin, J., L.C. Bohm, and J.T. Wack. 1982. Control, coping, and aging: Models for research and intervention. *Applied Social Psychology Annual* 3: 153–80.

Rotter, J.B. 1966. Generalized expectancies for internal versus external control of reinforcement. *Psychological Monographs* 80: 1–28.

Ryckman, R.M., and M.X. Malikiosi. 1975. Relationship between locus of control and chronological age. *Psychological Reports* 36: 655–8.

Ryff, C.D. 1982. Self-perceived personality change in adulthood and aging. *Journal of Personality and Social Psychology* 42: 108–15.

Salthouse, T.A. 1985. Speed of behavior and its implications for cognition. In *Handbook of the Psychology of Aging,* 2d ed., edited by J.E. Birren and K.W. Schaie, 400–26. New York: Van Nostrand Reinhold Co.

Salthouse, T.A. 1989. Age-related changes in basic cognitive processes. In *The Adult Years: Continuity and Change,* edited by M. Storandt and G.R. Vanden Bos, 5–40. Washington, D.C.: American Psychological Association.

Salthouse, T.A. 1990. cognitive competence and expertise in aging. In *Handbook of the Psychology of Aging,* 3d ed., edited by J.E. Birren and K.W. Schaie, 311–19. New York: Academic Press.

Salthouse, T.A., and R. Kail. 1983. Memory development throughout the life span: The role of processing rate. In *Life-Span Development and Behavior,* Vol. 5, edited by P.B. Baltes and O.G. Brim, Jr., 89–116. New York: Academic Press.

Schaie, K.W. 1990. Intellectual development in adulthood. In *Handbook of the Psychology of Aging,* 3d ed., edited by J.E. Birren and K.W. Schaie, 291–310. New York: Academic Press.

Schwartz, A.N., and R.W. Kleemeier, 1965. The effects of illness and age upon some aspects of personality. *Journal of Gerontology* 20: 85–91.

Siegler, I.C., and P.T. Costa, Jr. 1985. Health behavior relationships. In *Handbook of the Psychology of Aging,* 2d ed., edited by J.E. Birren and K.W. Schaie, 144–66. New York: Van Nostrand Reinhold Co.

Staats, S. 1974. Internal versus external locus of control for three age groups. *International Journal of Aging and Human Development* 5: 7–10.

Steuer, J., A. LaRue, J.E. Blum, et al. 1981. "Critical loss" in the eighth and ninth decades. *Journal of Gerontology* 36: 211–13.

Stones, M.J., and A. Kozma. 1989. Age, exercise, and coding performance. *Psychology and Aging* 4: 190–4.

Troll, L.E., and E.M. Parron. 1981. Age changes in sex roles amid changing sex roles: The double shift. In *Annual Review of Gerontology and Geriatrics,* Vol. 2, edited by C. Eisdorfer, 118–43. New York: Springer Publishing Co.

Valliant, G.E. 1977. *Adaptation to Life.* Boston: Little, Brown and Co.

Ward, R.A. 1977. The impact of subjective age and stigma on older persons. *Journal of Gerontology* 32: 227–32.

Willis, S. 1985. Towards an educational psychology of the older adult learner: Intellectual and cognitive bases. In *Handbook of the Psychology of Aging,* 2d ed., edited by J.E. Birren and K.W. Schaie, 818–47. New York: Van Nostrand Reinhold Co.

Wolk, S., and J. Kurtz. 1975. Positive adjustment and involvement during aging and expectancy for internal control. *Journal of Consulting and Clinical Psychology* 43: 173–8.

Woodruff-Pak, D.S. 1990. Mammalian models of learning, memory, and aging. In *Handbook of the Psychology of Aging,* 3d ed., edited by J.E. Birren and K.W. Schaie, 235–58. New York: Academic Press.

Woodruff, D.S., and J.E. Birren. 1972. Age changes and cohort differences in personality. *Developmental Psychology* 6: 252–9.

Chapter 4

The Older Adult's Adjustment to the Rehabilitation Setting

Robert J. Hartke

Hospitalization at any age is a highly stressful event (Wilson-Barnett 1979). It is a change of environment thrust upon an individual already coping with the threat of physical illness. How a patient adjusts to the hospital environment is critical to successful outcome, particularly when the patient is expected to remain in the environment for an extended period of time and play an active role in the therapeutic process. These special expectations are routinely part of hospitalization in a rehabilitation facility. In addition, the rehabilitation environment and its emotional implications must be sufficiently well tolerated so that patients can direct energies to learning in therapies and emotionally adjusting to their disabilities. This chapter will explore the unique problems encountered by older adults in making this adjustment as they invest meaning into the hospitalization event and confront a very active milieu where comfort is placed secondary to the drive for independence.

For the purposes of this discussion, the hospital environment is being considered in a broad manner to include the objective, physical environment as well as the subjective, perceived environment. Significant others (e.g., family, other patients, and the treatment team) are also included as part of the environment, as are the ethic and philosophy of the rehabilitation hospital setting. Likewise, the patient's adjustment to the hospital is defined as both intrapersonal (i.e., the older adult's personal sense of acclimation to the environment) and behavioral (i.e., ability to effectively function in the setting). It is assumed that this adjustment will influence cooperation and functional progress throughout the hospital stay.

The chapter will include an examination of relevant theoretical perspectives on the ecology of aging and their application to the hospital setting. The hospital experience will be described both in general and specifically as it relates to the older adult in a rehabilitation setting. Treatment strategies for increasing adjustment will be described with either the person or the environment as the focus of intervention, and a case study will illustrate these treatment ideas. In conclusion, questions in need of further research will be raised.

ECOLOGICAL MODELS AND AGING

Numerous ecological models pertinent to aging have been developed, primarily to address problems of long-term housing options for older adults (institutional and community). These models can serve as a rich source of concepts for understanding the problems of hospital adaptation in older adults. They provide a framework for identifying critical factors in the patient/hospital environment fit. Each perspective highlights different aspects of this fit. While the congruence and adaptation models focus on the more objective factors of environmental demands and the individual's skill level and needs, the cognitive and phenomenological models emphasize the importance of subjective factors, such as the individual's cognitive and emotional interpretation of the external environment. Both perspectives contribute to an understanding of the older adult's adjustment to the hospital/institutional setting. Extensive review and critique of these models and others are found in Lawton 1977; Parr 1980; Rapoport 1982; and Scheidt and Windley 1985.

Congruence and Adaptation Models

Kahana's congruence model of ecology in older adults focuses on the interaction between individual need and environmental press (demand) for need fulfillment (Kahana 1982; Kahana and Kahana 1983). An environment which is congruent with the older adult's needs results in a "good fit" and a sense of well-being. Elders' adaptation to the environment is the negotiation of this congruence to change the environment to suit their needs, altering their hierarchy of needs to fit the existing environment, or changing to a new environment altogether. Congruence is most important as the older adult's capabilities and perceptions become more limited and the environment becomes more restricted. Kahana specifies several environmental dimensions as important in operationalizing congruence, depending upon the population discussed. For vulnerable, institutionalized older adults, these are: the degree to which the environment (1) is segregated, (2) allows for privacy and personal autonomy, (3) provides structure, (4) is stimulating, (5) allows for affective expression, and (6) requires impulse control.

This model has implications for assessment and intervention. The concepts of optimal congruence, critical personal needs, and environmental attributes required for well-being can be useful factors to consider in reference to disabled older adults in a rehabilitation setting. This model prompts the professional to conceptualize how individuals in a particular setting, such as a rehabilitation unit, are a "good or bad match" with the environment. It can also direct the professional to counsel the elder in negotiating incongruities in the person/environment fit as a means of promoting adjustment.

Similar to Kahana's congruence paradigm of person/environment fit, Lawton and Nahemow's adaptation model (1973; Lawton 1982; Lawton et al. 1990) specifically focuses on competence and environmental demand. This model views adaptation as a product of the transaction between environmental demand and an individual's competence. Adaptation, environment, and competence are more objectively defined in this model. For example, competence is collectively defined as capacities in areas of health, functional health, cognition, time use, and social behavior (Lawton 1987). Lawton (1986) conceives of environmental demands as flowing from interpersonal, sociocultural, and physical dimensions. Adaptation is measured by more external sources (e.g., self-care, social behavior, quality of affect). More subjective factors, such as personality style and the individual's perception of the environment, are conceived as mediating factors to the person-environment transaction.

As shown in Figure 4-1, the model is bipolar and describes a homeostatic range in the relationship between competence and environmental demand. Excessively high demand (or press) results in an overwhelming environment, while exceedingly low demand creates an understimulating, boring environment. Neither of these imbalances allows for optimal adjustment. However, a positive adaptation is not just the point at which competence perfectly matches demand on the average (*adaptation level*), but consists of a range of demand tolerable by an individual with a given competence level. Thus, mildly lower demand relative to competence may be positively experienced as supportive and comforting (*zone of maximum comfort*), and mildly higher demand relative to competence may be positively experienced as activating and challenging (*zone of maximum performance*).

The *environmental docility hypothesis* (Lawton and Nahemow 1973; Lawton and Simon 1968) is an important corollary to the model. This hypothesis proposes that those of higher competence can adapt to a wider range of intensity in environmental demand, while the less competent can only effectively operate within a narrow range of environmental variation. Alternately stated, the more capable, resourceful person is flexible and less bound to environmental demands, but the more impaired, impoverished person's adaptation is vulnerable to environmental pressures.

Lawton has also proposed the *environmental proactivity hypothesis* to clarify the application of the adaptation model to the more competent elder. In this corollary, he emphasizes the role of the higher functioning older adult in actively shaping the environment to meet needs as well as preferences. He states (1987,

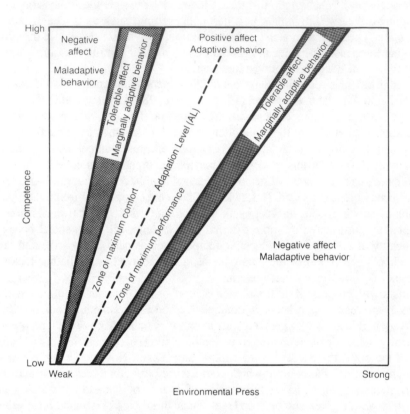

Figure 4-1 The Adaptation Model. *Source:* "Ecology and the Aging Process," by M.P. Lawton and L. Nahemow. In C. Eisdorfer and M.P. Lawton (Eds.), *Psychology of Adult Development and Aging*. Copyright 1973 by the American Psychological Association. Reprinted by permission.

37), "As competence increases, the environment becomes a potential source of increasing diversity in the person's ability to satisfy needs." Thus, with increasing competence, environmental press encompasses not only greater challenge, but also opportunity for enrichment. Lawton emphasizes, however, that less competent older adults also have a drive for autonomy (to exercise choice and preference), despite their increased dependence, and that this attribute must be considered in all environmental settings, including institutions.

Lawton and Nahemow's model more clearly specifies that intervention to facilitate adaptation may be formulated with either the individual or the environment as the target. In addition, the individual may be involved as an active initiator or passive recipient. For instance, individuals can be helped to a higher level of competence (e.g., through physical rehabilitation) to meet the press of the environment, they can be assisted to change the environment (or their view of it) themselves, or the environment can be engineered or redesigned to meet an unalterable competence level.

As two of the more developed and researched models of environmental adaptation in older adults, the congruence and adaptation perspectives provide new conceptual opportunities for comprehending the rehabilitation hospital setting and the older adult's adjustment to it. These formulations underscore the importance of delineating the needs of the older patient and the environmental features which may be consistently critical to a reasonable adaptation to the hospital.

The central role which competence plays in Lawton and Nahemow's adaptation model may be of particular use in understanding patient adjustment in the rehabilitation setting, for it is an alteration in one or more competencies which prompts such a hospitalization. Broadly, the goal of rehabilitation might be conceived as facilitating a new adaptive person/environment fit in view of altered competency (Coulton 1984). Adjustment to the rehabilitation hospital environment itself is not only necessary for this new fit to be discovered and learned, it can also become a prototype for adjustment after discharge. Further, Lawton and Nahemow's *environmental docility hypothesis* (i.e., the less competent, the more environmentally reactive) and Lawton's *environmental proactivity hypothesis* (i.e., the more competent, the more environmentally proactive) provide a framework for differentiating which patients may need the greatest attention for hospital adjustment and the optimal target of intervention. While substantial effort devoted to environmental engineering may successfully enhance the adjustment of the less competently functioning patient, attention to the individual and higher order needs (e.g., amount of personal control) may be salient to the more competent patient.

Cognitive and Phenomenological Perspectives

Cognitive and more phenomenological perspectives place greater emphasis on the cognition and perception (i.e., attributions or interpretations) of the older adult in environmental adjustment. Perhaps the single most important message from these cognitive/phenomenological approaches is the need to develop an appreciation for the complex and wide range of individual differences in how environmental adjustment is managed—often in unique, ingenious ways.

Schooler's stress response perspective (1982) emphasizes individual perceptions in environmental adjustment. Generalizing from Lazarus's cognitive theory of stress and coping (1966), he conceives of environmental adaptation as a stress response, particularly when responding to environmental hazard, as the older adult must often do. The individual's cognitive organization of an environmental event is the central theme in this perspective. Appraisal of threat and assessment of available coping skills are the operative factors in environmental adaptation. With hospitalization being undeniably a stressful event, this conceptualization of adaptation has merit in characterizing the internal (cognitive/perceptual) process of coping.

Howell (1980, 1983, 1985) approaches environmental adaptation in older adults from a highly subjective, phenomenological viewpoint. She is representative of a school of thought which is opposed to the reductionistic attempts to classify and quantify the person/environment fit. This approach to environmental adaptation places the emphasis squarely on the individual as being the critical source of environmental representation. As such, the person/environment fit is highly idiosyncratic. Howell postulates that older person-environment transactions are best understood by exploring the individual's history of *psychoenvironmental experiences* (the interweaving of life events with environment that invests the external setting with meaning) and perceived relevance of the current context. In her own words (1980, 430–31),

> . . . the built environment is encoded, on encounter, as a hypothetical construct for which the individual has contextual and historical matches. The intrapsychic processes and social behaviors of older people in various environments can thus be best understood through exploring the nature of these constructs . . .

Environmental adaptation for older people is therefore a fluid, dynamic process, continuously redefined by life experience. The environment becomes an integral part of identity.

While the rigorous theoretician may object to the slippery concepts which are so difficult to operationalize in these perspectives, both Schooler and Howell's accentuation of the individual is useful in explaining hospital adjustment. Understanding, and possibly influencing, the older patient's perception of the hospital experience may be the principal means of facilitating adjustment to a temporary, at times unalterable environment. Such questions as the meaning the older patient has invested in the disability and hospitalization events (e.g., the beginning of old age or dying), the symbolic meaning of specific areas or objects in the hospital, and the personalization of space (e.g., at bedside) are all important in becoming sensitive to and facilitating the older adult's adjustment.

THE HOSPITAL EXPERIENCE

Hospitalization is a dual admission. Literally, it involves being granted admission into a medical facility. Symbolically, it involves admission to oneself that an illness is serious, perhaps potentially life-changing or life-threatening. An individual suspends life activities and takes on the role of patient without full certainty of the outcome. Such an event constitutes a crisis filled with a multitude of negative feelings and adaptive tasks (Moos 1977).

Purtillo (1984) describes hospitalization at any age in the form of losses, including loss of self, home, privacy, and autonomy and control. Loss of self is at least temporarily apparent in the suspension of normal life activities (personal roles and relationships) with which one identifies. A hospital wrist band speaks to a new identity. Illness and hospitalization can also lead to a more permanent alteration of self should both become the occasion for diagnosis of disease or disability.

Loss of the comfort and security of home is readily apparent in the hospital experience. The patient has highly restricted options for extending and structuring the environment. As Kornfeld (1977, 239) states, "The hospital patient must, for the most part, accept the environment as given." There is minimal opportunity for personalized additions beyond the bedside table. In addition, the anchors of daily experience are lost (e.g., individualized rituals, favorite activities) and are replaced with unfamiliar, imposed routines and unpredictable events. Hospitalization involves a profound loss of privacy. Intrusion is experienced at the level of one's body, psyche, and immediate personal space. The request for display of the healing incision, the ubiquitous hospital gown, doors without locks, and curtains as walls are just a few of the interpersonal and environmental examples of hospital intrusion. Lack of confidentiality and solitude to allow for emotional reintegration are frequent examples of psychic intrusion.

To the extent that a hospital takes on institutional characteristics, patients surrender autonomy and control, and experience a loss of independence (Arling et al. 1986; Cooke 1987; Ryden 1985). Kleemeier (1959) and Pincus and Wood (1970) delineate dimensions of the institutional environment. Stated in the extreme, these dimensions include segregation and confinement, enforced congregation, regulation and standardization, and stratification of inhabitants. While one must be careful in generalizing to the hospital setting, parallels can easily be found which bear upon the patient's loss of autonomy. Doctor's "orders," leaving the hospital "against medical advice" as opposed to being "discharged," and the regimentation of scheduling are examples of this phenomenon. In contrast to a prison (the extreme institution), patients agree in principle to such institutionalization upon admission in exchange for efficient, quality care. They exercise overriding control by their consent. However, the threat of illness, death, and the authoritarian structure of medical institutions are mediating factors which dilute this sense of choice and independence.

Special Problems of the Hospitalized Older Adult

The hospital experience takes a more specific form when the patient is an older adult. Older people bring unique, age-related variables to the crisis of illness and hospitalization, such as their greater life experiences and the strengths and weaknesses inherent in aging. The meaning invested in the hospitalization event and hospital setting is usually distinctly different for the older adult. The event can signal the beginning of an identification as old for a formerly robust individual. For example, Mezey (1979) found an increase in subjective age evaluation in a sample of older adults hospitalized for surgical procedures from which they were expected to fully recover. Images of further decline and even death, rather than restoration, reinforced by realistic fear of leaving the hospital more debilitated than at admission, can be prominent for the frail older adult. Accompanying this fear is the image of hospitalization as the transition to permanent institutional living.

Temporarily surrendering control and independence is a difficult fact of hospitalization at any age. However, for the older adult, surrendering independence can be particularly demoralizing because of fear that it will be a permanent loss. Frail older adults are especially faced with the developmental task of rebalancing independence and dependence as they are unable to do all things for themselves. They, as well as the health professionals who deal with them, must continually assess the realism of their expectations for independence and accept the legitimacy of new dependencies. Rehabilitation for a disabling event directly confronts this issue and can invest the hospitalization with intense feelings of anxiety and shame.

Older adults are frequently described as functioning at a more delicate physical homeostasis due to natural aging processes and lack of reserve. Hospitalization can disrupt the older adult's equilibrium in a number of areas, either spontaneously (e.g., disruption of physical operations such as eating, sleeping, elimination) or iatrogenically (e.g., drug reactions or overdose) (Gillick et al. 1982). Risk of such disruption increases when one considers the likelihood of premorbid chronic illness coexisting with a new disability. In terms of Lawton and Nahemow's environmental docility hypothesis (1973), this less competent older adult is more sensitive to the effects of the environmental change precipitated by hospitalization. Evidence of this phenomenon, called *relocation shock*, is well documented in the observation of increased mortality with relocation of unprepared older adults (Bourestom 1984; Pastalan 1983) and increased prevalence of confusion due to hospitalization and immobilization (Campbell et al. 1986; Williams et al. 1985a, 1985b). In the hospital environment, the need for close attention to the balance of environmental stimulation of the older adult illustrates this homeostatic fragility factor very well. With reduced rate of processing, performance speed, and altered sensory thresholds, the extremes of over- and understimulation may be more easily experienced by the older adult. (Chances are increased even further by the unfortunate and expensive loss of sensory prosthetics—dentures, glasses, and hearing aids.)

The loss of home and accompanying loss of comfort and security may be particularly relevant to the adjustment process of the hospitalized older adult. Inability to individualize the environment and preserve the familiar and routine have serious repercussions for the older patient. As Howell (1985) and Rowles (1987) have suggested, the meaning of home for an older person may be strongly tied to identity, and the radical change of hospitalization can signal loss of a sense of self, independence, self-esteem, and dignity. Temporarily leaving home can be more disorganizing when it implies a fear of permanent loss and institutionalization. The potential for disruption of security attained through the environment is illustrated in Lawton's (1985, 515) observation that frail older adults often create a "control center" in their home. He consistently found the center of activity to be a comfortable chair strategically located and surrounded by sources of communication, assistance, and information (television, telephone, window, table with medicines, newspaper). Such a configuration allowed for security and control over the broader, largely unused, environment. Hospitals rarely provide the freedom or time to create this or other environmental coping strategies. In addition, they pose a new set of problems by presenting a strange, larger, and inevitably more physically and mentally challenging environment with which to interact.

The interpersonal environment must also be considered in discussing the impact of hospitalization on older adults. The hospitalized older adult is required to adopt a new support system (hospital staff and other patients) and frequently suspends or loses a prior interpersonal system of peers. This isolation is often moderated by the presence of extended family who can play a critical role in supporting the patient and facilitating hospital adjustment. However, rehabilitation treatment teams are often youth-oriented and provide few role models for older patients. The age/cohort difference can accentuate Hirst's (1983) sociological observation of a hospital staff as a metaphorical family, with shared experiences and technical language, and the patient as the outsider. For the older adult, understanding the organizational structure of hospital personnel may also be difficult. For example, it may be puzzling to the older adult to differentiate a nurse from a clinical nurse specialist, or to understand how a trusted community family practitioner relates to the admitting physiatrist at a rehabilitation facility. Identification of communication patterns or simply keeping names and faces straight is often impossible for the older adult, particularly when staff rotate and shift changes are made. Frequently, the treatment team does not take the time to explain these relationships and changes. Nahemow (1983), in writing on the patient-physician milieu, proposes that older patients frequently harbor anger and resentment at the humiliation of being placed in yet another subservient role in relation to the powerful, younger physician. Such feelings can intensify the sense of shame frequently harbored by older patients dealing with their own prejudices about physical disability. These underlying feelings, left unexpressed and unresolved, can also hinder open and clear communication on health matters.

Isolation of the hospitalized older person can also be appreciated when considering the support system left behind at admission. Peers or spouses may be unable to visit frequently due to their own frailties or fears of travel. Davies and Peters (1983) found that hospitalized older adults rated "thinking about home" (i.e., worries about the people at home and safety of the domicile) as a highly significant stressor for them. Research by Wilson-Barnett (1979) on hospital stress also supports this conclusion. The older adult is sometimes woven into an intricate web of interdependence (with spouses, siblings, or friends) through which they mutually compensate for diminished physical and financial resources by sharing tasks and costs. Hospitalized older adults have the worry of this balance of dependency being disrupted in their absence. Worries about home may also extend to other living familial substitutes which require daily attention. The preoccupation of the elder who has been forced to leave a cherished domestic pet unattended can become a critical issue in hospital adjustment.

The Rehabilitation Environment

The older adult usually experiences the rehabilitation setting as a link in a chain of events. Often transferring to a rehabilitation hospital/unit from an acute care facility, it becomes yet another strange environment to which the older adult must acclimate. All of the problems in hospital adjustment noted above may be reinstated, including the possibility of a confusional state with the relocation (labeled *translocation confusion* by Smith 1986). In addition, the specialized features of rehabilitation uniquely interact with aging issues.

Upon admission to a rehabilitation hospital, the older adult encounters what might be called the *rehabilitation ethic*. This ethic places a high value on independence at the cost of comfort. It considers strain and pain as potentially leading to a good outcome and states that accepting dependence is most often avoidable. This ethic is laudable and speaks strongly to the process of adjustment to disability, but, for the older adult, it can confound the age-appropriate dilemma of negotiating a positive self-image in the face of declining physical prowess. The older adult is often struggling with how to prioritize independencies (i.e., where is it most important to be independent?) as physical frailties present themselves. Physical comfort may be seen as just reward for a life of work and sacrifice. Coming to terms with this ethic and how it is operationalized by the treatment team is very important to hospital adjustment and a successful rehabilitation outcome.

In this context, the older adult finds him/herself in an environment where evaluations are conducted and performance is measured with expected goals in mind. The hospitalization becomes a training program to build strength and compensate for permanent weaknesses. The older adult is often emotionally unprepared for this school-like atmosphere, a setting they have not experienced since the early years of their lives. Their role shifts from patient to student. The mode of participation shifts distinctly from passive to active. The older adult is often filled with performance anxiety and, given the physical nature of the education, can question his/her stamina and become fearful of being physically overextended. Aitken (1982) speculates that such performance anxiety and fears of failure may have been instrumental in her finding that older rehabilitation patients had lower self-concept scores than those in acute or skilled care facilities.

The rehabilitation setting is quite different, although appearing much like a regular hospital. Required clothing frequently changes to sweat suits or other exercise tolerant dress. Patients are made more mobile via carts and wheelchairs and may travel frequently to different locations in the hospital building for therapies. This makes fellow patients and their disabilities more highly visible and traumatizing. The equipment utilized may appear frightening and strange. One can only speculate on the range of feelings of an elder who sees a patient transferred via a Hoyer Lift or enters a large physical therapy gymnasium for the first time at a peak treatment hour. The level and type of stimulation in the environment and its meaning differ from that of home or other medical care facilities, and the older patient must adjust.

Finally, the interpersonal milieu of the rehabilitation setting has unique features which relate to the older adult's hospital adjustment. The interdisciplinary team common to rehabilitation expands the number of relationships that older adults must negotiate in their new, temporary support system. The relationships demand greater skill at communication as the elder is asked to collaborate in goal setting and teaching over a longer hospital stay. The staffing level may shift to include paraprofessional personnel, and the kind of attentiveness provided to meet patients' needs changes to foster independence. Patients are expected to be more self-initiating in basic personal care. Needs are not anticipated as much so that requests for attention must be made; waiting time often increases. All of these factors can prompt the older patient to conclude that this new kind of hospital is overwhelming or not appropriately caring and protective of them.

Undoubtedly, the rehabilitation hospital experience offers distinct stresses and challenges to the older patient. The developmental stages of later life and the unique features of physical rehabilitation interact to require a new person/environment fit. Successful adjustment to the rehabilitation environment is critical to the desired outcome of returning to maximum capacity. This requires the effort of the patient and the treatment team's appreciation of the impact of the environment on the older patient. With this increased sensitivity, the team will be in a position to consider a range of interventions to facilitate the new person/environment fit.

INTERVENTIONS

Person-Oriented Intervention: The Older Adult Patient

It is important to note that hospital adjustment can be addressed prior to admission, particularly to the rehabilitation setting where entry is usually anticipated. The efficacy of preadmission preparation can be aided by the successful use of preparation programs in relocation of older adults (Bourestom 1984; Pastalan 1983). Such intervention can provide a wealth of information to the patient, begin the establishment of appropriate attitudes toward the rehabilitation process, and provide the receiving rehabilitation unit with important information that can promote an optimal personal and environmental approach to the patient. The end result is a more informed, consenting patient with an enhanced sense of control over the hospital experience. Preadmission preparation interventions can take a variety of forms and, given the diverse ways a patient may enter rehabilitation, it is best to have a range of options available. Preparation can be as elaborate as a personal interview by a rehabilitation staff member or a visit by the patient to the rehabilitation facility, and as simple as provision of printed material or a telephone call to the patient.

Once the older adult has reached the rehabilitation facility, further person-oriented intervention or counseling is possible to promote adjustment to the new environment. Again, generalization from literature on relocation would suggest that both individual and group interventions are possible, although groups are likely to be more effective with cognitively higher functioning patients (Pastalan 1983). Patient-focused intervention necessitates increased contact time between the older adult and staff at a critical period, the first days of hospitalization, to concentrate specifically on how the individual is fitting into the setting. This increased time and communication allows for information exchange, building patient skill for coping with the setting, emotional support, and enhancement of personal control. Counseling older adults regarding their adjustment to the hospital environment provides the opportunity for a reciprocal flow of information. Through sensitive inquiry, the team can discover misconceptions and knowledge deficits that the older adult is unable to formulate into questions. Information about team structure, hospital rules and regulations, and possible schedules of activities (therapeutic or otherwise) increases familiarity with the rehabilitation environment and instills a renewed sense of security and comfort. In addition, effective communication will also yield the patient's unique perspective of the hospital experience, which is essential to facilitating adjustment.

While the need for such empathic understanding may be self-evident, treatment teams are at risk of losing the patient perspective in effectively carrying out their work (Kornfeld 1977). Rehabilitation staff are pushed by time constraints, desensitized by their familiarity with the environment, and are emotionally defended in order to adequately function in a setting where witnessing catastrophe is the norm. Time spent discovering the older adult's experience allows for the temporary suspension of these variables and the opportunity to gain invaluable information for facilitating adjustment. In addition, such communication can uncover discrepancies between patient's and staff's perceptions of stressors. Davies and Peters (1983) compared the ratings of older patients and their primary nurses on various hospital stresses. They found least discrepancy in perceived stress related to physical illness and most discrepancy on the stressful impact of the hospital environment and routine. Further, patients saw the stress of these factors increasing during their hospital stay, while nurses perceived the stress as decreasing.

Counseling for improved hospital adjustment can also involve skill building and providing emotional support. Teaching older adults how to cope with the losses and frustrations of the rehabilitation milieu should be considered an important aspect of facilitating their adjustment. While angry, demanding patients may dismiss this as a way to excuse the hospital from being more flexible in satisfying their needs, skill building can be introduced with the more self-serving rationale of assisting them in getting what they want and need. Examples of areas frequently found deficient are interpersonal skills in dealing with staff (e.g., negotiating conflict, assertiveness), problem solving in difficult hospital predicaments (e.g., getting to an important therapy on time), and stress reduction skills (e.g., relaxation training).

Members of the treatment team should never underestimate the power of emotional support provided during counseling of recently admitted older rehabilitation patients. Allowing them an opportunity to ventilate feelings, reveal fears, and decrease their isolation is an easily missed means of assisting poorly adjusting patients. In surveying case studies on dealing with difficult older patients, English and Morse (1988, 35) found the most frequently effective intervention to be "taking time to sit and talk with the patient." This intervention may be too quickly ruled out as time consuming, indistinctive (easily done by anyone), and at times, too emotionally draining to the clinical staff.

Lack of control is frequently described as a prominent stressor that encompasses many complaints of the hospitalized patient (Dennis 1987). Hospital adjustment counseling on this issue can be complex but is worthy of special consideration. Studies of locus of control, older adults, and hospitalization require careful interpretation. An internal locus of control (i.e., belief that outcome depends upon one's own behavior or characteristics) has generally been associated with better adjustment and health behaviors in older adults (Kuypers 1971, 1972; Strickland 1978). However, it has also been found that an external locus of control (i.e., belief that outcome depends upon circumstances or people beyond the individual) leads to better adjustment for older adults in institutionalized or high-constraint environments (Cicirelli 1987; Felton and Kahana 1974; Ziegler and Reid 1979). Finally, it is generally accepted that promoting a sense of personal control leads to better hospital adjustment. Given that hospitalization and physical disability are high-constraint circumstances, these disparate findings make it difficult to know how to counsel the older patient who is frustrated by the experience of lack of control in the rehabilitation setting.

Rothbaum et al. (1982) distinguish different types of control, providing a useful means of addressing these issues in hospital adjustment counseling. They propose two levels of control by suggesting that people not only attempt to change the environment to suit their needs (*primary control*), but also change themselves to accommodate inalterable environmental circumstances (*secondary control*). This secondary level of control (of which they delineate four subtypes) is characterized as a more passive, inward process, but nonetheless results in a perception of control. It includes an *interpretive* subtype, in which control is established by understanding and deriving meaning from seemingly uncontrollable events, and a *vicarious* subtype, in which control is established by alignment with others perceived as more powerful. Rothbaum and his associates view healthy adaptation as an optimal coordination of both primary and secondary levels of control. This further elaboration of control attribution is of particular relevance to disabled older adults who may be questioning their ability to control their lives in the face of physical deterioration and mounting environmental constraints (of which hospitalization is a glaring confrontation). Counseling to promote a balance of primary and secondary control can help older patients restore a sense of choice in how external forces affect them, facilitating hospital, as well as overall, adjustment.

Discussion of the issue of control allows the clinician to discern the patient's pattern of beliefs about control attribution, such as internal versus external locus of control (Rotter 1966). Cicirelli (1987) suggests a further option for facilitating hospital adjustment—arranging treatment conditions congruent to the patient's belief system. For example, the treatment team can find ways for the highly internal patient to exert control in the environment, while placing the patient who finds control in powerful others with therapists who are self-assured and dominant in their style. Person-oriented intervention yields information that is valuable in shaping the environment to suit the patient's needs. Intervention to increase hospital adjustment is one of dynamic interplay between person-oriented and environment-oriented approaches.

Environment-Oriented Intervention: The Rehabilitation Hospital

Adjustment is also facilitated by attention to the setting itself. The rehabilitation hospital environment should not only be examined for how it impedes functioning, but also for how it could be manipulated to enhance and advance optimal functioning in the older adult. Environmental features which are relevant to hospital adjustment vary with the individual's competence and hierarchy of needs. As developed in Lawton and Nahemow's adaptation model (1973), the environment becomes more critical for less competently functioning older persons who have less capacity to assimilate or compensate for their surroundings. As stated in Kahana's congruence model (1982), the individual's hierarchy of needs will also impact on the person/environment fit. Thus, the gravely ill elder may be most comfortable in a highly constrained hospital environment designed for efficient delivery of care (Wolk and Telleen 1976; Rowe and Weinert 1987). In contrast, the medically stable, physically disabled elder who is cognitively intact likely functions best in a very different hospital environment.

The rehabilitation setting as a hospital environment is unique in that it must tolerate a wide diversity of patient competencies and needs. For example, patients may have severe physical disabilities, yet be mentally intact, or they may be physically quite competent, but disordered in their thinking and behavior. In addition, patients may remain in the rehabilitation environment for extended periods. Thus, there is the constant dilemma of negotiating an environment designed for medical efficiency with the flexibility needed to accommodate a wide variety of patients in their temporary home. Ideally, the rehabilitation hospital environment should be viewed as a set of components that can be assembled in varying configurations or individualized to fit a specific patient. Subenvironments can also be identified (such as the bedroom, the dining area, and the therapy area) with features to be varied to suit individuals and their activities in these arenas.

A rehabilitation team has an armamentarium of devices at its disposal to plug into a patient's environment as prostheses to compensate for weaknesses or enhance strengths. These are often derived from different therapeutic disciplines and must be organized in an understandable, useful fashion for the treatment team. The task of environmental intervention for better hospital adjustment then becomes one of analyzing the patient's needs and competencies, and conducting a systematic inventory of the environment to select and arrange its parts to maximize patient function and satisfaction as much as possible. Such effective communication and planning is the signature of a well-functioning interdisciplinary treatment team and a hallmark of rehabilitation. Hiatt (1990) discusses the contributions of various disciplines in addressing the adequacy of the environment and the dilemmas in coordinating and operationalizing effective changes for older adults.

General environmental features are described in Exhibit 4-1 as a suggested way of organizing a treatment team's thoughts about environmental adjustment for the older patient. They are adapted from Lawton (1986) and Windley and Scheidt (1980) who attempted to develop taxonomies of environmental features pertinent to the older person. The nine features listed in Exhibit 4-1 were chosen for their potential usefulness in the specific setting of the rehabilitation hospital. The first four features (safety, accessibility, legibility, and stimulation) may be pre-eminent when considering environmental adjustment for the less competent, while the subsequent four features (control, personalization, social integration, and comfort/aesthetics) may become more important when addressing the environment in the hospital adjustment of the higher functioning older adult. The final feature, adaptability, emphasizes the need for flexibility to individualize the environment and accommodate changes in the patient as recovery progresses. A full discussion of the ramifications of each of these features in the design of the environment is beyond the scope of this chapter. However, to more explicitly illustrate the process of environmental intervention, two frequently arising problems in hospital adjustment for older persons, confusion and comfort, have been chosen for further discussion.

Confusion

Transitory confusion is a common complication of hospitalization in older adults regardless of whether their medical problem involves mental impairment. Estimates of its incidence range from 10 to 50 percent in a variety of studies (as reported by Williams et al. 1985a). An acute confusional state in an older patient should precipitate medical investigation for a potentially reversible physiological cause. However, environmental factors in the hospital setting can contribute to confusional states or, when manipulated, can also facilitate mental clearing (Campbell et al. 1986; Williams et al. 1985a).

The change of living patterns, the strange surroundings, and alteration in sensory input are factors which are particularly amenable to environmental correction. Assuring a simplified, routine flow of events in the environment can re-establish a pattern (albeit a new one) for the older adult. Use of schedules and caregiving personnel that remain constant reorder the environment. The details of and appliances in the environment can also be used to increase familiarity and orientation. Bedside family pictures, reminiscence, and visits by family and friends can render the setting more familiar by association with these meaningful faces and events. Introduction of calendars, appliances (e.g., TV, radio, clock), newspapers and magazines, and even familiar scents (a favorite cologne or perfume), has an orienting effect when placed in the environment or used in therapeutic interaction. Finally, attention to correction of sensory decrements (assuring proper placement of visual and/or auditory aides) and balancing the amount of stimulation in the environment provide the older adult with accurate

Exhibit 4-1 Environmental Features

Safety
An important and often most fully realized feature in a hospital setting due to the details of building codes and medical necessity. Safety is often in conflict with other important environmental goals, such as control and aesthetics.

Accessibility
The degree to which the environment allows for easy movement from one point to another and manipulation of objects in the setting. In a hospital setting, this is a feature usually well operationalized in general, but often specific deficits of the individual patient can still be a problem. For example, the interaction of sensory changes and accessibility can be a particular problem for older adults.

Legibility
The extent to which the environment is understandably organized and assists in orientation, predictability, and direction finding. Uniformity in institutional design can sacrifice the orienting quality of variety and uniqueness. Strategic use of environmental components becomes important, such as signs, symbols, clocks, etc. This feature is particularly important when dealing with a less competent older adult.

Stimulation
The pace of activity, sensory stimulation emanating from the environment, and density (crowding) of the environment. For the older person, senses show an age decrement and rate of information processing decreases. Balancing stimulation to prevent over or under-stimulation can be a problem in arranging an optimal environment for the older adult.

Control
How the environment is arranged to promote independence and personal control. This can range from the amount of private space provided to the patient to choices built into the setting (such as controls for lights, bed, appliances, etc.). The need for a private space, a personal territory over which the individual has primary control, is universally accepted as essential for emotional health.

Personalization
Allows the patient to claim a space as his or her own. This can range from placement of furniture to decoration with personalized articles, such as pictures or memorabilia. This can be of great importance as it permits attachment and continuity. There is a wide range of options for personalization, many of which are unduly sacrificed for the sake of safety and medical efficiency.

Social Integration
Strategic design of space for comfortable active and passive socialization. Furniture placement is important to facilitate nondefensive interaction. Watching others while slightly removed is the preference of some, while direct social contact is preferred by others. Hospital social areas are often mistakenly located away from the hub of activity.

Comfort/Aesthetics
Creation of a warm, inviting atmosphere through design and decoration. This feature is often in conflict with legibility, the functional attributes of the environment, and the ease of its maintenance.

Adaptability
The flexibility of the setting to accommodate the unique needs of the individuals introduced into it. This feature addresses the issue of how easily the environment can be changed to meet the needs and desires of the individual patient. This can range from the ability to rearrange furniture to changes to accommodate a specific disability.

Source: Lawton 1986; Windley and Scheidt 1980.

input that is paced at an understandable rate. These interventions address the features of legibility, stimulation, and personalization listed in Exhibit 4-1. These environmental strategies may be implemented and then withdrawn as a temporary confusional state resolves. In the case of a more chronically confused patient (e.g., a cognitively impaired elder), a more comprehensive management plan is required for long-term implementation (see Chapter 8).

Comfort

The lack of comfort in the hospital environment is a common complaint of older adults (English and Morse 1988). This is especially true in the rehabilitation setting where daily performance for physical recovery is emphasized. Special environmental considerations to increase comfort are of significant importance in helping the older patient adjust to the rehabilitation setting. In this instance, conceptualization of sub-environments in the hospital is of value. For example, in terms of the adaptation model (Lawton and Nahemow 1973), therapy environments might be best structured as *zones of maximum performance* (where demand is modestly higher than competence) to facilitate learning, while the older patient's hospital room might be best engineered as a *zone of maximum comfort* (where competence is modestly higher than demand) to allow for rest and recuperation. Since the environment where therapy is provided is associated with effort and sometimes pain, the setting for rest and relaxation (e.g., the bedroom) can be engineered as an island of comfort, where greater convenience, privacy, control, and personalization are structured into the environment. This can be accomplished by examining the use of furniture (e.g., the need for a wheelchair versus a comfortable stationary chair); setting up the environment to be convenient rather than challenging (e.g., decreasing waiting time to meet a need); and encouraging personal items associated with comfort (e.g., a favorite blanket or pillow), rather than viewing them as superfluous or a safety risk.

Such an approach to the older patient's environment requires members of the team to suspend some of their long-held beliefs about discouraging dependency (the sick role) and using every aspect of daily care as a teaching opportunity. The interpersonal environment can also indirectly promote comfort through such commonplace but often forgotten techniques as a courteous approach, respectful of the older patient's longevity, avoidance of infantilization (Fitzsimons 1985), and the sensitive use of touch. These interventions concern the features of control, personalization, and comfort/aesthetics listed in Exhibit 4-1.

The Case of Mrs. J.

The following case study illustrates the person-oriented and environment-oriented approaches described above.

Mrs. J. was a 91 year old woman with a moderate subcortical dementia. She was moderately dysarthric making communication laborious, and she was quite frail and dependent for activities of daily living. Her initial hospital adjustment was tenuous as she frequently cried out and moaned at night, was inconsistently cooperative in therapies, and was reported by the nursing staff to be refusing medications.

In Mrs. J.'s case, person-oriented intervention for hospital adjustment was crucial. When the treatment team took the extended time necessary to talk with her, an engaging woman with highly intact interpersonal skill emerged. While possessing only sketchy knowledge of her condition and hospital stay, Mrs. J. easily disclosed her background as a former political organizer and later in life, as a hospital volunteer. She could both identify with and respect the position of the team, as well as bolster her self-esteem, through reminiscence as the organizer of a hospital volunteer program. Further counseling uncovered the needs being expressed through her problematic behavior. Her crying out at night was prompted by her lack of knowledge about the nursing intercom system, complicated by her age-related sensory decrements and stroke-related perceptual deficits. Her decreased motivation in therapies stemmed from a fear of being worked too hard, and her medication refusal appeared to be connected to confusion about the medication and fears of choking (she had a moderate dysphagia). Explanation and education about these matters (how to use the intercom, how therapies were scheduled, her medications and how they could be made more palatable) were effective in satisfying these needs. The counseling also showed that the patient developed supportive relationships quite rapidly and that these could be used to provide her with reassurance, and to uncover information about her and the reason for her behavior.

Both structural and interpersonal environmental interventions were also carried out with Mrs. J. Given her mental and physical frailties and fears of being overextended, her space of activity was kept fairly constricted to promote comfort and security. It was kept enriched, however, through interpersonal variation. Her therapies were conducted on the nursing unit and scheduled to accommodate her low energy. Nonphysically-oriented appointments (speech therapy, visits from psychologist and social worker) were conducted at bedside to allow the patient greater comfort. Given the patient's interpersonal skill, she responded best to an environment that used other people, rather than objects, to orient her and provide her with information. A special effort was made to provide her with a consistent caregiver, and information about her hospital stay was repeated to her frequently to decrease her confusion. A trusted younger sister, who was supportive of her and visited or called frequently, was also of considerable assistance in this latter objective.

Mrs. J.'s ultimate hospital adjustment was a mixture of success and failure. While the interventions noted above were successful in promoting her emotional adjustment, the patient was unable to make sufficiently rapid progress physically to remain in the rehabilitation hospital setting. She was discharged to an extended-care facility for a less intensive therapy program. The objective of increasing the patient's comfort and security in the rehabilitation setting was achieved, but the environment could not be adequately altered and paced to accommodate her frailty. With this patient, the most valuable information in intervening for hospital adjustment came from her self-report. The meaning she invested in the hospital environment, her knowledge and skill deficits and assets, as well as her fears became apparent and could be utilized in directing appropriate interventions toward her and her environment.

CONCLUSION

Adjusting to the rehabilitation setting poses a unique set of problems for older patients and their treatment team. An adequate adjustment is also a prerequisite to the work of therapy and acceptance of disability. In addressing this issue, this chapter has focused primarily on the psychology of the older patient in responding to the hospitalization event and the environment of rehabilitation.

Theoretical perspectives on the ecology of aging are useful in understanding the specific problem of older patient/hospital environment fit. The perspectives described attest to the importance of considering the older patient's needs, competencies, interpretation of stress, and subjective meaning given to the environment. Consideration of these factors helps to ascertain the target and content of intervention needed for increased hospital adjustment.

Exploration of the hospital experience is also fruitful in understanding how to facilitate adjustment to the rehabilitation setting. While any hospitalization prompts the experience of a series of losses, the older adult and the team in a rehabilitation setting are faced with special challenges. The active, independence-seeking approach of rehabilitation can confound resolution of older-age-appropriate conflicts, cause performance anxiety, and promote perception of the environment as threatening, incomprehensible, and uncaring.

Intervention to increase adjustment is often a dynamic mix of person- and environment-oriented approaches. Increasing knowledge and skill, providing emotional support, and promoting a sense of personal control are important objectives of patient counseling for hospital adjustment. Environmental intervention can be organized around the older adult's needs and competencies. Given the wide range possible in these areas, a flexible environment is highly desirable, although admittedly very difficult to achieve in a hospital. Manipulation of the setting for better patient adjustment begins with identifying critical environmental features and cataloging the environmental prostheses available for use by the treatment team. Once achieved, this allows for individualization of the environment to maximize the patient's adjustment.

Implementation of interventions for hospital adjustment can be difficult. Frequently, it is argued that they are too time-consuming. However, a treatment team will ultimately expend a great amount of time and effort to achieve rehabilitation goals with the poorly adjusted patient. More streamlined interventions can be developed if the assumptions made in this chapter could be validated and elaborated through further research. For example, the critical needs of the older adult in adjusting to the rehabilitation setting should be more precisely identified. An important corollary of this research question is one of identifying which older patients are at risk of poor adjustment in entering a rehabilitation facility (e.g., Steels 1976; Williams et al. 1985a). While the generally frail older adult may obviously be at risk, it is important to differentiate any individual personality and emotional factors which may make adjustment to rehabilitation hospitalization problematic. For example, it is frequently observed that more intact older adults, who defend against fears of aging with aggressive independence, are unable to tolerate hospitalization well due to the prospect of decline and the enforced dependence that it represents.

More stringent measurement of the environment (e.g., its affective quality and the level of demand it places on patients) is greatly needed. While various attempts have been made to develop environmental measures (Moos and Lemke 1985; Parr 1980), many are not clinically efficient, and there is little evidence that they have been directly applied to the rehabilitation environment. Most literature available provides anecdotal evidence of the effectiveness of certain types of interventions in specific situations. However, more research into factors critical to adjustment and instrumentation is required before specific interventions can be rigorously examined. Finally, the issue of rehabilitation hospital adjustment is related to the broader question of which older patients benefit most from which level of rehabilitation care (e.g., acute hospital level rehabilitation, skilled nursing facility, or day hospital). As raised in the case study presented, the older patient's hospital adjustment is closely related to the overall appropriateness of placement at that level of care.

Hospital adjustment for the older patient is critical, at times difficult, but by no means, impossible. Older patients have resources to rise to the challenges presented by a disability and the rehabilitation milieu. They require treatment teams sensitive to their needs who will work in concert with them for a realistic adjustment. Despite the loss and fear engendered by hospitalization, it can be a positive experience for many. The older patient can also emerge from the event with a sense of efficacy at having coped well with the rigors of rehabilitation and disability. A rehabilitation team alert to hospital adjustment issues increases the possibility for such a positive resolution.

REFERENCES

Aitken, M.J. 1982. Self-concept and functional independence in the hospitalized elderly. *The American Journal of Occupational Therapy* 36: 243–50.

Arling, G., E.B. Harkins, and J.A. Capitman. 1986. Institutionalization and personal control: A panel study of impaired older people. *Research on Aging* 8: 38–56.

Bourestom, N. 1984. Psychological and physiological manifestations of relocation. *Psychiatric Medicine* 2: 57–90.

Campbell, E.B., M.A. Williams, and S.M. Mlynarczyk. 1986. After the fall—confusion. *American Journal of Nursing* 86: 151–4.

Cicirelli, V.G. 1987. Locus of control and patient role adjustment of the elderly in acute-care hospitals. *Psychology and Aging* 2: 138–43.

Cooke, M. 1987. Part of the institution. *Nursing Times* 83(23): 24–7.

Coulton, C.J. 1984. Person-environment fit and rehabilitation. In *Rehabilitation Psychology: A Comprehensive Textbook,* edited by D.W. Krueger, 119–29. Gaithersburg, Md.: Aspen Publishers.

Davies, A.D.M., and M. Peters. 1983. Stresses of hospitalization in the elderly: Nurses' and patients' perceptions. *Journal of Advanced Nursing* 8: 99–105.

Dennis, K.E. 1987. Dimensions of client control. *Nursing Research* 36: 151–6.

English, J., and J.M. Morse. 1988. The 'difficult' elderly patient: Adjustment or maladjustment? *International Journal of Nursing Studies* 25: 23–39.

Felton, B., and E. Kahana. 1974. Adjustment and situationally-bound locus of control among institutionalized aged. *Journal of Gerontology* 29: 295–301.

Fitzsimons, V.M. 1985. Maintaining a positive environment for the older adult. *Orthopaedic Nursing* 4: 48–51.

Gillick, M.R., N.A. Serrell, and L.S. Gillick. 1982. Adverse consequences of hospitalization in the elderly. *Social Science and Medicine* 16: 1033–8.

Hiatt, L.G. 1990. Environmental factors in rehabilitation of disabled elderly people. In *Aging and Rehabilitation II: The State of the Practice,* edited by S.J. Brody and L.G. Pawlson, 150–164. New York: Springer Publishing Co.

Hirst, S.P. 1983. Understanding the difficult patient. *Nursing Management* 14: 68–70.

Howell, S.C. 1980. Environments as hypotheses in human aging research. In *Aging in the 1980's: Psychological Issues,* edited by L.W. Poon, 424–32. Washington, D.C.: American Psychological Association.

Howell, S.C. 1983. The meaning of place in old age. In *Aging and Milieu: Environmental Perspectives on Growing Old,* edited by G.D. Rowles and R.J. Ohta, 97–107. New York: Academic Press.

Howell, S.C. 1985. Home: A source of meaning in elders' lives. *Generations* 9: 58–60.

Kahana, E. 1982. A congruence model of person-environment interaction. In *Aging and the Environment: Theoretical Approaches,* edited by M.P. Lawton, P.G. Windley, and T.O. Byerts, 97–121. New York: Springer Publishing Co.

Kahana, E., and B. Kahana. 1983. Environmental continuity, futurity, and adaptation of the aged. In *Aging and Milieu: Environmental Perspectives on Growing Old,* edited by G.D. Rowles and R.J. Ohta, 205–28. New York: Academic Press.

Kleemeier, R.W. 1959. Behavior and the organization of the bodily and the external environment. In *Handbook of Aging and the Individual,* edited by J.E. Birren, 400–51. Chicago: University of Chicago Press.

Kornfeld, D.S. 1977. The hospital environment: Its impact on the patient. In *Coping with Physical Illness,* edited by R.H. Moos, 237–49. New York: Plenum Medical Book Co.

Kuypers, J.A. 1971. Internal-external locus of control and ego functioning correlates in the elderly. *The Gerontologist* 11: 39.

Kuypers, J.A. 1972. Internal-external locus of control, ego functioning, and personality characteristics in old age. *The Gerontologist* 12: 168–73.

Lawton, M.P. 1977. The impact of the environment on aging and behavior. In *Handbook of the Psychology of Aging,* edited by J.E. Birren and K.W. Schaie, 276–301. New York: Van Nostrand Reinhold Co.

Lawton, M.P. 1982. Competence, environmental press, and the adaptation of older people. In *Aging and the Environment: Theoretical Approaches,* edited by M.P. Lawton, P.G. Windley, and T.O. Byerts, 33–59. New York: Springer Publishing Co.

Lawton, M.P. 1985. The elderly in context: Perspectives from environmental psychology and gerontology. *Environment and Behavior* 17: 501–19.

Lawton, M.P. 1986. *Environment and Aging.* Albany, N.Y.: Center for the Study of Aging.

Lawton, M.P. 1987. Environment and the need satisfaction of the aging. In *Handbook of Clinical Gerontology,* edited by L.L. Carstensen and B.A. Edelstein, 33–40. New York: Pergamon Press.

Lawton, M.P., E.M. Brody, and A.R. Saperstein. 1990. Social, behavioral, and environmental issues. In *Aging and Rehabilitation II: The State of the Practice,* edited by S.J. Brody and L.G. Pawlson, 133–49. New York: Springer Publishing Co.

Lawton, M.P., and L. Nahemow. 1973. Ecology and the aging process. In *Psychology of Adult Development and Aging,* edited by C. Eisdorfer and M.P. Lawton, 619–74. Washington, D.C.: American Psychological Association.

Lawton, M.P., and B.B. Simon. 1968. The ecology of social relationships in housing for the elderly. *Gerontologist* 8: 108–15.

Lazarus, R. 1966. *Psychological Stress and the Coping Process.* New York: McGraw-Hill.

Mezey, M. 1979. Stress, hospitalization, and aging. *ANA: Clinical and Scientific Meetings,* 123–33. Kansas City, Mo.: American Nurses' Association.

Moos, R.H., ed. 1977. *Coping with Physical Illness.* New York: Plenum Medical Book Co.

Moos, R.H., and S. Lemke. 1985. Specialized living environments for older people. In *Handbook of the Psychology of Aging,* 2d ed., edited by J.E. Birren and K.W. Schaie, 864–89. New York: Van Nostrand Reinhold Co.

Nahemow, L. 1983. Working with older people: The patient-physician milieu. In *Aging and Milieu: Environmental Perspectives on Growing Old,* edited by G.D. Rowles and R.J. Ohta, 171–86. New York: Academic Press.

Parr, J. 1980. The interaction of persons and living environments. In *Aging in the 1980's: Psychological Issues,* edited by L.W. Poon, 393–406. Washington, D.C.: American Psychological Association.

Pastalan, L.A. 1983. Environmental displacement: A literature reflecting older-person/environment transactions. In *Aging and Milieu: Environmental Perspectives on Growing Old*, edited by G.D. Rowles and R.J. Ohta, 189–203. New York: Academic Press.

Pincus, A., and V. Wood. 1970. Methodological issues in measuring the environment in institutions for the aged and its impact on residents. *Aging and Human Development* 1: 117–26.

Purtillo, R. 1984. *Health Professional/Patient Interaction*, 3d ed. Philadelphia: W.B. Saunders Co.

Rapoport, A. 1982. Aging-environment theory: A summary. In *Aging and the Environment: Theoretical Approaches*, edited by M.P. Lawton, P.G. Windley, and T.O. Byerts, 132–49. New York: Springer Publishing Co.

Rothbaum, F., J.R. Weisz, and S.S. Snyder. 1982. Changing the world and changing the self: A two-process model of perceived control. *Journal of Personality and Social Psychology* 42: 5–37.

Rotter, J.B. 1966. Generalized expectancies for internal versus external control of reinforcement. *Psychological Monographs* 80, no. 609: 1–28.

Rowe, M.A., and C. Weinert. 1987. The CCU experience: Stressful or reassuring? *Dimensions of Critical Care Nursing* 6: 341–8.

Rowles, G.D. 1987. A place to call home. In *Handbook of Clinical Gerontology*, edited by L.L. Carstensen and B.A. Edelstein, 335–53. New York: Pergamon Press.

Ryden, M.B. 1985. Environmental support for autonomy in the institutionalized elderly. *Research in Nursing and Health* 8: 363–71.

Scheidt, R.J., and P.G. Windley. 1985. The ecology of aging. In *The Handbook of the Psychology of Aging*, 2d ed., edited by J.E. Birren and K.W. Schaie, 245–58. New York: Van Nostrand Reinhold Co.

Schooler, K.K. 1982. Response of the elderly to environment: A stress-theoretical perspective. In *Aging and the Environment: Theoretical Approaches*, edited by M.P. Lawton, P.G. Windley, and T.O. Byerts, 80–96. New York: Springer Publishing Co.

Smith, B.A. 1986. When is "confusion" translocation syndrome? *American Journal of Nursing* 86: 1280–1.

Steels, M.M. 1976. Perceptual style and the adaptation of the aged to the hospital environment. *Association of Rehabilitation Nurses* 1: 9–14.

Strickland, B.R. 1978. Internal-external expectancies and health-related behaviors. *Journal of Consulting and Clinical Psychology* 46: 1192–1211.

Williams, M.A., E.B. Campbell, W.J. Raynor, et al. 1985a. Reducing acute confusional states in elderly patients with hip fractures. *Research in Nursing and Health* 8: 329–37.

Williams, M.A., E.B. Campbell, W.J. Raynor, et al. 1985b. Predictors of acute confusional states in hospitalized elderly patients. *Research in Nursing and Health* 8: 31–40.

Wilson-Barnett, J. 1979. *Stress in Hospital: Patient's Psychological Reactions to Illness and Health Care*. New York: Churchill Livingstone.

Windley, P.G., and R.J. Scheidt. 1980. Person-environment dialectics: Implications for competent functioning in old age. In *Aging in the 1980's: Psychological Issues*, edited by L.W. Poon, 407–23. Washington, D.C.: American Psychological Association.

Wolk, S., and S. Telleen. 1976. Psychological and social correlates of life satisfaction as a function of residential constraint. *Journal of Gerontology* 31: 89–98.

Ziegler, M., and D.W. Reid. 1979. Correlates of locus of desired control in two samples of elderly persons: Community residents and hospitalized patients. *Journal of Consulting and Clinical Psychology* 47: 977–9.

Chapter 5

The Assessment of Rehabilitation Potential: Cognitive Factors

Dorene M. Rentz

Efforts to curb escalating health care costs among older adults has caused rehabilitation professionals to struggle with the concept of *rehabilitation potential* and how to select appropriate geriatric candidates for inpatient rehabilitation admissions. Currently, professionals use subjective rather than formal selection criteria because there has been no consensus in the literature about who would make a successful rehabilitation candidate. Without the establishment of formal standards, it is feared that negative cultural values and individual biases about aging may directly affect these clinical decisions (Becker and Kaufman 1988). Older adults with mental deterioration may be particularly affected, especially when denial of rehabilitation treatment might forestall institutional placement.

This chapter will define the rehabilitation potential of cognitively impaired elders and attempt to establish selection criteria for choosing appropriate inpatient rehabilitation candidates. While it is recognized that emotional factors are equally important for success in rehabilitation, these issues will be extensively addressed in Chapter 6 and will not be covered here. Also, the limitation of this criteria to an inpatient program is deliberate and meant to address the needs of professionals who are asked to assess hospitalized elders ready for discharge from acute care settings but unable to return home. However, this limited focus is not meant to imply that rehabilitation is done best only on an inpatient basis. In fact, many fine outpatient and home programs exist to address the rehabilitation needs of those elders dwelling in the community, and sometimes outpatient settings are especially optimal for patients with cognitive decline.

The basic questions addressed in this chapter are whether cognitively impaired elders can benefit from inpatient rehabilitation services and, if so, what programmatic changes are needed to enhance their success. Rehabilitation potential will be formally defined and a hypothetical discussion will ensue about what minimum but essential cognitive factors should be present for cognitively impaired elders to succeed in achieving rehabilitation goals. Assessment techniques for evaluating the presence of these cognitive factors will be presented and areas of future research will be explored.

DEFINITION OF TERMS

The concept of *rehabilitation potential* has never been formally defined in the literature, despite the fact that investigators have directly addressed the topic (Heller et al. 1984; Klingbeil 1982; Reynolds et al. 1959; Sussman 1972). Since rehabilitation programs differ from acute care medical settings in several important ways, assessing the patient's capability of actively cooperating with treatment is an important component of any rehabilitation consult. This chapter will define rehabilitation potential as the prognostic indicator of how the patient will perform within a standard inpatient rehabilitation program. This would involve an estimation of the patient's personal strengths (i.e., level of motivation/cooperation, cognitive status, and personality constellation), medical complications, and familial support as they interface with the therapies and rehabilitation environment. In essence, the assessment of rehabilitation potential estimates the individual's capability of cooperating with a rehabilitation program and making measured functional gains in ambulation and self-care. It also appraises whether the patient's current quality of life can be improved upon despite chronic or multiple disabilities.

Four other terms are frequently misunderstood in the rehabilitation literature and should be formally defined. They are *effectiveness, benefit, cost effectiveness* and *cost benefit*. These terms bear a direct relationship to rehabilitation potential because they reflect the interface that must exist between the personal strengths of the individual, the efficacy of the rehabilitation program, and the outcomes attained from participation.

The *effectiveness* of a rehabilitation program implies that objective functional gains were achieved through treatment (i.e., activities of daily living (ADL) and mobility status) and maintained after discharge. *Benefit* more subjectively implies the quality of life achieved by the individual following treatment (Feigenson 1979). *Cost effectiveness* compares functional gain with monetary value. It implies efficient delivery of service with the goal of the greatest functional gain through the least expensive form of treatment. *Cost benefit* also compares monetary expenditures to functional gains but assesses whether improved quality of life has been achieved. It theoretically implies that patients could be denied treatment because the costs outweigh the perceived benefit to the patient (Berkowitz 1984; Johnston and Keith 1983).

PROGNOSTIC INDICATORS OF SUCCESS OR RISK IN REHABILITATION

Deciding which older patients would benefit from a rehabilitation program is sometimes very difficult. Most physicians and rehabilitation professionals would admit that they base their decisions on a subjective estimate of a patient's potential rather than standardized protocols or objective criteria. In a survey of physicians conducted by Becker and Kaufman, a subjective estimate of *recovery potential* was used to determine applicability for rehabilitation. Recovery potential involved five components: "state of health before the stroke, level of cognitive impairment, severity of the stroke, ability of the patient to tolerate an intensive therapy program and age" (1988, 461). Other clinicians emphasized cognitive factors such as verbal and nonverbal comprehension of directions, memory, and the generalization of training (Anderson and Kottke 1978). Gryfe (1979) felt that behavioral factors such as the patient's motivation and cooperation were important to be a successful rehabilitation candidate.

Predictors of success or failure in rehabilitation have also been derived from more objective scientific investigations employing multivariate statistical methods. However, most of these studies used a stroke patient population and cannot be generalized to other geriatric patient groups. The results indicated that no single factor denoted a rehabilitation risk but rather that emotional, cognitive, and physical factors taken in combination tended to have more predictive capacity. Table 5-1 lists these studies and the variables which predicted poor rehabilitation outcome. A major criticism, however, is that most of the dependent measures were often informally constructed rating scales and tabulations of multiple physical, psychological, and laboratory variables derived from the patient's medical chart. Due to these diverse methodologies, no consensus emerged in the variables for predicting outcome. Consequently, no definitive criteria could be derived from these studies which reliably differentiated the patient who was likely to benefit from intensive rehabilitation from the patient who was likely to do poorly or to recover spontaneously. Use of outcome studies also implies that the patient's individual rehabilitation *performance* can predict rehabilitation *potential*. As noted later in this chapter, this may or may not be a fair method of assessing the applicability of rehabilitation treatment versus custodial placement.

If the prognostic indicators listed in Table 5-1 were utilized to assess the most cost-effective use of rehabilitation services, they would suggest that rehabilitation be limited to well-motivated, physiologically younger patients who were cognitively intact with a moderate level of disability. However, these criteria tend to endorse ageism biases. In contrast, most geriatric specialists believe that

Table 5-1 Factors Predicting Poor Rehabilitation Outcome

Study	Subjects	Predictive Factors
Anderson et al. 1974	N = 262 CVA Mean age— not reported	—Perceptual loss —Low motivation —Confusion/disorientation —Withdrawal/apathy —Extended time since onset —Previous CVA —Nystagmus —Low blood pressure —Extended period of unconsciousness post CVA
Carey et al. 1988	N = 6,194 Multiple Dx CVA	—Old age —Shortened length of stay —Poor functional ability at time of admission
Feigenson et al. 1977	N = 248 CVA Mean age = 67	—Severe weakness —Perceptual or cognitive dysfunction —Inability to walk —Incontinence —Homonymous Hemianopsia —Low motivation
Fullerton et al. 1988	N = 206 CVA Mean age = 70	—Perceptual loss —Altered level of consciousness —Severe limb weakness —Mental status changes —Dysphasia —Impaired electrocardiogram
Kotila et al. 1984	N = 154 CVA Mean age = 61	—Old age —Acute-stage hemiparesis —Intellectual/Memory loss —Visuoperceptual deficits —Nonadequate emotional reactions —Living alone
Lehmann et al. 1975	N = 114 CVA Mean age— not reported	—Extensive lesions —Previous history of CVA and cardiovascular disease —Perceptual loss —Low education —Old age
Osberg et al. 1988	N = 89 CVA Mean age— not reported	—Severity of illness —Old age —Wheelchair use —Poor social support

even older patients with poor prognostic signs can achieve some independence which would make rehabilitation worthwhile and consequently, cost-effective (Dombovy et al. 1986; Feigenson et al. 1977; Klingbeil 1982; Lehmann et al. 1975; Sussman 1972). These opinions corroborate other gerontologists who believe that elders who stay active and maintain a modicum of independence (even despite custodial placement) have a propensity toward greater psychological well-being and possibly longer life spans. Increasing their activity status was shown to improve life satisfaction and morale (Langer et al. 1984; Stones and Kozma 1986; Stones et al. 1989).

THE IMPACT OF COGNITIVE DYSFUNCTION ON
REHABILITATION POTENTIAL

In the past, standard rehabilitation programs were considered less applicable for patients with chronic cognitive dysfunction than individuals with other chronic illnesses such as heart disease or stroke (Reifler and Teri 1986). The predominant rationale was that rehabilitation is a relearning program and patients with deteriorated mental conditions were considered unable to learn and cooperate with rehabilitation treatment. Consequently, cognitive dysfunction was often considered a hallmark of a poor rehabilitation risk and was associated with poor rehabilitation outcomes and increased mortality (Beals 1972; Kotila et al. 1984; Miller 1978; Schuman et al. 1981). These opinions were derived from several research efforts.

A study examining the effectiveness of a standard rehabilitation program for those with and without cognitive dysfunction found that patients with normal cognition improved from standard rehabilitative techniques but those with mild, moderate, or severe cognitive deficits did not benefit (Schuman et al. 1981).

Cognitive dysfunction was implicated as a negative predictor of recovery and long range prognosis for hip fracture patients. Cognitively compromised patients tended to have poor ambulatory outcomes and high mortality rates (Beals 1972; Miller 1978).

Multiple regression studies of patients undergoing stroke rehabilitation also found cognitive variables highly predictive of poor rehabilitation outcomes. The cognitive functions implicated were overall intellectual decline, the inability to learn, memory dysfunction, visuoperceptual deficits, motor impersistence, word dysfluency, apraxia, agnosia, and perseveration (Klingbeil 1982; Kotila et al. 1984; Novack et al. 1987).

Efficacy of Rehabilitation for Cognitively Impaired Patients

While the above studies demonstrate that cognitive dysfunction is associated with poorer rehabilitative outcomes, several researchers have found that some patients with cognitive impairments have shown improvement, particularly when changes were made in the treatment program.

Barnes (1984) studied 70 postsurgical hip fracture patients with an average of 82 years who were admitted to a rehabilitation center specializing in geriatrics. He found that motivation, orientation, and alertness did not play a significant role in whether a patient returned to preambulatory status. In fact, 47 percent of his successfully rehabilitated patients were cognitively impaired. While his method of using orientation as an assessment of cognitive dysfunction has been criticized as crude (Hielema 1984), it is still noteworthy that patients who were disoriented could participate in rehabilitation and achieve a good rehabilitation outcome. These positive outcomes might possibly be attributed to the specialized geriatric focus of the rehabilitation program.

Jackson (1984) evaluated the efficacy of a geriatric rehabilitation unit versus a nonrehabilitation medical unit with limited physical therapy services. The diagnoses of both patient groups were common to rehabilitation and included arthritis, general debility, cerebral vascular accidents, and disorders of the cardiac, respiratory, and urinary tracts. The groups were matched for age, severity of illness, functional status, and cognitive ability at the beginning of the study. After a six week period, she found that the patients in the geriatric rehabilitation unit displayed significantly greater mental status and functional changes than the patients treated on the traditional medical service. These changes included increased ability in communication, social skills, self-care, balance, ambulation, and sleep patterns, with a diminishment in restlessness, confusion, and incidence of incontinence.

Jackson attributed the differences to staff education in geriatrics, ongoing training sessions, regularly planned interdisciplinary conferences, development of individualized treatment plans, and environmental modifications which emphasized a *wellness* rather than an *illness* model. On the geriatric rehabilitation unit, the staff encouraged patients to wear their own daytime clothes, participate in group activities, eat with others at a table, take greater control in decision making, and become independent in moving freely about the ward. The other group, treated in the traditional medical model, received routine medical care, followed their prescribed medical regimes, wore dressing gowns, and ate meals at bedside. A few had prescribed exercise programs, but there were no regularly planned interdisciplinary patient assessment conferences or individualized treatment plans.

The improved outcomes in this study provide evidence that a trained and motivated staff in geriatrics can make a difference in improving a patient's rehabilitation outcome even when mental status is impaired. Individualizing treatment regimes to match the patient's cognitive ability level was an essential component of the program.

Brody and associates (1971) used rehabilitation principles with moderate to severely demented elders and found that significant gains could be achieved if they enhanced the current potential strengths of the person. Essential to successful outcomes was the treatment of all *excess disabilities* which interfered with the patient's residual cognitive skills (see Chapter 8 in this text). Meyer and associates (1986) also found that cognition improved for multi-infarct dementia patients when excess disabilities were controlled. Longitudinally, however, Brody and associates (1974) found that treatment gains in their patients with moderate to severe dementia were not maintained. They concluded that this patient population would need sustained treatment input to preserve treatment efficacy.

Izzo and associates (1986) were able to utilize rehabilitation techniques to improve transfers, balance, ambulation, swallowing, memory, visual screening, and vertical gaze paralysis in a patient with progressive supranuclear palsy. These rehabilitation efforts enabled this patient to live independently until progressive deterioration made this prohibitive. An essential component of this patient's rehabilitation potential was her supportive family. They received ongoing education to provide caregiving at home and counseling services to assist with eventual custodial placement.

Rogers and associates (1987) treated a 90 year old institutionalized and severely disoriented woman. After 5 1/2 weeks of twenty 30 to 45 minute sessions involving intensive sensory stimulation, this patient made impressive gains in orientation, attention, concentration, self-feeding, mobility, communication, and cooperation with caregiving. Improvements were attributed to the patient's increasing ability to attend to tasks and imitate the examiner. Treatment sessions eventually stimulated overlearned, familiar skills which generalized to everyday activities on the unit.

Moderately impaired Alzheimer disease patients and survivors of severe closed head injury have also been shown to learn and retain motor and perceptual tasks (Eslinger and Damasio 1986; Ewert et al. 1989; Grosse et al. 1988). Called procedural learning, this aspect of memory processing is an essential component of rehabilitation. These studies demonstrated that patients with dementia or severe amnesia could successfully acquire and retain new skills while remaining disoriented and amnesic for day to day events.

Based on the principles of occupational therapy, a systematic, graduated program was designed by Levy (1989). It suggested therapeutic activities for patients at varying stages of cognitive disability. The goals of therapy were designed to accommodate deficiencies in attention, goal directed behavior, and self-initiated actions. Imitation of very familiar behavioral patterns was suggested in patients at lower levels of cognitive ability. Environmental modifications were advocated to compensate for a person's cognitive limitations.

In summary, these studies suggest that severity of cognitive status does not have to exclude a patient from consideration for rehabilitation. However, certain conditions were required for successful treatment outcomes. For example, regionalizing care into disability-oriented or geriatric units improved the rate of home placements and ambulatory status at time of discharge (Feigenson 1979; Feigenson et al. 1979; Liem et al. 1986; Schuman et al. 1980). These variables were associated with lower mortality and improved quality of life (Beals 1972; Liem et al. 1986; Miller 1978). Individualizing treatment programs to match an individual's ability level was necessary for acquiring gains in improved self-care and, in some instances, enhanced length of independent living. The presence of family support and their willingness to implement home treatment programs and utilize appropriate community services were required for the maintenance of treatment gains. Utilizing procedural learning improved patients' functional capacity despite continued disorientation and memory loss. Also, the treatment of excess disabilities enhanced attentional skills thereby optimizing patients' cognitive reserves and interest in the environment (Brody et al. 1971; Meyer et al. 1986).

In each instance, however, the progressive nature of the illness eventually led to a deterioration in functional status. This is probably the primary impediment to the maintenance of any rehabilitation gains demonstrated in these studies. However, geriatric rehabilitation considers family training to be as important as the patient's attainment of rehabilitation goals. Training focuses on behavioral and physical management and is conducted by all members of the interdisciplinary team. They provide information on the patient's strengths and deficits and capacity to manage independently or with a particular level of supervision. Such information, in conjunction with the team's recommendation, facilitates the family's decision-making process regarding their ability to care for the patient at home or resort to custodial care. This form of family education is often an unacknowledged but very important benefit of the rehabilitation of this patient group.

EVALUATING REHABILITATION POTENTIAL: COGNITIVE FACTORS

As mentioned above, the evaluation of rehabilitation potential in cognitively impaired elders has often been guesswork among specialists. When doubt occurs as to whether a patient would be appropriate, most professionals advocate the provision of a short trial of inpatient rehabilitation therapy. Once the patient is admitted, the interdisciplinary team provides a comprehensive assessment of the patient's potential for making treatment gains. Chapters 6 and 7 of this text discuss selected standardized instruments most often used for assessing emotional and cognitive status. From these measures, an inference can be made early-on in the rehabilitation admission as to whether the patient can successfully participate from a cognitive/emotional standpoint.

However, with rehabilitation resources becoming limited, a lengthy, comprehensive inpatient assessment is not cost-effective. Rehabilitation specialists need to find a way to assess rehabilitation potential prior to admission that will not be biased against age and cognitive status. This would involve modifying the goals that rehabilitation can accomplish for this patient group and determining which cognitive skills are necessary in order to be successful. In contrast to the goals of younger, more intact patients, goals for cognitively impaired geriatric patients are often small and focus on enhancing self-care skills and family education for home management. Patients who fail to succeed in achieving acceptable functional outcomes have often been assigned treatment regimes which exceeded their cognitive and/or physical capacity and led to uncooperative behaviors and aborted rehabilitation stays. (Chapter 8 discusses management issues and appropriate treatment modifications in more detail.)

Even when programs are adapted to geriatric individuals and treatment teams have the expertise to modify goals to the patient's ability level, the rehabilitation evaluator is still required to assess the patient's personal strengths for succeeding in a rehabilitation program. Some objective guidelines exist for assessing level of motivation, cooperation, and personality constellation required for optimum rehabilitation potential. However, the literature is inconclusive as to which cognitive strengths or level of alertness is necessary for benefiting from a rehabilitation program (Kemp 1984).

Given the success of those cognitively impaired elders in the above cited studies, one could objectively hypothesize that rehabilitation success is possible if the patient possesses only three basic cognitive components: (1) attention (Brody et al. 1971, 1974; Levy 1989; Rogers et al. 1987); (2) procedural learning (Eslinger and Damasio 1986; Ewert et al. 1989; Levy 1989); and (3) a capacity to imitate or follow nonverbal directions (Izzo et al. 1986; Levy 1989; Rogers et al. 1987). Perhaps, other cognitive abilities such as language, memory, orientation, perception, and problem-solving skills, which seem essential to traditional rehabilitation, are not necessary for geriatric patients to benefit from treatment and be discharged home. Self-care skills, such as the ability to get in and out of bed, use a toilet, dress, and eat are well entrenched habits from years of practice. It is possible that a cognitively impaired elder may only require a minimum of cognitive reserve to relearn them.

However, most rehabilitation professionals use one of several standardized mental status instruments (such as the Mini Mental State Exam or the Kahn Goldfarb Mental Status Questionnaire described in Chapter 7) for assessing rehabilitation potential. Sole use of such instruments would fail to directly elicit attention, procedural learning, and imitation and would unintentionally eliminate many cognitively impaired elders from participating in a rehabilitation program.

To avoid this, the evaluator should utilize additional bedside techniques which incorporate the use of the environment and observational skills. This may require the patient to perform tasks which would mimic treatment behaviors. The following sections describe a few methods for assessing these three basic cognitive skills.

Attention

Attention encompasses three interrelated aspects: sustained attention, selective attention, and attentional capacity (Albert 1988). Attentional capacity generally involves the person's ability to perform two tasks at the same time. It is commonly known that most older adults are limited in this capacity and cannot manipulate two tasks simultaneously. Consequently, those who work with older people know that instructions and tasks should be given simply and one at a time.

Sustained attention involves the ability to focus on a simple task and perform it without losing track of the object of the task. Most older adults will usually have adequate abilities to sustain attention. If patients are distractible, prohibiting them from staying task-focused, then a possible delirious or confusional state has occurred. Efforts to rehabilitate these individuals might be premature until their mental condition clears.

Simple bedside tests have been developed for assessing sustained attention. A common measure is repetition of digits. This requires the examiner to recite a series of numbers and then requests that the patient repeat them. An adequate performance would consist of between four and seven digits forward. Another common measure of sustained attention is the test of *Vigilance*. A nice feature of this test is that it measures both auditory and visual modalities and one form could replace the other depending on the patient's sensory losses. This test requires the patient to indicate the letter "A" from a series of letters presented in a random fashion by either underlining the letter or tapping a pencil when the letter is recited. Strub and Black (1977, 19) provide further elaboration of this simple bedside measure. Several standardized tests also include simple measures of sustained attention with normative data for older adults. The reader is referred to the Wechsler Memory Scale—Revised (Wechsler 1987) and the Dementia Rating Scale (Mattis 1988) for examples of verbal and visual attention span tests.

Selective attention is the capacity to attend to relevant while ignoring irrelevant stimuli. This component is important for most rehabilitation settings since numerous patients are usually treated at the same time in large therapy rooms. Patients would have to be able to attend to the directions of their individual therapist while ignoring all the other activity that is going on around them.

Assessment of adequate selective attention can be done in several ways. Observations of the patient's ability to attend during the evaluation interview is probably the simplest test. Another, more traditional assessment measure is a target detection task. The patient is presented with a spatial array and asked to circle the target stimuli in the presence of an array of nontargets. Targets should be modified according to the patient's ability to recognize them. For example, letters, shapes, or colors, could be used. Selective attention is generally well preserved in older adults and can be evaluated through these simple methods (Gilmore et al. 1985; Nissen and Corkin 1985; Wright and Elias 1979).

Procedural Learning

Squire (1986) defined procedural learning as the activation of knowledge which is associated with motor and perceptual skills. These skills were acquired incrementally early in life and have become habituated to the individual. For example, standing, walking, or eating are examples of procedural skills. This type of knowledge is implicit and not in conscious awareness. It is accessible only through performance, that is, by engaging in the skills or operations in which the knowledge is embedded. Procedural learning is generally activated through priming preexisting representations which were embedded in sensory or motor modalities. This can be done through imitation or by actually guiding the individual through a task. However, the acquired information can only be accessed through the same sensory modality in which the material was initially learned.

Another important feature of procedural activation is that it is not language dependent. Most learning in humans is based on language. Called declarative memory, this type of learning is explicit, accessible to conscious awareness, and includes the facts, episodes, lists, and routes of everyday life. It can be declared, that is, brought to mind verbally as an idea or nonverbally as an image. For example, one's fifth grade teacher can be recalled as a name, or as an image of the teacher's face.

Recent studies have shown that patients with memory loss have a striking dissociation in their ability to learn and retain these different types of information (Brooks and Baddeley 1976; Cohen and Squire 1980; Corkin 1968; Eslinger and Damasio 1986; Ewert et al. 1989; Heindel et al. 1988; Squire et al. 1984). While the patients in these studies had difficulty recalling declarative knowledge (i.e., common words, unfamiliar faces, or verbal directions), they often retained the capacity to learn and remember motor and perceptual tasks. This implies that while declarative or verbal memory processing may be impaired, skill acquisition can still be activated. This information has important implications for rehabilitation. Physical and occupational therapies usually involve the activation of skills that are often deeply embedded in acquired procedural knowledge such as walking, dressing, and basic self-care tasks. These studies suggest that patients with severe cognitive limitations may be able to successfully activate procedural tasks and learn and retain new skills based on procedural learning paradigms.

Specific tests which can elicit procedural learning at the bedside are still undeveloped. Examples of procedural tasks used in research have been mirror reading (Squire et al. 1984), Porteus mazes (Porteus 1959), and pursuit rotor (Corkin 1968), but these tasks are somewhat esoteric and difficult to conduct at bedside. However, the performance of simple activities of daily living may be tested as a way of assessing procedural learning (Ewert et al. 1989). This would require the evaluator to be behaviorally active with the patient rather than verbally active. Imitation and task setup would replace verbal commands. For example, providing a washcloth and basin should facilitate awareness of bathing, a basic procedural task in humans. Patients may be unable to completely perform the task because of a debilitated state but, nevertheless, it is the basic awareness of the procedure that should be assessed. If procedural learning can be demonstrated, the goals of geriatric rehabilitation may be accomplished despite the lack of other higher cognitive abilities, such as language, visuoperception, problem solving, insight, and judgment.

Imitation

Imitation is the capacity to follow the example of another without the aid of verbal directions. This task is different from the type of praxic tasks usually tested on mental status examinations, which involve the performance of an act to a given verbal command. Patients are apraxic when they cannot motorically perform a command because there is a breakdown between the ideational association of what is requested and the ability to carry out the motor movement. Consequently, apraxia is defined as a defect in motor planning, or the integrative steps that precede skilled or learned movements (Strub and Black 1977, 119). However, when the verbal command component is removed, apraxic patients are often able to imitate the examiner performing the task because muscle strength, motor coordination, and sensation are intact.

Most rehabilitation involves language dependent learning. Therapists are trained to give verbal commands and the patient is expected to understand and carry out these commands. Retention of rehabilitation strategies is often elicited through a verbal recitation of the previous day's lesson. These strategies often fail with cognitively impaired elders since many of them have disabling aphasias, agnosias and apraxias. Consequently, these patients have poor outcomes when language dependent rehabilitation techniques are used. However, if the patient is able to imitate the examiner and procedural learning remains intact, then these patients should be able to regain simple ADL skills which would ease the care-giving burden. Programmatic adaptations which involve nonverbal imitation to elicit procedural learning appear essential if this patient population is to be successfully rehabilitated.

There are no standardized bedside tests developed to elicit imitation abilities. However, with a little imagination the examiner, using readily available accessories found in the hospital room, should have no difficulty determining whether a patient can imitate. Demonstrations should involve well-learned motor skills and actual objects should be used. For example, the toothbrushing motion should have a toothbrush in hand; hair combing should have a brush in hand, and so on. If the patient has adequate attentional abilities and good motor capacities despite weakness, then imitation should be possible.

POTENTIAL CRITERIA FOR ASSESSING CANDIDACY TO REHABILITATION

The information provided in this chapter can be summarized into suggested criteria for assessing the rehabilitation potential of cognitively impaired elders. An outline of these criteria is presented in Exhibit 5-1.

The assessment of rehabilitation potential currently involves an estimation of the patient's personal strengths (i.e., level of motivation, cooperation, cognitive status, and personality constellation) as well as medical complications and familial support. How these personal characteristics interface with the endurance required to participate in a rehabilitation program are also considered. Patients must be able to withstand a given number of hours of therapy per day and achieve the goals of rehabilitation within a reasonable length of time.

Cognitively impaired elders have often been denied a trial of rehabilitation because they lacked the personal characteristics to do well. However, the research

---

Exhibit 5-1 Criteria for Assessing Rehabilitation Potential of Cognitively Impaired Elders

—Cognitive factors such as sustained and selective attention, procedural learning and imitation
—Staff sensitivity to the treatment of excess disabilities
—The establishment of disability-oriented or geriatric units with trained and motivated staff
—Treatment based on functional rather than neurological deficits
—The expertise to design individualized treatment programs based on the patient's preserved strengths
—Motivated families and caregivers who are interested in implementing treatment regimens at home

presented in this chapter suggests that rehabilitation potential is not just inherent in the patient but, more importantly, involves an interaction with the program to which the patient is admitted. Many outcome studies have shown that cognitively impaired patients do poorly if they are admitted to standard rehabilitation units which require language dependent learning. However, the patient's poor outcome may not have been due to weak rehabilitation potential but rather to the failure of a program which was unable to tap or utilize the patient's true rehabilitation potential. In other words, unless both personal and programmatic components are operative, then cognitively impaired elders will show insufficient rehabilitation potential to benefit. This suggests that using patient outcome variables as a means of establishing criteria for rehabilitation potential is probably insufficient. Programmatic variables should also be considered.

In summary, the assessment of rehabilitation potential in cognitively impaired elders should consider the following personal, environmental, and staff factors:

1. Does the patient possess a minimum of cognitive reserve (i.e., the capacity to stay task-focused, utilize procedural processes, and imitate)?
2. Is the unit designed to be conducive to the cognitive deficiencies and disorientation of the disabled elder?
3. Is the rehabilitation team trained in geriatrics and enthusiastic about working with elders?
4. Do they have the expertise to design an individualized treatment plan which coincides with an older patient's cognitive and physical ability levels?
5. Is the team sufficiently motivated to work with elders who may not achieve the treatment gains that younger patients can accomplish through similar efforts?
6. Are programmatic goals practical, focused on basic self-care skills, and realistic to the needs of older adults?
7. Does the rehabilitation team appreciate the involvement of families and are families willing to help utilize the information they receive to implement changes in the home environment or to assist in decision-making processes?

AREAS OF FUTURE RESEARCH

The studies presented in this chapter demonstrate that research in geriatric rehabilitation and, particularly, the rehabilitation potential of cognitively impaired elders is in its infancy. Since more and more older adults are consumers of rehabilitation services, it is apparent that empirical research with this patient population is warranted.

The need for rehabilitation programs to evaluate the efficacy of their standard approaches for geriatric patients is one important area requiring future research. Most standard techniques have not been designed for this patient population and do not take into consideration the special needs of the older adult. Empirical investigations which can establish the components of successful rehabilitation among geriatric patients should continue. However, practical goals and specialized outcome criteria valid for older adults should be established. In addition, better outcome measures should be refined from the ones currently in use. These measures should be sensitive enough to detect even small changes in functional status; items measured should be relevant to geriatric patients, including those who are cognitively impaired. Outcome measurement could be further advanced through the employment of interval and ratio rather than ordinal data in order to provide a more objective and accurate sense of treatment efficacy. Merbitz and associates (1989) provide a comprehensive review of how our functional outcome measures can be improved.

As proposed in this chapter, further research is needed on the cognitive components necessary to be successful in rehabilitation. Based on these findings, formal mental status procedures could be developed to assist in the evaluation of an elder's rehabilitation potential from a cognitive perspective.

Another important area of future research involves the development of treatment paradigms which can enhance rehabilitation outcomes in cognitively impaired elders. Delineating treatment activities which are appropriate to specific cognitive ability levels is essential to the rehabilitation of this patient population. Levy (1989) provides an excellent example for occupational therapists. Other therapies should also consider how their treatment paradigms can be adapted to various cognitive capacities. Outcome studies generated from this type of programmatic focus would better substantiate preselection criteria and assist in formally establishing the level of cognitive ability necessary to achieve a good rehabilitation outcome.

While the development of specialized programs should enhance the treatment outcome of some patients, these efforts may be cost-prohibitive in a traditional rehabilitation setting. Research efforts should be directed toward determining where cognitively impaired elders can most cost-effectively benefit from treatment. This may mean programs where professionals provide rehabilitation in the home, treatment paradigms in nursing homes, or specialized units outside hospital environments (such as day care centers, etc.) that incorporate traditional rehabilitation concepts into their programs. These programs would be able to provide individualized, long-term treatment without the institutional or Medicare rules which currently constrain standard rehabilitation units. These alternative treatment settings could then be compared with custodial care institutions to determine how cost-effective and cost-beneficial their programs actually are.

Finally, further research is needed in the area of the pharmacological enhancement of cognition. While such efforts have failed to help patients learn declarative information, little work has been done to enhance procedural learning while measuring habituated ADL skills.

CONCLUSION

Rehabilitation was founded on the premise that innovative environments can be constructed to foster independence in populations once thought to be untreatable. Cognitively impaired elders, the new consumers of rehabilitation, are currently in need of these kinds of environments. They are also in need of treatment teams that can concentrate more on the severity of their disabilities than their potentials for improvement. This chapter suggests that enhanced quality of life for cognitively impaired elders should be the next new horizon to which rehabilitation medicine directs its expertise.

REFERENCES

Albert, M. 1988. Cognitive function. In *Geriatric Neuropsychology,* edited by M. Albert and M. Moss, 33–53. New York: Guilford Press.

Anderson, T., N. Bourestom, F. Greenberg, et al. 1974. Predictive factors in stroke rehabilitation. *Archives of Physical Medicine and Rehabilitation* 55: 545–53.

Anderson, T., and F. Kottke. 1978. Stroke rehabilitation: A reconsideration of some common attitudes. *Archives of Physical Medicine and Rehabilitation* 59: 175–81.

Barnes, B. 1984. Ambulation outcomes after hip fracture. *Physical Therapy* 64: 317–20.

Beals, R. 1972. Survival following hip fracture. *Journal of Chronic Diseases* 25: 235–44.

Becker, G., and S. Kaufman. 1988. Age, rehabilitation, and research: Review of the issues. *The Gerontologist* 28 (4): 459–68.

Berkowitz, M. 1984. Benefit-cost analysis in rehabilitation medicine. In *Functional Assessment in Rehabilitation Medicine,* edited by C. Granger and G. Gresham, 154–71. Baltimore: Williams and Wilkins.

Brody, E., M. Kleban, M. Lawton, et al. 1974. A longitudinal look at excess disabilities in the mentally impaired aged. *Journal of Gerontology* 29: 79–84.

Brody, E., M. Kleban, M. Lawton, et al. 1971. Excess disabilities of mentally impaired aged: Impact of individualized treatment. *The Gerontologist* 11(2), pt. 1: 124–32.

Brooks, D., and A. Baddeley. 1976. What can amnesic patients learn? *Neuropsychologia* 14: 111–22.

Carey, R., J. Seibert, and E. Posavac. 1988. Who makes the most progress in inpatient rehabilitation? An analysis of functional gain. *Archives of Physical Medicine and Rehabilitation* 69: 337–43.

Cohen, M., and L. Squire. 1980. Preserved learning and retention of pattern-analysing skill in amnesia: dissociation of knowing how and knowing that. *Science* 210: 207–9.

Corkin, S. 1968. Acquisition of motor skill after bilateral medial temporal-lobe excision. *Neuropsychologia* 6: 255–65.

Dombovy, M., B. Sandock, and J. Basford. 1986. Rehabilitation for stroke: A review. *Stroke* 17: 363–9.

Eslinger, P., and A. Damasio. 1986. Preserved motor learning in Alzheimer's disease: Implications for anatomy and behavior. *The Journal of Neuroscience* 6: 3006–9.

Ewert, J., H. Levin, M. Watson, et al. 1989. Procedural memory during posttraumatic amnesia in survivors of severe closed head injury. *Archives of Neurology* 46: 911–16.

Feigenson, J. 1979. Stroke rehabilitation: Effectiveness, benefits, and cost. Some practical considerations. *Stroke* 10: 1–3.

Feigenson, J., H. Gitlow, and S. Greenberg. 1979. Disability oriented stroke unit: A major factor influencing stroke outcome. *Stroke* 10: 5–8.

Feigenson, J., F. McDowell, P. Meese, et al. 1977. The factors influencing outcome and length of stay in a stroke rehabilitation unit. Part 1. Analysis of 248 unscreened patients—Medical and functional prognostic indicators. *Stroke* 8: 651–6.

Fullerton, C., G. MacKenzie, and R. Stout. 1988. Prognostic indices in stroke. *Quarterly Journal of Medicine*, n. 5., 66, vol. 250: 147–62.

Gilmore, G., T. Tobias, and F. Royer. 1985. Aging and similarity grouping in visual search. *Journal of Gerontology* 40: 586–92.

Grosse, D., R. Wilson, and J. Fox. 1988. Maze learning in Alzheimer's disease. Paper presented at the International Neuropsychological Society Meeting, Vancouver, B.C.

Gryfe, C. 1979. Reasonable expectations in geriatric rehabilitation. *Journal of the American Geriatrics Society* 27: 237–8.

Heindel, W., N. Butters, and D. Salmon. 1988. Impaired learning of a motor skill in patients with Huntington's disease. *Behavioral Neuroscience* 102: 141–7.

Heller, B., R. Barker-Bausell, and M. Ninos. 1984. Nurses' perceptions of rehabilitation potential of institutionalized aged. *Journal of Gerontological Nursing* 10: 23–7.

Hielema, F. 1984. Commentary. *Physical Therapy* 64: 320–1.

Izzo, K., P. DiLorenzo, and A. Roth. 1986. Rehabilitation in progressive supranuclear palsy: Case report. *Archives of Physical Medicine and Rehabilitation* 67: 473–6.

Jackson, M. 1984. Geriatric rehabilitation on an acute-care medical unit. *Journal of Advanced Nursing* 9: 441–8.

Johnston, M., and R. Keith. 1983. Cost-benefits of medical rehabilitation: Review and critique. *Archives of Physical Medicine and Rehabilitation* 64: 147–54.

Kemp, B. 1984. Psychosocial and mental health issues in rehabilitation of older persons. In *Aging and Rehabilitation: Advances in the State of the Art,* edited by S. Brody and G. Ruff, 122–58. New York: Springer Publishing Co.

Klingbeil, G. 1982. The assessment of rehabilitation potential in the elderly. *Wisconsin Medical Journal* 81: 25–7.

Kotila, M., O. Waltimo, M. Niemi, et al. 1984. The profile of recovery from stroke and factors influencing outcome. *Stroke* 15: 1039–44.

Langer, E., P. Beck, R. Janoff-Bulman, et al. 1984. An exploration of the relationships among mindfulness, longevity, and senility. *Academic Psychology Bulletin* 6: 211–26.

Lehmann, J., B. DeLateur, R. Fowler, et al. 1975. Stroke rehabilitation: Outcome and prediction. *Archives of Physical Medicine and Rehabilitation* 56: 383–9.

Levy, L. 1989. Activity adaptation in rehabilitation of the physically and cognitively disabled aged. *Topics in Geriatric Rehabilitation* 4: 53–66.

Liem, P., R. Chernoff, and W. Carter. 1986. Geriatric rehabilitation unit: A 3-year outcome evaluation. *Journal of Gerontology* 41: 44–50.

Mattis, S. 1988. *DRS Dementia Rating Scale: Professional Manual.* Odessa, Fla.: Psychological Assessment Resources.

Merbitz, C., J. Morris, and J. Grip. 1989. Ordinal scales and foundations of misinference. *Archives of Physical Medicine and Rehabilitation* 70: 308–12.

Meyer, J., B. Judd, T. Tawakina, et al. 1986. Improved cognition after control of risk factors for multi-infarct dementia. *Journal of the American Medical Association* 256: 2203–9.

Miller, C. 1978. Survival and ambulation following hip fracture. *The Journal of Bone and Joint Surgery* 60-A: 930–3.

Nissen, M., and S. Corkin. 1985. Effectiveness of attentional cueing in older and younger adults. *Journal of Gerontology* 40: 185–91.

Novack, T., G. Haban, K. Graham, et al. 1987. Prediction of stroke rehabilitation outcome from a psychologic screening. *Archives of Physical Medicine and Rehabilitation* 68: 729–34.

Osberg, J., G. DeJong, S. Haley, et al. 1988. Predicting long-term outcome among post-rehabilitation stroke patients. *Archives of Physical Medicine and Rehabilitation* 67: 94–103.

Porteus, S. 1959. *The Maze Test and Clinical Psychology.* Palo Alto, Calif.: Pacific Books.

Reifler, B., and L. Teri. 1986. Rehabilitation and Alzheimer's disease. In *Aging and Rehabilitation: Advances in the State of the Art,* edited by S. Brody and G. Ruff, 107–21. New York: Springer Publishing Co.

Reynolds, F., M. Abramson, and A. Young. 1959. The rehabilitation potential of patients in chronic disease institutions. *Journal of Chronic Diseases* 10: 152–9.

Rogers, J., C. Marcus, and T. Snow. 1987. Maude: A case of sensory deprivation. *The American Journal of Occupational Therapy* 41: 673–6.

Schuman, J., E. Beattie, D. Steed, et al. 1981. Geriatric patients with and without intellectual dysfunction: Effectiveness of a standard rehabilitation program. *Archives of Physical Medicine and Rehabilitation* 62: 612–18.

Schuman, J., E. Beattie, D. Steed, et al. 1980. Rehabilitative and geriatric teaching programs: Clinical efficacy in a skilled nursing facility. *Archives of Physical Medicine and Rehabilitation* 61: 310–15.

Squire, L. 1986. Mechanisms of memory. *Science* 23: 1612–19.

Squire, L., N. Cohen, and J. Zouzounis. 1984. Preserved memory in retrograde amnesia: sparing of a recently acquired skill. *Neuropsychologia* 22: 145–52.

Stones, M., B. Dornan, and A. Kozma. 1989. The prediction of mortality in elderly institution residents. *Journal of Gerontology* 44: 72–9.

Stones, M., and A. Kozma. 1986. Happiness and activities as propensities. *Journal of Gerontology* 41: 85–90.

Strub, R., and F. Black. 1977. *The Mental Status Examination in Neurology.* Philadelphia: F.A. Davis Co.

Sussman, N. 1972. Rehabilitation potential of the aging. *Pennsylvania Medicine* 75: 36–8.

Wechsler, D. 1987. *Wechsler Memory Scale—Revised.* New York: Psychological Corp.

Wright, L., and J. Elias. 1979. Age differences in the effects of perceptual noise. *Journal of Gerontology* 34: 704–8.

Chapter 6

The Assessment of Rehabilitation Potential: Emotional Factors

Richard R. Trezona, Jr.

Successful physical rehabilitation of the older patient depends, in part, upon the patient's ability to learn a variety of new skills, which range in complexity from the acquisition of simple motor skills to the relearning of social and family roles. The elder rehabilitation patient must also be able to form therapeutic relationships with the treatment staff and mobilize the energy needed to participate in an intensive daily rehabilitation program. The elder patient's potential to meet the learning and interpersonal demands of an inpatient rehabilitation program will be strongly influenced by the patient's emotional status at the time of admission to a rehabilitation program. The purpose of this chapter is to discuss the relationship between the older patient's emotional state and the potential for participation in a physical rehabilitation program.

In order to explore the relationship between emotional states and the potential for rehabilitation with older adults, a variety of topics will be discussed. These include the effects of emotional states, particularly anxiety, upon learning and performance; the emotional impact of disability upon older adults; and the influence of emotional factors on rehabilitation outcomes. Special considerations in the emotional assessment of older adults, both practical and psychometric, will be presented. Instruments that may prove useful in the evaluation of emotional states with older rehabilitation patients are discussed. Finally, emotional factors that may prove critical in predicting successful rehabilitation will be proposed, as well as suggestions for areas of future research.

DEFINITION OF TERMS

Terms such as *affect, emotions,* and *mood* are frequently used interchangeably by professionals and laypeople alike. Consequently, there is often confusion as to what these terms actually mean. A brief review of the definition of these respective terms will help clarify how they will be used in this chapter. The American Psychiatric Association (1987) defines *affect* as a pattern of observable behaviors which is the expression of a subjective feeling. Examples of affect include anger, sadness, or happiness. Affective states are regarded as varying over time and are changeable. This definition of affect is contrasted with that of *mood,* which refers to a pervasive and sustained emotion that colors an individual's perception of the world. Moods are less variable than affects, and exert a more powerful influence over how people interpret their experience. Examples of mood would include anxiety, depression, and elation. For purposes of this chapter, the term *emotional status* will be used in the broadest sense, and include both affect and mood states. Both affect and mood will be considered since either can influence the rehabilitation potential of older adults.

THE RELATION BETWEEN EMOTIONAL STATUS AND AROUSAL

The distinction between the terms emotion and mood has also been addressed by Buss (1973), who believes that these terms can be differentiated from one another on the basis of the level of arousal underlying each of them. Emotions are classified as high arousal states and are likely to alter the person's relation to the environment, prompting pursuit of some course of action. Moods are characterized by moderate levels of arousal, and their effects are localized within the individual. Moods are of a moderate time duration, whereas emotions are of a short duration. Buss notes that emotions and moods have motivational properties which cause people to act on their environment. The older rehabilitation patient is likely to be in a high state of emotional arousal after the experience of disability and prolonged hospitalization, which can influence a variety of emotional and behavioral responses.

There is evidence of age-related differences in how emotions are experienced by older adults. Schultz (1985) reviewed studies on biological and neural changes with aging and concluded that the older adult reaches higher levels of arousal compared with the young when confronted with novel stressful situations. He states that older adults require more time to return to baseline levels once they have been aroused. Thus, Schultz concludes that the intensity and duration of emotions may increase with age.

THE RELATION BETWEEN EMOTIONAL STATUS AND LEARNING

If the rehabilitation environment is conceptualized as a learning environment, then those variables which influence learning need to be more fully understood. Emotional states, particularly anxiety, have been shown to exert a powerful influence on an individual's ability to learn (Spielberger 1972).

Spence's Drive Theory

The drive theory of Spence (1958) is a useful model for understanding the effects of anxiety on learning. Spence proposes that each organism, including humans, has a repertoire of responses available. These responses are arranged in a hierarchy based upon the individual's past learning history. The probability of a response occurring depends upon the strength of a particular habit (H), and the level of drive (D). Drive has motivational properties and impels the organism to take some action. Examples of drive in Spence's theory include hunger, thirst, and anxiety. Spence proposes that the relationship between drive and habit is multiplicative and summarizes their relationship in the following equation: Response (R) = f($H \times D$). Consequently, for a single response, the higher the level of drive, the stronger the response.

The Spence model can be used to make predictions about the relationship between anxiety and learning under various conditions. If anxiety is conceptualized as a drive, then increases in anxiety ought to increase the rate of learning and improve performance. This prediction holds true, however, only in those situations in which the task to be learned is relatively simple and the correct response is dominant on the habit strength hierarchy. In complex learning situations, in which there are a number of competing response tendencies, all of which are relatively weak in habit strength, anxiety will only serve to increase the habit strength of many incorrect responses. As learning progresses, the correct response will begin to occur more frequently and it will successively move up in the habit strength hierarchy. Eventually, the correct response will become dominant, and what began as a complex task with many competing, incorrect responses, will become a simple task with a dominant, correct response.

Spence's drive theory can also be used to explain how skills are learned in a rehabilitation setting. For example, when patients are confronted with the task of relearning how to walk, they may have many competing responses which are incorrect, or in improper sequence. As physical therapy progresses, those responses which are correct will move up the response hierarchy and incorrect responses will drop out. With continued repetition, the originally complex task of relearning how to walk becomes a simple task.

Yerkes-Dodson Law

Spence's drive theory can be used to explain experimental phenomena such as the Yerkes-Dodson law. The Yerkes-Dodson law states that learning is greatest at a mid-range of anxiety, which is neither too high nor too low. According to drive theory, low levels of anxiety do little to facilitate learning because the motivation they provide is too weak to affect performance. High levels of anxiety interfere with learning since the drive state is so high that there are too many competing responses. The Yerkes-Dodson law further states that the relationship between drive and performance varies according to the complexity of the task. A higher drive level is optimal when the task is simple; less drive is optimal when the task is complex. As applied to human learning situations, the Yerkes-Dodson law predicts that a small amount of anxiety is insufficient to improve performance, whereas a moderate amount of anxiety energizes the person and facilitates performance. Additional increases in anxiety are likely to be disruptive for learning.

The rehabilitation environment places a high value on performance and the patients are subjected to frequent evaluations of their progress. Consequently, anxiety regarding performance is likely to be common in older patients. If the patient experiences too high a level of anxiety, then performance in therapy is likely to deteriorate. This deterioration is even more probable if the task to be relearned is complex in nature. In addition, the older rehabilitation patient may not have the familial, cognitive, and social resources available to mediate the effects of anxiety.

EMOTIONAL STATUS AND ILLNESS IN THE OLDER ADULT

The emotional status of older rehabilitation patients, and consequently their performance in rehabilitation, can be adversely affected by the psychological impact of a major disabling illness or injury in a number of ways. The disabled elder is subject to feelings of helplessness, loss of control, and diminished self-esteem. There is some empirical evidence from the gerontology literature to support the contention that physical illness has a proportionately greater impact on the emotional well-being of the older adult. For example, Larson (1978) reviewed the literature on factors which are related to measures of subjective well-being in samples of people 65 years and older. His findings indicated that of all the elements of an older person's life situation, physical health was most strongly related to feelings of well-being. Larson's review found that older adults who were ill or physically disabled were much less likely to express contentment with their lives. This data supports the salience of health as one ages and the increased sensitivity of elders to physical decline. In a recent study, Reich and associates (1989) investigated the effects of two major life stressors—recent physical disability and conjugal bereavement—on the mental health of older adults. The sample for this study consisted of 246 adults between the ages of 60 and 80 who were interviewed over a period of ten months. The average age of the sample was about 70 years, and 80 percent of the sample were women. Subjects in the disabled and bereaved groups were compared with a control group who were not experiencing these stressors, but were selected from a sample matched on age, sex, and socio-economic status. The disabled group was defined by its scores on a self-report measure of limitations of daily activities. Dependent variables in this study were measures of psychological distress and psychological well-being.

The results of the Reich study revealed that physical disability has far-reaching psychological consequences for older adults. Reich found that the disabled subjects were significantly more emotionally distressed than their control group counterparts at all of the interview periods. Compared to the control group, the disabled demonstrated higher levels of anxiety, depression, helplessness/hopelessness, and even confused thinking. Furthermore, the elders in the disabled group showed that their psychological distress was of a longer duration when compared with the bereaved sample. Disabled subjects also reported much lower levels of self-esteem than did the bereaved sample, and these feelings persisted over the course of the study.

Reich and associates (1989) hypothesized several possible explanations for the finding that the bereaved group made an almost full recovery over the course of the study while the disabled group demonstrated a much less positive change in psychological functioning. One explanation put forth is that the disabled patients had to continually confront the stressful effects of their condition, whereas the bereaved patients were able to move beyond their loss over time. Consequently, members of the disabled group were forced to cope on a daily basis with the chronic problems of a disability. Another explanation for the findings is that the disabled group sustained a more permanent and negative change in self-esteem and self-concept. This alteration in self-concept, as a result of a physical disability, may become permanent and contribute to continued feelings of low self-esteem and hopelessness in disabled older adults.

EMOTIONAL STATUS AND REHABILITATION OUTCOME

There are few studies which have empirically examined the relationship between affective variables and rehabilitation outcomes in older adults. The vast majority of studies in this area have used demographic variables, such as age, to predict success in rehabilitation programs.

Anderson and associates (1974) used a sample of 233 patients with a diagnosis of completed stroke. They collected data on variables which predicted long-term functional recovery after participation in an inpatient rehabilitation program. Predictor variables included physiological, neurological, behavioral-personality, speech, and demographic variables. The success of rehabilitation outcome was measured by improvement in self-care activities and functional communication. Psychological tests and behavioral measures that proved to have some predictive validity for improvement in self-care included behavioral ratings by staff, the Wechsler Memory Scale (a measure of verbal and figural memory), performance subtests of the Wechsler Adult Intelligence Scale (measures of nonverbal intelligence), and the Porteus Maze test (a measure of route finding). Only two variables from the psychological test battery were predictors of improvement in functional communication. These variables were the exhibitionism scale of the Edwards Personal Preference Survey (EPPS), and the schizophrenia scale of the Minnesota Multiphasic Personality Inventory (MMPI). The exhibitionism scale correlated positively with functional communication, perhaps because it assesses the degree to which one is outgoing, assertive, and sociable. The schizophrenia scale was negatively correlated with functional communication. This may be because this scale includes items on confused and disordered thinking, social withdrawal, and apathy. The inability of the Anderson study to find a stronger relationship between psychological factors and rehabilitation outcome could be due to the selection of more enduring personality variables as measured by the MMPI and the EPPS, in contrast to instruments that measure specifically emotional states.

Using an unscreened sample of stroke patients (mean age of 67), Feigenson and associates (1977) retrospectively studied the factors which influenced outcome and length of stay in a stroke rehabilitation unit. These researchers found that a severe organic mental syndrome, severe perceptual dysfunction (denial, neglect, visual-spatial disorientation), and poor motivation coupled with hemiparesis predicted poor performance on all outcome measures. Although the concept of motivation was not well defined in this study, it does emphasize the importance of this variable when assessing rehabilitation potential.

Hyman (1971) investigated the effects of patients' self-concept (stigma, self-esteem), attitudes toward their life situation (loneliness, social integration, home and job satisfaction), and attitudes towards their illness (dependency, secondary gain, belief in supernatural causes of their illness) on motivation and functional improvement in an inpatient rehabilitation setting. The sample consisted of patients who had sustained a stroke less than six months prior to admission. The results revealed that feelings of stigma were associated with decreased motivation and lower functional improvement, especially for those patients who anticipated social contacts following discharge. Feelings of loneliness were related to lower levels of motivation at admission and four weeks into the rehabilitation program. Loneliness was also related to lower functional improvement at discharge. Dependency was associated with low motivation at admission and at a four-week interval. The combination of two variables, dependency and feelings of loneliness, were the most robust predictors of motivation and functional improvement.

Nickens (1983) reviewed a series of studies that examined the psychosocial factors related to the occurrence and outcome of hip fractures. Nickens found that when particular psychosocial factors are present before the fracture, then more positive outcomes are likely. These factors include not living alone, regular social contacts and visiting, ability to manage household responsibilities, and the absence of an organic brain syndrome. Nickens points out the lack of inclusion of psychological variables in the studies that he reviewed. In future studies, he advocates the use of such factors as the role of depression and recent loss, personality type, and hopelessness associated with pending institutional placement.

These studies point out a few factors which are relevant when estimating rehabilitation potential and provide preliminary evidence for the importance of considering emotional factors in rehabilitation. However, the relatively low number of studies available for review indicates that rigorous investigation is needed in this area. Considering the increased frequency of depression in older adults, for example, it seems that more extensive research into how it impacts on high energy, goal-directed rehabilitation activities would be of great benefit in working with this age group.

SPECIAL CONSIDERATIONS IN THE ASSESSMENT OF EMOTION IN OLDER ADULTS

Certain characteristics of older adults should be taken into consideration when attempting to make an assessment of their emotional status. If these characteristics are ignored, the level of cooperation of the patients may be poor, and the clinical information that is gathered may be of questionable validity. The need for these special considerations when communicating with and assessing older adults is even more critical when applied to a rehabilitation setting. For example, the effects of multiple disabilities can complicate assessment and exacerbate the usual problems encountered when evaluating elders. The following factors have been identified as critical prerequisites to obtaining accurate information about the emotional state of the older rehabilitation patient.

Rapport

Before an effective assessment can begin, the patient needs to become socially engaged with the interviewer. This is accomplished through the establishment of rapport. With older patients, additional time may need to be devoted to the task of rapport building. Older patients may be unfamiliar with psychological assessment procedures and feel threatened or anxious when placed in an evaluative situation. Time needs to be allowed for the patient to become comfortable with the assessment situation and the interviewer. The disparity in age between the interviewer and the older patient can also be a factor when establishing rapport. This is particularly true in rehabilitation settings where the treatment staff tends to be much younger than the patients. Rapport can be facilitated by explaining the nature of the assessment and by prompting reminiscence where appropriate to communicate interest and bolster self-esteem. Starting the interview with a topic area that is first mentioned by the patient is another method of promoting rapport.

Social Reinforcement

Older patients may require regular reinforcement in the form of attention and verbal encouragement in order to continue with an assessment interview. The delivery of these social reinforcers can be particularly important when the patient is discussing a topic that is especially sensitive or embarrassing. Embarrassment or shame concerning a decrement in functioning can be particularly common in disabled elders. Social reinforcement should be delivered randomly, on a noncontingent basis, so as to not selectively influence the type of information that a patient provides. Regular social reinforcement is also a way of reducing the tendency toward cautiousness found in older adults (Botwinick 1978) and is especially important in evaluation situations.

Pacing

The pace of the interview will require tailoring to the unique needs of elders. Older patients, particularly those with sensory or cognitive loss, will require additional time to respond to questions. Older patients without functional speech may require extra time to communicate their responses through the use of writing, mechanical device, or a letter board. If the patient is not given an adequate opportunity to respond, then rapport will suffer and the patient's frustration may mount to the point of refusing to continue with the assessment.

Length of the Interview

The length of the interview may have to be modified when assessing older patients. Elders generally fatigue more easily and may require several interviews of shorter duration. This is particularly true for older rehabilitation patients whose physical tolerance for participation in an interview might be limited by decreased endurance and deconditioning. The patient's ability to participate in an interview may also be influenced by reduced attention or other cognitive-related deficits.

Sensory Deficits

Sensory deficits in the older patient need to be recognized and accommodated when conducting an assessment. As Botwinick (1978) points out, there are a variety of sensory changes which accompany aging, including progressive declines in visual acuity, hearing, taste and smell, and tactile sensation. The interviewer needs to recognize these potential deficits and help the older patient compensate. Such factors as adequate lighting, reduction of glare and extraneous noise, use of large print reading materials and adequate speech volume, as well as temperature comfort should all be routinely checked before starting an interview.

USE OF THE CLINICAL INTERVIEW TO ASSESS EMOTIONAL FACTORS

The individual clinical interview can provide a rich source of data for assessing the influence of emotional factors on an elder's potential to participate successfully in rehabilitation. A clinical interview provides an opportunity to build rapport with the patient and to observe behaviors in a more natural setting. Compared with psychometric evaluation (to be discussed later), clinical interviews pose less threat to the elder and engender less resistance. The clinical interview also allows for greater flexibility than formal testing procedures. The evaluator can choose to explore different areas of emotional functioning in detail as they arise.

There are several areas that warrant investigation when assessing emotional factors which could influence the older adult's rehabilitation potential. Exploring the meaning that the disability holds for the elder is of critical importance during the evaluation. It is likely that a physical disability will have highly individualized implications for the elder, representing the person's unique developmental and cultural history. Asking questions about prior experience with disability (either personal or with family and friends) may elicit these meanings. Sudden disability may confront an elder with personal mortality and be the precipitant to a self-image of being old. It may signify ultimate physical decline, dependency, and loss of cherished roles. While most older adults will view disability negatively, it should not be forgotten that some may have witnessed or directly experienced positive coping with physical limitations in the past and may be encouraged that they will be able to compensate for the limits of their present condition.

Coping style and its effectiveness should also be explored. Discussing prior losses and how they were handled will give the clinician some clues as to the likely ways an elder will cope with the new disability. Frequently, older patients have lost a significant person in their lives (be it a spouse, child, parent, or close friend). A history of withdrawal and depression with poorly resolved grief, or a view of oneself as a victim of circumstance beyond any personal control may not bode well for adjustment to disability and efforts at rehabilitation. In contrast, elders who have been able to reach out to others for support in times of trouble, have resumed activities in a reasonable amount of time after a loss, and have developed a sense of reshaping their lives in the face of unwanted change will likely exhibit more adaptive coping.

A well-conducted clinical interview will also provide the examiner with a sense of the older person's personality and typical defense mechanisms, as well as current mood and affective expression. Such information will be derived from both the content and process of the interview. The patient's developmental history, with a focus on past and present adaptational levels, will allow for hypotheses about personality. Asking directly about mood and observing its congruence with the patient's current emotional expression can be informative. Checking one's own reaction to patients will invariably yield valuable information about their impact on others. While there are few well-researched guidelines regarding personality and rehabilitation potential, clinical experience suggests that people who have a passive/dependent, hysterical, suspicious, or antisocial nature will conflict with staff and perform poorly in rehabilitation settings. On the other hand, older patients who possess qualities of assertiveness, curiosity, and initiative, have demonstrated a capacity for intimacy, and are able to set and work toward goals find greater affinity with the philosophy of rehabilitation (Kemp 1990).

Information from the interview can guide clinicians in the choice of more formal psychometric instruments to complete their understanding of the older patient's emotional status and rehabilitation potential. Whether the instruments are to be administered in an interview format or completed independently (i.e., via paper and pencil), the open-ended clinical interview can facilitate rapport and accurate responses to these more directed measures.

USE OF PSYCHOLOGICAL TESTS WITH ELDERS: PSYCHOMETRIC CONSIDERATIONS

As Kane and Kane (1981) have noted, many psychological tests and rating scales designed for use with older adults often fail to meet established standards of test construction and validation. These standards include the establishment of age-appropriate norms, acceptable levels of reliability, and construct validity. The lack of normative data for older adults is the most frequently encountered and most serious drawback of tests used with elders. Schaie and Schaie (1977) comment that unsophisticated clinicians often assume that normative data for younger adults can be extended upward to older populations without compromising the validity of the test. However, when norms developed for younger samples are applied to elders, the potential for misdiagnosis increases. Consequently, a well-functioning older individual may be incorrectly identified as having significant psychopathology or cognitive dysfunction when inappropriate norms are applied.

The reliability of a test refers to the consistency of the measure over time. Test reliability is an important factor to consider when using tests with older adults since their performance can easily vary from one assessment period to the next. The older adult's performance can be influenced by changes in motivation, fatigue, memory, inattention, and physical health. Therefore, establishing a test's baseline reliability is important when applying it to the older adult.

Construct validity is the degree to which a hypothetical construct or trait is being measured by a test instrument. It is particularly important to consider construct validity in tests used with older adults because the trait to be measured can manifest itself differently than with a younger population. For example, the presentation of depression in older patients can be much different than in younger patients (Gaylord and Zung 1987). The older depressed patient might appear more apathetic, report more somatic complaints, and minimize subjective distress. As a result, tests designed to measure depression in elders need to sample these symptom areas if the test is to have good construct validity. All too frequently, tests are applied with the assumption that the trait to be measured manifests itself in the same fashion in younger and older populations alike.

SELECTED INSTRUMENTS FOR ASSESSING EMOTIONAL STATUS

There are few instruments which have been specifically designed to assess the emotional status of the older patient. The majority of scales that have been developed are used to assess depression, and they will be discussed in detail in Chapter 9. However, the following is a suggested list of measures that may prove useful when assessing the emotional aspects of rehabilitation potential in older adults. These scales were selected on the basis of their frequent use with older patients, their relevance to rehabilitation potential, and because of their established reliability and validity.

State-Trait Anxiety Inventory

The State-Trait Anxiety Inventory (STAI) (Spielberger et al. 1970) is a self-report measure of anxiety derived from Spielberger's 1966 conceptual distinction between anxiety as a state and anxiety as a trait. State anxiety is defined as a transitory anxiety condition which varies in intensity and fluctuates over time. Trait anxiety is conceptualized as a more stable and enduring disposition towards anxiety proneness. State anxiety can increase rapidly in reaction to a specific threatening situation, particularly those situations involving a threat to one's self-esteem, such as evaluative situations. Trait anxiety, on the other hand, remains relatively consistent across situations. Spielberger notes, however, that individuals high in trait anxiety experience increases in state anxiety more frequently than low trait anxiety individuals and respond to a greater variety of situations as threatening.

The STAI measures state and trait anxiety on separate scales. When completing the state anxiety scale, subjects are asked to indicate how they feel at the moment. This contrasts with the trait anxiety scale in which subjects are asked to indicate how they generally feel. Individuals completing the STAI must be able to understand this distinction and respond to the inventory items accordingly. Each scale consists of 20 items relating to the subjective experience of anxiety. Subjects are required to rate themselves on a four point continuum for each statement, with higher scores indicating greater subjective anxiety. Spielberger and associates (1970) state that a fifth or sixth grade education is required to complete the inventory without assistance. Although the STAI was originally normed on college and high school students and medical and psychiatric patients, McDonald and Spielberger (1983) report a series of studies on the use of the STAI with older adults. Modifications of the STAI were made to adjust for impairments of vision and memory. For example, large print was used, and response alternatives were printed beside each item. The results of these studies indicated that the STAI was valid for collecting information on the anxiety levels of older individuals. Findings revealed that state anxiety levels did not vary as a function of age, although older female subjects reported a higher level of state anxiety than males. Subjects living at home who indicated a large number of physical complaints were higher in state anxiety as compared with those who reported fewer complaints. The STAI has also been used to assess the effectiveness of relaxation training with geriatric patients (DeBerry 1982).

Self-Rating Anxiety Scale and Anxiety Status Inventory

The Zung Self-Rating Scale (SAS) (Zung 1971) has now been used with older adults to make information on reliability, validity, and age-adjusted norms available (Zung 1983). The SAS was designed to assess anxiety as a clinical disorder rather than as a trait or affective state. The scale is composed of 20 items related to anxiety symptoms, and subjects rate themselves on a four-point scale as to the frequency of the symptom. The first five items of the SAS refer to affective components of anxiety (nervousness, panic), while the final fifteen items refer to physical manifestations of anxiety (trembling, dizziness, fainting). Therefore, with the SAS, anxiety can be rated on both psychic and somatic dimensions.

The Anxiety Status Inventory (ASI) (Zung 1971) is an observer rating scale, and is designed as an analogue scale to the SAS. The ASI has the advantage of providing a mechanism for rating patients in those situations when they cannot complete an inventory. The ASI requires the clinician to rate the patient on a four-point scale using the same fifteen items of the somatic dimension from the SAS.

The SAS and ASI may have limits on their applicability in a rehabilitation setting because of the large proportion of somatic items on these scales. The changes in physical functioning which accompany chronic illness and disability may result in an overestimation of the prevalence of anxiety in the older rehabilitation population on such scales.

Sandoz Clinical Assessment—Geriatrics

The Sandoz Clinical Assessment-Geriatrics (SCAG) (Shader et al. 1974) is an observer rating scale in which subjects are rated on eighteen items using a seven-point scale ranging from "not present" to "severe." Several domains are rated including emotional, behavioral, cognitive, and interpersonal functioning. The SCAG was originally developed for use in psychopharmacological research with older adults. The scale also provides the rater with an opportunity to rate overall functioning.

Shader and associates (1974) report satisfactory inter-rater reliability (average reliability coefficient across dimensions was .75) and adequate concurrent validity using the SCAG with other mental status measures. Kane and Kane (1981), however, point out that the SCAG is subject to the same criticisms as many of the other geriatric rating scales in that the SCAG items and their rating scale are not behaviorally anchored, limiting the reliability of the results. Consequently, comparisons between individuals are difficult.

The SCAG does have some potential advantages in its use with older rehabilitation patients. The scale was designed to assess psychological functioning in elders. It is easy to administer and does not require the patient to read or to fill out a questionnaire. The SCAG also assesses areas which may be predictive of rehabilitation outcome, such as motivation, initiation, hostility, and uncooperativeness.

Symptom Checklist 90—Revised

The Symptom Checklist 90—Revised (SCL-90-R) (Derogatis 1975) is a self-report inventory that is designed to measure psychological distress. For each item, subjects indicate the degree of distress that they are experiencing on a five-point scale, ranging from *0* (not at all) to *4* (extreme). Nine primary dimensions of distress are assessed: somatization, obsessive-compulsive patterns, depression, anxiety, hostility, phobic anxiety, paranoid ideation, interpersonal sensitivity, and psychoticism. Three global indices are also derived which are distinct from the nine affective subscales. The General Severity Index combines information on the number of symptoms and intensity of distress, while the Positive Symptom Total reflects only the number of symptoms. The Positive Symptom Distress Index is a pure measure of distress intensity, adjusted for the number of symptoms reported. The SCL-90-R was normed on psychiatric outpatients, psychiatric inpatients, and nonpatient normals.

The SCL-90-R has been used increasingly in the medical and rehabilitation literature. The scale has been utilized to measure psychological distress in patients with cancer (Rogentine et al. 1979), chronic pain (Viernstein 1982), and sleep disorders (Kales et al. 1980). The SCL-90-R was recently used with a sample of patients with severe chronic obstructive pulmonary disease (mean age 62 years) to study the relationship between activity level and emotional factors (Beck et al. 1988). The SCL-90-R has several features which support its use with older adults in rehabilitation settings. The scale covers a variety of emotional states that may impact on rehabilitation outcome. Subscales of the SCL-90-R can be administered separately to assess particular emotional states. The SCL-90-R is gaining wider use in medical settings, and additional data on various diagnostic groups and age categories should be forthcoming. Disadvantages of the SCL-90-R include the length of the instrument, the absence of normative data for elders, and items dealing with somatic problems which may be normal in older adults.

SALIENT EMOTIONAL FACTORS IN REHABILITATION

Psychologists and other mental health professionals are frequently called upon to comment on the rehabilitation potential of patients, including older adults, based upon the assessment of emotional factors which may influence the rehabilitation process. As previous sections of this chapter have indicated, there are few empirical studies to guide the clinician in determining what emotional factors might be most predictive of successful rehabilitation outcomes. The lack of formal research on predictors of rehabilitation outcome is particularly apparent in the case of the older adult. Despite this state of affairs, several emotional factors will be suggested as areas that could be of particular relevance in estimating rehabilitation potential in older patients (see Exhibit 6-1).

Exhibit 6-1 Emotional Factors To Consider in Evaluation of Rehabilitation Potential

- Anxiety
- Depression
- Psychic Energy
- Perceived Self-Efficacy
- Disengagement

Anxiety

Anxiety is an important variable to assess when estimating potential for rehabilitation with older adults. The application of the Yerkes-Dodson law to rehabilitation settings predicts that there is an optimal range of anxiety for the acquisition of new skills in therapy situations. Too low an anxiety level (for example, patients in a denial phase of adjustment) would not mobilize the patient to learn new activities. An anxiety level which is too high would have an interfering effect on skill acquisition. There is research (Backman and Molander 1986) to suggest that older adults are particularly vulnerable to the deleterious effects of anxiety, especially when they are compared with younger people.

Depression

Depression is another significant factor to consider when estimating rehabilitation potential. Epidemiological studies of the prevalence of depression in older community residents (Gurland et al. 1980) places the incidence at 13 to 15 percent. Among disabled older adults, the prevalence rises to 20 to 30 percent (Blazer and Williams 1980). Therefore, older rehabilitation patients may be particularly susceptible to developing a depressive reaction during their rehabilitation.

Depression can affect several areas of functioning that are critical to the rehabilitation process. Depressed patients have less energy to invest in therapies and may show little interest in resuming previously enjoyable activities. Depressed patients can withdraw from treatment staff and resist efforts to engage them in group activities. The depressed person's interpersonal manner, with increased irritability and complaints, as well as a sense of hopelessness, can alienate treatment staff. The cognitive aspects of depression, including impaired memory and concentration, also interfere with learning in therapy situations.

Psychic Energy

Psychic energy is a concept related to depression and particularly relevant to the arduous task of rehabilitation. The rehabilitation patient must be able to mobilize a certain level of energy to invest in therapy activities and use for the formation of therapeutic relationships. It will be quite difficult for successful rehabilitation to occur if the patient does not have the emotional energy to meet the physical and psychological demands of intensive rehabilitation. Older adults may have even less psychic energy to extend outside themselves, given their tendency toward interiority. The likelihood of multiple medical problems which can deplete their physical energy levels will impact upon how psychic energy is used as well.

Perceived Self-Efficacy

The concept of perceived self-efficacy as outlined by Bandura (1977) deserves consideration as an important variable in assessing rehabilitation potential. Bandura defines perceived self-efficacy as a person's judgment of capability to carry out a course of action that is required to attain a particular goal or achieve a level of performance. Self-efficacy theory focuses beyond the skills required for a task to the judgment of whether the task can be successfully executed. Bandura notes that people often have the required skills but do not apply them.

Bandura and his colleagues have discovered that perceived self-efficacy influences an individual's performance in a variety of ways. Bandura and Cervone (1983, 1986) found that judgment of self-efficacy was an important factor in determining how much effort people would expend on a task and how long they would persist when confronted with obstacles. They discovered that with stronger self-efficacy, subjects' efforts were more persistent and vigorous. Further, judgment of self-efficacy can also influence emotional reactions and thought processes. Persons who judge themselves as unable to cope with environmental demands tend to dwell on their deficiencies and overestimate potential difficulties (Meichenbaum 1977; Beck 1976).

Bandura (1986) hypothesizes that decreased self-efficacy in older adults stems from reappraisals (and misappraisals) of their capabilities given age-related declines in physical and/or cognitive status. He believes that a declining sense of self-efficacy in older adults can start a self-perpetuating process of diminishing belief in their cognitive and behavioral functioning. Bandura has applied self-efficacy principles to the treatment of a variety of medical problems, including the treatment of arthritis in older patients (McLeod 1986).

The notion of self-efficacy seems to be especially useful when assessing the potential for rehabilitation in older adults. Older rehabilitation patients are confronted with a variety of therapy tasks, many of which may seem insurmountable. Patients make an estimation of their ability to accomplish these tasks. High perceived self-efficacy would lead to greater persistence in the face of failure and the ability to build upon successive achievements. Low perceived self-efficacy leads to avoidance of tasks that are judged too difficult.

Disengagement

An assessment of the older rehabilitation patient's degree of disengagement can be important when assessing potential for rehabilitation. The concept of disengagement in the later years of life was first introduced by Cumming and Henry (1961). Based upon interviews with older adults, Cumming and Henry proposed that elders become more withdrawn, display decreased involvement with activities and relationships, and become more preoccupied with their own norms and philosophy of life. Since its inception, disengagement theory has undergone criticism and revision (see Botwinick 1978). For example, Carp (1966) found that disengagement can be a selective process in which withdrawal takes place in some areas, such as leisure, but not in other areas, such as family involvement, where engagement might actually increase.

An evaluation of the degree of disengagement in the older rehabilitation patient might be predictive of potential for rehabilitation, and suggest areas for intervention. Older patients who are highly disengaged and internalized may be difficult for staff to involve in therapy. Highly disengaged patients might not find the opportunity for increased socialization through rehabilitation to be a desirable goal. By discovering those areas in which the patient remains engaged, the clinician can advise the treatment team on what types of functioning remain most relevant for the patient. This determination can maximize the congruence in goal setting between the patient and treatment staff, and reduce frustration on both sides.

AREAS FOR FUTURE RESEARCH

There is an obvious need for empirical research to identify which emotional variables are predictive of successful rehabilitation outcomes with older adults. The preceding section of this chapter recommends variables that can be included in research studies in this area. Variables such as anxiety, depression, and perceived self-efficacy are logical choices for exploratory studies. Progress in identifying emotional factors related to positive rehabilitation outcomes with the older patient will depend upon the development of valid and reliable measures for assessing these variables. Very few instruments have been exclusively designed for use with the older adult and normed on older samples. Even further, few have been widely used with the older adult in a rehabilitation setting.

Research on the emotional factors influencing rehabilitation with older adults also suffers from a lack of clarity in the literature on what constitute normal emotional and personality changes with age (Neugarten 1977). Existing research on changes in personality and emotional status during aging is often contradictory and dependent upon the methodology employed. Therefore, with no clear data, it is difficult to separate out those emotional changes due to normal aging from the emotional reactions to disability in older adults. In addition, there is very little research on the emotional consequences of acquiring a severe physical disability in late life.

The identification of the emotional variables that influence rehabilitation outcomes with the older adult has practical implications for treatment. Once these factors are identified, criteria can be established for screening older patients for their preparedness to participate in a physical rehabilitation program. An understanding of the role of emotional factors in rehabilitation with the older adult would also help clinicians identify those patients who are at risk for performing poorly in a rehabilitation setting. When high risk patients are identified, appropriate interventions can be instituted to increase their readiness for the ambitious task of physical rehabilitation.

REFERENCES

American Psychiatric Association. 1987. *Diagnostic and Statistical Manual of Mental Disorders,* 3d ed. Washington, D.C.: American Psychiatric Association.

Anderson, T.P., N. Boureston, F.R. Greenberg, et al. 1974. Predictive factors in stroke rehabilitation. *Archives of Physical Medicine and Rehabilitation* 55: 545–53.

Backman, L., and B. Molander. 1986. Adult age differences in the ability to cope with situations of high arousal in a precision sport. *Psychology and Aging* 1: 133–9.

Bandura, A. 1977. Self-efficacy: Toward a unifying theory of behavioral change. *Psychology Review* 84: 191–215.

Bandura, A. 1986. *Social Foundations of Thought and Action: A Social Cognitive Theory.* Englewood Cliffs, N.J.: Prentice Hall.

Bandura, A., and D. Cervone. 1983. Self-evaluative and self-efficacy mechanisms governing the motivational effects of goal systems. *Journal of Personality and Social Psychology* 45: 1017–28.

Bandura, A., and D. Cervone. 1986. Differential engagement of self-reactive influences in cognitive motivation. *Organizational Behavior and Human Decision Processes* 38: 92–113.

Beck, A.T. 1976. *Cognitive Therapy and Emotional Disorders.* New York: International Universities Press.

Beck, J.G., S.K. Scott, R.B. Teague, et al. 1988. Correlates of daily impairment in COPD. *Rehabilitation Psychology* 33: 77–84.

Blazer, D., and C.D. Williams. 1980. Epidemiology of dysphoria and depression in an elderly population. *American Journal of Psychiatry* 37: 439–44.

Botwinick, J. 1978. *Aging and Behavior.* New York: Van Nostrand Reinhold Co.

Buss, A. 1973. *Psychology: Man in Perspective.* New York: John Wiley and Sons.

Carp, F.M. 1966. *A Future for the Aged.* Austin, Tex.: University of Texas Press.

Cumming, E., and W. Henry. 1961. *Growing Old: The Process of Disengagement.* New York: Basic Books.

DeBerry, S. 1982. The effects of meditation-relaxation on anxiety and depression in a geriatric population. *Psychotherapy: Theory, Research, and Practice* 19: 512–21.

Derogatis, L.R. 1975. *The SCL-90-R.* Baltimore: Clinical Psychometric Research.

Feigenson, J.S., F.H. McDowell, P. Meese, et al. 1977. Factors influencing outcome and length of stay in a stroke rehabilitation unit: Part 1. Analysis of 248 unscreened patients—medical and functional prognostic indicators. *Stroke* 8: 651–6.

Gaylord, S.A., and W.W.K. Zung. 1987. Affective disorders among the aging. In *Handbook of Clinical Gerontology,* edited by L.L. Carstensen and B.A. Edelson, 76–95. New York: Pergamon Press.

Gurland, B., L. Dean, P. Cross, et al. 1980. The epidemiology of depression and dementia in the elderly: The use of multiple indicators of these conditions. In *Psychopathology in the Aged,* edited by J.D. Cole and J.E. Barrett, 37–62. New York: Raven.

Hyman, M.D. 1971. Social psychological determinants of patients' performance in stroke rehabilitation. *Archives of Physical Medicine and Rehabilitation* 3: 217–26.

Kales, A., C.R. Soldatos, A.B. Caldwell, et al. 1980. Somnambulism: Clinical characteristics and personality patterns. *Archives of General Psychiatry* 37: 1406–10.

Kane, R.A., and R.L. Kane. 1981. *Assessing the Elderly: A Practical Guide to Measurement.* Lexington, Mass.: Lexington Books.

Kemp, B. 1990. The psychosocial context of geriatric rehabilitation. In *Geriatric Rehabilitation,* edited by B. Kemp, K. Brummel-Smith, and J.W. Ramsdell, 41–57. Boston: College Hill Press.

Larson, R. 1978. Thirty years of research on the subjective well-being of older Americans. *Journal of Gerontology* 33: 109–25.

McDonald, R.J., and C. Spielberger. 1983. Measuring anxiety in hospitalized geriatric patients. In *Series in Clinical and Community Psychology: Stress and Anxiety,* edited by A.G. Shering, 135–43. Washington, D.C.: Hemisphere Publishing.

McLeod, B. 1986. Rx for health: A dose of self-confidence. *Psychology Today* 18: 46–50.

Meichenbaum, D.H. 1977. *Cognitive-behavior Modification: An Integrative Approach.* New York: Plenum.

Neugarten, B.L. 1977. Personality and aging. In *Handbook of the Psychology of Aging,* edited by J.E. Birren and K.W. Schaie, 626–49. New York: Van Nostrand Reinhold Co.

Nickens, H.W. 1983. A review of the factors affecting the occurrence and outcome of hip fracture, with special reference to psychosocial issues. *Journal of the American Geriatrics Society* 31: 166–70.

Reich, J.W., A.J. Zautra, and C.A. Guarnaccia. 1989. Effects of disability and bereavement on the mental health and recovery of older adults. *Psychology and Aging* 4: 57–65.

Rogentine, D.S., D.P. Van Kammen, B.H. Fox, et al. 1979. Psychological factors in the prognosis of malignant melanoma: A prospective study. *Psychosomatic Medicine* 41: 647–55.

Schaie, K.W., and J.P. Schaie. 1977. Clinical assessment and aging. In *Handbook of the Psychology of Aging,* edited by J.E. Birren and K.W. Schaie, 692–723. New York: Van Nostrand Reinhold Co.

Schultz, R. 1985. Emotion and affect. In *Handbook of the Psychology of Aging,* 2d ed., edited by J.E. Birren and K.W. Schaie, 531–43. New York: Van Nostrand Reinhold Co.

Shader, R.I., J.S. Harmatz, and C.A. Salzman. 1974. A new scale for clinical assessment in geriatric populations: Sandoz Clinical Assessment-Geriatric (SCAG). *Journal of the American Geriatrics Society* 22: 107–13.

Spence, K.W. 1958. A theory of emotionally based drive (D) and its relation to performance in simple learning situations. *American Psychologist* 13: 131–41.

Spielberger, C.D. 1966. Theory and research on anxiety. In *Anxiety and Behavior,* edited by C.D. Spielberger, 3–20. New York: Academic Press.

Spielberger, C.D. 1972. Anxiety as an emotional state. In *Anxiety: Current Trends in Theory and Research,* vol. 1, edited by C.D. Spielberger, 23–49. New York: Academic Press.

Spielberger, C.D., R.L. Gorsuch, and R.E. Lushene. 1970. *State-trait Anxiety Inventory.* Palo Alto, Calif.: Consulting Psychologists Press.

Viernstein, M.D. 1982. Psychological testing for chronic pain patients. In *Diagnosis and Treatment of Chronic Pain,* edited by N.H. Hendler, D.M. Long, and T.N. Wise, 43–52. Boston: John Wright PSG.

Zung, W.W.K. 1971. A rating instrument for anxiety disorders. *Psychosomatics* 12: 371–9.

Zung, W.W.K. 1983. Self-rating scales for psychopathology. In *Assessment in Geriatric Pharmacology,* edited by T. Crook, S. Ferris, and R. Bartus, 145–52. New Canaan, Conn.: Mark Powley Associates.

Chapter 7

The Neuropsychological Assessment of Dementia in a Rehabilitation Setting

Dorene M. Rentz

The population of patients admitted to inpatient rehabilitation is growing older. This is the result of advances in medical technology and increased survivorship among people over the age of 65 (Findley and Findley 1987). These statistics have important implications for rehabilitation because many older patients have cognitive impairments in addition to their physical disabilities (Garcia et al. 1984; Luxenberg and Feigenbaum 1986). In fact, a recent epidemiological report suggests that cognitive disorders among elders living in the community are greater than previously estimated and increase substantially with age (Evans et al. 1989; U.S. Congress 1987).

As cognitively impaired elders enter rehabilitation programs, the treatment team will be required to understand the behavioral and functional deficits associated with various cognitive disorders and dementia syndromes. Such knowledge will help facilitate treatment interventions, maximize rehabilitation potential, and provide appropriate education to the family.

The purpose of this chapter is to define the neuropsychological and behavioral sequela of those cognitive disorders most likely to be seen in an inpatient rehabilitation setting. Psychometric instruments for determining the severity, progressivity, and functional status of these patients will be discussed. Chapter 8 will focus on behavioral management.

DIFFERENTIAL DIAGNOSIS OF COGNITIVE DECLINE

Cognitive change among older adults does not always imply a chronic dementia, despite the prevalence of dementing illnesses among individuals as they age. Cognitive changes may be due to normal aging, individual variations, premorbid abilities, and acute illness. This section will discuss the most frequently seen syndromes which can alter mental function and present the neuropsychological and behavioral criteria for making a differential diagnosis.

135

The reader is referred to Cummings and Benson's (1983) excellent work for a more comprehensive discussion of the pathophysiology and laboratory investigations of these and all other cognitively disordered syndromes. Chapter 3 discusses normal cognitive changes in older adults.

Definitions and Classifications

Dementia is a term that will be used in this chapter to refer to the persistent cognitive changes, observed in elders, that have resulted from an acquired illness. These changes represent a decline in both mental and social functioning from a previous level of performance. The key terms in this definition are *acquired* and *persistent*. *Acquired* symptomatology implies that the abilities were already within the behavioral domain of the individual and are now dysfunctional. This distinguishes dementia from mental retardation or learning disabilities where the cognitive functions were never developed. The *persistence* of the symptoms differentiates dementia from *delirium*, which produces a fluctuating attentional state causing temporary confusion and loss of mental function. *Delirium* is characterized by an abrupt onset, short duration, impaired memory, incoherence of thought and conversation, hallucinations, and evidence of systemic illness (Cummings and Benson 1983; American Psychiatric Association 1987). Dementia, on the other hand, involves a variety of neuropsychological and behavioral symptoms including a persistent loss of recent and long-term memory; inability to think abstractly; impaired judgment; impairment of higher cortical functions such as language, praxis, and gnosis; inability to perform self-care tasks; emotional instability; disorientation; and personality change (American Psychiatric Association 1987; Cummings and Benson 1983). The definition of dementia excludes those patients with isolated neuropsychological disturbances such as aphasia or amnesia that occur with focal brain lesions. The term organic brain syndrome, which has often been used interchangeably with the term dementia, is now considered obsolete (Cummings and Benson 1983).

A diagnosis of dementia does not imply any specific cause. In fact, more than 60 different conditions can produce a dementia (Katzman 1986). The most commonly seen dementias among geriatric patients admitted to a rehabilitation setting are degenerative, vascular, toxic, and reversible. Exhibit 7-1 lists the major categories under which the dementias are classified. Multiple sclerosis and normal pressure hydrocephalus are also sometimes seen in rehabilitation settings. (For more information on these disorders see Shukla and associates (1980) and van den Burg and associates (1987).)

Cummings and Benson (1983) propose subdividing the dementias into three major categories: cortical, subcortical, and mixed. Despite the widespread use of this classification system, the term *subcortical dementia* has come under extensive criticism in the literature since its introduction by Albert and associates (1974). Some investigators claim that subcortical dementia can be separately

Exhibit 7-1 Major Classifications of the Dementias

Degenerative Dementias
- Alzheimer disease*
- Parkinson's disease (some cases)*

Vascular Dementias
- Multi-infarct dementia*
- Subcortical dementias (i.e., Binswanger, Lacunar, Angular Gyrus syndrome)*

Anoxic Dementia (i.e., cardiac arrest, etc.)

Traumatic Dementias (i.e., head injury, etc.)

Infectious Dementias (i.e., AIDS, herpes encephalitis, etc.)

Normal Pressure Hydrocephalus

Multiple Sclerosis (some cases)

Toxic Dementias
- Alcohol-related dementia*

Auto-Immune Disorders (i.e., lupus erythematosus, AIDS, etc.)

Reversible Dementias*

*refers to those dementias discussed in the chapter

---

identified as a clinical syndrome by its characteristic features of forgetfulness, slowed thought processes, alterations in mood and personality (particularly apathy and depression), plus a reduced ability to manipulate acquired knowledge (Cummings and Benson 1983, 1984; Huber et al. 1986a). Others report that the distinction is inaccurate because neuropathological evidence does not support it (Mayeux et al. 1983; Whitehouse 1986). This chapter will use the term subcortical dementia to describe the classic clinical syndrome mentioned above, in order to distinguish it from the cortical dementias which include aphasias, agnosias, and apraxias.

DEMENTIAS COMMON TO REHABILITATION SETTINGS

The most prevalent cause of cognitive decline in older adults is Alzheimer's disease. Therefore, it is reasonable to suspect that elders admitted to rehabilitation may have this illness. Given its prevalence in the population, it will be described in greater detail.

Alzheimer's Disease

Diagnostic Criteria

A biological marker for Alzheimer's disease has not been found. Therefore, Alzheimer's disease is not definitively diagnosed until death. The histopathological features of granulovacuolar degeneration, neurofibrillary tangles, and neuritic (senile) plaques confirm the diagnosis. In 1984, a work group under the auspices of the Department of Health and Human Services Task Force on Alzheimer's Disease (McKhann et al. 1984) published what has been widely adopted as the clinical criteria used for the probable diagnosis of Alzheimer's disease.

Probable Alzheimer's disease can be diagnosed with confidence if there is a typical insidious onset of dementia (as previously defined above) which is progressive, but not caused by any other systemic or central nervous system disease known to produce memory loss and cognitive decline. The diagnosis is exclusionary and based on the results of a medical history; neurologic, psychiatric, and clinical examination; neuropsychological tests; and laboratory studies.

Subtypes

Various subtypes of Alzheimer's disease have been discussed in the literature (Becker et al. 1988; Bondareff et al. 1987; Botwinick et al. 1986; Chui et al. 1985; Martin et al. 1986; Mayeux et al. 1985). Some investigators believe that Alzheimer's disease is not one, but several different biologic disorders with different levels of severity and rates of progression (Becker et al. 1988; Botwinick et al. 1986; Chui et al. 1985). The subtypes currently distinguished involve early versus late onset; presence or absence of family history; rapid or slow progression; and the initial presence of focal deficits which progress into a diffuse Alzheimer-type disorder. The focal deficits may involve the initial presentation of a pronounced amnesic syndrome, language disturbance, or visuospatial abnormality (Becker 1988; Knesevich et al. 1985; Martin et al. 1986).

Clinical Course

Initially, an Alzheimer-type dementia presents with forgetfulness. This phase involves subjective memory complaints such as forgetting where one has placed familiar objects or the names of familiar people. However, there are no demonstrable memory deficits on clinical exam (Reisberg et al. 1982). The illness progresses to a mild dementia where the patient experiences difficulty with recent memory of sufficient severity that it interferes with daily functioning; orientation to person and place but disorientation to day; moderate difficulty with complex problem solving; inability to function independently in community affairs; difficulty with performance of home tasks; and abandonment of hobbies and interests. Social judgment, however, continues to be intact; occasional prompting may be necessary for self-care tasks. A moderate dementia phase follows where the deficits are now recognized in casual encounters and restlessness becomes apparent. There is severe memory loss for both recent and remote information; disorientation to time and place; impairment in problem solving and social judgment; only simple chores are performed within the home; and the patient requires assistance in dressing, hygiene, and personal care. In severe dementia, intellectual functioning is globally deteriorated and patients need continual supervision (Bayles and Kaszniak 1987; Hughes et al. 1982).

Neuropsychological and Behavioral Characteristics

Research investigating the neuropsychological deficits in Alzheimer's disease has been prolific over the last ten years. The areas of function most commonly studied involve memory, intelligence, attention, language, visuospatial skills, and personality/behavioral changes.

It is universally accepted that memory is disturbed early in the course of the disease with difficulty in the acquisition of new information being the first and most salient symptom to emerge. Research investigations have shown that the memory impairment in Alzheimer's disease involves both poor encoding and retrieval processes (Kopelman 1985; Ober et al. 1985) along with poor recognition recall (Moss et al. 1986). Episodic memory (i.e., memory for specific personally experienced events) shows a decline in the early stages of the disease (Martin et al. 1985). Semantic memory (i.e., memory for general principles, associations, and rules) declines in moderate to severe stages (Martin and Fedio 1983; Ober et al. 1985; Weingartner et al. 1981). There have been some recent investigations, however, which suggest that procedural processing (i.e., motor and perceptual skills that are acquired by practice) may be preserved (Eslinger and Damasio 1986; Nissen et al. 1987).

Intellectual decline also appears early in the disease course, involving impairments in manipulating acquired knowledge (Cummings and Benson 1983); abstraction; proverb interpretation (Albert 1988); sequencing; set maintenance; set shifting (Albert and Moss 1984); and calculations (Cummings and Benson 1983). In contrast, attention and concentration skills are intact even for mild to moderately impaired patients (Vitaliano et al. 1986).

The language disturbance in Alzheimer's disease has many of the manifestations of an aphasic disorder, despite the absence of focal lesions. The spontaneous verbal output is agrammatical and has an empty, vague quality, lacking specific content words and using words of indefinite reference (e.g., "It's the thing we have so you can do it for me somewhat"). Patients typically make anomic/semantic errors but literal paraphasias are rarely seen until late in the disease course (Bayles and Kaszniak 1987). Comprehension and verbal fluency become progressively impaired. However, spelling, writing, reading aloud, and repetition are all maintained (Bayles and Kaszniak 1987; Cummings and Benson 1986).

Visuoperceptive, visuospatial, and visuomotor deficits may become apparent early in the disease course (Albert 1988; Albert and Moss 1984). The geographical disorientation, apraxia, and poor spatial reasoning which result, tend to impair the patient's ability to navigate in the environment. Poor visual discrimination contributes to perceptual errors, which exacerbate confrontation naming problems (Bayles and Kaszniak 1987). Unilateral neglect, however, is not noted.

Personality changes often occur simultaneously with the cognitive changes and are sometimes the first manifested signs of Alzheimer's disease. These changes continue to occur across the disease span (Rubin et al. 1987). Patients become progressively indifferent, apathetic, irritable, and sad (Petry et al. 1988). Depression is a frequent symptom in early stages of the disease and is often a reaction to the awareness of cognitive decline (Lazarus et al. 1987; Reding et al. 1985; Shuttleworth et al. 1987). In middle and late phases the predominant personality features are indifference and apathy.

Petry and associates (1988) asked spouses of Alzheimer patients to note changes in personality before and after disease onset. In general, they found patients to be more immature, passive, withdrawn, unreasonable, and self-absorbed. Behavioral changes could not be attributed entirely to the intellectual decline and were not primarily a release of premorbid personality traits. The evidence suggested that the behavioral changes represented a uniform behavioral profile produced by the illness.

Different rates of progression have also been found in Alzheimer's disease (Becker et al. 1988; Botwinick et al. 1986; Chui et al. 1985; Rentz et al. 1986). Some suggest that early onset, language abnormalities, or the presence of a family history may be predictive of the rapidly progressive variety (Becker et al. 1988; Folstein and Breitner 1981; Heston et al. 1981; Seltzer and Sherwin 1983); others find no clear identifiable variables which differentiate rapid from slow progressors (Botwinick et al. 1986; Chui et al. 1985; Rentz et al. 1986).

Multi-Infarct Dementia

Multi-infarct dementia (MID) is the term used to denote the cognitive disorder resulting from the additive effects of large and small infarcts in both grey and white matter producing a loss of brain tissue (Hachinski et al. 1974). The neuropsychological and behavioral deficits in MID have been shown to resemble those of Alzheimer's disease and can be mistaken for it (Brinkman et al. 1986; Perez et al. 1975), but there are a few distinguishing characteristics. The onset of cognitive dysfunction is usually sudden rather than insidious, and the progression is described as *step-wise*. This produces spotty or patchy deficits which give the appearance of some preserved areas of ability in the presence of obvious impairments. Sometimes a lateralizing pattern is observed but, in general, no particular pattern of deficits emerges. Sudden changes in symptoms, or fluctuations in the disease course, are thought to reflect new infarctions.

The *Ischemic Score* by Hachinski and his co-workers (1975) was developed to quantify the clinical features of MID in an effort to differentiate this disorder from Alzheimer's disease. As shown in Exhibit 7-2, they found that patients with Ischemic scores of four or less were more likely to have Alzheimer's disease while those with seven or more points were patients diagnosed as having multi-infarct dementia. Five clinical features were of particular value in predicting the presence of cerebral infarction. They included abrupt onset, step-wise deterioration, history of stroke, and focal neurologic signs and symptoms (Burst 1983). However, it should be noted that the presence of one or more strokes does not exclude the presence of a coexisting Alzheimer's disease. A high Ischemic score may identify patients who have had a stroke, but a high score does not necessarily mean that the stroke either caused or contributed to the dementia.

Neuropsychiatric symptoms of MID and Alzheimer's disease were investigated by Cummings and associates (1987). They found that both Alzheimer and MID patients tend to have paranoid delusions with equal frequency, usually involving elementary misbeliefs concerning theft or infidelity. Hallucinations in

---

Exhibit 7-2 Hachinski Ischemic Score

Feature	Score
Abrupt onset	2
Step-wise deterioration	1
Fluctuating course	2
Nocturnal confusion	1
Relative preservation of personality	1
Depression	1
Somatic complaints	1
Emotional incontinence	1
History of hypertension	1
History of strokes	2
Evidence of associated atherosclerosis	1
Focal neurological symptoms	2
Focal neurological signs	2

Source: Reprinted from *Archives of Neurology*, Vol. 32, pp. 632–637, with permission of the American Medical Association, © 1975.

both illnesses were rare. Depression frequently occurred in both groups but depressive symptomatology was more severe in MID patients, particularly among women.

Subcortical Vascular Dementias

Some investigators believe that changes in the deep white matter of the brain, not multiple infarcts, produce a dementia state (Janota 1985). This white matter degeneration may cause disconnection of a relatively intact cerebral cortex, resulting in a subcortical dementia (Roman 1987). Binswanger's disease is the term historically applied to this form of white matter degeneration, which results from persistent hyper/hypotension and causes small strokes or hypoperfusion of the watershed areas. Binswanger's disease, once thought to be rare, is being observed more frequently since the advent of more sophisticated brain imaging techniques such as computed tomography (CT) and magnetic resonance imaging (MRI). However, some investigators have found that not all patients who present with white matter changes on CT or MRI evidence the type of dementia produced by Binswanger's disease (Rao et al. 1989). They prefer to call these observed radiographic changes *leukoaraiosis* (Hachinski 1987). Others claim that evidence of leukoaraiosis is more closely associated with the symptoms of an Alzheimer-type dementia (Steingart et al. 1987).

A lacunar state is another condition similar to Binswanger's disease (Roman 1987). Lacunae, cavitary infarcts of two to fifteen millimeters in diameter, occur due to hypertension affecting small penetrating arteries in the diencephalon, brainstem, or deep cerebral white matter. A subcortical dementia occurs when lacunae are present in large numbers.

The neuropsychological sequela of Binswanger's disease or a lacunar state is characterized by a slowness of thought and motor processes, reduced spontaneity, inability to manipulate acquired knowledge, inability to generate effective problem-solving strategies, and a paucity/poverty of thought. Impaired spontaneous recall, poor concentration, divided attention, diminished concern, and blunting of affect are also observed (Brown and Marsden 1988; Cummings and Benson 1984; Huber et al. 1986a). Patients, particularly with lacunae, are also known to present with a pseudobulbar palsy, dysarthria, dysphagia, weakness, bradykinesia, small-stepped gait, hyperreflexia, Babinski signs, and incontinence (Burst 1983).

Angular Gyrus syndrome is a symptom complex, sometimes mistaken for Alzheimer's disease. It results from lesions in the posterior portion of the middle cerebral artery territory and includes a fluent aphasia, alexia, agraphia, plus constructional disturbances. Focal motor and/or sensory changes may be absent and the lesions may be too small to be detected by CT. Differentiating signs of Angular Gyrus syndrome include intact memory, preserved visuospatial skills, and an awareness/frustration over language problems. Subtle right-sided neurologic findings, asymmetric electroencephalogram (EEG), and minor asymmetries on CT may provide supportive evidence for an Angular Gyrus syndrome (Cummings and Benson 1983).

Parkinson's Disease

Parkinson's disease is an extrapyramidal disorder that results from an idiopathic degeneration of neurons, producing Lewy bodies in the basal ganglia and substantia nigra. This neuronal degeneration causes a depletion of dopamine essential to the regulation of movement. The term *parkinsonism* is used rather than Parkinson's disease if the patient has sparing of the substantia nigra. Both Parkinson's disease and parkinsonian-type syndromes have the clinical presence of rigidity, tremor, bradykinesia, masked facies, and abnormal gait (Lechtenberg 1982).

There is some disagreement as to the proportion of Parkinson's disease patients who eventually develop cognitive changes. The most recent prevalence estimates suggest 10 to 35 percent (Brown and Marsden 1987; Mayeux et al. 1988). Those patients who do develop cognitive decline tend to be older (over age 70) and have a more rapid progression of illness, greater physical disability, and reduced survival rates (Mayeux et al. 1988).

The pathophysiological and neuropsychological features of the dementia in Parkinson's disease vary and have been found to involve subcortical, frontal, and global impairments. The subcortical features are characterized by forgetfulness, mental slowing, personality changes, and an impaired ability to manipulate acquired knowledge (Cummings and Benson 1983). The fronto-subcortical features include deficits in sequencing, shifting, acquiring, and maintaining conceptual sets; slowed initiation; and distractability (Albert 1978; Cools et al. 1984; Flowers and Robertson 1985; Lees and Smith 1983). Patients with more global impairments have problems with visuospatial discrimination, orientation, memory, and language (Boller et al. 1984; Brown and Marsden 1986; Chui et al. 1986; Huber et al. 1986b).

The unusual presence of cortical deficits in some Parkinson's disease patients has led to the speculation that Parkinson's disease can coexist with an Alzheimer's dementia. Histopathological evidence of Alzheimer's disease has been found in some Parkinson's patients (Alvord et al. 1974; Boller et al. 1979) but not all (Chui et al. 1986; Perry et al. 1985). These conflicting pathophysiological and neuropsychological findings have led to the speculation that Parkinson's disease may be a heterogeneous disorder with no predictable pattern of deficits or clinical course (El-Awar et al. 1987).

Depression is a common psychiatric symptom observed in Parkinson's disease and etiological explanations vary. Some claim it is a realistic reaction to a progressive, crippling illness (Taylor et al. 1986), linked predominantly to the severity of cognitive impairment rather than the severity of motor involvement (Cummings and Benson 1983; Mayeux et al. 1981). Levodopa, the medication used to treat Parkinson's disease, may be the cause of the depression (Mindham et al. 1976) as well as the reduction in brain monoamines associated with a basal ganglia disorder (Cummings and Benson 1983).

Alcohol-Related Dementia

Alcohol is known to produce a variety of behavioral and neuropsychological disorders. Chronic alcoholics initially present with Wernicke's encephalopathy, an acute illness characterized by mental confusion, inattention, drowsiness, ocular paralysis, and ataxia of gait (Lechtenberg 1982). This syndrome is essentially a biochemical disorder due to a thiamine deficiency and is reversible.

Sixty percent of alcoholics who survive Wernicke's disease may develop Korsakoff's psychosis, a syndrome characterized by an amnesia involving the sudden loss of recent memory (Cutting 1978; Korsakoff 1889). Confabulation, the inability to remember past events in their correct chronological sequence, affective blandness, and passivity differentiate these patients from other alcohol abusers (Lezak 1983).

An alcoholic dementia syndrome results from long-term alcohol abuse, along with the associated symptoms of repeated head trauma and seizures. The cardinal features which differentiate the dementia state from Korsakoff's psychosis are diminished intellectual ability and concrete thinking, mental rigidity, and impaired visuomotor performance. Patients with an alcohol dementia may also present with prominent frontal lobe deficits such as difficulty maintaining a cognitive set, impersistence, deficient motor inhibition, and perseveration. They tend to perform poorly on speed-dependent visual scanning tasks and have impaired motor control and motor integration. Short-term memory deficits are prominent, but remote memory is better preserved. Alcoholic dementia is considered to be the result of alcohol-induced cerebral atrophy (Lezak 1983).

Pseudodementia or the Cognitive Decline of Depression

Pseudodementia is a term used to describe the syndrome in which dementia is mimicked or caricatured by functional psychiatric illness, particularly depression (Wells 1979). Contemporary thought has shifted away from the use of this term as it risks implying that the symptomatic older adult must be either depressed or demented, but could not be both (Haggerty et al. 1988). Recent studies suggest that depression and dementia frequently coexist (Kral 1983; Lazarus et al. 1987; McAllister and Price 1982; Morstyn et al. 1982; Shuttleworth et al. 1987). In such cases, when the depression is recognized and treated the demented patient can show functional improvement, even though still cognitively compromised. Patients with a predominant depression, who are treated with appropriate tricyclic antidepressants or electroconvulsive therapy, will show improvement in both function and cognition (Gershon and Herman 1982).

In contrast to patients with dementia, depressed patients have a sudden onset and rapid progression of symptoms with the characteristic vegetative changes in sleep, appetite, and energy (Gershon and Herman 1982). Cohen and associates (1982) found that depressed patients demonstrated recent memory loss, a slowness of mentation and movement, cognitive confusion, and a tendency to give up as tasks became complex. They found that these impairments, along with lowered intellectual scores, were primarily due to diminished motivation, drive, attention, and energy rather than structural brain damage.

In general, the apraxias, anomias, aphasias, and agraphias typically seen in a dementia patient are not evident (Bayles and Kaszniak 1987). Rather, the neuropsychological features of a pseudodementia include: attention and concentration deficits; memory deficiencies; psychomotor slowing; inefficient mental flexibility; expressive language difficulties (predominantly inarticulation and mumbling); and impaired comprehension when information is presented in a rapid manner. Naming, repetition, word production, spelling, writing, and reading are all within normal limits (Lezak 1983; Weingartner and Silberman 1984). Weingartner and associates (1981) closely examined the memory deficits of depressed patients and found that they tended to use weak or incomplete encoding strategies, which produced poor initial registration of information into memory. Repetition, organization, and structure facilitated learning for the depressed patients but not for those with dementia. On word fluency tests, depressed patients were noted to demonstrate an augmentation of words to category stimuli, while dementia patients failed to benefit from the cognitive structure and produced more words to letter stimuli. On visuospatial tasks, depressed patients tended to do poorly because of the novelty of the tasks and the energy it took to learn them. The errors were generally careless ones, but no visuoconstruction deficits were evident (Cohen et al. 1982). Behaviorally, depressed patients tended to exaggerate their perceived cognitive deficits, while demented patients frequently concealed their disabilities or seemed oblivious to them. Depressed patients also tended to make self-critical, derogatory comments about their performance and frequently reported saddened affect and feelings of anhedonia (Gershon and Herman 1982).

Reversible Dementias

Until recently dementia was regarded as a permanent, irreversible, and progressive disorder that led inevitably to disability and death. It is now known that 10 to 30 percent of patients presenting with dementia states have illnesses which are treatable. Interventions to correct a structural or metabolic condition have been known to restore intellectual function. Exhibit 7-3 lists the treatable causes of dementia. Dementias that cannot be reversed by medical or surgical intervention may still have treatable aspects. Cognitive reserves may be impeded by drugs, minor infections, dehydration, depression, or social and sensory deprivation. Appropriate identification and minimization of these factors may aid substantially in the management of demented individuals (Cummings 1983).

THE NEUROPSYCHOLOGICAL ASSESSMENT OF DEMENTIA

In clinical practice, the neuropsychological evaluation is usually undertaken to aid in the diagnosis, management, treatment, and long-range planning of patients with brain disorders (Lezak 1986). In cases of suspected dementia, neuropsychological testing has played an integral role because the degenerative diseases of old age are not often reliably identified by laboratory tests or neuroradiologic techniques (de Leon et al. 1980; Miller 1983; Weisberg 1979).

Exhibit 7-3 Reversible Dementias

Obstructive hydrocephalus

Psychiatric disorders (depression, anxiety, psychosis)

Drugs (sedatives, hypnotics, anti-anxiety agents, anti-depressants, anti-arrhythmics, anti-hypertensives, anti-convulsants, anti-psychotics, drugs with anticholinergic side effects)

Nutritional disorders (B-6 deficiency, Thiamine deficiency, B-12 deficiency or pernicious anemia, Folate deficiency and Marchiafava-Bignami disease)

Metabolic disorders (hyper/hypothyroidism, hypercalcemia, hyper/hyponatremia, hypoglycemia, kidney failure, liver failure, Cushing syndrome, Addison's disease, hypopituitarism, carcinoma)

Source: Adapted from R. Katzman, et al. 1986. *Accuracy of Diagnosis and Consequences of Misdiagnosis of Disorders Causing Dementia,* contract report prepared for the Office of Technology Assessment, U.S. Congress.

Neuropsychological test profiles have also been useful in differentiating between normal aging and dementia as well as identifying patterns of deficits which distinguish among the dementias (Fuld 1978; Gainotti et al. 1980; Kaszniak 1986; Lezak 1986). This is particularly true in cases of probable Alzheimer's disease, where the diagnosis is exclusionary of any systemic illness and is based on behavioral criteria involving cognitive and personality changes (Poeck 1988; Spinnler and Della-Sala 1988).

Elders who are admitted to rehabilitation settings with newly acquired physical disabilities may have developed or had preexisting cognitive disorders that are currently affecting their rehabilitation performance. In these situations, the neuropsychological evaluation can be used for assisting the treatment staff in designing individualized physical and occupational therapies that would maximize the patient's learning potential. It can also provide the family with information on the progressivity of the disease course, identify ways of responding that would capitalize on the patient's strengths, specify areas where supervision may be needed, and assist in long-range decisions regarding competency for managing one's affairs and living independently.

Approaches to Neuropsychological Assessment

Neuropsychologists take one of several approaches to performing a neuropsychological assessment. These include the formal battery approach which correlates behavior with brain function and distinguishes between functional and organic disorders (Reitan 1986); the information processing approach which analyzes a complex skill into its functional components (McKenna and Warrington 1986); the qualitative approach which is based on history and clinical observation (Goldberg and Costa 1986); and the Boston Process approach which assesses the qualitative nature of a behavior by use of psychometric instruments (Milberg et al. 1986).

For the evaluation of dementia, particularly within a rehabilitation setting, a combination of each of these approaches is relevant. A battery of tests can provide information on a wide range of cognitive abilities that are necessary for rehabilitation. Those standardized tests which supply normative data on healthy elders are particularly useful because they permit a comparison between normal changes associated with aging and the patient's current performance. The Boston Process approach is applicable when the examiner needs to move beyond the rigors of standardization in order to compensate for the motor, sensory, attentional, and latent response deficits associated with aging. The information processing approach, on the other hand, is beneficial to physical, occupational, and speech therapists because it can define those impaired functional components which interfere with the performance of a complex task. With this information, the therapists can more usefully direct their work toward helping the patient compensate for those impaired processes. The qualitative examination is frequently a part of every evaluation because it involves the estimation of the patient's premorbid performance and the assessment of whether the current behavioral changes are a deviation from the patient's usual behavioral repertoire.

The Neuropsychological Test Battery for Assessment of Dementia

Along with the decision as to which neuropsychological approach to utilize, the examiner is faced with the challenge of deciding which neuropsychological tests would be useful and cost-effective for assessing dementia. Screening instruments, despite the advantage of their brevity and ease of administration, are often inadequate alone. Such tests as the Mini-Mental State Examination (Folstein et al. 1975), which now contains age specific norms for older adults (Bleecker et al. 1988); a Modified Mini-Mental State for Alzheimer patients (Teng et al. 1987); and the Short Test of Mental Status, which has a high sensitivity and specificity in patients with dementia (Kokmen et al. 1987), are typically insensitive to very mild dementia states and lack sufficient specificity to differentiate among the various dementing disorders (Anthony et al. 1982; Kaszniak 1986). On the other hand, comprehensive test batteries such as the Halstead Reitan Battery (Reitan 1979) are lengthy and contain subtests which tend to be too difficult for general application except where the dementia is mild (Kaszniak 1986).

Most experienced neuropsychologists recommend an individualized battery approach which samples a range of cognitive functions that target behaviors relevant to the diagnosis of dementia, including: general intelligence, memory, attention, language, perception, praxis, and personality change (Fuld 1978; Gainotti et al. 1980; Lezak 1986). Also included would be measures which stage the severity of the dementia and determine its progressivity. These neuropsychological functions correlate with DSM-III-R criteria and other widely referenced sources (Cummings and Benson 1983; McKhann et al. 1984). For a comprehensive review of all the tests available for the assessment of dementia see Kaszniak's (1986) excellent chapter. The following subsections describe a few of the tests available for assessing the severity, progressivity, and degree of cognitive dysfunction involved in dementia states. Included will be those tests which have current norms and adequate reliability and validity with older adults. Exhibit 7-4 summarizes these tests.

General Intelligence

Decline in intellectual functioning is an essential feature of a dementing illness, and necessitates the inclusion of formal intelligence measures in the as-

Exhibit 7-4 Measures Used in a Dementia Evaluation

Diagnostic Measures
- DAT Diagnostic Inventory (Cummings and Benson 1986)
- Hachinski Ischemic Score (Hachinski et al. 1975)

Screening Tests
- Mini-Mental State Exam (Folstein et al. 1975)
- Modified Mini-Mental State Exam (Teng et al. 1987)
- Short Test of Mental Status (Kokmen et al. 1987)

Intellectual Measures
- Wechsler Adult Intelligence Scale—Revised (Wechsler 1981)
- Short Form of the WAIS-R (Silverstein 1982; Satz and Mogel 1962)
- Ravens Coloured Progressive Matrices (Raven 1984)
- Wechsler Deterioration Index (Wechsler 1958)
- Estimating Premorbid IQ using Demographics (Wilson et al. 1978)
- Estimating Premorbid IQ—National Adult Reading Test (Nelson 1982)
- Estimating Premorbid IQ—Revised National Adult Reading Test (Blair and Spreen 1989)

Memory Measures
- Wechsler Memory Scale (Wechsler 1945)
- Russell Revision of the Wechsler Memory Scale (Russell 1988, 1975)
- Wechsler Memory Scale—Revised (Wechsler 1987)
- California Verbal Learning Test (Delis et al. 1987)

Language Measures
- Multilingual Aphasia Examination (Benton and Hamsher 1983)
- Aphasia Screening Test (Reitan 1981)
- Boston Naming Test (Kaplan et al. 1983)
- Boston Diagnostic Aphasia Battery (Goodglass and Kaplan 1983)

Visuospatial Measures
- Benton Line Orientation Test (Benton et al. 1978)
- Benton Facial Recognition Test (Benton and van Allen 1968)
- Hooper Visual Organization Test (Hooper 1983)

Dementia Severity Rating Measures
- Mattis Dementia Rating Scale (Mattis 1988, 1976)
- Global Deterioration Scale (Reisberg et al. 1982)
- The Alzheimer's Disease Rating Scale (Rosen et al. 1984)
- Clinican Dementia Rating Scale (Hughes et al. 1982)
- Blessed Dementia Scale (Blessed et al. 1968)
- Haycox Behavioral Scale (Haycox 1984)

Progressivity Measure
- Rapidity Index (Rentz et al. 1988, 1986)

sessment battery (Kaszniak 1986). However, estimations of a patient's premorbid intellectual status continue to be a problem for the neuropsychologist.

The Wechsler Adult Intelligence Scale-Revised (WAIS-R) (Wechsler 1981) has been the most commonly studied measure for estimating intellectual status in older patients with and without dementia (Brinkman and Braun 1984; Fuld

1984; Satz et al. 1987). However, normative data extend only to age 74 and the higher age ranges of the WAIS-R sample have been criticized (Albert 1988). The deterioration index developed by Wechsler (1958) for measuring intellectual decline among normal older adults has not been useful with dementia patients (Kaszniak 1986). WAIS-R subtest profile patterns for differentiating between Alzheimer's disease, other forms of dementia, and normal aging (Fuld 1982, 1983, 1984) are also of limited usefulness (Brinkman and Braun 1984; Hendrichs and Celinski 1987; Satz et al. 1987). Shortened versions of the WAIS-R produce a quick estimate of the Full Scale IQ score but should be interpreted conservatively and used qualitatively (Satz and Mogel 1962; Silverstein 1982).

Ravens Coloured Progressive Matrices (Raven et al. 1984) has wide appeal among neuropsychologists because it was designed for use with organically impaired adults from ages 65 to 80. It is often considered a *culture-fair* test since it requires neither language nor academic skills for success; it is, however, influenced by educational level (Lezak 1983). Methods for estimating premorbid intellectual performance have been developed for the Ravens (Barona et al. 1984; Wilson et al. 1978) but the formulas fail to discriminate reliably between groups of normal and brain-damaged subjects (Klesges et al. 1985). A revision of the National Adult Reading Test (Nelson 1982) was found to be a better predictor of premorbid IQ but additional validation studies are needed (Blair and Spreen 1989).

Since quantitative measures for ascertaining degree of deterioration from a previous level of performance are currently unreliable, a qualitative estimation is generally made based on assumptions about the patient's educational and occupational attainments. Comparisons are then made to current test scores. Since premorbid test results are rarely available, retesting in six months to one year allows decline to be measured from the original test data.

Memory

Memory loss is another diagnostic feature of dementia. The Wechsler Memory Scale (WMS) (Wechsler 1945), despite its reported weaknesses (Prigatano 1978), is the most widely used test of memory decline. The Wechsler Memory Scale—Revised (WMS-R) (Wechsler 1987), has attempted to address the shortcomings of the WMS and now includes normative data for elders up to age 74. Butters and associates (1988) found the WMS-R to have good clinical utility for differentiating amnesic and demented patients.

For those who are unable to administer the entire WMS or WMS-R, Russell (1975) devised a scoring system for the Logical Memory and Visual Reproduction subtests. These tests provide a sample of the patient's verbal and visual memory performance with a delayed recall component. Abikoff and associates

(1987) and Russell (1988) recently reported normative data containing age and education corrections prorated to age 80 and above. Storandt and associates (1984, 1986) found the Logical Memory subtest a powerful discriminator between early Alzheimer patients and healthy older controls, but this discriminating factor did not apply later in the course of the illness.

Other memory measures such as the California Verbal Learning Test (Delis et al. 1987) are used for assessing learning capacity over a number of trials. This particular measure was modeled after the Rey Auditory Verbal Learning Test (Rey 1964) but contains norms to age 80.

Other Disorders of Higher Cortical Function

While memory and intellectual decline are essential for the diagnosis of dementia, other higher cortical functions are also affected and should be evaluated in a comprehensive neuropsychological assessment. These functions include attention, language, praxis, and visuoperception.

Attention

Disorders of attention (as mentioned previously and discussed more comprehensively in Chapter 5) can differentiate a dementia from a reversible disorder or an acute confusional state. The auditory Digit Span subtest of the WAIS-R and WMS batteries is most commonly used and norms to age 74 are found in both manuals (Wechsler 1987, 1981). Storandt and associates (1986) found that performance on the Digit Span subtest becomes progressively impaired in longitudinally studied patients with Alzheimer's disease but may not be useful in discriminating between early dementia states and healthy controls.

Language

The most commonly used measure for assessing language in dementia has been the Boston Diagnostic Aphasia Examination (Goodglass and Kaplan 1983). Normative data are grouped by age and educational level through age 85 (Borod et al. 1980). The Boston Naming Test, a subtest of the larger Boston examination (Kaplan et al. 1983), has recently published norms to age 80 and above (van Gorp et al. 1986). The Multilingual Aphasia Examination (Benton and Hamsher 1983) is useful for assessing patients of particularly lower educational status. Education corrections are computed downward to the sixth grade on some subtests, but age corrections are only to age 69. The Reitan-Indiana Aphasia Screening Test (Reitan 1981) does not contain norms for older adults, but is widely used as a qualitative assessment for reading, writing, spelling, naming, comprehension, constructional praxis, calculations, and left/right orientation.

Praxis and Visuoperception

Constructional praxis has been assessed in dementia patients through the Block Design subtest of the WAIS-R (Danziger and Storandt 1982) and drawing tasks (Bayles and Kaszniak 1987; Storandt et al. 1984). Eslinger and Benton (1983) found that the Benton Facial Recognition Test (Benton and van Allen 1968) and the Benton Line Orientation Test (Benton et al. 1978) had good validity for assessing the progressive visuoperceptive deterioration in dementia patients and dissociating patients of varying dementia etiologies from normal controls. Normative data are available on both these measures to age 84 (Benton et al. 1981). The Hooper Visual Organization Test (Hooper 1983) provides norms for those with lower educational levels but age corrections extend only to age 69.

Behavioral and Personality Change

Several scales for rating behavioral and personality change in dementia exist (Haycox 1984; Reisberg et al. 1982) but two scales have had the widest use in the literature. These are the Clinical Dementia Rating (CDR) scale (Hughes et al. 1982) and the Blessed Dementia Scale (Blessed et al. 1968). The CDR was developed and used in a large longitudinal study to stage dementia severity. It contains categories such as cognitive status, community affairs, home and hobbies, and personal care. The Blessed Dementia Scale contains items involving the performance of everyday activities as well as changes in personality, interests, and drive. Noncognitive behaviors are also addressed in the Alzheimer's Disease Assessment Scale (Rosen et al. 1984), which measures the severity of behaviors such as agitation, depression, concentration, appetite, and psychotic features.

Severity and Progressivity

In a comprehensive neuropsychological evaluation, the clinician is naturally expected to express an opinion on the severity, progressivity, and prognosis of the dementia. Age-education adjustments of formal cognitive performance are felt to be the most reliable method for grading cognitive severity (Spinnler and Della-Sala 1988), and these types of measures are recommended when selecting instruments for a dementia battery. Along with the CDR mentioned above, another widely used measure for staging severity of dementia is the Mattis Dementia Rating Scale (Mattis 1976, 1988). This scale has high test-retest reliability, is relatively quick to administer, and has been used in large epidemiological studies. A valuable feature of this instrument is its selection of items geared toward lower ability levels. This overcomes the problem of patients not being able to perform the tasks required of more complex standardized instruments.

Repeat neuropsychological testing generally provides information on the progressivity of the disease course. This implies the rate at which change is taking place, its regularity, and whether the changes that are occurring fill the expected pattern (Lezak 1986). Another method for assessing rate of progression in patients with Alzheimer's disease was devised by Rentz and associates (1986). Based on a single testing session and utilizing measures calculated to give a premorbid cognitive score of zero, progressivity was measured as a ratio of cognitive severity over estimated duration of illness. This Rapidity Index was longitudinally tested in a small repeat sample with patients keeping their predicted classifications of slow, moderate, or fast progression (Rentz et al. 1988).

History of Cognitive Decline: The Family Interview

Taking a history of cognitive decline from a reliable informant is an essential part of any dementia evaluation. Since many patients with dementia have maintained social and verbal skills, a false sense of competence may be communicated, which could mislead the unsuspecting examiner. Therefore, a family member, who is in daily contact with the patient, is more apt to provide the most information regarding the patient's actual functional status.

The objective of a cognitive history is to establish the nature of the earliest symptoms, the time at which they first occurred, and the progression of the symptoms over time. Questions should cover topics such as memory loss, confusional behavior, disorientation, psychiatric traits, changes in daily activities, loss of previously acquired skills, and current coping style. A helpful technique is to ask the family what the patient was like two years ago compared to behavior today. This usually provides an estimate of functional deterioration and date of onset. Information should also be obtained regarding the patient's educational level; work history; relevant habits (i.e., drinking, smoking, and drug use); school history; learning problems; and previous medical and psychiatric conditions (Lezak 1986). Exhibit 7-5 provides a sample of questions that may facilitate a cognitive history interview.

Obtaining accurate information is sometimes difficult. Unless the decline had a sudden onset, most behavior is usually perceived by family members as symptomatic of normal aging or an exaggeration of a previous personality style. In addition, some family members may deny, or become defensive, when asked to describe deficits in their loved one. Consequently, most of the interview questions may not be answered directly. However, the questions may trigger a discussion that could yield a behavioral description of significant value to the alert interviewer.

Exhibit 7-5 Guidelines for Conducting a Family Interview

Onset and Nature of Earliest Symptoms
How did you first become aware something was wrong?
When did this occur?
What was the main symptom that caused you to look for help?

Symptom Progression
Describe the patient's memory loss?
    Does the patient forget significant events and conversations?
    How soon will the patient forget the event? (a week, day, hour, or minute)
    Is the patient aware of his/her declining memory?
    Does he/she write information down in order to remember?
    How long has he/she been using this strategy?
What does the patient do now that is uncharacteristic of his/her previous way of acting?
    Does the patient tend to repeat him/herself?
    Does the patient dwell in the past?
    Is he or she more withdrawn or isolated?
    Is the patient more self-centered?
    Does the patient disregard the feelings of others?
    Does the patient initiate things on his/her own?
    Is the patient sexually inappropriate?
    Does the patient demonstrate nonpurposeful activities?
What were the patient's favorite activities or skills? Is he/she still interested in them? Can he/
    she still perform them?
How does the patient spend the day? In what way are his or her activities different from one
    year ago?
Has the patient ever failed to recognize familiar people or surroundings?
Has the patient ever gotten lost in familiar surroundings? e.g., neighborhood, yard, home, etc.
Has the patient neglected his or her personal care needs? e.g., dressing, bathing, toileting, eat-
    ing.
Is the patient's personality different from his or her usual self? In what way is he or she dif-
    ferent? e.g., withdrawn, blunted affect, emotional outbursts, childish behaviors, stub-
    bornness, suspiciousness, humorlessness, silliness, sexual promiscuity/perversity, rigid-
    ity, lack of spontaneity, etc.
How did the patient cope with previous stressful situations? How is the patient coping now?

Current Difficulties in Management at Home
What difficulties have you encountered in managing the patient at home?
    Does the patient sleep through the night?
    Does the patient wander restlessly?
    Is the patient more confused as nighttime approaches?
    Is the patient incontinent?
    How is the patient's appetite? Eating habits?
    How is the patient with strangers? Old friends? Family?
    What causes the patient to be particularly agitated?
    Has the patient become aggressive, violent or hurt anyone?
How would the patient cope with hospitalization/institutionalization?

Historical Information
Educational level; work history; relevant habits such as drinking, smoking and drug abuse;
    school history, learning problems, and previous medical conditions.
Has anyone else in the patient's family had similar symptoms of cognitive decline or been
    diagnosed as having a dementing illness?

Families are also known to tolerate a wide range of abnormal behaviors before seeking medical intervention. The most frequently reported complaints at the time of initial interview usually involve impaired memory; failure to recognize familiar people; and unusual, bizarre, or violent behavior. For example, almost all families complain that patients repeatedly ask the same questions and cannot remember what they were immediately told. They report that the patient may fail to recognize loved ones or confuse a spouse for a parent or a child for a sibling. Sometimes these failures in recognition cause the patient to become aggressive or violent, and delusions of persecution or infidelity are commonly reported. Sometimes the behavior is suggestive of the agnosias and apraxias commonly seen in dementia. For example, patients may put cornflakes in the coffeemaker, give away precious heirlooms, or take apart the house because they are "looking for their home." Patients may also inappropriately apply make-up, dress incorrectly, or put on clothing unsuitable to the weather. Families also report disruptions in the sleep-wake cycle and find their loved ones doing laundry at 2:00 A.M., or wandering the house or streets at night. It is particularly alarming to family members when the patient can no longer handle finances, balance a checkbook, make change, drive a car, or perform previously well learned skills.

The cognitive history interview is often viewed by family members as extremely valuable and sometimes stress-reducing because they receive a rationale for understanding the patient's behaviors. Suggestions regarding behavioral management may be addressed at this time, enabling the family to feel more in control of the situation. In regard to the cognitive evaluation, it is obvious that the cognitive history is essential for determining the functional severity of the dementia state. Depending on the quality of data obtained, the rehabilitation clinician may now be able to make long-range predictions regarding competency for independence, the management of personal affairs, or the level of supervision necessary in the home.

Reporting Neuropsychological Data

The findings of the cognitive evaluation are generally communicated at interdisciplinary team conferences and in a neuropsychological test report. A dementia evaluation should answer the following questions: level of alertness; cortical versus subcortical features; onset characteristics (i.e., abrupt versus insidious); progressivity (i.e., slow, moderate, or rapid); features of the memory loss; behavioral changes; placement considerations; and competency issues. These features are particularly relevant for diagnosis of the type of dementia involved and may provide useful information to the team regarding the patient's current adaptive abilities or behavioral expectations. Recommendations should stress the strengths that therapists may utilize, as well as potential areas of frustration and failure.

Predicting whether the patient is capable of independent self-care and competent decision making is another area of great importance to the treatment team. A determination of the patient's competence should include not only cognitive, but functional abilities as well.

Mental and functional competence compose different, yet interrelated skills. Mental competence involves three components: (1) the capacity to recognize that a purposeful, decision-making response is required; (2) the ability to process the decision (i.e., the capacity to review past experience, obtain more information, compute information, and predict outcomes or consequences); and (3) the implementation of the resolution (Alexander 1988). Functional competence, on the other hand, usually implies the ability to carry out daily responsibilities and self-care tasks safely and appropriately (Kapust and Weintraub 1988). While neuropsychological testing has been successful in predicting mental competence (Alexander 1988; Heaton and Pendleton 1981), it has not always predicted functional competence (Baird and Blaum 1989). Weintraub and associates (1982) found a double dissociation of function in two dementia cases where the extent of cognitive impairment was not reflective of the degree of functional impairment in daily-living activities. In fact, cognitive faculties and daily-living activities may deteriorate at different rates. The availability of an interdisciplinary team in the functional assessment of the patient is a unique contribution that rehabilitation can make. Ideally, any competency evaluation of an older adult should entail not only a comprehensive cognitive assessment but a functional assessment as well.

CONCLUSION

Rehabilitation is dedicated to helping people reach their highest attainable level of functioning. Historically, rehabilitation professionals have not viewed people with dementing illnesses as viable therapy candidates. However, it has become increasingly clear that evaluation and treatment in a rehabilitation setting can make a unique contribution to the maintenance and management of patients dually diagnosed with both physical and cognitive illnesses. The intention of this chapter has been to provide an overview of the cognitive disorders often seen in rehabilitation settings and discuss the value of neuropsychological assessment in these cases.

REFERENCES

Abikoff, H., J. Alvir, G. Hong, et al. 1987. Logical memory subtest of the Wechsler Memory Scale: Age and education norms and alternate-form reliability of two scoring systems. *Journal of Clinical and Experimental Neuropsychology* 9: 435–48.

Albert, M. 1988. Alzheimer's disease and other dementing disorders. In *Geriatric Neuropsychology*, edited by M. Albert and M. Moss, 145–78. New York: Guilford Press.

Albert, M., and M. Moss. 1984. The assessment of memory disorders in patients with Alzheimer disease. In *Neuropsychology of Memory*, edited by L.R. Squire and N. Butters, 236–46. New York: Guilford Press.

Albert, M. 1978. Subcortical dementia. In Alzheimer's disease: Senile dementia and related disorders. *Aging*, vol. 7, edited by R. Katzman, R.D. Terry and K.L. Bick, 173–80. New York: Raven Press.

Albert, M., R. Feldman, and A. Willis. 1974. The 'subcortical dementia' of progressive supranuclear palsy. *Journal of Neurology, Neurosurgery and Psychiatry* 37: 121–30.

Alexander, M. 1988. Clinical determination of mental competence: A theory and a retrospective study. *Archives of Neurology* 45: 23–6.

Alvord, E., L. Forno, and J. Kusske. 1974. The pathology of parkinsonism: A comparison of degenerations in cerebral cortex and brainstem. *Advances in Neurology* 5: 175–93.

American Psychiatric Association. 1987. *Diagnostic and Statistical Manual of Mental Disorders*, 3d ed., revised. Washington, DC: American Psychiatric Association.

Anthony, J., L. LeResche, U. Niaz, et al. 1982. Limits of the 'Mini-Mental State' as a screening test for dementia and delirium among hospital patients. *Psychological Medicine* 12: 397–408.

Baird, A., and C. Blaum. 1989. *Performance of Older Adults in the Neuropsychological Laboratory and the Real World*. Presented at the Annual Meeting of the International Neuropsychological Society, Vancouver, B.C.

Barona, A., C. Reynolds, and R. Chastain. 1984. A demographically based index of premorbid intelligence for the WAIS-R. *Journal of Consulting and Clinical Psychology* 52: 885–7.

Bayles, K., and A. Kaszniak. 1987. *Communication and Cognition in Normal Aging and Dementia*. Boston: Little, Brown and Company.

Becker, J., J. Huff, R. Nebes, et al. 1988. Neuropsychological function in Alzheimer's disease: Patterns of impairment and rates of progression. *Archives of Neurology* 45: 263–8.

Becker, J. 1988. Working memory and secondary memory deficits in Alzheimer's disease. *Journal of Clinical and Experimental Neuropsychology* 10: 739–53.

Benton, A., and K. Hamsher. 1983. *Multilingual Aphasia Examination*. Iowa City: AJA Associates.

Benton, A., P. Eslinger, and A. Damasio. 1981. Normative observations on neuropsychological test performances in old age. *Journal of Clinical Neuropsychology* 3: 33–42.

Benton, A., N. Varney, and K. Hamsher. 1978. Visuospatial judgment: A clinical test. *Archives of Neurology* 35: 364–7.

Benton, A., and M. van Allen. 1968. Impairments in facial recognition in patients with cerebral disease. *Cortex* 4: 344–58.

Blair, J., and O. Spreen. 1989. Predicting premorbid IQ: A revision of the National Adult Reading Test. *The Clinical Neuropsychologist* 3: 129–36.

Bleecker, M., K. Bolla-Wilson, C. Kawas, et al. 1988. Age-specific norms for the Mini-Mental State Exam. *Neurology* 38: 1565–8.

Blessed, G., B. Tomlinson, and M. Roth. 1968. The association between quantitative measures of dementia and of senile change in the cerebral grey matter of elderly subjects. *British Journal of Psychiatry* 114: 797–811.

Boller, F., D. Passafiume, N. Keefe, et al. 1984. Visuospatial impairment in Parkinson's disease: Role of perceptual and motor factors. *Archives of Neurology* 41: 485–90.

Boller, F., T. Mizutani, U. Roessmann, et al. 1979. Parkinson disease, dementia and Alzheimer disease: Clinicopathological correlations. *Annals of Neurology* 7: 329–35.

Bondareff, W., C. Mountjoy, M. Roth, et al. 1987. Age and histopathologic heterogeneity in Alzheimer's disease: Evidence for subtypes. *Archives of General Psychiatry* 44: 412–17.

Borod, J., H. Goodglass, and E. Kaplan. 1980. Normative data on the Boston Diagnostic Aphasia Examination, Parietal Lobe Battery and the Boston Naming Test. *Journal of Clinical Neuropsychology* 2: 209–15.

Botwinick, J., M. Storandt, and L. Berg. 1986. A longitudinal, behavioral study of senile dementia of the Alzheimer type. *Archives of Neurology* 43: 1124–7.

Brinkman, S., J. Largen, L. Cushman, et al. 1986. Clinical validators: Alzheimer's disease and multi-infarct dementia. In *Clinical Memory Assessment of Older Adults*, edited by L. Poon, 307–13. Washington, D.C.: American Psychological Association.

Brinkman, S., and P. Braun. 1984. Classification of dementia patients by a WAIS profile related to central cholinergic deficiencies. *Journal of Clinical Neuropsychology* 6: 393–400.

Brown, R., and C. Marsden. 1988. Subcortical dementia: The neuropsychological evidence. *Neuroscience* 25: 363–87.

Brown, R., and C. Marsden. 1987. Neuropsychology and cognitive function in Parkinson's disease: An overview. In *Movement Disorders*, 2d ed., edited by C. Marsden and S. Fahn, 99–123. London: Butterworths.

Brown, R., and C. Marsden. 1986. Visuospatial function in Parkinson's disease. *Brain* 109: 987–1002.

Burst, J. 1983. Dementia and cerebrovascular disease. In *The Dementias*, edited by R. Mayeux and W.G. Rosen, 131–47. New York: Raven Press.

Butters, N., D. Salmon, C. Cullum, et al. 1988. Differentiation of amnesic and demented patients with the Wechsler Memory Scale—Revised. *The Clinical Neuropsychologist* 2: 133–48.

Chui, H., J. Mortimer, U. Slager, et al. 1986. Pathologic correlates of dementia in Parkinson's disease. *Archives of Neurology* 43: 991–5.

Chui, H., E. Teng, V. Henderson, et al. 1985. Clinical subtypes of dementia of the Alzheimer type. *Neurology* 35: 1544–50.

Cohen, R., H. Weingartner, S. Smallberg, et al. 1982. Effort and cognition in depression. *Archives of General Psychiatry* 39: 593–7.

Cools, A., J. Van den Bercken, M. Horstink, et al. 1984. Cognitive and motor shifting aptitude disorder in Parkinson's disease. *Journal of Neurology, Neurosurgery and Psychiatry* 47: 443–53.

Cummings, J., B. Miller, M. Hill, et al. 1987. Neuropsychiatric aspects of multi-infarct dementia and dementia of the Alzheimer type. *Archives of Neurology* 44: 389–93.

Cummings, J., and D. Benson. 1986. Dementia of the Alzheimer type: An inventory of diagnostic clinical features. *Journal of the American Geriatrics Society* 34: 12–19.

Cummings, J., and D. Benson. 1984. Subcortical dementia: Review of an emerging concept. *Archives of Neurology* 41: 874–9.

Cummings, J., and D. Benson. 1983. *Dementia, a Clinical Approach*. Woburn, Mass.: Butterworth Publishers.

Cummings, J. 1983. Treatable dementias. In *The Dementias*, edited by R. Mayeux and W. Rosen, 165–83. New York: Raven Press.

Cutting, J. 1978. The relationship between Korsakov's syndrome and 'alcoholic dementia.' *British Journal of Psychiatry* 132: 240–51.

Danziger, W., and M. Storandt. 1982. Psychometric performance of healthy and demented older adults: A one year follow-up. Presented at the Annual Meeting of the Gerontological Society of America, Boston, Mass.

de Leon, M., S. Ferris, and A. George. 1980. Computed tomography evaluations of brain-behavior relationships in senile dementia of the Alzheimer's type. *Neurobiology of Aging* 1: 69–79.

Delis, D., J. Kramer, E. Kaplan, et al. 1987. *California Verbal Learning Test: Adult Version Manual.* New York: The Psychological Corp., Harcourt Brace Jovanovich.

El-Awar, M., J. Becker, K. Hammond, et al. 1987. Learning deficit in Parkinson's disease: Comparison with Alzheimer's disease and normal aging. *Archives of Neurology* 44: 180–4.

Evans, D., H. Funkenstein, M. Albert, et al. 1989. Prevalence of Alzheimer's disease in a community population of older persons: Higher than previously reported. *Journal of the American Medical Association* 262: 2551–6.

Eslinger, P., and A. Damasio. 1986. Preserved motor learning in Alzheimer's disease: Implications for anatomy and behavior. *The Journal of Neuroscience* 6: 3006–9.

Eslinger, P., and A. Benton. 1983. Visuoperceptual performances in aging and dementia: Clinical and theoretical implications. *Journal of Clinical Neuropsychology* 5: 213–20.

Findley, T., and S. Findley. 1987. Rehabilitation needs in the 1990s: Effects of an aging population. *Medical Care* 25: 753–63.

Flowers, K., and C. Robertson. 1985. The effect of Parkinson's disease on the ability to maintain a mental set. *Journal of Neurology, Neurosurgery and Psychiatry* 48: 517–29.

Folstein, M., and J. Breitner. 1981. Language disorder predicts familial Alzheimer's disease. *Johns Hopkins Medical Journal* 49: 145–7.

Folstein, M., S. Folstein, and P. McHugh. 1975. "Mini-Mental State": A practical method for grading the cognitive state of patients for the clinician. *Journal of Psychiatric Research* 12: 189–98.

Fuld, P. 1984. Test profile of cholinergic dysfunction and of Alzheimer type dementia. *Journal of Clinical Neuropsychology* 6: 380–92.

Fuld, P. 1983. Psychometric differentiation of the dementias: An overview. In *Alzheimer's Disease,* edited by B. Reisberg, 201–10. New York: Free Press.

Fuld, P. 1982. Behavioral signs of cholinergic deficiency in Alzheimer dementia. In *Alzheimer's Disease: A Report of Progress in Research,* edited by S. Corkin, K. Davis, J. Growdon, et al., 193–6. New York: Raven Press.

Fuld, P. 1978. Psychological testing in the differential diagnosis of the dementias. In Alzheimer's disease: Senile dementia and related disorders. *Aging,* vol. 7, edited by R. Katzman, R. Terry, and K. Bick, 185–93. New York: Raven Press.

Gainotti, G., C. Caltagirone, C. Masullo, et al. 1980. Patterns of neuropsychologic impairment in various diagnostic groups of dementia. In Aging of the brain and dementia. *Aging,* vol. 13, edited by L. Amaducci, 245–50. New York: Raven Press.

Garcia, C., J. Tweedy, and J. Blass. 1984. Underdiagnosis of cognitive impairment in a rehabilitation setting. *Journal of the American Geriatrics Society* 32: 339–42.

Gershon, S., and S. Herman. 1982. The differential diagnosis of dementia. *Journal of the American Geriatrics Society* 30, supplement: 858–66.

Goldberg, E., and L. Costa. 1986. Qualitative indices in neuropsychological assessment: An extension of Luria's approach to executive deficit following prefrontal lesions. In *Neuropsychological Assessment of Neuropsychiatric Disorders,* edited by I. Grant and K. Adams, 48–64. New York: Oxford University Press.

Goodglass, H., and E. Kaplan. 1983. *The Assessment of Aphasia and Related Disorders,* 2d ed. Philadelphia: Lea and Febiger.

Hachinski, V., L. Iliff, E. Zilhka, et al. 1975. Cerebral blood flow in dementia. *Archives of Neurology* 32: 632–7.

Hachinski, V., N. Lassen, and J. Marshall. 1974. Multi-infarct dementia. A cause of mental deterioration in the elderly. *Lancet* 2: 207–10.

Hachinski, V., P. Potter, and H. Mersky. 1987. Leuko-araiosis. *Archives of Neurology* 44: 21–23.

Haggerty, J., R. Golden, D. Evans, et al. 1988. Differential diagnosis of pseudodementia in the elderly. *Geriatrics* 43: 61–74.

Haycox, J. 1984. A behavioral scale for dementia. In *Dementia in the Elderly*, edited by C. Shamoian, 2–13. Washington, D.C.: American Psychiatric Press.

Heaton, R., and M. Pendleton. 1981. Use of neuropsychological tests to predict adult patients' everyday functioning. *Journal of Consulting and Clinical Psychology* 49: 807–21.

Hendrichs, R., and M. Celinski. 1987. Frequency of occurrence of a WAIS dementia profile in male head trauma patients. *Journal of Clinical and Experimental Neuropsychology* 9: 187–90.

Heston, L., A. Mastri, E. Anderson, et al. 1981. Dementia of the Alzheimer type. *Archives of General Psychiatry* 38: 1085–90.

Hooper, H. 1983. *Hooper Visual Organization Test (VOT) Scoring Key*. Los Angeles: Western Psychological Services.

Huber, S., E. Shuttleworth, G. Paulson, et al. 1986a. Cortical vs. subcortical dementia: Neuropsychological differences. *Archives of Neurology* 43: 392–4.

Huber, S., E. Shuttleworth, and G. Paulson. 1986b. Dementia in Parkinson's disease. *Archives of Neurology* 43: 987–90.

Hughes, C., L. Berg, W. Danziger, et al. 1982. A new clinical scale for the staging of dementia. *British Journal of Psychiatry* 140: 566–72.

Janota, I. 1985. Letters to the editor. *Lancet*, (19 Jan.): 174.

Kaplan, E., H. Goodglass, S. Weintraub, et al. 1983. *Boston Naming Test*. Philadelphia: Lea and Febiger.

Kapust, L., and S. Weintraub. 1988. The home visit: Field assessment of mental status impairment in the elderly. *The Gerontologist* 28: 112–15.

Kaszniak, A. 1986. The neuropsychology of dementia. In *Neuropsychological Assessment of Neuropsychiatric Disorders*, edited by I. Grant and K. Adams, 172–220. New York: Oxford University Press.

Katzman, R. 1986. Alzheimer's disease. *New England Journal of Medicine* 314: 964–74.

Klesges, R., L. Fisher, M. Vasey, et al. 1985. Predicting adult premorbid functioning index. *Clinical Neuropsychology* 7: 1–3.

Knesevich, J., F. Toro, J. Morris, and E. LaBarge. 1985. Aphasia, family history, and the longitudinal course of senile dementia of the Alzheimer type. *Psychiatry Research* 14: 255–63.

Kokmen, E., J. Naessens, and K. Offord. 1987. A short test of mental status: Description and preliminary results. *Mayo Clinic Procedures* 62: 281–8.

Kopelman, M. 1985. Rates of forgetting in Alzheimer's-type dementia and Korsakoff's syndrome. *Neuropsychologia* 23: 623–38.

Korsakoff, S. 1889. Psychic disorder in conjunction with peripheral neuritis. Translated by M. Victor and P.I. Yakovlev (1955). *Neurology* 5: 394–406.

Kral, V. 1983. The relationship between senile dementia (Alzheimer type) and depression. *Canadian Journal of Psychiatry* 28: 304–6.

Lazarus, L., N. Newton, B. Cohler, et al. 1987. Frequency and presentation of depressive symptoms in patients with primary degenerative dementia. *American Journal of Psychiatry* 144: 41–5.

Lechtenberg, R. 1982. *The Psychiatrist's Guide to Diseases of the Nervous System*. New York: John Wiley & Sons.

Lees, A., and W. Smith. 1983. Cognitive deficits in the early stages of Parkinson's disease. *Brain* 106: 257–70.

Lezak, M. 1986. Neuropsychological assessment. In *Geropsychological Assessment and Treatment: Selected Topics*, edited by L. Teri and P. Lewinsohn, 3–33. New York: Springer Publishing Co.

Lezak, M. 1983. *Neuropsychological Assessment*, 2d ed., New York: Oxford University Press: 192–6.

Luxenberg, J., and L. Feigenbaum. 1986. Cognitive impairment on a rehabilitation service. *Archives of Physical Medicine and Rehabilitation* 67: 796–8.

Martin, A., P. Brouwers, F. Lalonde, et al. 1986. Towards a behavioral typology of Alzheimer's patients. *Journal of Clinical and Experimental Neuropsychology* 8: 594–610.

Martin, A., C. Cox, P. Brouwers, et al. 1985. A note on different patterns of impaired and preserved cognitive abilities and their relation to episodic memory deficits in Alzheimer's patients. *Brain and Language* 26: 181–5.

Martin, A., and P. Fedio. 1983. Word production and comprehension in Alzheimer's disease: The breakdown of semantic knowledge. *Brain and Language* 19: 124–41.

Mattis, S. 1988. *DRS Dementia Rating Scale: Professional Manual*. Odessa, Fla.: Psychological Assessment Resources.

Mattis, S. 1976. Mental status examination for organic mental syndrome in the elderly patient. In *Geriatric Psychiatry*, edited by R. Bellack and B. Karasu, 77–103. New York: Grune and Stratton.

Mayeux, R., Y. Stern, R. Rosenstein, et al. 1988. An estimate of the prevalence of dementia in idiopathic Parkinson's disease. *Archives of Neurology* 45: 260–2.

Mayeux, R., Y. Stern, and S. Spanton. 1985. Heterogeneity in dementia of the Alzheimer's type: Evidence of subgroups. *Neurology* 35: 453–61.

Mayeux, R., Y. Stern, J. Rosen, et al. 1983. Is subcortical dementia a recognizable clinical entity? *Annals of Neurology* 14: 278–83.

Mayeux, R., Y. Stern, J. Rosen, et al. 1981. Depression, intellectual impairment, and Parkinson disease. *Neurology* 31: 645–50.

McAllister, T., and T. Price. 1982. Severe depressive pseudodementia with and without dementia. *American Journal of Psychiatry* 139: 626–9.

McKenna, P., and E. Warrington. 1986. The analytical approach to neuropsychological assessment. In *Neuropsychological Assessment of Neuropsychiatric Disorders*, edited by I. Grant and K. Adams, 31–47. New York: Oxford University Press.

McKhann, G., D. Drachman, M. Folstein, et al. 1984. Clinical diagnosis of Alzheimer's disease: Report of the NINCDS-ADRDA work group under the auspices of Department of Health and Human Services Task Force on Alzheimer's disease. *Neurology* 34: 939–44.

Milberg, W., N. Hebben, and E. Kaplan. 1986. The Boston process approach to neuropsychological assessment. In *Neuropsychological Assessment of Neuropsychiatric Disorders*, edited by I. Grant and K. Adams, 65–86. New York: Oxford University Press.

Miller, V. 1983. Lacunar stroke. *Archives of Neurology* 40: 129–34.

Mindham, R., C. Marsden, and J. Parkes. 1976. Psychiatric symptoms during l-dopa therapy for Parkinson's disease and their relationship to physical disability. *Psychological Medicine* 6: 23–33.

Morstyn, R., G. Hochanadel, and E. Kaplan. 1982. Depression vs. pseudodepression in dementia. *Journal of Clinical Psychiatry* 43: 197–9.

Moss, M., M. Albert, N. Butters, et al. 1986. Differential patterns of memory loss among patients with Alzheimer's disease, Huntington's disease and alcoholic Korsakoff's syndrome. *Archives of Neurology* 43: 239–46.

Nelson, H. 1982. *Nelson Adult Reading Test Manual.* London: The National Hospital for Nervous Diseases.

Nissen, M., D. Knopman, and D. Schacter. 1987. Neurochemical dissociation of memory systems. *Neurology* 37: 789–94.

Ober, B., E. Koss, and R. Friedland. 1985. Processes of memory failure in Alzheimer-type dementia. *Brain and Cognition* 4: 90–103.

Perez, F., V. Rivera, J. Meyer, et al. 1975. Analysis of intellectual and cognitive performance in patients with multi-infarct dementia, vertebrobasilar insufficiency with dementia and Alzheimer's disease. *Journal of Neurology, Neurosurgery and Psychiatry* 38: 533–40.

Perry, E., M. Curtis, D. Dick, et al. 1985. Cholinergic correlates of cognitive impairment in Parkinson's disease: Comparisons with Alzheimer's disease. *Journal of Neurology, Neurosurgery and Psychiatry* 48: 413–21.

Petry, S., J. Cummings, M. Hill, et al. 1988. Personality alterations in dementia of the Alzheimer type. *Archives of Neurology* 45: 1187–90.

Poeck, K. 1988. A case for neuropsychology in dementia research. *Journal of Neurology* 235: 257.

Prigatano, G. 1978. Wechsler memory scale: A selective review of the literature. *Journal of Clinical Psychology* 34: 816–32.

Rao, S., W. Mittenberg, and L. Bernadin. 1989. Neuropsychological test findings in subjects with leukoaraiosis. *Archives of Neurology* 46: 40–4.

Raven, J., J. Court, and J. Raven. 1984. *Manual for Raven's Progressive Matrices and Vocabulary Scales: Section 2, Coloured Progressive Matrices.* London: H.K. Lewis and Co.; San Antonio, Tex.: Psychological Corporation.

Reding, M., J. Haycox, and J. Blass. 1985. Depression in patients referred to a dementia clinic. *Archives of Neurology* 42: 894–6.

Reisberg, B., S. Ferris, M. deLeon, et al. 1982. The global deterioration scale for assessment of primary degenerative dementia. *American Journal of Psychiatry* 139: 1136–9.

Reitan, R. 1986. Theoretical and methodological bases of the Halstead-Reitan neuropsychological test battery. In *Neuropsychological Assessment of Neuropsychiatric Disorders,* edited by I. Grant and K. Adams, 3–30. New York: Oxford University Press.

Reitan, R. 1981. *Reitan-Indiana Aphasia Screening Test.* Tucson, Ariz.: Reitan Neuropsychology Laboratories.

Reitan, R. 1979. *Manual for Administration of Neuropsychological Test Batteries for Adults and Children.* Tucson, Ariz.: Reitan Neuropsychology Laboratories.

Rentz, D., M. Moulthrop, K. Rupar, et al. 1988. *The Validity and Clinical Utility of a Rapidity Index in Alzheimer's Disease.* Presented at the Annual Meeting of the International Neuropsychological Society, Vancouver, B.C.

Rentz, D., M. Moulthrop, and D. Luchins. 1986. *Rapidity of Disease Progression in Alzheimer Type Dementia.* Unpublished doctoral dissertation. Presented at the Annual Meeting of the American Psychological Association, New York, 1987.

Rey, A. 1964. *L'Examen Clinique en Psychologie.* Paris: Presses Universitaires de France.

Roman, G. 1987. Senile dementia of the Binswanger type. *Journal of the American Medical Association* 258: 1782–8.

Rosen, W., R. Mohs, and K. Davis. 1984. A new rating scale for Alzheimer's disease. *American Journal of Psychiatry* 141: 1356–64.

Rubin, E., J. Morris, and L. Berg. 1987. The progression of personality changes in senile dementia of the Alzheimer's type. *Journal of the American Geriatrics Society* 35: 721–5.

Russell, E. 1988. Renorming Russell's version of the Wechsler Memory Scale. *Journal of Clinical and Experimental Neuropsychology* 10: 235–49.

Russell, E. 1975. A multiple scoring method for the assessment of complex memory functions. *Journal of Consulting and Clinical Psychology* 43: 800–9.

Satz, P., W. van Gorp, H. Soper, et al. 1987. WAIS-R marker for dementia of the Alzheimer type? An empirical and statistical induction test. *Journal of Clinical and Experimental Neuropsychology* 9: 767–74.

Satz, P., and S. Mogel. 1962. An abbreviation of the WAIS for clinical use. *Journal of Clinical Psychology* 18: 77–9.

Seltzer, B., and I. Sherwin. 1983. A comparison of clinical features in early- and late-onset primary degenerative dementia. *Archives of Neurology* 40: 143–6.

Shukla, D., B. Singh, and R. Strobos. 1980. Hypertensive cerebrovascular disease and normal pressure hydrocephalus. *Neurology* 30: 998.

Shuttleworth, E., S. Huber, and G. Paulson. 1987. Depression in patients with dementia of Alzheimer type. *Journal of the National Medical Association* 79: 733–6.

Silverstein, A. 1982. Two- and four-subtest short forms of the Wechsler Adult Intelligence Scale-Revised. *Journal of Consulting and Clinical Psychology* 50: 415–18.

Spinnler, H., and S. Della-Sala. 1988. The role of clinical neuropsychology in the neurological diagnosis of Alzheimer's disease. *Journal of Neurology* 235: 258–71.

Steingart, A., V. Hachinski, C. Lau, et al. 1987. Cognitive and neurologic findings in demented patients with diffuse white matter lucencies on computed tomographic scan (Leuko-Araiosis). *Archives of Neurology* 44: 36–9.

Storandt, M., J. Botwinick, and W. Danziger. 1986. Longitudinal changes: Patients with mild SDAT and matched health controls. In *Handbook of Clinical Memory Assessment of the Older Adult*, edited by L.W. Poon et al., 277–84. Washington, D.C.: American Psychological Association.

Storandt, M., J. Botwinick, W. Danziger, et al. 1984. Psychometric differentiation of mild senile dementia of the Alzheimer type. *Archives of Neurology* 41: 497–9.

Taylor, A., J. Saint-Cyr, A. Lang, et al. 1986. Parkinson's disease and depression: A critical reevaluation. *Brain* 109: 279–92.

Teng, E., H. Chui, L. Schneider, et al. 1987. Alzheimer's dementia: Performance on the Mini-Mental State Examination. *Journal of Consulting and Clinical Psychology* 55: 96–100.

U.S. Congress, Office of Technology Assessment. 1987. *Losing a Million Minds: Confronting the Tragedy of Alzheimer's Disease and Other Dementias*. Washington, D.C.: U.S. Government Printing Office.

van den Burg, W., A. van Zomeren, J. Minderhoud, et al. 1987. Cognitive impairment in patients with multiple sclerosis and mild physical disability. *Archives of Neurology* 44: 494–501.

van Gorp, W., P. Satz, M. Kiersch, et al. 1986. Normative data on the Boston Naming Test for a group of normal older adults. *Journal of Clinical and Experimental Neuropsychology* 8: 702–5.

Vitaliano, P., J. Russo, and A. Breen. 1986. Functional decline in the early stages of Alzheimer's disease. *Psychology and Aging* 1: 41–6.

Wechsler, D. 1987. *Wechsler Memory Scale—Revised*. New York: Psychological Corporation.

Wechsler, D. 1981. *WAIS-R Manual*. New York: Psychological Corporation.

Wechsler, D. 1958. *The Measurement and Appraisal of Adult Intelligence*, 4th ed. Baltimore: Williams and Wilkins.

Wechsler, D. 1945. A standardized memory scale for clinical use. *Journal of Psychology* 19: 87–95.

Weingartner, H., and E. Silberman. 1984. Cognitive changes in depression. In *Neurobiology of Mood Disorders*, edited by R. Post and J. Ballenger, 121–35. Baltimore: Williams and Wilkins.

Weingartner, H., W. Kaye, S. Smallberg, et al. 1981. Memory failures in progressive idiopathic dementia. *Journal of Abnormal Psychology* 90: 187–96.

Weintraub, S., R. Baratz, and M. Mesulam. 1982. Daily living activities in the assessment of dementia. In Alzheimer's disease: A report of progress. *Aging*, vol. 19, edited by S. Corkin et al., 189–92. New York: Raven Press.

Weisberg, L. 1979. Computed tomography in the diagnosis of intracranial disease. *Annals of Internal Medicine* 91: 87–105.

Wells, C. 1979. Pseudodementia. *American Journal of Psychiatry* 136: 895–9.

Whitehouse, P. 1986. The concept of subcortical and cortical dementia: Another look. *Annals of Neurology* 19: 1–6.

Wilson, R., G. Rosenbaum, G. Brown, et al. 1978. An index of premorbid intelligence. *Journal of Consulting and Clinical Psychology* 46: 1554–5.

Chapter 8

Management of the Cognitively Impaired Older Patient

Dorene M. Rentz

Management of disruptive and dysfunctional behaviors is of special concern to rehabilitation professionals who are required to treat cognitively impaired elders with a newly acquired physical disability. Specialized treatment programs which have been developed for younger cognitively disordered patients are often not available for older rehabilitation patients with cognitive illnesses. Consequently, when older adults sustain a disability requiring inpatient rehabilitation, the treatment team is asked to manage and treat these patients utilizing traditional rehabilitation programs designed for younger, more intact individuals. The patient's successful adjustment and sustained cooperation with treatment can become a major challenge for those who must work with the patient on a day-to-day basis. Due to multiple cognitive and behavioral losses, these patients tend to disrupt therapy sessions, the nursing floor, and other patients on the rehabilitation unit. Management of disruptive behaviors is essential, not only for the welfare of others, but also for the patient's achievement of rehabilitation goals.

While many of the cognitive impairments sustained by elders cannot be remediated, the behavioral manifestations usually accompanying cognitive disorders are treatable. However, the term *therapy* may not be the correct word to use when describing the treatment of cognitively impaired older adults, since it implies a treatment that cures the basic cause of an illness so that the illness will not recur (Lawton 1980). These patients have organic brain disorders due to neuronal tissue loss. Consequently, the word *prosthesis* is probably the more useful term to distinguish management interventions with this patient population (Lindsley 1966). Prosthetics assumes the unchangeable quality of the basic condition and the prosthesis, or method found for managing the disruptive behavior, must be continuously applied in order to compensate for the disability associated with the condition. While rehabilitation professionals are specialists in the area of prosthetics for numerous physical disabilities, behavioral prosthetics for enhancing rehabilitation cooperation among older, cognitively impaired patients are a relatively new frontier.

This chapter will discuss the theoretical foundations for understanding and analyzing disruptive behaviors as they occur in an inpatient rehabilitation setting and describe the types of behavioral prostheses available to manage these behaviors. The focus on an inpatient setting is not intended to imply that these techniques are useful only in this environment; they may generalize to other outpatient settings as well. The chapter will also identify possible etiologies of catastrophic reactions and comment on staff issues in caring for the older patient with cognitive and behavioral decline.

THEORETICAL UNDERSTANDING OF BEHAVIORAL MANAGEMENT

Human behavior is considered a functional and dynamic relationship between a person and the environment. Behaviors operate upon environmental events and are strengthened, maintained, or extinguished in association with their consequences. In normal situations, this means that disruptive behaviors can usually be modified by educating the individual, altering the environment, or changing the consequences of an action in order to produce appropriate conduct. However, problematic behaviors exhibited by older, cognitively impaired persons have an interactive quality affecting biological, psychological, and sociological components that operate on specific environments (Eyde and Rich 1983; Hoyer et al. 1975; Labouvie-Veif et al. 1974). Consequently, these individuals are usually deficient in learning new information or adapting to environmental changes (Perez 1980). Disruptive behaviors often occur because of patients' inability to understand what is expected of them and adapt. Since patient cooperation is essential for rehabilitation, a major goal is to facilitate the patient's understanding of and comfort with treatment. This may require a great deal of practical ingenuity and an enormous amount of compassion (Heston 1983). It will also require a solid understanding of what precipitates and maintains the disruptive behaviors that lead to cooperation failures. Effective and humane management more successfully happens when everyone on the treatment team understands what behaviors typically occur in these patients and which ones can be reduced through environmental modifications, interactional adjustments, or the elimination of unnecessary stressors.

Types of Disruptive Behaviors

Not all behavioral or affective disabilities in this patient population are the direct result of brain damage. Some may be unrelated to or exacerbating the organic condition (Lawton 1980). Kahn (1965) introduced the term *excess disability* for those situations where the magnitude of the disturbance in functioning is greater than might be accounted for by the basic physical illness or cerebral pathology. Brody (1971) expanded the term to include those conditions which may compound the cognitive losses but have the potential for being treatable, such as depression, acute confusional states, or a deficient environment.

For the purposes of this chapter, two major types of disruptive behaviors will be discussed: (1) those behaviors that are indigenous to disorders of cognition such as disorientation and forgetfulness; and (2) those behaviors which occur as a result of internal or environmental stressors such as agitation, yelling out, or combativeness (Hussian 1981). Table 8-1 lists these behavioral disturbances based on their type.

The first category of behaviors is referred to as chronic, organically caused behaviors since they occur as a direct result of tissue loss. These behaviors are more likely managed in a prosthetic way. The second category of behaviors is stress-related and has an acute, driven quality, which arises out of anxiety or agitated depression. Diminished cognitive resources cause the patient to become overwhelmed when mastery of the situation is unobtainable (Verwoerdt 1980). These behaviors are more likely treatable if the external or environmental demands are modified to compensate for the patient's declining ability to adapt (Lawton and Nahemow 1973; Lawton 1981).

Table 8-1 Types of Behavioral Disturbances

Chronic Behavioral Disturbances	*Acute Behavioral Disturbances*
• Disinhibition	• Irritability
• Misapprehension	• Overactivity
• Forgetfulness/disorientation	• Catastrophic reactions
• Altered sleep patterns	• Emotional outbursts
• Confusion	• Noisy behavior
• Wandering	• Sudden withdrawal from activities
• "Sundowning"	• Fearfulness
• Night walking	• Agitation
• Eating problems	• Paranoid reactions
• Dressing and bathing problems	• Violence and aggression
• Sexual exposure	• Territoriality
• Losing or hiding things	• Depression
• Repetitive questions/actions	• Anxiety reactions
• Communication problems	
• Incontinence	

Progressively Lowered Stress Threshold Model

Based on the psychological theories of stress, coping, and adaptation set forth by Lazarus (1966), Coyne and Lazarus (1981), and Selye (1980), Hall (1986) developed a conceptual model called the Progressively Lowered Stress Threshold. This model incorporated the pathophysiology of brain cell loss, cognitive dysfunction, and environmental factors as they impact on disruptive behavior. While Hall and Buckwalter (1987) applied this theory to dementia patients, it may also be applied to cognitively disordered patients in the rehabilitation environment.

Hall and Buckwalter (1987) noted that patients with dementia exhibit three main types of behavior: *baseline, anxious,* and *dysfunctional.* The proportions of each behavior type change with the progression of the disease. Baseline behavior is normative behavior and is characterized as a generally calm state. The person is able to communicate needs, respond to communications, and is oriented to the environment based on the limits of neurologic deficits. Anxious behaviors occur when the demented patient feels stress. The patient loses eye contact and avoids offending stimuli. However, the caregivers are still able to make or maintain contact with the patient. If the stress level is allowed to continue or increase, dysfunctional behavior results. In this state, the patient is unable to effectively communicate with others and is unable to use the environment in a functionally appropriate manner. This results in what has been called *catastrophic* behavior (i.e., irritability, agitation, fearfulness, panic, combativeness, or sudden withdrawal). The Progressively Lowered Stress Threshold model suggests that if environmental demands are modified to account for the patient's cognitive and emotional deficits, the patient's anxiety will be reduced and catastrophic behaviors can be abated.

This model is instructive in conceptualizing the stress of an inpatient rehabilitation setting, particularly for the older, cognitively impaired adult. When patients are on a rehabilitation unit, a certain amount of anxiety is necessary for the patient to learn new adaptive techniques. However, even with cognitively intact patients, anxiety can become detrimental when the environmental demand exceeds a person's competence to perform successfully. The band for optimal anxiety is particularly narrow in cognitively impaired elders and rehabilitation professionals are challenged to keep the patient within the zone where maximum performance potential is possible (Lawton 1981). Otherwise, catastrophic behaviors will result.

A typical morning on a rehabilitation unit can illustrate how challenging this might be. Patients are required to wash, dress, and toilet themselves early in the morning in order to get out to the day area where breakfast is served. After breakfast, patients receive their medication and are ushered off for a full day of therapies. Usually, these tasks are performed in a rushed manner since everyone usually gets up and dresses at the same time. For the patient with cognitive impairments, the task of washing, dressing, and toileting may already be highly stressful because of planning deficits and the inability to process multiple stimuli. While the anxiety generated may have been optimal for performing the self-care tasks of morning ADLs, it may be exceeded if the patient is now required to manage breakfast and therapies. Consequently, the patient may feel incapable of meeting all the required demands. Anxiety heightens and dysfunctional behavior results (see Figure 8-1). When this occurs, patients become irritable and combative or withdrawn and noncompliant.

Hall and Buckwalter (1987) propose that normative, baseline behavior can be maintained by controlling the factors related to stress. These factors include:

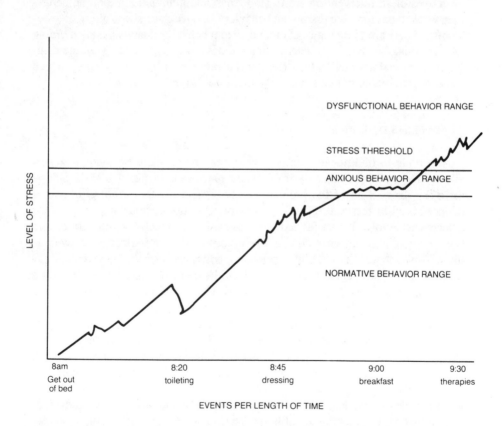

Figure 8-1 Progressively Lowered Stress Threshold Model. *Source:* Adapted from *Archives of Psychiatric Nursing,* vol. 1, 399–406, with permission of the W.B. Saunders Co., © 1987.

(1) fatigue and other physical conditions such as acute illness, discomfort, pain, and medication reactions; (2) environmental stressors such as change in the environment, caregiver or routine; and (3) internal or external demands for the patients to function beyond the limits of their cognitive and emotional reserves. In the above example, a rest period between dressing and breakfast would have provided a more comfortable transition between tasks and may have helped the patient stay within the normative behavior range.

ANALYSIS FOR BEHAVIORAL INTERVENTION

A behavioral analysis is the method usually used to determine the etiology of a behavioral disturbance and to brainstorm possible intervention strategies. The objectives of an intervention are to strengthen and maintain appropriate behaviors, weaken or eliminate disruptive behaviors, and teach or shape alternative behaviors. There are three major components to a behavioral analysis: (1) defining the disturbing behavior; (2) determining the desired change; and (3) implementing the appropriate intervention. Exhibit 8-1 provides a list of guidelines which can assist the rehabilitation team in making a behavioral analysis.

The Problem Definition

According to traditional operant approaches, the problem behavior is generally defined by a detailed analysis of: (1) the antecedents which led to the behavior; (2) a description of the problem behavior; and (3) the reinforcing consequences used in responding to the behavior. Questions which inquire into the antecedents involve the social and physical setting in which the behavior occurs (i.e., where did it happen and who was involved when it happened) as well as the person's thoughts or feelings prior to performance of the behavior. A description of the problem entails a reference to its frequency (e.g., how often does it occur); its intensity (mild, moderate, severe) and its duration (minutes, hours, days) as well as to what escalates, modifies, or interrupts it. The patient's current physical, cognitive, and psychological status are also important informational points when describing the problem behavior. The reinforcing consequences are discerned by asking what happened after the behavior, and how the person felt about the consequences. These may be judged as positive, negative, or neutral.

While many behaviors can be understood with reference to the here and now, it is important to expand information gathering to include the patient's developmental history and functioning at home prior to admission. For example, knowing that the patient premorbidly became anxious in new situations and has re-

Exhibit 8-1 Analysis of Disturbing Behavior

1. Define the disturbing behavior.
   a. What is the behavior?
   b. What does the behavior mean?
   c. When does it occur?
   d. How often does it occur?
   e. What precedes, escalates, modifies, or interrupts it?
   f. What is the usual outcome of the behavior?
2. Identify those disturbed by the behavior.
   a. Who is disturbed?
   b. What feelings are evoked?
   c. What happens following the disturbance?
3. Where does the disturbing behavior occur?
   a. Who are the significant others involved?
   b. Describe the activity and noise level?
   c. Where does the disturbing behavior not occur?
4. What is the current status of the person behaving in a disturbing manner?
   a. Physical status
   b. Social/psychological status
   c. Cognitive status
   d. Health status
5. Determine the desired change.
   a. Change the meaning of the behavior
   b. Change the response to the behavior
   c. Change the specific behavior itself
6. Determine the type of intervention strategy which would be appropriate and effective.
   a. Brainstorm a range of interventions geared to the needs of the person, treatment team, and others on the unit
   b. Choose a simple, flexible, humane, cost-effective plan
   c. Set a reachable goal
   d. Inform those who need to know and stress consistent implementation
   e. Evaluate effectiveness

cently become less competent even in familiar environments is useful for understanding the patient's current behavioral disruptions.

Probably the most challenging part of defining problem behavior is understanding the personal context out of which the behavior occurs. Theoretically, this implies that the behavior has a meaning originating within a person's life history or subjective experience. Therefore, long-standing personality characteristics and daily behavior patterns will not be easily modified. Often patients with cognitive impairments are not accommodating to the hospital regime because they think they are at home and do not understand why they cannot do what they have always done at a particular time of day. This usually leads to conflicts between the treatment team's agenda to perform therapy and the patient's failure to comply. Since reorientation to the hospital environment often fails, helping the staff understand these life-long behaviors can be a major goal in managing the team's level of anxiety and willingness to work with the patient. Family members are often important sources of information regarding these daily behavior patterns and can assist the team in structuring hospital activities to parallel the patient's habits at home.

Besides having meaning within the context of a person's life, behavior also occurs as a response to the external stressors of a current situation. Understanding the environmental context which led to the disruptive behavior is equally challenging. Often these environmental precipitants are the result of institutional policies, schedule demands, or personality clashes which may be impossible to modify for the comfort of a single patient. For example, consistency in caregivers is an important intervention for disoriented patients. Staff shortages, insurance limitations, and institutional policies may make the provision of a privately-hired 24-hour caregiver unfeasible. Therefore, despite awareness of what might be successful in controlling the patient's disruptions, many of these interventions may be impossible to implement.

A complete definition of the problem behavior will require gathering information from all relevant sources using both formal and informal methods. Interdisciplinary team conferences, interviews with all relevant parties, and development of special charting forms which tabulate behavioral disruptions when they occur constitute more formal methods of gathering behavioral data. Accuracy of the information is assured if a description of the problem behavior is obtained from at least two team members who are in 80 to 90 percent agreement as to the antecedents, description, and consequences of the behavior. Data can be gathered from therapists, family members, and nursing staff who have observed the patient's behavior and made their own observations of the patient throughout the day in various settings.

Determining the Desired Change

Once all the information is gathered, the next part of the analysis is determining the desired change. Prior to determining what changes are necessary, the team must first decide whether the problem behavior is modifiable or of sufficient severity to justify the focused energy needed to change the team's response patterns (Eyde and Rich 1983). For example, is the disturbed behavior the result of deficiencies in the person or the environment and is it modifiable (i.e., chronic or acute)? Is the behavior an exaggerated response to stimuli found naturally within the environment which are unchangeable (e.g., paranoid ideations due to the use of public address systems)? If the behavior is modifiable and of sufficient severity that change is necessary, then behaviors can be altered from one of several perspectives: changing the meaning of the behavior, changing the response to the behavior, or changing the behavior itself. Theoretically, meaning and response changes usually involve interventions that are staff and environment focused, while behavioral interventions are focused directly on the patient. An appropriate focus can be determined by considering the cognitive and emotional capacities of the individual patient and/or the flexibility of the staff and the environment. Very often, staff who are frustrated by the behavior will emphasize the need for the patient to change and lose sight of the other options available through external or environmental modifications. Whatever interventions are decided upon, they should be evaluated for their realism and generalizability. Interventions which could be practiced in the hospital and eventually implemented in the home following discharge are the most ideal. However, not all interventions can be generalized to the home setting because of environmental constraints and the undue burden it places on family members to implement them.

Interventions focused on directly changing the patient's behavior have been quite successful using operant psychology paradigms, even in severely impaired older adults. Operant techniques decrease the frequency of an inappropriate behavior while reinforcing the behavior that should continue. Successful attempts have been reported in dealing with participation in activities (McClannahan and Risley 1975), social interaction (Hoyer et al. 1974), and pathological screaming (Baltes and Lascomb 1975; Garfinkle 1979). Contingent positive reinforcement on a continuous schedule and stimulus control procedures worked the best for this cognitively impaired population (Hussian 1981). Success is predicated, however, on how much control one has over contingencies in the environment or over available and workable reinforcers.

Implementing the Appropriate Intervention

Once the behavior and realistic change have been defined, an intervention strategy can be designed and implemented. The major objective of any intervention strategy is to promote a maximal level of safe functioning and quality of life for both the patient and hospital staff. Intervention strategies are the most effective when they are based on the remaining skills of the patient. As mentioned in Chapter 7, patients with cognitive disorders have a wide and varying range of functional abilities. Once the patient's strengths and weaknesses are assessed, strategies can be developed around the maintenance of existing skills.

The goal of all intervention strategies is parsimony (i.e., keeping it simple, flexible, and cost-effective). It is critical that any intervention strategy be fully communicated and agreed upon by all members of the treatment team because interventions will need to be consistently implemented on every shift (i.e., 24 hours per day) in order for them to be effective. A before-treatment measure should be performed in order to evaluate the effectiveness of the treatment plan. This involves documenting the frequency of the disruptive behavior prior to implementation of the intervention strategy. Once the plan is initiated, behavioral changes should be documented within a specified trial period. Team members should be aware that the disturbing behavior is likely to escalate initially and should not be discouraged. Regular follow-up evaluations should be performed by the team to determine the effectiveness of the strategies. Adjustments can be made if the interventions are not effective.

THE ETIOLOGY AND MANAGEMENT OF DISRUPTIVE BEHAVIORS

Behavioral disruptions in this patient population often have a variety of overlapping biopsychosocial etiologies which makes the identification of the antecedents and consequences of a behavior a challenging problem for eventual modification. Understanding the source of a behavior is an important diagnostic step toward managing it. For the purposes of this chapter, four major sources of dysfunctional behavior will be considered. They include: (1) organic or physically related causes, (2) environmental causes, (3) cognitive causes, and (4) emotional causes. Management strategies will be discussed within the context of these basic etiologies and a separate section will address pharmacological treatments. However, it should be kept in mind that behavior is complex and often not the result of a single etiology. Consequently, the behavioral and pharmacological strategies mentioned below will be applicable across several etiological categories.

Physical Causes

More than at any other time in life, physical disruptions in older individuals can cause behavioral disorders. When combined with cognitive frailty, these physical stressors often lead to catastrophic reactions. However, disruptive behavior resulting from a physical stressor should be considered an "excess disability" (Brody et al. 1971; Kahn 1965), which is currently complicating the patient's cognitive status and is treatable. Once it is treated, or removed, the patient will be able to utilize remaining cognitive reserves and disruptive behavior should abate.

The most serious of the physical stressors is the acute confusional state, also known as delirium. Acute confusional states are common in older adults, particularly following surgery, illness, or medication changes (Mesulam and Gerschwind 1976). Since the clinical symptoms are similar to a dementia, they are frequently overlooked in a patient with a history of cognitive decline. Misdiagnosis can lead not only to increased morbidity, but also to mortality. The major causes of an acute confusional state are cardiovascular disorders, infection or fever, drug intoxication, metabolic and nutritional disorders, neurological disorders, and disorders related to hospitalization (e.g., excessive or deficient sensory input, sleep loss, etc.) (Albert 1988a). Agitation and physical aggression often coincide with elevated blood glucose levels, active congestive heart failure, elevated blood urea nitrogen (BUN), and mild myocardial infarction (Hussian 1981). Once the patient has been identified as confused, the cause of the disordered behavior must be determined through a complete medical work-up (Albert 1988b). Even if the metabolic disturbance or systemic illness is diagnosed and treated in the primary care hospital, the cognitive and behavioral residuals of the delirium often take a long time to clear and persist in the rehabilitation environment.

Fatigue causes disruptive behaviors more frequently than any other etiological factor. Rehabilitation, by its very nature, pushes patients to their maximum performance, inducing high levels of fatigue. For the cognitively impaired patient, this can be extremely detrimental and rehabilitation teams must be constantly vigilant to the patient's stamina. Scheduling more strenuous activities after a period of sleep, encouraging frequent rest periods during the day, and refraining from several hours of unbroken activity can eliminate disruptions.

Other physical causes of acute behavioral disturbance may be illness, medication reactions, sensory losses, and pain and discomfort due to immobility, poor positioning, hunger, or bowel and bladder fullness. The disruptive behaviors resulting from these physical etiologies are often noted to be confusion, agitation, combativeness, emotional outbursts, continual shouting, and visual hallucinations. At these times, patients attempt to get out of bed, or out of their wheelchair, producing falls and further injuries (Albert 1988a). During therapies, they are frequently noncompliant, highly distracted, or fall asleep. Until these physical etiologies are addressed, cooperation with rehabilitation therapies and the learning of new techniques will be minimal. However, daily contact by the therapists and the practice of familiar routines may facilitate rehabilitation progress while these issues are being treated. Behavioral interventions for managing these disruptive behaviors involve controlling the physical environment as much as possible and raising the team's awareness of the problem and its source. The techniques described elsewhere in this chapter and in Chapter 4 of this text are applicable here.

Environmental Causes

Another common cause of acute disruptive behaviors involves environmental stressors. Due to the patient's limited cognitive and emotional capacities, any changes in the environment, caregiver, or routine often precipitate disorientation, confusion, agitation, and panic. The fact that the patient is in the hospital has already lowered the patient's stress threshold. Additional hospital-induced stressors, such as unfamiliar people; lack of privacy; multiple competing stimuli from television, radio, noise, unfamiliar voices, and public address announcements, commonly cause a free-floating anxiety which can escalate to a catastrophic reaction (see Figure 8-1).

Environmental manipulation is difficult to achieve in rehabilitation settings, but is essential if environmentally-induced behaviors are to be eliminated. This patient population benefits the most from a structured setting, consistent caregivers, frequent personal contact, expressions of attention, and balanced levels of stimulation. Excessive noise and interaction with many people can only be tolerated on a limited basis, so removal from group situations and frequent rest breaks are helpful in managing the irritability that results from overstimulation. When removal is not possible because of the demands of therapy, distractions and snacks have been successfully used to calm agitated patients (Cherry and Rafkin 1988). Disrupted sleep-wake cycles and sun downing (i.e., nocturnal confusion) are also responsive to environmental modifications such as having the patient do more strenuous exercises closer to nightfall; using night lights and other devices to orient the patient in the dark; withholding fluids after dinner if night urination is the cause of the problem; or accepting odd behaviors such as letting the patient sleep in a chair, or in street clothes (Mace and Rabins 1981).

Cognitive Causes

The patient's cognitive impairments in memory, communication, insight, judgment, and problem solving are another common cause of disruptive behaviors. Since traditional rehabilitation therapies are often didactic, requiring patients to learn new adaptive techniques, patients with cognitive impairments are often asked to understand and perform tasks which are too complex for them. This situation creates unusual stress for these individuals, frequently resulting in violent outbursts and sudden acts of aggression toward therapists and caregivers.

Fasano (1986) found that clear directions, one step commands, elimination of choices, pacing, repetition, and simplifying tasks into small components worked well to counteract the processing and planning deficits of this patient population. Patients will require more time to comprehend and perform a task. Therefore, waiting a few seconds and repeating a request facilitates performance. Cues and prompts supplied immediately when the patient is having difficulty also alleviate the patient's frustration. When language is significantly disrupted, interpretive strategies may be necessary to decipher what patients mean by the words they use. For example, "I want to go home" may mean, "I feel lost." "My mother is coming" may mean, "I want someone to understand where I am coming from." Reassurances, eye contact, and body language are excellent sources of communication with these patients. Misrecognitions, resulting from sensory losses and/ or visual agnosias, can lead to increased suspiciousness and paranoia because patients fail to recognize family members, caretakers, therapists, or their own room. Utilizing other sensory modalities, (i.e., hearing a familiar voice, smelling a familiar perfume) may help patients recall the face or situation they cannot identify. Misrecognitions might also be associated with the inappropriate use of objects (i.e., misperceiving hand cream for toothpaste, or voiding in receptacles that look like a toilet). Bright colors to code and identify such things as the patient's room, bathroom, and wheelchair can be helpful. Much of the hallucinatory behavior that is the result of misperceptions can be minimized if public address systems are kept to a minimum, mirrors and life-like pictures are removed, and the staff move slowly into the visual field of these patients.

Emotional Causes

Disruptive behaviors can also result from emotional causes such as anxiety, depression, lowered self-esteem, attention seeking, fear, and suspiciousness. Many of these emotional reactions occur simultaneously, but they will be discussed separately for the sake of clarity.

Anxiety states in cognitively impaired elders are frequently free-floating and often based on a fearful anticipation of loss, fear of disease and disability, fear of failure to adapt and be acceptable within the social context, and fear of a new and strange environment. To patients with cognitive impairments, hospitalization often means that their families intend to "put them away" or think "they are crazy." Consequently, combative and noncompliant behaviors usually result from rigidity, the need for control, and the fear of loss of competence. If anxious behavior can be identified as excessive negative anticipation, interventions can be structured to increase the patient's control over the environment and participation in short- and long-range decisions; therapy activities that reinforce the patient's sense of competency can also be devised (Eyde and Rich 1983).

Depression is another common etiology of noncompliance in a rehabilitation setting. Symptoms such as insomnia, despair, lethargy, anorexia, loss of interest, and numerous somatic complaints are frequently seen in older patients admitted to the hospital. (See Chapter 9 for a complete discussion of this topic.) However, in cognitively impaired patients depression may be the result not only of organic changes, but of viewing experiences, oneself, and the future negatively. Feelings of powerlessness, helplessness, and worthlessness predominate. Inactivity and isolation often exacerbate a depression. Within a rehabilitation environment, these patients should be encouraged to socialize with others by sitting out in the dayroom or watching television with small groups of people. Staff need to provide consistent reinforcement for positive statements and ignore negative self-comments. Pharmacological management, which is discussed in the following section, should also be considered.

Lowered self-esteem can generate disruptive behaviors, particularly in a rehabilitation setting where performance is accentuated. As mentioned earlier, rehabilitation therapies frequently require patients to perform complex tasks beyond their capacities. Due to their retained ability to read nonverbal messages (Edelson and Lyons 1985), patients perceive themselves as having failed to live up to what is expected of them. As with cognitively intact persons, these failures represent a threat to the patient's self-esteem and competence (Beck and Heacock 1988). Territoriality (e.g., pushing others away from their dining table), as well as attempts at concealing their memory deficits are ways in which cognitively impaired patients retain a sense of competence. Withdrawal from social interactions may be the result of cognitive deficits and overstimulation, but it can also be attributed to lowered self-esteem. Meeting new people or keeping up with a social conversation is difficult, and these patients often avoid these situations. Social interactions work best when they are limited, and occur in a quiet surrounding, devoid of noisy activity. However, if patients become anxious, agitated, fidgety, and express a desire to leave, this generally signals the need for respite.

Attention-seeking behaviors (while common among many patient groups) are also seen in this patient population. For example, patients quickly learn that agitated, aggressive, or combative behaviors are likely to gain the attention they want even from a busy staff. In cognitively impaired patients, the attention that results instinctively reinforces this behavior. Providing attention during calm periods, or on a regular basis, while ignoring more agitated behavior may eliminate these disruptions. However, the staff must be sure that the agitation is merely an attention-seeking device and not an attempt to communicate other physical or environmental stressors that are impacting on the patient at the time. In addition, attention-seeking behaviors may also indicate the patient's fears caused by the unfamiliarity of the situation. Acknowledging these fears and providing encouragement usually address these needs (Fasano 1986).

Fear, suspiciousness, and paranoid reactions are another common cause of behavioral disturbance. The sensory, social, cognitive, and environmental deprivations that cognitively impaired older adults experience often blur the distinction between inner and external reality. Along with memory loss and confusion, these elders tend to experience only fragments of reality. Paranoid ideations are often their attempt to put these pieces into some meaningful, consistent order.

Staff should be encouraged to be sensitive to the fact that this experience is frightening and upsetting to the patient and should address these fears. Careful attention to the content of what is said may also give insight into whether the patient is responding to a real life event and needs assistance. However, patients will often take a self-protective stance, make false accusations, or hide personal items because they feel threatened by environmental stimuli they do not understand. When suspicious behavior predominates, it is always important to reassure patients that they are safe and that their concerns are being taken seriously. However, team members should carefully monitor whether the delusions are getting worse or more exaggerated. If environmental modifications and reassurances fail, medications may be necessary.

Pharmacological Management

In early and mild stages of cognitive decline, nonpharmacologic management of behavioral abnormalities is usually preferred (Salzman 1988). However, as the decline progresses, acute disruptive and injurious behaviors are sometimes managed with medications, used in conjunction with behavioral and environmental interventions (Jenike 1985). It cannot be emphasized enough that elders are very sensitive to drug interactions; medications for behavioral management should be used judiciously.

Medication management can be divided into two general categories: simple behavioral control and symptomatic relief (Maletta 1985). Behaviors requiring simple but immediate control include aggressiveness, combativeness, agitation, fearfulness, belligerence, and unprovoked outbursts of rage. Neuroleptics are the psychotropic drugs most commonly used for the treatment of these behaviors. Although they are reliably and predictably effective in controlling agitated behavior, side effects are common and behavioral control may not be complete (Salzman 1988). No differences are reported in treatment effectiveness among the neuroleptics but different researchers will state a preference for one drug over another based upon potential side effects (Goldman and Lazarus 1988; Lovett et al. 1987; Salzman 1987a, 1987b; Volicer 1988). Extrapyramidal effects are sometimes noted with haloperidal (Haldol) which limits its usefulness in rehabilitation. Long-term use of neuroleptics can also cause tardive dyskinesia, and patients with underlying brain disease, such as dementia, are at particular risk for developing this syndrome (Goldman and Lazarus 1988).

Behaviors which benefit from symptomatic relief include delusions, hallucinations, anxiety, and depression. Neuroleptics are the drugs of choice for controlling delusions and hallucinations but are best used as a last resort when environmental manipulations prove unsuccessful (Jenike 1985). Anxiety, apprehension, and depression frequently occur in the early stages of a progressive disorder, when patients have some awareness of their cognitive deficits. Short-acting benzodiazepines have been found effective in controlling anxiety. However, these drugs are known to produce deleterious side effects including sedation, ataxia, disorientation, confusion, and disinhibition and should be used with caution. As the severity of the cognitive disorder progresses to a moderate or severe state, benzodiazepines are contraindicated due to the presence of these adverse behavioral and cognitive side effects (Salzman 1988). Depression (or symptoms resembling depression) is also seen in early stages of dementia. As cognition declines, emotional lability or total flatness of affect, with sleep and appetite impairment, are observed. Antidepressant therapy has been successful in alleviating depressive symptomatology and concomitantly improving cognitive function (Salzman 1988). Low doses of doxepin (Sinequan) or desipramine (Norpramin) were found effective in some patients with cognitive disorders (Reifler et al. 1986). Patients placed on a course of therapy with these drugs should be monitored for a range of anticholinergic, sedative, hypotensive, and cardiac side effects that may be especially dangerous in this age group (Maletta 1985). Maprotiline (Ludiomil) and trazodone (Desyrel) are often considered more beneficial because of their low anticholinergic properties. However, these drugs can also cause postural hypotension, marked sedation, and, in some cases, seizures (Maletta 1985). Monoamine oxidase inhibitors (MAOIs) improve mood (Jenike 1985), but they can produce increased agitation and psychosis (Salzman 1986).

Psychostimulants, such as methylphenidate (Ritalin), have been used successfully in withdrawn, apathetic, and low-energy patients with dramatic effects (Goldman and Lazarus 1988). This class of drugs has been known to improve appetite in some patients and may be useful for the medically ill patient who cannot tolerate tricyclic side effects. Although controlled and long-term studies have not been done, some geriatricians feel this class of drugs is safe, effective, and unlikely to result in physical tolerance (Goldman and Lazarus 1988). Others feel they are not useful because they possess a brief duration of action, cause occasional rebound of depression, have psychologically addicting properties and cardiovascular effects, and risk growing drug tolerance (Maletta 1985).

It is apparent that the use of drugs for behavior management must be weighed against the potential for creating adverse side effects, medical complications, or drug interactions. Pharmacological interventions for the management of disruptive and symptomatic behaviors should be considered as only one component of an otherwise multimodal treatment approach. Patients who are placed on drugs should also be carefully monitored and reevaluated for dosage reduction or medication termination, should their level of alertness or performance in therapies decline.

STAFF ISSUES IN CARING FOR THE COGNITIVELY IMPAIRED PATIENT

The symptoms and concomitant disruptive behaviors that occur with cognitive disorders often make caring for this patient population a challenging and burdensome task. The feelings most often reported are depression, anger, and guilt, which eventually lead to staff burnout, excessive staff turnover (Committee on Aging 1988), and sometimes elder abuse (U.S. Congress 1987).

Two of the major difficulties for staff are the concentrated supervisory care which these patients require and the unrewarding nature of working with those who are disruptive or accusatory. Recently, a number of books and articles have appeared in the academic literature which address the special needs that staff and family caregivers face in dealing with this patient population (Kahan et al. 1985; Rheaume et al. 1988; Wilder et al. 1983; Zarit et al. 1980; Zarit et al. 1986). Some of the major interventions have involved specialized training and education for staff and family; lower patient-to-staff ratios; a concerned and motivated administration; support groups which facilitate discussion of emotional reactions and problem solving; and frequent respites or vacations.

When dealing with cognitively declining older adults, it is extremely important to educate both the professional and paraprofessional staff on the normative aging process and the special needs of patients with cognitive illnesses. Learning about cognitive decline should increase the staff's understanding of the chronic and sometimes progressive nature of the illness and its impact on behavior. With enhanced understanding, staff are more empathic and accepting of behaviors which would otherwise be viewed as deliberate or manipulative. Specialized training in communication techniques is another important topic for an educational seminar. Staff should be encouraged to explore and learn interactive skills which enable them to communicate on a level that the cognitively impaired patient can comprehend (Rhcaume et al. 1988). Finally, staff benefit from knowledge about family reactions in caring for a loved one with a cognitive illness. Relatives of the patient bring their confusion, grief, anger, and guilt with them when they visit the patient, often adding to the stress of the treatment staff. Learning ways to counteract families' unrealistic expectations, understanding the concepts of prolonged grieving, and providing information regarding support networks alleviate the staff's sense of humiliation, helplessness, and anger when problems with family members are encountered.

In addition to an orientation training program, staff respond positively to regular continuing education sessions. These sessions should focus on providing staff with support as well as information on new developments in the field. Some professionals report that continuing education has been an important strategy in augmenting the staff's motivation in working with this patient population as well as reducing staff turnover (U.S. Congress 1987). Kahan and associates (1985) found that educational support groups were also beneficial to family members and that the acquisition of new knowledge was an important ingredient in reducing the perception of burden as well as levels of depression.

The initiation of weekly support groups for the treatment team is another important means of alleviating the stress of dealing with a cognitively impaired older population. These groups generally meet at a regular time and are run by a consulting mental health professional. Confidentiality is imperative as staff members need the reassurance that no administrative repercussions will result from honest expression of their feelings and attitudes. The purpose of the support group is to help members of the treatment team identify and cope with emotional reactions and/or ambivalent feelings engendered by treating this patient population. Rehabilitation teams generally expect to help people progress in function. Patients who are disruptive, uncooperative, and have progressively deteriorating illnesses can tend to make staff members feel that these patients are inappropriately admitted to rehabilitation units. The availability of a support group can assist staff members in identifying their feelings about caring for cognitively impaired patients who will only deteriorate further despite their efforts. They also allow staff to ventilate their frustrations and guilt so that these emotional feelings do not interfere with the professional care of the patient. In addition to a weekly support group, daily problem-solving sessions are also important. This format helps to foster participation in decision making on the unit, which can be an important administrative means of supporting staff.

When the above intervention strategies have been used on treatment units with cognitively impaired elders, staff burnout has been minimized. Edelson and Lyons (1985) note that burnout and high staff turnover usually occur when the staff feels unsupported and the patient-staff ratio is too high. An increase in behavioral outbursts can also be a sign of staff dissatisfaction, since patients with cognitive impairments remain sensitive to nonverbal communications and respond negatively to staff members' irritability and impatience (Edelson and Lyons 1985). While education and the availability of support groups can reduce staff dissatisfaction and increase morale, ultimately there are some staff who cannot comfortably work with cognitively disordered patients. When necessary, such staff members should be counseled and reassigned to a different patient population (Cherry and Rafkin 1988).

CONCLUSION

Management and care of the cognitively impaired patient is a difficult endeavor. However, the principles of intervention are similar for many problems and settings. Perhaps the most important concept is that fairly simple interventions, based on an understanding of the levels of brain impairment and the meaning of the patients' behaviors within the context of their lives and new environment, are often very helpful. All too often, families are told that nothing can be done. In fact, success in managing the patient through a rehabilitation program can provide new hope and direction for the family.

REFERENCES

Albert, M. 1988a. Acute confusional states. In *Geriatric Neuropsychology*, edited by M. Albert and M. Moss, 100–14. New York: Guilford Press.

Albert, M. 1988b. Assessment of cognitive dysfunction. In *Geriatric Neuropsychology*, edited by M. Albert and M. Moss, 57–81. New York: Guilford Press.

Baltes, M., and S. Lascomb. 1975. Creating a healthy institutional environment for the elderly via behavior management. *International Journal of Nursing Studies* 12: 5–12.

Beck, C., and P. Heacock. 1988. Nursing interventions for patients with Alzheimer's disease. *The Nursing Clinics of North America: Alzheimer's Disease* 23: 95–124.

Brody, E., M. Kleban, M. Lawton, and H. Silverman. 1971. Excess disabilities of mentally impaired aged: Impact of individualized treatment. *The Gerontologist* 11 (No. 2, Part 1): 124–132.

Cherry, D., and M. Rafkin. 1988. Adapting day care to the needs of adults with dementia. *The Gerontologist* 28: 116–20.

Committee on Aging. 1988. *The Psychiatric Treatment of Alzheimer's Disease*. New York: Brunner/Mazel Publishers: 53–96.

Coyne, J., and R. Lazarus. 1981. Cognitive style, stress perception and coping. In *Handbook on Stress and Anxiety*, edited by I. Kutash and L. Schlesinger, 144–59. San Francisco: Jossey Bass.

Edelson, J., and W. Lyons. 1985. *Institutional Care of the Mentally Impaired Elderly*. New York: Van Nostrand Reinhold Co.

Eyde, D., and J. Rich. 1983. *Psychological Distress in Aging*. Gaithersburg, Md.: Aspen Publishers: 123–165.

Fasano, M. 1986. *Creative Care for the Person with Alzheimer's*. New Jersey: Brady Publications.

Garfinkle, R. 1979. Brief behavior therapy with an elderly patient. *Journal of Geriatric Psychiatry* 12: 23–5.

Goldman, L., and L. Lazarus. 1988. Assessment and management of dementia in the nursing home. *Clinics in Geriatric Medicine: Clinical and Policy Issues in the Care of the Nursing Home Patient* 4: 589–600.

Hall, G. 1986. A conceptual model for planning and evaluating nursing care of the client with Alzheimer's disease or a related disorder. Paper presented at the 1986 Annual Meeting of the American Association of Neuroscience Nurses.

Hall, G., and K. Buckwalter. 1987. Progressively lowered stress threshold: A conceptual model for care of adults with Alzheimer's disease. *Archives of Psychiatric Nursing* 1: 399–406.

Heston, L., and J. White. 1983. *Dementia: A Practical Guide to Alzheimer's Disease and Related Illnesses*. New York: W.H. Freeman and Co.

Hoyer, W., B. Mishara, and R. Reidel. 1975. Problem behaviors as operants: Applications with elderly individuals. *Gerontologist* 15: 452–6.

Hoyer, W., R. Kafer, S. Simpson, et al. 1974. Reinstatement of verbal behavior in elderly mental patients using operant procedures. *Gerontologist* 14: 149–52.

Hussian, R. 1981. *Geriatric Psychology*. Baltimore, Md.: Van Nostrand Reinhold Co.

Jenike, M. 1985. *Handbook of Geriatric Psychopharmacology*. Littleton, Mass.: PSG Publishing Co.

Kahan, J., B. Kemp, F. Staples, et al. 1985. Decreasing the burden in families caring for a relative with a dementing illness: A controlled study. *Journal of the American Geriatric Society* 33: 664–9.

Kahn, R. Comments. 1965. *Proceedings of the York House Institute on the Mentally Impaired Aged*. Philadelphia: Philadelphia Geriatric Center.

Labouvie-Veiff, G., W. Hoyer, M. Baltes, et al. 1974. Operant analysis of intellectual behavior in old age. *Human Development* 17: 259–72.

Lawton, M. 1981. Sensory deprivation and the effect of the environment on management of the patient with senile dementia. In Clinical Aspects of Alzheimer's Disease and Senile Dementia. *Aging*, vol. 15, edited by N. Miller and G. Cohen, 227–51. New York: Raven Press.

Lawton, M. 1980. Psychosocial and environmental approaches to the care of senile dementia patients. In *Psychopathology in the Aged*, edited by J. Cole and J. Barrett, 265–80. New York: Raven Press.

Lawton, M., and L. Nahemow. 1973. Ecology and the aging process. In *Psychology of Adult Development and Aging*, edited by C. Eisdorfer and M. Lawton. Washington, D.C.: American Press.

Lazarus, R. 1966. *Psychological Stress and the Coping Process*. New York: McGraw-Hill.

Lindsley, O. 1966. Geriatric behavioral prosthetics. In *New Thoughts on Old Age*, edited by R. Kastenbaum. New York: Springer Publishing.

Lovett, W., D. Stokes, L. Taylor, et al. 1987. Management of behavioral symptoms in disturbed elderly patients: Comparison of trifluoperazine and haloperidol. *Journal of Clinical Psychiatry* 48: 234–6.

Mace, N., and P. Rabins. 1981. *The 36-Hour Day*. Baltimore: The Johns Hopkins University Press.

Maletta, G. 1985. Medications to modify at-home behavior of Alzheimer's patients. *Geriatrics* 40: 31–42.

McClannahan, L., and T. Risley. 1975. Design of living environments for nursing home residents: Increasing participation in recreation activities. *Journal of Applied Behavioral Analysis* 8: 261–8.

Mesulam, M., and N. Gerschwind. 1976. Disordered mental states in the postoperative period. *Urologic Clinics of North America* 3: 199–215.

Perez, F. 1980. Behavioral studies of dementia: Methods of investigation and analysis. In *Psychopathology in the Aged*, edited by J.O. Cole and J.E. Barrett, 81–95. New York: Raven Press.

Reifler, B., E. Larson, E. Teri, et al. 1986. Dementia of the Alzheimer's type and depression. *Journal of the American Geriatric Society* 34: 855–9.

Rheaume, Y., K. Fabiszewski, J. Brown, et al. 1988. In *Clinical Management of Alzheimer's Disease*, edited by L. Volicer, K. Fabiszewski, Y. Rheaume, et al., 201–22. Gaithersburg, Md.: Aspen Publishers.

Salzman, C. 1988. Treatment of agitation, anxiety and depression in dementia. *Pharmacology Bulletin* 24: 39–42.

Salzman, C. 1987a. Treatment of agitation in the elderly. In *Psychopharmacology: The Third Generation of Progress*, edited by H. Meltzer, 1167–76. New York: Raven Press.

Salzman, C. 1987b. Treatment of the elderly agitated patient. *Journal of Clinical Psychiatry* 48: 19–22.

Salzman, C. 1986. Caution urged in using MAOIs with the elderly. *American Journal of Psychiatry* 143: 118–19.

Selye, H. 1980. The stress concept today. In *Handbook on Stress and Anxiety,* edited by I. Kutash and L. Schlesinger, 124–44. San Francisco: Jossey Bass.

U.S. Congress, Office of Technology Assessment. 1987. *Losing a Million Minds: Confronting the Tragedy of Alzheimer's Disease and Other Dementias,* OTA-BA-323. Washington, D.C.: U.S. Government Printing Office.

Verwoerdt, A. 1980. Anxiety, dissociative and personality disorders in the elderly. In *Handbook of Geriatric Psychiatry,* edited by E. Busse and D. Blazer, 368–89. New York: Von Nostrand Reinhold Co.

Volicer, L. 1988. Drugs used in the treatment of Alzheimer dementia. In *Clinical Management of Alzheimer's Disease,* edited by L. Volicer, K. Fabiszewski, Y. Rheaume, et al., 185–200. Gaithersburg, Md.: Aspen Publishers.

Wilder, D., J. Teresi, and R. Bennett. 1983. Family burden and dementia. In *The Dementias,* edited by R. Mayeux and W. Rosen, 239–51. New York: Raven Press.

Zarit, S., P. Todd, and J. Zarit. 1986. Subjective burden of husbands and wives as caregivers: A longitudinal study. *The Gerontologist* 26: 260–6.

Zarit, S., K. Reever, and J. Bach-Peterson. 1980. Relatives of the impaired elderly: Correlates of feelings of burden. *The Gerontologist* 20: 649–54.

Chapter 9

Assessment and Treatment of Depression in the Older Rehabilitation Patient

Richard R. Trezona, Jr.

Depression is the most frequently occurring mental disorder in late life (Blazer and Williams 1980). Left untreated, depression in older adults can last for several months (Blazer 1982) and have devastating effects on emotional, social, cognitive, and physical functioning. The risk of suicide also increases steadily with age, and the rate of suicide is four times as great in those 85 and older as compared with adolescents (Stoudemire and Blazer 1985). The prevalence of depression in older adults is of special concern since this age group tends to underutilize available mental health services and medical professionals are frequently untrained to deal with their emotional problems (Chaisson-Stewart 1985).

Accurate assessment and prompt treatment of depression in the older rehabilitation patient is also essential. The duration of inpatient rehabilitation is often brief and of an intensive nature (several hours of therapy per day). Therefore, older rehabilitation patients must mobilize their psychological and physical resources quickly in order to participate maximally. Failure to engage in the rehabilitation process soon after admission can result in poorer functional outcomes, increased dependency, and placement in more restrictive environments. This chapter will focus on the special issues involved in the assessment and treatment of depression in older rehabilitation patients. Prevalence of depression in older adults, problems of differential diagnosis, theoretical models, and assessment instruments will be discussed. In addition, treatment approaches will be presented with special emphasis on behavioral and cognitive-behavioral strategies.

DEFINITION OF DEPRESSION

The issue of how depression is defined becomes important when reviewing research on its prevalence and treatment in older adults. Many of the apparent inconsistencies in this area have resulted from confusion over definitions of depression. The meaning of the term depression varies depending upon the context in which it is used. Depression can refer to variations in normal emotional expression, or it may refer to a more intense dysphoric mood and be regarded as a symptom. Finally, depression can refer to a group of symptoms and diagnostic signs which constitutes a clinical syndrome. A prime example of defining depression as a clinical syndrome is the definition used by the *Diagnostic and Statistical Manual of Mental Disorders* (DSM-III-R) of the American Psychiatric Association (1987). There are a variety of terms used to characterize dysphoric states in later life which are distinct from depression and require definition. These terms include *grief reaction*, *adjustment disorder*, and *demoralization*.

Depression should be distinguished from grief reactions. Normal grief is defined as an expected reaction to loss which is characterized by crying, feelings of emptiness, insomnia, preoccupation with the deceased, and sometimes social withdrawal. Normal grief reactions generally last from six months to one year after which time adaptation to the loss is achieved. Symptoms may subsequently reappear on significant anniversaries, such as birthdays and holidays. Sometimes a normal grief reaction can develop into a more severe form of pathological grief. This state is characterized by severe depression, severe anniversary reactions, refusal to relinquish belongings of the deceased, deterioration in health, and panic attacks (Brown and Stoudemire 1983).

Blazer (1989) notes that the onset of a depressed mood and expressions of hopelessness in older adults are often in reaction to an identifiable event. In these cases, Blazer argues that an adjustment disorder with depressed mood is the correct diagnosis using DSM-III-R criteria. An adjustment disorder is applicable to those individuals who exhibit a maladaptive reaction to an identifiable trauma. Blazer points out that elders face a host of potential traumas including loss of social roles, physical illness, retirement and economic losses, difficulty with children, and relocation.

Stoudemire and Blazer (1985) make a distinction between clinical depression and demoralization in older adults. They define demoralization as a state in which a person feels trapped and helpless by overwhelming circumstances. Demoralization can be caused by increasing social, physical, and economic stressors to which elders are particularly susceptible.

PRESENTATION OF DEPRESSION IN OLDER ADULTS

The presentation of depression in older adults may be qualitatively different from depression in younger age groups. Klerman (1983) notes that depressed older adults often deny being depressed and do not report feelings of sadness or dysphoria. Rather, the depressed older individual often presents with signs of memory or concentration problems, apathy, lack of drive, or somatic problems. Zung (1980) reports that guilt and introjection of hostility or unacceptable impulses were relatively unimportant factors in late life depression. Instead, Zung found that depression in older adults was more likely to be related to feelings of inferiority and loss of self-esteem. The nature of psychotic depression is also reported to be different in elders. Meyers and associates (1984) compared the prevalence of delusions in people who suffered the onset of depression before age 60 with those who sustained their depression after age 60 in a sample of 50 patients hospitalized for endogenous depression. They found that depressions with onset after age 60 were more frequently accompanied by delusions as compared with those of earlier onset. In the older sample, delusions of persecution or of having an incurable illness were more common than delusions associated with guilt.

The indirect expression of depression in older adults and the lack of hard clinical signs have given rise to the term *masked depression* to describe this affective disorder in late life. In masked depressions, individuals deny depressive affect but manifest other signs that indicate that a depression can be diagnosed. Ban (1984) describes masked depressions as characterized by phasic appearance of autonomic or somatic symptoms, diurnal fluctuations, mild inhibition of thinking, dysthymic mood changes, fatigue, and an anxious sense of failure or nonspecific apprehension.

It is not surprising to find that depression is underdiagnosed in older adults, given the tendency for them to deny depression, the atypical manner in which depression may be presented in this age group, and ageistic notions of depression held by many medical professionals. Underdiagnosis of depression may be particularly common in medical settings. In a recent study, Rapp and associates (1988) compared nonpsychiatric house physicians' ability to detect depression in a randomly selected sample of older medical inpatients with base rates of depression established through clinical interviews using Research Diagnostic Criteria (Spitzer et al. 1978). A blind review of medical records revealed that physicians were able to detect depression in only 8.7 percent of those cases diagnosed as depressed.

PREVALENCE OF DEPRESSION IN OLDER ADULTS

The commonly held belief that the prevalence of depression increases with age is far from consistently substantiated. Estimates of the prevalence of depression in elders vary widely, depending upon how depression is defined, the types of samples that are employed, and the methodology used to gather data. Blazer and Williams (1980) surveyed older community based residents and found the prevalence of substantial depressive symptoms to be 14.7 percent. However, only 3.7 percent of this sample met the criteria for diagnosis of a major depressive disorder. In a prospective study using a large community sample, age 55 and older, Phifer and Murrell (1986) examined the number of people who became depressed over a six month interval. They found that 10.7 percent of their sample met the criteria for depression based on the Center for Epidemiological Studies Depression Scale (CES-D) (Radloff 1977). Phifer and Murrell discovered that health and social support were significant predictors of depression, while other factors such as age, sex, education, marital status, and early parental death did not discriminate between depressed and nondepressed individuals. These estimates of depression in older adults can be contrasted with estimates for the prevalence of depression in the general population, which range from 4 to 9 percent for females and 2 to 3 percent for males (American Psychiatric Association 1987). Therefore, depending upon the criteria employed, it may be difficult to consistently demonstrate substantial differences in the prevalence of major depression in older adults.

In a comprehensive review of the literature on depression and aging, Newmann (1989) concluded that a definitive answer to the question of whether depression increases in late life is not possible due to the conceptual and methodological problems which plague this research. Newmann points out that there are two distinct measurement approaches to assessing depression in aging research. One approach treats depression as a continuous variable which can vary in intensity and severity. This approach has its roots in psychometric research and relies on standardized screening scales to assess depression. The alternative approach regards depression as a discrete variable in which a categorical distinction is made between the presence or absence of a depressive disorder. This approach has its origins in psychiatry and relies on interviews to determine if an individual's symptoms conform to a set of inclusionary or exclusionary criteria. Newmann's analysis of previous research indicates that studies utilizing the psychometric approach suggest that levels of depression are highest among the youngest and oldest age cohorts, and lowest in the middle years. The clinical diagnostic approach yields exactly the opposite relationship: highest rates for depression are observed in the middle aged, somewhat lower rates for the youngest age cohort, and the lowest rates among the oldest age cohort. Therefore, contradictory findings regarding the relationship between age and depression may be an artifact of the types of measures employed.

Prevalence of Depression in Disabled Older Adults

The prevalence of depression in disabled people across the life span was studied by Turner and associates (1985). Using a community-based sample of disabled people in Ontario, Canada, they screened for depression in three age groups: 18 to 44 years, 45 to 65 years, and 65 or older. They found that the prevalence of depression was lowest among older adults, compared to the younger age groups, when using the Center for Epidemiological Studies Depression Scale. Although the older disabled sample reported lower rates of depression relative to younger disabled adults, the frequency of depression (nearly 30 percent) still represents a significant complication of physical disability.

There are also many contradictory findings in the literature on the occurrence of depression in rehabilitation settings. Depression is often associated with disabling illnesses such as stroke (Robinson and Benson 1981), Parkinson's disease (Mindham 1974), multiple sclerosis (Kahana et al. 1971), and head injury (Lezak 1978). However, Gans (1981) reports that rehabilitation staff tend to overestimate the prevalence of depression in their patients. Gans contends that staff often mistake extreme emotional reactions, such as grief, regression, or demoralization, for depression. Caplan (1983) also observed that various disciplines in rehabilitation settings use a variety of different data to diagnose depression in their patients.

DIFFERENTIAL DIAGNOSIS

Differential diagnosis between depression and other disorders is extremely important for the older rehabilitation patient who may present with a multitude of symptoms. Accurate diagnosis is essential for expedient treatment and optimizing rehabilitation outcomes.

Physical Illness and Depression

The DSM-III-R makes a distinction between depressions which are caused by known medical disorders and those which are not related to an organic etiology. The former are labeled as an *organic mood syndrome*. The treatment of a depression precipitated by organic factors is much different than that of a *major depression* in that resolution of the organic illness may cause the depression to remit. Misdiagnosis of an organic mood syndrome can lead to unnecessary delays in the treatment of the underlying medical cause of the depression or to inappropriate treatment of the depressive symptoms. Therefore, a complete medical examination and review of the patient's medical history is required to rule out an organic cause of a depression. This is particularly true for the older rehabilitation patient who may enter a rehabilitation setting with multiple medical problems.

Ban (1984) notes that there are many neurological, endocrine, nutritional, and metabolic disorders that can result in depressive-like symptoms in the older patient. These disorders include many neurologic conditions (e.g., symptoms of multiple sclerosis, normal pressure hydrocephalus, and temporal lobe tumors). Endocrine disorders such as hypothyroidism, adrenal insufficiency, and hyperparathyroidism can be mistaken for depression. Metabolic disorders with an associated decrease in sodium and/or potassium, or an increase in serum calcium can mimic depression. Also, Ouslander (1984) states that the effects of fever, dehydration, decreased cardiac output, electrolyte disturbances, and hypoxia can be misdiagnosed as depression. Finally, infectious diseases, especially viral illness, can be accompanied by depressive-like symptoms.

Pseudodementia

Wells (1979) defines *pseudodementia* as a syndrome in which patients with psychiatric disturbances demonstrate cognitive impairments which mimic dementia. The term was originally applied to depressed patients but has come to be applied to other psychiatric disorders as well, such as mania and schizophrenia. Cummings and Benson (1983) observe that use of the term *pseudo* dementia is unfortunate since it implies that the cognitive dysfunction associated with depression is somehow less real than in an organically based dementia. The primary value of the term may be in its role of alerting clinicians to make more careful diagnoses when confronted with an older patient with complaints of cognitive inefficiency or memory loss.

Estimates of the prevalence of pseudodementia vary widely depending upon the method for assessing it and the type of sample used. Most studies suggest a prevalence rate of approximately 10 percent for patients evaluated for a history of progressive mental deterioration (Cummings and Benson 1983). For example, Feinberg and Goodman (1984) found that between 5 to 15 percent of thoroughly evaluated patients with a presumed diagnosis of dementia will be diagnosed with depression at follow-up.

There have been a number of attempts to distinguish the clinical features of pseudodementia from dementia. One of the most frequently cited is the work of Wells (1979). Wells proposed that pseudodementia and dementia can be differentiated on the basis of their clinical course and history, the subjective complaints and behavior presented, and the differences in memory and intellectual dysfunctions (refer to Chapter 7 for a complete discussion of this topic). The diagnosis of depression and dementia should not be regarded as mutually exclusive. As Jenike (1988) points out, many patients suffer from both an organically-based intellectual impairment and depression. This is especially true of patients in the early stages of a dementing illness who have an awareness of their intellectual decline. Jenike notes that treatment of a depression in demented persons can have significantly beneficial effects on their behavior even though the cognitive deficits persist. Demented patients who are treated for depression become less negativistic and more interested in hobbies and social activities. In addition, family members report improvement in the patient's mood (Jenike 1988).

The coexistence of dementia and depression in late life is so common that some researchers (Christison and Blazer 1988) suggest that the frequency of pseudodementia is actually overestimated. Jenike (1988) goes so far as to suggest that depression in older adults is often times a warning sign of undetected dementia. In support of this assertion, Reding and associates (1985) followed 225 patients referred to a dementia clinic over a three year period. Of the patients initially thought to be depressed, 57 percent went on to develop a dementia. Retrospective analysis revealed that many of those thought to be depressed had some sign of organicity on initial evaluation, however subtle. Those depressed individuals who later developed dementia had evidence of cerebrovascular, extrapyramidal, or spinocerebellar disease; significant evidence of ischemia; impairment of mental status; or confusion on low doses of tricyclic antidepressants.

MODELS OF DEPRESSION

Various models of depression can be specifically applied to older adults. This section will describe *learned helplessness, behavioral,* and *cognitive* models of depression, and discuss their application to the rehabilitation setting.

Learning theorists, such as Lewinsohn and associates (1969) and Seligman (1975), emphasize the relationship between depression, reductions in the frequency of positive reinforcers in the environment, and loss of control. Cognitive theorists, such as Beck (1967), focus on the role of negative belief systems in predisposing a person to developing depression. Psychoanalytic theorists (Freud 1959; Zetzel 1965) emphasize the importance of loss of significant objects, ambivalence towards lost loved ones, and the acceptance of inevitable loss (see Chapter 11 on treatment for a further discussion of this approach).

Learned Helplessness Model

One extension of learning theory that has received considerable attention in the rehabilitation literature is the learned helplessness model of depression proposed by Seligman and his colleagues (Seligman 1975; Seligman and Maier 1967). The learned helplessness model of depression was derived from a series of experiments which studied the effects of inescapable shock on laboratory animals. In these studies, Seligman was able to produce a depressive-like state in animals by placing them in inescapable, uncontrollably aversive circumstances.

He compares their reaction to those of humans who become depressed when they believe their behaviors no longer positively impact on the environment.

Learned helplessness theory was reformulated by Abrahamson and associates (1978) when it became clear that the existing theory was too simplified and could not account for certain findings (e.g., helplessness followed uncontrollability for some subjects with particular personality traits but not for others). The reformulation of learned helplessness theory centered on the types of causal explanations that are used when an individual is confronted with a bad event. Abrahamson and associates proposed that causal explanations varied along three dimensions: internal versus external; stable versus unstable; and global versus specific. According to the revised theory, depression is most frequently associated with attributional styles that give internal, stable, and global explanations for bad events. In the words of Peterson and Seligman (1985, 926) this depressive attributional style concludes that "it's me, it's going to last forever, and it's going to affect everything I do," when confronted with negative events.

The learned helplessness paradigm has been useful in understanding the development of depression in rehabilitation settings. The experience of disability has many parallels with Seligman's experimental conditions that produced learned helplessness. In both instances, the onset of the aversive event is unpredictable, frequently beyond the control of the person. Initially, rehabilitation patients may respond with fear and anxiety when confronted with an uncontrollable event such as a stroke or spinal cord injury. Over time, however, the expression of fear can give way to depression when the aversive event continues and appears inescapable. Consequently, rehabilitation patients lose their motivation to respond and initiation of behaviors decreases significantly. The opportunity to learn new, adaptive behaviors is lost due to the expectation that no responses will produce the desired outcome (i.e., ambulation, speech, feeding). According to the revised version of learned helplessness theory, rehabilitation patients are likely to experience depression if they attribute the cause of the disability to themselves (internal), view the effects of the disability as unchangeable (stable), and see the disability as affecting all aspects of their functioning (global).

Behavioral Model

Behavioral theorists, such as Lewinsohn and associates (1969, 1985) provide another perspective on the development of depression with older adults in rehabilitation settings. They view depression as a consequence of reduction in response-contingent positive reinforcement. This reduction in positive reinforcement results in a decreased frequency of behavior and associated feelings of dysphoria that are characteristic of depression. Lewinsohn and associates (1976) proposed that a reduction in response-contingent reinforcement may occur when reinforcers lose their effectiveness, become unavailable, or the individual lacks the skills to elicit them. Consequently, treatment of depression focuses on identifying target behaviors through goal setting, self-monitoring relationships between mood and events, increasing the frequency of pleasant events, managing aversive events, and social skills training. The central assumption of behavioral theories of depression is that the behavior of depressed people does not result in reinforcement sufficient to sustain a behavior, or that the behavior results in an aversive outcome. Applied to the circumstances of rehabilitation, a behavioral model suggests that disabled individuals are prone to depression because their behaviors no longer result in positive reinforcement (at least initially), or the consequences of their actions have an aversive result.

Cognitive Model

Cognitive theories of depression, such as the one proposed by Beck (1967, 1976), assume that depression is caused by unrealistic and distorted thoughts, beliefs, and images (i.e., cognitions). According to Beck's theory, a person's affect and behavior are largely determined by the way in which the person views the world, the self, and the future. Depressed individuals have a tendency to view the world as full of barriers and demands; perceive themselves as inadequate or worthless; and see the future as pessimistic. Beck (1967) calls these three beliefs the *negative triad* of depression.

Beck (1967) also describes several common errors and distortions that depressed individuals make when processing information. These errors include drawing conclusions on the basis of an isolated event (overgeneralization), overestimating the magnitude of an undesirable event (magnification), underestimating the significance of a desirable event (minimization), and all-or-none thinking. Cognitive psychotherapy focuses on identifying and modifying these dysfunctional thoughts and substituting more reasonable beliefs. Older rehabilitation patients often harbor distorted beliefs about themselves and their future as described by Beck (e.g., "my life is over"), and they frequently process information about their rehabilitation performance in biased and distorted ways (e.g., "this task is absolutely impossible").

MEASUREMENT OF DEPRESSION IN OLDER ADULTS

Beyond the clinical interview, the assessment of depression can be facilitated by the use of standardized instruments. The utilization of formal tests to assess depression in elders is particularly indicated given the tendency of medical professionals to underdiagnose depression in this age group. The following is a description of suggested instruments to assess depression in older rehabilitation patients. These tests were selected on the basis of their use with older adults and their potential applicability in a medical setting.

Table 9-1 summarizes information on the format, length, and traditional cutoff scores for severity of depression for each of the instruments discussed. It should be noted that cutoff scores may vary depending upon the goal of assessment (screening for further diagnostic workup, selection for treatment studies, use as an outcome variable). Furthermore, the instruments vary in their sensitivity and specificity with different cutoff ranges (e.g., Rapp et al. 1988).

Geriatric Depression Scale

The Geriatric Depression Scale (GDS) (Yesavage et al. 1983) is one of the few depression measures that has been specifically designed for use with elders. The scale avoids the use of somatic items which can often confound the assess-

Table 9-1 Measures To Assess Depression in the Older Adult

Instrument	Format	Number of Items	Cutoff Scores			
			Normal	Mild	Moderate	Severe
Geriatric Depresson Scale (Yesavage et al. 1983)	Self-report Yes/No	30	0-10	11-20	21-30	Same
Beck Depression Inventory (Beck, et al. 1961)	Self-report Rating scale	21	0-9	10-15	16-23	24-63
Self-Rating Depression Scale (Zung 1965)	Self-report Rating scale	20	Below 50	50-59	60-69	70-99
Hamilton Rating Scale for Depression (Hamilton 1960)	Interviewer Rating scale	17	0-6	7-17	18-24	+25

ment of depression in this age group. For example, questions regarding sleep disturbance or change in appetite are not included on the GDS. Inquiries into areas that older adults may find offensive, such as sexual functioning, are also excluded. The format of the GDS is designed to be simple and straightforward and does not use a rating scale, which often requires the patient to make judgments about gradations in their depressive symptoms. The GDS has been found to have acceptable reliability and validity (Yesavage et al. 1983).

There are several advantages to using the GDS with older rehabilitation patients. The avoidance of somatic items reduces the chances of overestimating the severity of depression with this population based on somatic items alone. The relatively simple format and ease of administration are advantageous when screening patients with sensory and/or cognitive impairments. In addition, the GDS can be verbally administered to the patient by the clinician if the patient cannot complete it independently.

Beck Depression Inventory

The Beck Depression Inventory (BDI) (Beck et al. 1961) is one of the most frequently used self-report measures of depression in the psychiatric literature (Shaw et al. 1985). Scale items were clinically derived and designed to measure both attitudes and symptoms of depression. Content areas include vegetative signs, mood, and cognitive symptoms of depression.

Gallagher and associates (1983) studied the appropriateness of using the BDI with an older sample (mean age 68.9 years) seeking psychological treatment. Subjects were classified as not depressed, mildly depressed, and moderate to severely depressed using BDI cutoff scores. Categories of depression as determined by the BDI were then compared with diagnoses of depression utilizing the Research Diagnostic Criteria (RDC) (Spitzer et al. 1978). Findings indicated that only 16.7 percent of the subjects were misclassified by BDI cutoff scores. The BDI was most accurate in classifying major depressive episodes, and least accurate in classifying minor depressive episodes. Gallagher and associates conclude that the BDI is useful as a screening instrument for depression in older adults.

Despite its promise, the BDI does have some disadvantages for use with older adults, particularly for rehabilitation populations. The rating scale format of the BDI requires subjects to make relatively fine distinctions between items which may be confusing for the older patient. Patients must also have sufficient short-term memory to retain the definitions between points on a rating scale for a given item. Patients need sufficient reading skill and visual acuity to complete the BDI. The length of the BDI might be fatiguing for an older patient to complete, particularly if mental and physical stamina are low secondary to physical illness. In order to circumvent some of these problems, the BDI can be administered verbally, and a 13-item short form of the inventory can be used (Beck and Beck 1972).

Self-Rating Depression Scale

The Self-Rating Depression Scale (SDS) (Zung 1965) is a self-administered questionnaire that was originally designed to assess the severity of depression in subjects with a primary diagnosis of depressive disorder. The scale is intended to sample depressive symptoms from three domains: affect (2 items); somatic complaints (8 items); and psychological state (10 items).

Zung and Zung (1986) summarized studies which used the SDS to assess depression in older adults. They concluded that the SDS can be used with most older subjects, and has adequate concurrent validity with other measures of geriatric depression. Cross-sectional studies indicated that SDS scores were relatively stable until age 60, after which they increased with age. Zung and Zung interpreted this finding (increasing depression after age 60) as evidence of construct validity for the SDS. Consequently, clinicians using the SDS should be aware of Zung and Zung making the questionable assumption that increased depression is a normal part of later life, and that scores on the SDS will naturally be higher for older individuals.

Hamilton Rating Scale for Depression

The Hamilton Rating Scale for Depression (HRSD) (Hamilton 1960) is probably the most widely used interview measure of depression (Shaw et al. 1985). The scale was originally designed by Hamilton to assess the severity of depression in patients already diagnosed as depressed. Therefore, the scale was not originally intended as a diagnostic measure. The HRSD is completed following an interview with a patient, which Hamilton (1960) estimates to be approximately 30 minutes in duration. Although Hamilton suggested some guidelines for conducting the interview, he did not provide a standardized method for administration. In an attempt to standardize the administration of the HRSD, Whisman and associates (1989) have outlined a more structured format for the HRSD interview.

Hedlund and Vieweg (1979) provide a comprehensive review of the psychometric properties of the HRSD based on published studies. The HRSD was found to differentiate depressed individuals from normals. It also was sensitive to change in depression following psychopharmacological treatment of depression. O'Hara and Rehm (1983) found that acceptable levels of inter-rater reliability (r = .76) could be obtained for the HRSD using undergraduates with five hours of training. Inter-rater reliability coefficients increase with the raters' level of formal training (Ziegler et al. 1978).

The HRSD has had limited application with older adults, although results are generally encouraging. Agrell and Dehlin (1989) found that the HRSD correlated significantly (r = .65) with a global rating of depression derived from clinical examination in a sample of geriatric stroke patients. They also determined that the concurrent validity of the HRSD was relatively good as demonstrated by high positive correlations with other measures of depression, such as the Geriatric Depression Scale (r = .77), the Zung Self-Rating Scale (r = .70), and the Center for Epidemiological Studies Depression Scale (r = .74). Despite this promising preliminary data, the HRSD does have some disadvantages in its use with geriatric patients. The scale contains many somatic items, such as weight loss and insomnia, that could artificially inflate the depression scores of medically ill elders.

Comparisons among Measures of Depression with Older Adults

The development of specific measures to assess depression in older adults, as well as the application of existing measures to this population, has led to several studies which compare the relative merit of specific measures. For example, Rapp and associates (1988) found relatively high positive intercorrelations between the BDI, SDS, and GDS (ranging from .74 to .80) in a sample of geriatric medical inpatients. All three instruments showed moderate sensitivity and specificity, and psychometric properties were judged adequate. Internal consistency, concurrent validity, and discriminant validity were also at acceptable levels. However, the GDS and BDI both had somewhat higher reliability and validity coefficients than the SDS, and may be the most efficient of the screening instruments studied. In addition, Rapp and associates suggest that the somatic items on the BDI may be useful in diagnosing depression with frail elders, given the findings that somatic symptoms did differentiate between depressed and nondepressed patients using the Research Diagnostic Criteria.

Dunn and Sacco (1989) compared the psychometric properties of the GDS and SDS with a sample of older community based residents attending an adult activity center (mean age of 74 years). The internal consistency of each measure was good, although the correlation between the SDS and GDS was somewhat lower than reported elsewhere (r = .59). They also compared the scores from the SDS and GDS for the young-old (age 60 to 74) and the old-old (age 75 and above) in their sample. Neither scale showed significant differences between these two groups. Dunn and Sacco did find that there was a greater percentage of unanswered items for the SDS as compared to the GDS.

Agrell and Dehlin (1989) compared the validity of three examiner-rating scales of depression (Hamilton Rating Scale for Depression, the Comprehensive Psychopathological Rating Scale—Depression, and the Cornell Scale) with three self-rating scales (the Geriatric Depression Scale, the Zung Self-Rating Depression Scale, and the Center for Epidemiologic Studies Depression Scale) in a sample of 40 geriatric stroke patients. Subjects were selected from an outpatient day hospital, a geriatric rehabilitation unit, and a nursing home. All patients had sustained a stroke within 4 months to 2 1/2 years (mean of 14 months). Each instrument was compared with a clinical examination of the patient, resulting in a global rating of depression. Results showed that all instruments had a highly positive correlation with the global ratings of depression except for the Cornell Scale. This scale also had low intercorrelations with all other measures.

The decision as to which instrument to use when assessing depression with geriatric patients depends upon a number of factors including the purpose of the assessment (diagnosis versus measuring severity), the cognitive ability of the patient, and the importance of norms specialized to older adults. Self-report instruments such as the Beck Depression Inventory and the Geriatric Depression Scale will not be appropriate with cognitively compromised patients who do not have the intellectual capacity to follow the format. In these cases, the Hamilton Rating Scale for Depression, or another appropriate observation rating scale, may be more useful. The GDS does have the advantage of being normed on a geriatric population, and has no somatic items. The absence of somatic items is particularly helpful when assessing geriatric rehabilitation patients since they frequently have multiple medical problems of a chronic nature. The GDS also has the advantage of a simple yes/no format which reduces the chances of confusion over the meaning of degree points on a rating scale. The GDS and BDI also have superior psychometric properties as compared with the Zung Self-Rating Depression Scale.

The mental health professional in a rehabilitation setting is often confronted with the task of assessing depression in geriatric patients who have significant cognitive and/or communication deficits. In these cases, psychometric instruments will not be appropriate and the clinical interview, as well as other nontraditional and creative approaches, will be required. For example, unobtrusive observation of the patient on the nursing unit or during therapy can provide valuable information on the patient's emotional status, social functioning, and level of interest in activities. Soliciting feedback from the treatment team can also be a source of information when assessing depression, although caution must be exercised when relying upon impressions that might be less psychologically sophisticated or based on therapists' projections. Also, family members can provide important information on the patient's behavior and mood over time, and give a picture of the course of the patient's adjustment. Family members are also valuable sources of data on the patient's pre-illness personality and characteristic patterns of coping. They can assist the clinician in understanding how the patient coped with significant losses in the past, and whether the patient was predisposed to developing depressive symptoms in these situations.

TREATMENT OF DEPRESSION IN GERIATRIC REHABILITATION PATIENTS

Prompt treatment of depression is critical for successful rehabilitation outcomes with older adults. If a depression is allowed to continue, the older rehabilitation patient will have difficulty mobilizing the energy necessary to fully participate in a rehabilitation program. Such patients eventually become regarded by staff as lazy, unmotivated, or difficult patients, and therapeutic efforts are abruptly or gradually withdrawn. The following section addresses various treatments for depression in the geriatric rehabilitation patient (refer to Chapter 11 for a more psychodynamic approach to treatment).

Psychopharmacological Interventions

Historically, drug therapy has been the most frequently chosen course of action for management of depression in older adults (Blazer 1982). Tricyclics are most often prescribed, but, to a lesser extent, late life depressions are also treated with Monoamine Oxidase Inhibitors (MAOIs), stimulants, and lithium. Despite the use of these medications with elders, there is limited experimental research on their efficacy with this population (Veith 1982) and very limited research on their use with geriatric rehabilitation patients. Table 9-2 lists frequently prescribed antidepressants and their recommended dosages for geriatric patients.

There is a good deal of clinical evidence that antidepressant medications can have a number of adverse side effects when used with older adults (Gerner 1984; Salzman 1985). Anticholinergic side effects of tricyclic antidepressants include confusion, delirium, cognitive impairment, tachycardia, orthostatic hypotension, urinary retention, constipation, and worsening of glaucoma (Jenike 1988; Blazer 1982). Side effects such as postural hypotension can be especially problematic with older adults because they can lead to falls and possible fractures. In addition, proper dosing and the risk of polypharmacy (given the multitude of drugs prescribed to older adults) are frequent problems in the use of psychoactive medications with elders.

The inpatient rehabilitation setting does present unique problems when considering the use of antidepressants. Length of admission can be relatively brief (two to three weeks) which makes regulation of dosages and monitoring of potential side effects difficult. Also, the length of time required to ascertain the

Table 9-2 Antidepressants and Their Recommended Dosages for Geriatric Patients

Category	Generic Name	Brand Name	Dose Range (mg/day)
Tricyclics	Imipramine	Tofranil	25–300
	Desipramine	Norpramin	10–300
	Amitriptyline	Elavil	25–300
	Nortriptyline	Aventyl	10–150
	Doxepin	Sinequan	10–300
	Trimipramine	Surmontil	25–300
	Protriptyline	Triptil	10–40
Dibenzoxazepine	Amoxapine	Asendin	50–300
Tetracyclic	Maprotiline	Ludiomil	25–100
MAO Inhibitor	Phenelzine	Nardil	15–90
	Isocarboxazid	Marplan	10–60
	Tranylcypromine	Parnate	10–60
Trizazolopyridine	Trazodone	Desyrel	50–600
Bicyclic	Fluoxetine Hydrochloride	Prozac	Not Established

Sources: Davidson 1989, and Bezchlibnyk-Butler 1990.

benefit of antidepressant medication (often two to four weeks) makes it an inefficient adjunctive treatment in rehabilitation where there is an imperative for rapid, consistent involvement in therapies. The potential interactions between antidepressant medications and existing medications, such as antihypertensives, are frequently encountered problems. Finally, the multitude of chronic medical problems which are often present in older patients is another complicating factor when prescribing antidepressants since these medications can exacerbate existing medical conditions. For example, it is important to consider a limited medical work-up for cardiovascular status to assure adequate tolerance of commonly used tricyclic antidepressants.

Despite the preceding caution, limited evidence exists that antidepressant medications *can* be effective in treating depression in geriatric rehabilitation patients. For example, Lakshmanan and associates (1986) studied a sample of inpatients age 70 years or older who were part of a general medical rehabilitation unit. They found that low doses of doxepin over a three-week interval significantly reduced depressive symptoms compared with a placebo control group.

Electroconvulsive therapy (ECT) is another somatic treatment of depression with older adults. Although there is evidence (Weiner 1982) that ECT may be effective with certain types of late-life depression (major depression with melancholia, major depression with psychotic symptoms), it is not the treatment of choice initially, and should only be prescribed when other treatment modalities have been exhausted (Blazer 1989). ECT is rarely considered a treatment option in older rehabilitation patients, due to the number of complicating medical conditions (e.g., cardiac compromise) that are frequently encountered.

Environmental Interventions

Manipulations of the patient's environment can reduce feelings of helplessness and depression in the rehabilitation setting by facilitating a greater sense of mastery and control. According to a number of psychological theories (Deci 1980; Seligman 1975; White 1959) those people who possess a greater sense of control are better adapted and have a greater sense of well-being compared to those who experience less control. Geriatric rehabilitation patients are especially predisposed to feeling loss of control of their environments due to sensory, cognitive, and physical deficits, as well as the effects of institutionalization. There is a growing body of research on the effects of control on the adjustment of older adults in institutional settings (see White and Janson 1986 for a review). For example, Langer and Rodin (1976) demonstrated that when nursing home residents were given responsibility for a task (care of a plant) they showed significantly more activity, happiness, and alertness as compared with a non-responsibility control group.

The rehabilitation setting can present numerous opportunities for manipulation of environments, activities, and relationships to provide patients with a greater sense of control. For example, placement of objects such as call lights, telephones, bed controls, or assistive devices within reach allows patients to experience more control over their immediate environment. A sense of responsibility can also be engendered through participation in the planning of treatment goals. Providing patients with a voice in decisions about food, medical routines, scheduling of activities, and therapy tasks also provides a sense of control over their lives in the hospital. Members of a treatment team should not underestimate the impact of allowing a patient to make what may seem like a relatively minor decision.

When designing environmental interventions to increase feelings of control in older rehabilitation patients, it is important to match the opportunity for increased control to the level of the patient's functional abilities. If patients are expected to perform tasks that exceed their capacities due to disability, then a sense of failure and feelings of inadequacy are likely to result. Patients should not be inadvertently set up for failure experiences by the treatment team. In addition, patients cannot be expected to exert control over situations in which they have no control (frequently found in an institutional setting).

Behavioral Interventions

Behavioral interventions focus upon reducing depressive symptoms and sustaining positive reinforcers for the patient's efforts. It is easy to understand how the depressed older rehabilitation patient would find fewer activities reinforcing and emit fewer behaviors. The newly disabled elder is likely to discover that many formerly pleasurable activities such as speaking, eating, and ambulation are now aversive or punishing experiences. As these behaviors are no longer found to be reinforcing in the same manner as before, their frequency of occurrence decreases until they stop completely (extinction). The treatment team is faced with the task of finding reinforcers that will increase the likelihood of performance of target behaviors.

Potential reinforcers that can be utilized by the treatment team include verbal praise and encouragement, attention, and the opportunity to talk about a favorite topic. Observation of the patient in nontherapy situations can also provide clues as to possible reinforcers that can be integrated into therapy sessions.

The identification of activities which patients found pleasurable prior to their illness is another step in treating depression in geriatric rehabilitation patients. This can be accomplished by encouraging patients to discuss their daily routines before their illness, with particular emphasis on those activities or events that gave them enjoyment. These activities may include visits from family, going to lunch with friends, participation in church activities, cooking, reading, or listening to music. Family members are also a good source of information regarding activities that patients found pleasurable. Patients may express feelings of hopelessness when reviewing former activities, believing that these activities are no longer attainable. At these times, the application of cognitive approaches (to be discussed next) can counter these expressions of hopelessness.

It should not be assumed that all tasks are equally reinforcing for all patients, particularly with older adults whose interests and activities may become more restricted and defined over time. An indiscriminant approach to activity programs is not likely to reduce depressive symptoms with disabled older adults (Woods and Britton 1985). Therapists should explore the meaning that the activity has for the patient before prescribing it.

Behavioral approaches with geriatric rehabilitation patients can also focus on the development of social skills, including communication techniques and assertiveness training. The enhancement of social skills might be especially useful with disabled elders, who frequently become increasingly withdrawn when confronted with a newly acquired disability. Patients can be encouraged to practice social and communication skills with other patients and staff during their inpatient stay. With overly compliant and passive patients, assertiveness training can be useful in teaching them how to get needs met in an institutional environment.

Cognitive-Behavioral Interventions

Cognitive-behavioral treatments of depression center on the identification of dysfunctional automatic thoughts, evaluation of their reasonableness, and substitution of more realistic beliefs. This approach has been applied successfully with nondisabled elders (Gallagher and Thompson 1982; Steuer et al. 1984).

Older rehabilitation patients are particularly susceptible to expressing negative self-statements about themselves, their future, and their world. They often incorporate beliefs about themselves, such as "I am too old for rehabilitation"; "I am too sick to participate"; "I cannot do anything for myself"; or "I am not worth your efforts to help me." Dysfunctional beliefs about their future might include "I will never be able to enjoy life again"; or "I have nothing to live for." Maladaptive beliefs about their world can include "therapy is too painful"; or "there are too many things that people are asking me to do." Consequently, older rehabilitation patients may have several of the elements that constitute the negative triad of depression described by Beck (1976).

It becomes the task of the treatment team to help the older rehabilitation patient to examine the reasonableness of these automatic thoughts. Often in rehabilitation, these negative self-statements are articulated during activities outside of the therapy hour (e.g., when a patient is attempting dressing or ambulation). Depending upon the therapist's comfort and expertise in dealing with emotional issues, such thoughts might be questioned and processed at the time they occur or deferred for discussion with a more appropriate team professional. In addressing these thought patterns, the clinician might start by asking the patient to examine the evidence to support a particular conclusion. For example, is the fact that an individual required additional assistance with ambulation on a particular day evidence that the patient is backsliding and will never walk? The clinician can go on to ask the patient to examine alternative explanations for the event (e.g., the assignment of a new therapist, increased fatigue at the end of a therapy hour). Finally, patients might be asked if they are totally to blame for the event. Seligman (1981) notes that depressed persons tend to attribute failure to themselves rather than to external events and view their failures as the result of internal, stable personal characteristics.

Further treatment of depression in the older rehabilitation patient could focus on the substitution of more reasonable beliefs in place of dysfunctional thoughts.

Patients can be taught to replace their negative self-statements with more reasonable thoughts based on the available evidence. In the latter stages of treatment, patients might be taught to identify and modify "silent" assumptions which influence their world view. For instance, patients may examine the belief that they are unworthy or unlovable because they have a hemiplegia resulting from a stroke.

Cognitive-behavioral therapy will not be applicable to all geriatric rehabilitation patients. This approach requires that the patient have some capacity for self-reflection, the ability to generate and communicate alternative interpretations, and the intellectual capacity to understand the concepts involved. Cognitive-behavioral therapy probably works best with those elders who are verbal, well educated, and middle class (Gallagher and Thompson 1982). This approach may also work well with patients who utilize higher level defense mechanisms, such as intellectualization and rationalization (Lazarus 1989).

Family Interventions

Families play a critical role in the rehabilitation process, and their reaction to a disabled member has a significant impact on treatment outcome. The importance of the family in rehabilitation is no less significant for the older disabled patient, particularly when depressed. Blazer (1982) discusses the role of the mental health professional in family therapy with depressed older adults. Blazer emphasizes the need for accurate assessment of the family system, including family structure, quality of family interaction, family values, and degree of family support and tolerance for the older member. The identification of the various roles that family members play (e.g., patient, caretaker, facilitator, escapee) is important when attempting to understand the dynamics of the family in rehabilitation. Family conflicts and unresolved emotional issues (e.g., control, dependency, abandonment) that have been dormant for many years may reappear when a family is confronted with the stress of a newly disabled elder. Treatment of a family with a depressed elder member can include education about depression, emotional support for stressed family members, identification of unresolved family issues, counseling for these issues, and giving permission for respite to caregivers.

CONCLUSION AND RECOMMENDATIONS FOR
FURTHER RESEARCH

This chapter has emphasized the importance of prompt diagnosis and aggressive treatment of depression in geriatric rehabilitation patients. The chances of successful rehabilitation outcomes are greatly diminished if depression goes undetected and untreated. Older patients will be prevented from realizing their full rehabilitation potential if depression is a significant component of their clinical picture and is regarded as an inevitable untreatable consequence of their physical disability.

In order to enhance the probability of accurate diagnosis of depression in this population, clinicians and researchers need to devise better methods of assessment, including more valid psychometric instruments which are not overly sensitive to somatic symptoms. The development of observational scales to assess depression in older rehabilitation patients would be especially useful when applied to patients with cognitive and/or communication deficits. Treatment approaches need to be systematically evaluated, with special attention given to the differential effectiveness of various types of interventions for a geriatric rehabilitation population. In addition, the factors which might be predictive of the development of depression in older rehabilitation patients, such as lack of a confidant, need to be identified so that treatment strategies can be devised to address these variables.

REFERENCES

Abrahamson, L.Y., M.E.P. Seligman, and J. Teasdale. 1978. Learned helplessness in humans: Critique and reformulation. *Journal of Abnormal Psychology* 87: 49–74.

Agrell, B., and O. Dehlin. 1989. Comparison of six depression rating scales in geriatric stroke patients. *Stroke* 20: 1190–4.

American Psychiatric Association. 1987. *Diagnostic and Statistical Manual of Mental Disorders*, 3d ed., revised. Washington, D.C.: American Psychiatric Association.

Ban, T. 1984. Chronic disease and depression in the geriatric population. *Journal of Clinical Psychiatry* 45: 18–23.

Beck, A.T. 1967. *Depression: Clinical, Experimental, and Theoretical Aspects*. New York: Harper and Row.

Beck, A.T. 1976. *Cognitive Theory and the Emotional Disorders*. New York: International Universities Press.

Beck, A.T., and R.W. Beck. 1972. Screening depressed patients in family practice. A rapid technique. *Postgraduate Medicine* 52: 81–5.

Beck, A.T., C.H. Ward, M. Mendelson, et al. 1961. An inventory for measuring depression. *Archives of General Psychiatry* 4: 561–71.

Bezchlibnyk-Butler, K.Z., J.J. Jeffries, S.B. Bredin, et al. 1990. *Clinical Handbook of Psychotropic Drugs*, 2d ed. Toronto: Hogrefe & Huber.

Blazer, D.G. 1982. *Depression in Late Life*. St. Louis: C.V. Mosby.

Blazer, D.G. 1989. Affective disorders in late life. In *Geriatric Psychiatry*, edited by E.W. Busse and D.G. Blazer, 369–401. Washington, D.C.: American Psychiatric Press.

Blazer, D.G., and C. Williams. 1980. The epidemiology of dysphoria and depression in an elderly population. *American Journal of Psychiatry* 137: 439–44.

Brown, J.T., and A. Stoudemire. 1983. Normal and pathological grief. *Journal of the American Medical Association* 239: 213–16.

Caplan, B. 1983. Staff and patient perception of patient mood. *Rehabilitation Psychology* 28: 68–77.

Chaisson-Stewart, G.M. 1985. Tragedies of inappropriate or inadequate treatment. In *Depression in the Elderly: An Interdisciplinary Approach*, edited by G.M. Chaisson-Stewart, 44–55. New York: John Wiley and Sons.

Christison, C., and D.G. Blazer. 1988. Clinical assessment of psychiatric symptoms. In *Geriatric Neuropsychology*, edited by M.S. Albert and M.B. Moss, 82–99. New York: Guilford Press.

Cummings, J.L., and D.F. Benson. 1983. *Dementia: A Clinical Approach*. Boston: Butterworth.

Davidson, J. 1989. The pharmacologic treatment of psychiatric disorders in the elderly. In *Geriatric Psychiatry*, edited by E.W. Busse and D.G. Blazer, 524. Washington, D.C.: American Psychiatric Press.

Deci, E.L. 1980. *The Psychology of Self-Determination*. Lexington, Mass.: Heath.

Dunn, V.K., and W.P. Sacco. 1989. Psychometric evaluation of the Geriatric Depression Scale and the Zung Self-Rating Depression Scale using an elderly community sample. *Psychology and Aging* 4: 125–6.

Feinberg, T., and B. Goodman. 1984. Affective illness, dementia and pseudodementia. *Journal of Clinical Psychiatry* 45: 100–3.

Freud, S. 1959. Mourning and melancholia. In *Sigmund Freud: Collected Papers*, vol. 4, edited by E. Jones, 152–70. New York: Basic Books.

Gallagher, D., J. Breckenridge, J. Steinmetz, et al. 1983. The Beck Depression Inventory and Research Diagnostic Criteria: Congruence in an older population. *Journal of Consulting and Clinical Psychology* 51: 945–6.

Gallagher, D., and L.W. Thompson. 1982. Treatment of major depressive disorder in older adult outpatients with brief psychotherapies. *Psychotherapy: Theory, Research, and Practice* 19:482–90.

Gans, J. S. 1981. Depression diagnosis in a rehabilitation hospital. *Archives of Physical Medicine and Rehabilitation* 62: 386–9.

Gerner, R.H. 1984. Antidepressant selection in the elderly. *Psychosomatics* 25: 528–35.

Hamilton, M. 1960. A rating scale for depression. *Journal of Neurology, Neurosurgery and Psychiatry* 12: 56–62.

Hedlund, J.L. and B.W. Vieweg. 1979. The Hamilton Rating Scale for Depression: A comprehensive review. *Journal of Operational Psychiatry* 10: 149–62.

Jenike, M. 1988. Depression and other psychiatric disorders. In *Geriatric Neuropsychology*, edited by M.S. Albert and M.B. Moss, 115–44. New York, Guilford Press.

Kahana, E., V. Leibowitz, and M. Alter. 1971. Cerebral multiple sclerosis. *Neurology* 21: 1179–85.

Klerman, G.L. 1983. Problems in the definition and diagnosis of depression in the elderly. In *Depression and Aging: Causes, Care, and Consequences*, edited by L.D. Breslau and M.R. Haug, 3–19. New York: Springer Publishing.

Lakshmanan, M., L.C. Mion, and J.D. Frengley. 1986. Effective low dose Tricyclic antidepressant treatment for depressed geriatric rehabilitation patients. *Journal of the American Geriatrics Society* 34: 421–6.

Langer, E.J.,and J. Rodin. 1976. The effects of choice and enhanced personal responsibility for the aged: A field experiment in an institutionalized setting. *Journal of Personality and Social Psychology* 34: 191–8.

Lazarus, L.W. 1989. Psychotherapy with geriatric patients in the ambulatory care setting. In *Geriatric Psychiatry*, edited by E.W. Busse and D.G. Blazer, 567–91. Washington, D.C.: American Psychiatric Press.

Lewinsohn, P.M., T. Biglan, and A. Zeiss. 1976. Behavioral treatment of depression. In *Behavioral Management of Anxiety, Depression, and Pain*, edited by P. Davidson, 91–146. New York: Brunner/Mazel.

Lewinsohn, P.M., H.M. Hoberman, L. Teri, et al. 1985. An integrative theory of depression. In *Theoretical Issues in Behavior Therapy*, edited by R.R. Bootzin and S. Reiss, 331–59. New York: Academic Press.

Lewinsohn, P.M., M.S. Weinstein, and D.A. Shaw. 1969. Depression: A clinical-research approach. In *Advances in Behavior Therapy*, edited by R.D. Rubin and C.M. Frank, 231–49. New York: Academic Press.

Lezak, M.D. 1978. Subtle sequelae of brain damage: Perplexity, distractibility, and fatigue. *American Journal of Physical Medicine* 57: 9–15.

Mindham, R.S. 1974. Psychiatric aspects of Parkinson's disease. *British Journal of Hospital Medicine* 11: 411–14.

Meyers, B.S., B. Kalayam, and V. Mei-Tal. 1984. Late-onset delusional depression: A distinct clinical entity? *Journal of Clinical Psychiatry* 45: 347–9.

Newmann, J.P. 1989. Aging and depression. *Psychology and Aging* 4: 150–65.

O'Hara, M.W., and L.P. Rehm. 1983. Hamilton Rating Scale for Depression: Reliability and validity judgements of novice raters. *Journal of Consulting and Clinical Psychology* 51: 318–19.

Ouslander, J.G. 1984. Physical illness and depression in the elderly. *Journal of the American Geriatrics Society* 30: 593–9.

Peterson, C., and M.E.P. Seligman. 1985. The learned helplessness model of depression: Current status of theory and research. In *Handbook of Depression: Treatment, Assessment, and Research*, edited by E.E. Beckham and W.R. Leber, 914–39. Homewood, Ill.: Dorsey Press.

Phifer, J.F., and S.A. Murrell. 1986. Etiologic factors in the onset of depressive symptoms in older adults. *Journal of Abnormal Psychology* 95: 282–91.

Radloff, L.S. 1977. The CES-D Scale: A self-report depression scale for research in the general population. *Applied Psychological Measurement* 1: 358–401.

Rapp, S.R., S.A. Parisi, D.A. Walsh, et al. 1988. Detecting depression in elderly medical inpatients. *Journal of Consulting and Clinical Psychology* 56: 509–13.

Reding, M., J. Haycox, and J. Blass. 1985. Depression in patients referred to a dementia clinic: A three-year prospective study. *Archives of Neurology* 42: 894–6.

Robinson, R.G., and D.F. Benson. 1981. Depression in aphasic patients: Frequency, severity, and clinico-pathological correlations. *Brain and Language* 14: 282–91.

Salzman, C. 1985. Clinical guidelines for the use of antidepressant drugs in geriatric patients. *Journal of Clinical Psychiatry* 46: 38–44.

Seligman, M.E.P. 1975. *Helplessness: On Depression, Development, and Death*. San Francisco: W.H. Freeman.

Seligman, M.E.P. 1981. A learned helplessness point of view. In *Behavior Therapy for Depression: Present Status and Future Directions*, edited by L.P. Rehm, 123–41. New York: Academic Press.

Seligman, M.E.P., and S.F. Maier. 1967. Failure to escape traumatic shock. *Journal of Experimental Psychology* 74: 1–9.

Shaw, B.F., T.M. Vallis, and S.B. McCabe. 1985. The assessment of the severity and symptom patterns in depression. In *Handbook of Depression: Treatment, Assessment, and Research*, edited by E.E. Beckham and W.R. Leber, 372–407. Homewood, Ill.: Dorsey Press.

Spitzer, R.L., J. Endicott, and E. Robbins. 1978. Research and Diagnostic Criteria: Rationale and reliability. *Archives of General Psychiatry* 35: 773–82.

Steuer, J.L., J. Mintz, C.L. Hammen, et al. 1984. Cognitive-behavioral and psychodynamic group psychotherapy in treatment of geriatric depression. *Journal of Consulting and Clinical Psychology* 52: 180–9.

Stoudemire, A., and D.G. Blazer. 1985. Depression in the elderly. In *Handbook of Depression: Treatment, Assessment, and Research*, edited by E.E. Beckham and W.R. Leber, 556–86. Homewood, Ill.: Dorsey Press.

Turner, R.J., S. Noh, and D.M. Levin. 1985. Depression across the life course: The significance of psychosocial factors among the physically disabled. In *Depression in Multidisciplinary Perspective*, edited by A. Dean, 32–59. New York: Brunner/Mazel.

Veith, R.C. 1982. Depression in the elderly: Pharmacologic considerations in treatment. *Journal of the American Geriatrics Society* 30: 581–6.

Weiner, R.D. 1982. The role of electroconvulsive therapy in the treatment of depression in the elderly. *Journal of the American Geriatrics Society* 30: 710–12.

Wells, C.E. 1979. Pseudodementia. *American Journal of Psychiatry* 136: 895–900.

Whisman, M.A., K. Strosahl, A.E. Fruzzetti, et al. 1989. A structured interview version of the Hamilton Rating Scale for Depression: Reliability and validity. *Psychological Assessment: A Journal of Consulting and Clinical Psychology* 1: 238–41.

White, C.B., and P. Janson. 1986. Helplessness in institutional settings: Adaptation or iatrogenic disease? In *The Psychology of Control and Aging*, edited by M.M. Baltes and P.B. Baltes, 297–313. Hillsdale, N.J.: Lawrence Erlbaum.

White, R.W. 1959. Motivation reconsidered: The concept of competence. *Psychology Review* 66: 297–333.

Woods, R.T., and P.G. Britton. 1985. *Clinical Psychology with the Elderly*. Gaithersburg, Md: Aspen Publishers.

Yesavage, J.A., T.L. Brink, T.L. Rose, et al. 1983. Development and validation of a geriatric depression screening scale. *Journal of Psychiatric Research* 17: 37–49.

Zetzel, E. 1965. Metapsychology of aging. In *Geriatric Psychiatry*, edited by M.A. Berezin and S. Cath, 109–18. New York: International Universities Press.

Ziegler, V.E., D.A. Meyer, S.H. Rosen, et al. 1978. Reliability of video taped Hamilton ratings. *Biological Psychiatry* 13: 119–22.

Zung, W.W.K. 1965. A self-rating depression scale. *Archives of General Psychiatry* 12: 63–70.

Zung, W.W.K. 1980. Affective disorders. In *Handbook of Geriatric Psychiatry*, edited by E.W. Busse and D.G. Blazer, 338–367. New York: Van Nostrand Reinhold Co.

Zung, W.W.K., and E.M. Zung. 1986. Use of the Zung Self-Rating Depression Scale in the elderly. *Clinical Gerontologist* 5: 137–48.

Chapter 10

Transference and Countertransference in the Therapeutic Relationship with the Older Adult

Michael Horowitz

Development of an effective therapeutic relationship is essential in working with the older adult in a rehabilitation setting. It is apparent, however, that such helping relationships can be filled with difficulty, despite the supposed agreement of all parties concerned regarding who needs help and who is qualified to provide it.

This chapter focuses on *transference* and *countertransference* as they emerge in working with older adults in a rehabilitation setting. These two core concepts of psychoanalysis have been distilled for use in many areas of psychological work. They have not fully been capitalized upon, however, in medical or physical rehabilitation settings. It is hoped that this chapter will further the integration of these concepts into mainstream psychological work in rehabilitation settings.

Transference is typically defined as the patient's displacement of unconscious feelings, attitudes, and reaction onto the therapist. This phenomenon is thought to be a repetition of earlier primary relationships and reveals the patient's neurosis (Freud 1966). Transferences can involve both positive and negative feelings such as attachment, idealization, feelings of anger, or resentment. Therapeutic progress is made through an exploration and clarification of these distorted feelings. Countertransference is defined as the involvement of the therapist's own unconscious conflicts in the psychotherapeutic relationship, prompted by the patient's transference. It is generally accepted that therapists must be aware of how their own needs enter into relationships with patients in order to effectively work with them (Langs 1981).

Broader definitions of transference and countertransference are useful when considering them as part of patient/staff relationships in physical rehabilitation. In this situation, where there are a variety of therapy relationships (e.g., patient-psychologist, patient-nurse, patient-physiatrist, etc.), transference will be defined as the characteristic emotional style that the patient adopts toward any one of the different helping professionals encountered during the crisis of physical impairment. The stress of physical disability will prompt universal transference themes as well as stimulate dormant transference material unique to the individual. For example, seeking affection and physical closeness from staff may be a result of the patient's regression to infancy when mother was always present to provide physical attention.

Countertransference will be largely considered as the emotional response of the helping professional to the patient. The concept is further broadened to consider universal countertransference material in response to a physically damaged older adult, as well as more specific reactions unique to the individual rehabilitation therapist. An example would be the rehabilitation therapist who is easily frustrated by certain patients and had ailing parents who spurned their child's suggestions for improving their health.

Therapeutic relationships with older adults become fertile ground for many transferential issues in the rehabilitation setting. Communication in this setting is prone to confusion due to a number of factors:

1. Relationships between staff and patient are heightened by the stress of the onset of physical disability.
2. Staff and patient are placed in a situation of accelerated intimacy.
3. Functions normally private, such as toileting, are now very public.
4. Therapists are typically far younger than their patients.
5. Long-term patterns of living have often recently been disrupted.
6. Mortality is not just contemplated but stared in the face.
7. Continued life with a new disability awaits.

These and many other factors make for strong fluid transference reactions on the part of both patients and staff. The rehabilitation setting complicates what are already unique therapy relationships—when young therapists meet much older patients (Horowitz and Grunes 1987).

As described by Gans (1987) and Gunther (1987), the circumstances of the patient, the staff and the setting all contribute to this conflictual milieu. The patient faced with the emotional catastrophe of physical loss can regress to irrational, immature ways of coping and become emotionally volatile, disorganized, and needy. The staff are, in contrast, usually young, healthy, very goal-directed, and seemingly in control. They are consolidating their own identities and often have not yet experienced significant developmental milestones, such as commitment to a long-term relationship, parenting, grieving the loss of a significant other, or even aging itself. Their training in developing a therapeutic alliance may be minimal, and they often inaccurately look toward the success of their patients as the main measure of their professional competence. Nonmental health professionals account for the bulk of patient therapy contact time in a rehabilitation setting and these various specialists (physical therapists, nurses, physicians, occupational therapists, speech therapists, etc.) can engage in actions that, while routine for them, are highly provocative for the patient—toileting, dressing, moving a paralyzed or amputated limb, or in other ways confronting a deficit.

Finally, the setting itself can create stress due to the tension of emphasizing dependent, compliant behavior in the patient, while promoting the ethic of maximal independence. The patients can often find themselves in the position of hearing both "do as I say" and "think for yourself" from the staff. In fact, to use developmental stages as a metaphor, acute hospitalization is reminiscent of childhood with its restrictions and dependence. Rehabilitation is a type of adolescence culminating in a figurative adulthood represented by final discharge from the hospital and return to the community (Horowitz and Hartke 1988).

Failure to account for the dynamics of a rehabilitation relationship can sabotage otherwise well-formulated plans and lead to unexplained resistance, noncompliance, and/or benign social interaction in place of therapy. This chapter will present clinical examples and some tools for undoing psychodynamic barriers to effective rehabilitation treatment of the older adult. While rehabilitation mental health professionals may be most focused on these issues, the entire treatment team plays an important role in the constructive use of transference and countertransference.

FOUNDATIONS

Discussion of transference and countertransference in treatment of the older adult has received little attention to date in the psychological literature. The extant literature has focused primarily on overcoming a general bias against insight-oriented work with this group of patients (e.g., Pollock 1980). A group of mental health practitioners (e.g., Blau and Berezin 1982; Breslau 1980; Cath and Miller 1986; Gurian 1986; Hildebrand 1982; Hinze 1987; Knight 1986; Levin 1986; Sandler 1982; Sobel 1980; Wylie and Wylie 1987) have by now assembled a body of literature focusing on insight-oriented psychological treatment of the older adult. But as Colarusso and Nemiroff (1987, 1263) point out:

These ideas are just beginning to be integrated with clinical theory and practice. The elaboration of the interface between the rapidly expanding developmental theory of normal adulthood and clinical intervention with older patients is a psychiatric frontier.

Gutmann (1987) is among a growing group of developmental psychogerontologists who demonstrate that the later portion of life heralds continued normal development. The applicable aging literature, while not specifically dealing with physical rehabilitation, clearly suggests that modifying goals and expectations with this population is indicated. Aging is not only accompanied by inevitable losses but also unique developments in personality and world view.

Physical rehabilitation literature is quite understandably sparse on the topic of transference and countertransference in older adults. Gans (1983) made an important contribution to physical rehabilitation literature by openly discussing the common but uncomfortable feelings of hate in the rehabilitation setting. And Gunther (1971, 1977, 1979, 1987, 1988) has almost singlehandedly championed psychodynamic "knowing" in the area of physical rehabilitation. Gunther (1987) and Emener (1979) emphasize the inevitable burnout that results from not taking psychodynamic phenomena into account in work with rehabilitation patients. Knowledge of these depth phenomena is felt by these clinicians to be crucial. While this maxim may sound obvious, it is far from being universally accepted in the field of rehabilitation.

Another area of the literature that relates to transference and countertransference in rehabilitation work is that of prejudicial attitudes toward disability and aging. The formation of negative and patronizing social attitudes toward the disabled (Wright 1983) and older adults (Gutmann 1987) is a significant factor in the development of a negative collective countertransference. For example, Livneh (1982) outlined a number of these attitudes that play a role in creating unconscious conflict when interacting with disabled people. Among these attitudes are: (1) feelings that the disabled person must mourn—"he or she 'ought' to suffer and slowly adjust to such a misfortune" (p.339); and (2) guilt of being "able-bodied" (p.340). The first attitude may be specifically applied to older adults in that many see this phase of the life cycle as inevitably including suffering and incapacitation. Thus the disabled older adult is in danger of being seen by some as not worth the effort of or unable to benefit from treatment. This attitude may contribute to a phobic, avoidant stance vis-à-vis the older disabled individual. The guilt of being able-bodied may be intensified by the guilt of having the youth which the elder patient has lost. This guilt represents an impediment to viewing the older adult more clearly as a viable individual facing age-appropriate challenges. Staff struggling with unconscious guilt are in danger of responding to their own psychic discomfort and not the legitimate needs of the patient.

In dealing with the disabled older adult, one must add the prevalent social feeling that older adults are less worthy of our increasingly scarce treatment resources because they are no longer useful, have less time to live, and so on. They are easier to relegate to the "throwaway" pile of our society. No doubt, anxieties about our own and our parents' and elders' deaths are involved here as well. In the next section unconscious themes specific to working with older adults are examined.

TRANSFERENCE AND COUNTERTRANSFERENCE THEMES
SPECIFIC TO THE OLDER ADULT

In the fast-paced rehabilitation unit, where crises seem to be continuous, alliances can develop rapidly, along with a host of transference and countertransference feelings. Older adults have been noted to maintain the universal parental transference, even with much younger therapists (Apfel et al. 1984). Therapists of older adults must also contend with child and/or deceased spouse transferences. Rehabilitation therapists are faced with these strong emotional transference pulls and the countertransference illusion of facing one's aging or dead parent. They may, therefore, withdraw or overinvolve themselves emotionally, become overly controlling or demanding, or in some other way avoid a realistic examination of the patient's wants and needs.

Gutmann (1988) has proposed that geriatric workers are largely driven by one of two unconscious motivations for working with older adults. *Gerophiles* or lovers of older people have had positive experiences with their elders and wish to return some of what they have received from them by being supportive, giving, and so on. *Gerophobes* are fearful of the aging process. They have missed life experience with elders and are seeking to overcome this deficit. These concepts can be thought of as illustrating two extremes of the countertransference continuum. Both styles protect rehabilitation therapists from anxiety about their own vulnerabilities and may surface alone or in combination. The essential point is that if one is healing older adults, then the fantasy that he or she will not get sick or old is maintained. The gerophobic-gerophilic continuum provides one way of conceptualizing broad countertransference themes in work with older rehabilitation patients.

In the instance of the gerophilic extreme, countertransference may be acted out by being more supportive and controlling than necessary. Such countertransference will prompt more support and backup of the patient than is indicated. In this instance, the latent strengths and functional abilities of older patients may be missed. As an example, consider the older adult who achieves ambulatory status by the time of discharge from the hospital. It is not uncommon to find some of the patient's therapists requesting continued restriction of ambulation on the nursing unit within a day or two of discharge because the patient is viewed as "not quite ready yet." The therapists may harbor the fantasy that the patient will be fully protected by their surveillance, not considering that the patient will be without them very soon. Patients who do not want much help or decline it may be especially frustrating to the rehabilitation therapist with gerophilic tendencies and may provoke feelings of incompetence and low self-esteem. In contrast, the patient may have complaints of feeling patronized or treated as a child.

However, the same rambunctious, feisty patients may be precisely those who invigorate the work of therapists who have a gerophobic bent. This type of therapist is in danger of colluding with the patient in denying deterioration and the aging process. A rapid hospital discharge or avoidance of a lower-level patient may be an expression of gerophobic therapists' frustration at their own impotence to turn back the clock for their elders. Gerophobic therapists may involve themselves disproportionately with the interesting, more intact older patients.

Transference and countertransference dynamics can become complementary, serve to defend both staff and patients from underlying anxieties, and, hence, diminish the therapeutic effectiveness of the relationship. The parental transference of older adults can ignite universal countertransference reactions in younger treatment staff due to the discrepancy in age and roles. The social norm of elders guiding the younger generation is here reversed and can cause therapists to experience anxiety and feelings of inadequacy. In addition, older patients themselves may bring pressure to bear to create a more superficial climate in the therapy relationship, in the service of avoiding the experience of their therapist as a parent. Calling their therapists "honey" or "sonny" and detailing their physical aches and pains, older patients may mask their shame or guilt at being in need of help from someone who is younger. The treatment team may respond in kind by dropping a degree of formality which is important in maintaining the patient's dignity. This informality may represent both parties' attempts to deny their age discrepancy and pretend that they are peers. The team's mental health professional may be in a position to first notice such a dynamic and can therefore model and encourage a more appropriate stance toward the patient. An example of such inappropriate informality may be found in the case of therapists addressing elder patients by their first names or nicknames. Clearly, in any formal therapy situation addressing an older patient by their last name is most appropriate unless the patient clearly states a preference otherwise (and it is apparent to the therapist that this would foster a more adaptive relationship).

Treating staff can have countertransference reactions which complement the patients' fears and can collude with them in avoiding depth in the relationship. On a more conscious level, therapists may feel that they lack the life experience to sensitively help an older patient. At a deeper level, there is the immobilizing anxiety of having to help the parent who one has usually called on for help oneself. Furthermore, there can be panic over developing intimacy (physical or emotional) with the patient. For example, the tendency to avoid discussion of sexual material with this population can be linked to this panic. Regressed patients who act like children can thus be enraging to staff because they ignite these anxieties. These patients are most likely to require a great deal of physical intimacy and contact, as in toileting and dressing.

Another configuration of transference and countertransference feelings exhibited in working with older adults revolves around the patient's pull for the therapist to be a perfect child or spouse. This is often done to compensate for the sins and omissions of real spouses, children, or never-born children. The child transference is usually more idealizing and less ambivalent than the parental transference. But it is, therefore, potentially more burdensome and suffocating to some therapists; to others, it may be more tempting to manipulate for one's gratification and pleasure. Depending on their own conflicts with parental relationships, therapists may take flight from this evocation of guilt and burden by curtailing the treatment and/or trying to overcompensate and actually be the perfect son or daughter. The latter might bring out behavior such as making special requests of other team members on behalf of the patient or joining in condemnation of the patient's children, family, or the younger generation. The rehabilitation social worker, primary nurse, psychologist, and physiatrist who more frequently deal with the patient's family (or absence of family) may be especially vulnerable in this area.

Of major importance in making use of transference and countertransference dynamics is a good understanding of the older adult patient's premorbid personality and attitudes toward illness, aging, and health. The patient has not begun a new life with the onset of disability. Rather a life that has been lived in a particular manner until now has been impacted by disability. The style and behavior adopted by a patient can therefore not be understood merely as resulting from the disability or hospitalization. A well-understood history garnered from the patient and other informants often explains the style exhibited in the hospital and can inform treatment. Depression, for example, is very common in the older adult rehabilitation population. But knowing that a specific patient's depression is the outcome of having a life-long hysterical personality style, which has been disrupted by the disability, may allow the staff to offer some extra attention to the patient's physical appearance and, with minimal effort, relieve some of the depression (see Chapter 9 for a more extensive discussion of the treatment of depression).

It is very important to determine the adaptive value of the particular transference to the patient. What may seem pathological to the treatment team may be psychologically useful to the patient. For example, staff may see a patient who is hypervigilant about being mistreated by them as paranoid and ask the mental health professional in the treatment team to help resolve the paranoia. Closer inspection may reveal that this paranoid patient is projecting feelings of inadequacy and breakdown onto the environment in order to preserve a personal sense of integrity. A little paranoia may, in other words, go a long way in maintaining the psychological equilibrium of the disabled older adult. In this instance, the mental health professional's task may be to explain the nature and value of the patient's transference to the staff and family, not to resolve it. The rehabilitation setting is not necessarily appropriate for intense individual psychotherapy. Vulnerable states and characterological styles should be identified and necessary defenses respected and strengthened, not taken away (see Chapter 11 for further discussion of psychotherapy).

The mental health professional is uniquely able, by virtue of working in a multidisciplinary treatment team, to address the resistance and anxieties of patients and staff. In contrast to other members of the treatment team, mental health professionals most often enter into more reflective, nondemanding relationships with patients where clear, effective communication is given great priority. From this position, the pressure and anxiety of patients and staff can be alleviated by determining which disturbing mechanisms are operating unconsciously. Whether it is staff guilt, patient shame, or another dynamic, the manifest presentation is often some variant of anxiety. Anxiety on the unit should signal exploration of team dynamics.

CONSULTATION AND EDUCATION

While it is necessary to deal with the very pressing external realities in the rehabilitation setting, consideration of the patient's and staff's internal worlds, including transference and countertransference, is bound to increase the overall effectiveness of the team. The team's mental health professional is usually in the best position to understand these phenomena and consult with other members to facilitate understanding of transference/countertransference with the older adult. However, other experienced therapists may recognize the operation of such relationship dynamics and seek assistance with them.

As will be seen in the three case examples to be discussed, consultation may be on an individual case basis, such as being called in on the "problem" or "unmotivated" patient, or in providing an inservice to the treatment team on relationship issues. Conceptualizing transference and countertransference phenomena for a treatment team member can often expand options for resolving therapeutic impasses. Open discussion of these internal psychological processes can promote empathy and tolerance and relieve staff of the perception that they are responsible for changing the patient's behavior. The concept of countertransference can also help nonmental health staff appreciate the impact their attitudes and impressions have upon their behaviors and, hence, relationships with patients. Positive effects of the phenomena can be reinforced. For example, a patient's positive transference toward a team member can be used in an informed way to move through a difficult emotional period while staying focused on the tasks of rehabilitation. Negative effects, such as overinvolvement, avoidance, or rejection of the patient, can be neutralized.

When difficult relationship issues are opened up to staff, it is important that implementation is carried out responsibly. Manipulation of a positive transference must, for example, be weighed against the prospects of the patient functioning well when the transference figure is no longer present. Exploration of negative countertransference should not unleash open hostility toward the patient in question.

Consultation in this area should be done with care for another important reason: it challenges therapists with the potentially threatening task of looking at their own behavior and motivations as well as the patient's. Normalizing the concepts of transference and countertransference may help in this regard. They should be emphasized as normative concepts of everyday life rather than pathological phenomena that are being weeded out among the treatment team. Using less mysterious, analytic terminology and focusing on more universally experienced themes of transference and countertransference also help to relieve treatment team members of the feeling that they alone are subject to such influences. They must be assured that such a consultation will not lead to an indictment of their skill as a clinician. It is also important to emphasize that negative feelings toward their patients are sometimes inevitable, but acting upon those feelings in an uninformed way is clearly and necessarily avoidable.

Gunther (1988) indicates that staff are more likely able to identify with negative countertransference themes linked to characteristics of their patients because they are more salient to the therapist in a problematic therapy relationship. This may be the best place to begin in discussing relationship dynamics. Mental health professionals can facilitate such a discussion by sharing their own negative and difficult feelings about patients. Countertransference material related primarily to therapists' unique unconscious motivations and dynamics may be inappropriate to address as a consultant and colleague. When a therapist's psychological problem does appear to be the major difficulty, the situation is best handled via that team member's supervisor. Options might include a recommendation that the employee in question seek personal psychotherapy or that the patient involved be reassigned.

While individual consultation is usually case-specific, an inservice with the treatment team serves as a broader consciousness raising vehicle. It assists the team members in more strongly taking into account the power of their relationships with patients and appreciating that these relationships play as much of a role as technical skill in successful outcome. An effective inservice format is one that blends didactic explication of the concepts of transference and countertransference, case examples, and guided large or small group discussion. It is critical that the members of the team are able to share experiences and apply the concepts to themselves. Exhibit 10-1 enumerates questions that are suggested to prompt and guide such a discussion.

Exhibit 10-1 Discussion Guide for Staff Inservice

1. What are your feelings about older adults in general?
2. How did you become interested in working with older adults?
3. Who have been significant older adult figures in your life?
4. What are the memorable positive and negative features of the significant older adults you have had in your life?
5. Who do older patients tell you that you remind them of? (e.g., friend, child, spouse, or parent). Is there any consistency across patients in the responses that you get?
6. When treating an older adult which of their personality characteristics:
   (a) make it easy for you to relate to them?
   (b) tend to promote your becoming too emotionally involved?
   (c) make it difficult for you to relate to them?
   (d) make you want to avoid/minimize contact with them?
7. In your clinical experience, identify specific older patients with whom
   (a) you've had difficulty working with or avoided.
   (b) you've worked well with or with whom you've become overinvolved.
8. Can you identify transference or countertransference features of the relationships noted above? Can you think of ways to have better managed or improved the quality of these relationships?
9. Have you ever knowingly used the strength of a very positive relationship with a patient as a "power base" to change their thinking or behavior? How did you feel about this?
10. How do you respond (versus how do you *feel* like responding) when an older adult asks for reassurance or makes self-deprecating comments? How do you think you should respond?

Staff are typically eager to engage in such an interactive discussion. This is an inservice that they can experience as receiving something from the institution, not as a chore. They are being helped with their difficult feelings and their stress, not being required to only learn new information. Again, the use of oneself as an icebreaking example will enhance group participation. Therapists will be relieved to find out that even the mental health professional on a treatment team struggles with internal conflict in working with patients. The consultant conducting this inservice will get a more developed sense of the group psychology of the team and ideas for interventions.

CASE EXAMPLES

The following cases are offered as examples of how the rehabilitation team's mental health professional can intervene in difficult patient/staff relationships by assessing internal and external transference/countertransference dynamics. Depending on the composition of the treatment team, the designated mental health professional may be a consulting psychiatrist, psychologist, social worker, or a clinical nurse practitioner. In these examples, the team's mental health professional works via individual psychotherapy with the patient as well as behavioral and environmental consultation with the team and family. It should be stressed that an intervention based on an understanding of transferential dynamics can have many different manifestations and need not be solely verbal or take place in the psychotherapeutic realm. It is hoped that these examples will highlight the fact that the rehabilitation mental health professional not only works with the patient individually but operates as a consultant to all the parties involved.

Case A

Mr. A. was a 75-year-old retired executive who was active in various leisure activities and volunteered his time as a consultant. Two weeks after suffering a massive hip fracture necessitating a total hip replacement, he was admitted to a rehabilitation unit. He was found to be severely depressed and obsessed with his confinement to a wheelchair. His social worker and psychologist, feeling that some extra attention would "pick him up," made him one of their "special" patients. They wheeled him to therapy appointments when they saw him in the hall, made a point to stop and chat with him in the common area, and praised him for minor (to him) accomplishments on the unit. Theoretically, they understood their position as trying to replace lost psychological and physical functions. To their dismay, the patient's depression deepened.

In a case conference with a consultant it was suggested that there be exploration of the personal meaning of the disability and the care he was getting with the patient. Through a number of such individual sessions, the psychologist discovered that the patient experienced the staff's solicitous behavior as destroying his self-concept of being strong, reliant, and competent. This patient responded well when the focus of psychological treatment became a life review. Evocation of his past achievements restored a potent self-image and greater tolerance for his new limitations. In addition, after consultation with the patient about his preference in this matter, staff were instructed to let the patient initiate their assistance. In other words, he was allowed to undertake as much of his own care as possible. Mr. A. was now able to undertake rehabilitation therapy much more energetically. He returned home with 24-hour nursing care and resumed an active life as best he could.

Mr. A.'s history and personality demanded as much hands-off care as possible. The successful outcome of this case may be understood as a result of shifting the focus from the need of the team members to feel helpful to the need of the patient for autonomy.

Case B

Mrs. B. was an extremely regressed stroke patient who lived with an adult daughter. She was 81 years old, a widowed seamstress (with a third-grade education), and born in eastern Europe. She had never become fluent in English despite more than 50 years in the United States. A son kept in regular contact with mother and daughter but dealt primarily with monetary and household matters. In interviewing the mother and daughter together, the team's mental health professional found it difficult to distinguish between the two psychologically; they formed an emotional unit in their enmeshment. Each talked for the other and described the other's physical and emotional pains as if they were her own.

Mrs. B. demanded the same enmeshed overinvolvement of staff that she had from her daughter. She all but refused to engage in therapies and constantly complained abut poor treatment and/or lack of attention from the staff. Her daughter became omnipresent on the unit, trying to channel her mother's complaints to the staff and attempting to soothe the patient in lieu of therapy. The treatment team initially tried to attend to all of Mrs. B.'s demands but then became angry and ignored her. This led to an escalation of the mother's and daughter's histrionic behavior and to the involvement of the son. Forced to become involved, the son turned out to be quite irrational and belligerent, threatening the hospital with lawsuits and bombarding the administration and unit with angry phone calls and visits. Despite the family's anger, it became clear that they did not wish to take their mother home; nor were they willing to place her in a nursing home—the guilt and level of symbiotic attachment between mother and daughter were too great. The son strongly reinforced the notion that his sister was to care for their mother at home (which he did not share with them).

In this case the psychologist and the social worker assisted the team by explaining the mother and daughter's overinvolvement and the role of the son. This work with the treatment team helped relieve them of their guilty feelings for not meeting the patient's impossible standard. The daughter was asked to change her visiting from 12 to 14 to 2 to 4 hours per day and was actually quite relieved to be given permission to do so. Regular phone calls from the attending physiatrist to the son helped to quiet his demands. The son also appeared relieved to be able to de-escalate his involvement. The team psychologist held brief but frequent supportive meetings with the patient alone while the social worker met regularly and alone with the daughter. While the latter would not accept suggestions for psychological treatment for herself or geriatric day care for her mother, she was gratified by the social worker's individual attention. The patient continued to level malevolent charges at staff, but they were able to maintain appropriate levels of contact in the newly created interpersonal environment. The patient was discharged home under the daughter's care with visits from a nursing agency three times a week. The daughter kept in regular contact with the social worker by phone and in person when the mother came for outpatient appointments. This arrangement served in large part to restabilize this family system.

The case of Mrs. B. illustrates a situation where the treatment team was overwhelmed by guilt and anger. They responded overzealously at first and then withdrew completely. The magnitude of their response to Mrs. B. suggests that some strong anxieties were evoked by this older woman who acted like a child. To some extent, as in the case of Mr. A., less proved to be more as it was discovered that a well-regulated amount of contact distributed among team members was best for all parties. Mrs. B. is the prototype for the type of patient who is difficult for staff with gerophobic tendencies. However, the staff members leaning more in the gerophilic direction learned that no matter how Herculean their efforts, Mrs. B. would not see them as satisfactory.

Case C

Mrs. C. was a proud, independent, married, 75-year-old woman who denied her stroke and dementia-related deficits. Her 81-year-old husband was a healthy, polite gentleman who colluded in his wife's denial. He seemed to have mild dementia-related deficits as well. Mrs. C. was capable of returning to independent living with her husband. There were, however, some legitimate safety concerns. Mrs. C. flaunted her disdain for the staff's concerns while her husband acted oblivious to the whole issue.

After more extensive experience with both the patient and her husband, the team's mental health professional determined that little could be done to shift their attitudes. In psychodynamic terms, Mrs. C.

experienced the staff's interventions as too great a blow to her narcissism. Mr. C. was unconsciously too frightened by the assault to his family system that his wife's decline represented. He could not allow himself to hear what the staff was telling him.

In this case, the team's mental health professional needed to consult primarily with the patient's treatment team. The therapists needed assurances that they had not failed and an opportunity to vent their anger openly instead of bickering with the patient. A number of team meetings were conducted during which, among other things, the adaptive and defensive meanings of the couple's behavior were discussed. The goal became to help the team separate their view of their own competence from the behavior of this patient.

Subsequent to this consultation, the patient improved slightly in the area of safety, adopting some of her therapists' suggestions as her own. Clearly, removing some of the intensity between the treatment team and patient had been indicated. The treating therapists were better prepared to accept the absence of gratitude on the part of the patient and demonstrated some increased capacity to tolerate this partially positive outcome. The patient was discharged home with increased visits from her housekeeper. The extra visits were tolerated by the couple since they were not considered medical. The staff's anxiety was somewhat allayed knowing that someone would be checking on the couple more frequently.

Mrs. C. exemplified a most frustrating patient to the gerophilic therapist. She did not demand more help, she disdained any help. The result was that the team members working with her were demoralized. In contrast, this kind of patient may be appealing to therapists with gerophobic tendencies, consciously admiring her independence and unconsciously feeling relieved by the denial of illness and the patient's adoption of a parental role. In this situation there is danger in assuming that such patients are completely functional when they are not. In the case of Mrs. C., frustrated gerophilic therapists had to be assisted in lowering the investment of their own self-esteem in the outcome of one patient's case.

In these three case examples, the mental health professional worked to decrease support in the case of Mr. A., increase empathy in the case of Mrs. B., and defuse patient-staff conflict in the case of Mrs. C. Interventions are rarely as simple as being more supportive. The nonmental health professionals are probably already supplying more than adequate amounts of support. Mr. A. and Mrs. C. both had proud, independent personalities that required a particular approach to their rehabilitation. They both needed to maintain their psychological autonomy. Mrs. B. and Mrs. C. also manifested some elements of paranoia that were most likely necessary to them. They essentially said to the younger, healthy team: "You have the problem, not me," and therefore felt more able to tolerate their disabilities. This logic may not make rational sense to the rehabilitation staff and requires that they increase their psychodynamic comprehension. Therapeutic relationships laden with unrecognized transference and countertransference reactions can quickly escalate and be fraught with tension and conflict, to the bewilderment of both team and patient. Each of the three patients discussed here had very different rehabilitation agendas based on their own attitudes toward disability, aging, and health. The best possible resolution was achieved when staff were more fully informed of the patients' agendas (and their own) and arrived at acceptable compromises.

FUTURE TRENDS

The use of transference and countertransference material is still fairly novel in the rehabilitation setting. Members of the interdisciplinary treatment team and trainees should become more informed as to the salience of psychodynamics in their work. They can easily remain highly focused on their specific therapy tasks and lose sight of the effects of their patients' personalities and emotional states. This phenomenon can reinforce a view of older rehabilitation patients as unable to grapple with intrapsychic issues, promote seeing only their physical disability, and perpetuate ageism. Rehabilitation professionals have great potential for enhancing both patients' and staff's functioning by assuring that *psychological* phenomena such as transference and countertransference are addressed. Given their extensive and intensive clinical contact with patients, they will find that there are ample opportunities for research.

For example, Robiner (1987) examined the effects of patient and therapist age on transference in a psychotherapy analogue study. Older patients saw therapists, particularly younger ones, as similar to their children more often than younger patients. Older rehabilitation patients offer an excellent opportunity to pursue similar lines of research in an applied setting. Comparison of the differing transferences and countertransferences with disabled and nondisabled older adults is yet to be explored. The impact of disability on the older adult's fantasy life and ability to relate his life story are other questions needing to be addressed.

Gunther (1987) has discussed the very difficult nature of providing hard data to back up the effectiveness of the kinds of interventions discussed in this chapter. Given the consultative nature of much of the work on transference and countertransference, indirect measures of effectiveness should also be considered. Measuring staff burnout and distress on units where particular attention is also being paid to patient/staff dynamics is an approach worthy of consideration. Further, formally measuring the emotional climate of such a unit, and patient and staff satisfaction with treatment outcomes, may also help operationalize effectiveness of these interventions.

The two explanatory phenomena of gerophobic and gerophilic tendencies in professionals working with older adults await more formal operationalization and testing. These concepts have demonstrated clinical utility and should be further explored. Rehabilitation work will benefit from greater knowledge of who chooses to work in the field and their motivations.

In summary, consideration of transference and countertransference phenomena in the treatment of older rehabilitation patients holds promise as a clinically important and useful tool. At the same time, these phenomena and related psychological issues and effects should be examined empirically.

CONCLUSION

The greater number of older adults found in our rehabilitation units today demands sensitivity not only to different physical conditions but to psychological ones as well. The older adult brings his or her own developmental tasks to the rehabilitation setting; these tasks are usually quite different from those of the treating staff.

Failure to account for the psychodynamics of rehabilitation therapy relationships with older adults can lead to destructive acting out of conflicts and anxieties. Even the most well-formulated treatment plans may encounter resistance from patients. Treating staff may avoid therapeutic work or pursue a nonconsensual agenda.

Members of a rehabilitation treatment team must develop a more complex view of patients that includes their intrapsychic functioning and distinguishes the older patients' views about advanced age and disability from their own. The attitude that older adults are marginal to our *rehabilitative* efforts, that they are custodial patients, must be counteracted. Attention to the psychodynamics of patient-staff interactions offers new pathways for growth, rejuvenation, and development for both treatment team members and their older patients.

REFERENCES

Apfel, R.J., M. Fox, R.S. Isberg, et al. 1984. Countertransference and transference in couple therapy: treating sexual dysfunction in older couples. *Journal of Geriatric Psychiatry* 17: 203–14.

Blau, D. and M.A. Berezin. 1982. Neuroses and character disorders. *Journal of Geriatric Psychiatry* 15: 55–97.

Breslau, L. 1980. The faltering therapeutic perspective toward narcissistically wounded institutionalized aged. *Journal of Geriatric Psychiatry* 13: 193–206.

Cath, S. and N.E. Miller. 1986. The psychoanalysis of the older patient. *Journal of the American Psychoanalytic Association* 34: 163–77.

Colarusso, C.A., and R.A. Nemiroff. 1987. Clinical implications of adult developmental theory. *American Journal of Psychiatry* 144: 1263–70.

Emener, W.G. 1979. Professional burnout: Rehabilitation's hidden handicap. *Journal of Rehabilitation* 45: 55–8.

Freud, S. 1966. Transference. In *Introductory Lectures on Psychoanalysis*, edited and translated by J. Strachey, 431–48. New York: W.W. Norton and Co. (Original work published in 1920).

Gans, J.S. 1983. Hate in the rehabilitation setting. *Archives of Physical Medicine and Rehabilitation* 64: 176–9.

Gans, J.S. 1987. Facilitating staff/patient interactions in rehabilitation. In *Rehabilitation Psychology Desk Reference*, edited by B. Caplan, 185–218. Gaithersburg, Md.: Aspen Publishers.

Gunther, M.S. 1971. Psychiatric consultation in a rehabilitation hospital: A regression hypothesis. *Comprehensive Psychiatry* 12: 572–85.

Gunther, M.S. 1977. The threatened staff: A psychoanalytic contribution to medical psychology. *Comprehensive Psychiatry* 18: 385–97.

Gunther, M.S. 1979. The psychopathology of psychiatric consultation: A different view. *Comprehensive Psychiatry* 20: 187–98.

Gunther, M.S. 1987. Catastrophic illness and the caregivers: Real burdens and solutions with respect to the role of the behavioral sciences. In *Rehabilitation Psychology Desk Reference*, edited by B. Caplan, 219–43. Gaithersburg, Md.: Aspen Publishers.

Gunther, M.S. 1988. Personal communication.

Gurian, B.S. 1986. The myth of the aged as asexual: Countertransference issues in therapy. *Hospital and Community Psychiatry* 37: 345–6.

Gutmann, D.L. 1987. *Reclaimed Powers*. New York: Basic.

Gutmann, D.L. 1988. The two faces of gerontology. *Center on Aging Newsletter* 4, no. 1. Chicago: McGaw Medical Center of Northwestern University.

Hildebrand, H.P. 1982. Psychotherapy with older patients. *British Journal of Medical Psychology* 55: 19–28.

Hinze, E. 1987. Transference and countertransference in the psychoanalytic treatment of older patients. *International Review of Psychoanalysis* 14: 465–74.

Horowitz, M., and J. Grunes. 1987. *Therapeutic Use of Countertransference Reactions in Psychodynamic Therapy with Older Adults*. Paper presented to the 3rd Congress of the International Psychogeriatric Association, Chicago, Ill.

Horowitz, M., and R. Hartke. 1988. *Transference and Countertransference with Older Adults in a Rehabilitation Setting*. Paper presented to the 96th Annual Convention of the American Psychological Association, Atlanta, Ga.

Knight, B. 1986. *Psychotherapy with Older Adults*. Sage: Beverly Hills.

Langs, R., ed. 1981. *Classics in Psychoanalytic Technique*. New York: Aronson.

Levin, E.L. 1986. Lasting impressions. *Psychotherapy Patient* 2: 81–6.

Livneh, H. 1982. On the origins of negative attitudes toward people with disabilities. *Rehabilitation Literature* 43: 338–47.

Pollock, G.H. 1980. Aging or aged: Development or pathology. In *The Course of Life*, vol. 3, edited by S.I. Greenspan and G.H. Pollock, 549–85. Washington, D.C.: U.S. Government Printing Office.

Robiner, W.N. 1987. An experimental inquiry into transference roles and age. *Psychology and Aging* 2: 306–11.

Sandler, A.M. 1982. Psychoanalysis and psychoanalytic psychotherapy of the older patient. *Journal of Geriatric Psychiatry* 15: 11–32.

Sobel, E.F. 1980. Countertransference issues with the later life patient. *Contemporary Psychoanalysis* 16: 211–22.

Wright, B.A. 1983. *Physical Disability—a Psychosocial Approach.* New York: Harper and Row.

Wylie, H.W., Jr., and M.L. Wylie. 1987. The older analysand: Countertransference issues in psychoanalysis. *International Journal of Psychoanalysis* 68: 343–52.

Chapter 11

Psychotherapy with the Older Rehabilitation Patient

Robert J. Hartke and *Michael Horowitz*

Contemporary practice in geriatrics makes it increasingly clear that psychotherapy with older adults is a worthy enterprise. Older adults are no longer viewed as incapable of change or undeserving of the effort of psychotherapy. As societal barriers and individual prejudices are addressed, older adults are beginning to avail themselves of psychotherapeutic treatment. Onset of physical disability and the frequently ensuing rehabilitation hospitalization quite often place the older adult in contact with a mental health professional—indeed, in some instances, for the first time. It is a very appropriate time for older adults to address emotional issues with a professional outside of their ordinary support system. Rehabilitation staff concerned with the emotional well-being of the patient can play a very important role in the overall treatment and optimal adjustment of the physically disabled older adult, despite the fact that a physical disability is at the center of attention.

This chapter focuses upon the unique features of psychotherapeutic treatment with the older adult in the rehabilitation setting. A range of possible interventions is discussed with special emphasis on their applications to older adults. Treatment issues unique to older people, such as overcoming age-related prejudice, expanding the format of therapy beyond the traditional office session, and the use of reminiscence, are also explored. Distinguishing treatment of the premorbidly well-adapted versus poorly adapted elder is considered, and special issues in group intervention with older adults in rehabilitation are described. The practice of psychotherapy with older adults is quite a complex topic with full volumes addressing its many concerns (e.g., Butler and Lewis 1982; Sadavoy and Leszcz 1987). Consequently, this chapter is less than comprehensive by design. Areas such as psychopharmacology, family therapy, and other physical concomitants of emotional disturbance are deliberately omitted in order to avoid injustice to these complex issues through only cursory reference. In addition, some special treatment issues are discussed elsewhere in this text, particularly treatment with the depressed and less cognitively intact older adult. While it is acknowledged that psychotherapeutic treatment of older adults is a more *biopsychosocial* phenomenon (Kemp 1986), this chapter will primarily focus upon work with older adults individually and in groups and less upon the systems with which they interact.

CONTINUUM OF TREATMENT OF THE OLDER ADULT

The forms of intervention possible with the older adult in a rehabilitation setting can be organized along a continuum in respect to length and format of psychotherapy. Both Rechtschaffen (1959) and Kahana (1987) discuss therapy with older adults as ranging from environmental modification and support at one end of the spectrum to exploration and insight at the other, discriminating patient criteria for each type of intervention. In the present discussion, treatment will be described on a continuum ranging from crisis intervention through a variety of short-term to long-term, insight-oriented psychotherapies.

Crisis Intervention

Intervention at the time of crisis is largely conceived of as supportive, mobilizing a positive transference, allowing for emotional release, and providing emotional clarification and concrete problem solving where possible. Kahana (1987) describes the frail older person as predisposed to crisis due to the fragile homeostasis common to later years and associated with limited physical/cognitive reserves, diminished external resources, loss, and dependency.

Being confronted with a physical disability and admission to a rehabilitation hospital can precipitate a variety of emotional crises for the older adult. These can include problems in hospital adjustment resulting in a demand for premature discharge; severe depression with withdrawal or suicidal ideation; as well as the emotional sequelae of mental confusion, overmedication, pain, or unexpected medical complications. In these instances, psychotherapeutic treatment often takes the form of crisis intervention in which the practitioner gathers information to clarify the problem, supports the patient to restore a sense of control, and mobilizes emotional and tangible resources in the patient, staff, and family systems for conflict resolution. In the rehabilitation setting, crisis intervention can often involve assuming the role of arbitrator and coordinator among the older patient, family, and staff.

Short-Term Therapy

Several authors have reported success in applying short-term therapy techniques in work with older adults (Goldfarb and Sheps 1954; Grunes 1984;

Lazarus and Groves 1987; Sifneos 1987). In this age of cost containment and consolidation of treatment, time-limited psychotherapy has become the norm for the mental health professional working in a rehabilitation setting. With average length of stay shrinking, assessments must be abbreviated, interventions highly focused and intensively delivered in a few patient contacts. It is not uncommon for a rehabilitation team's mental health professional to have fewer than ten sessions with a patient during the hospital stay. Within these time constraints, the approach of the therapist can be varied, including supportive, counseling, and insight-oriented techniques. These roughly correspond to the objectives of treatment with older adults recommended by Butler and Lewis (1982): restitution, growth and renewal, and perspective.

A supportive approach identifies pre-existing coping or defense patterns and helps the patient re-establish their use in the face of physical change. Such coping patterns may be clinically perceived as more or less adaptive, but nonetheless functional for individuals over their lifetime. The older adult has an extensive history from which to discern coping patterns that may be adaptively brought to bear upon the current situation. A short-term supportive intervention involves understanding predominant emotional defense patterns in the patient, explaining their function to treating staff, and respecting their use by the patient during the course of hospitalization. This approach is particularly relevant for the premorbidly *emotionally frail* older adult who will need assistance in coping with the onset of physical disability, hospitalization, and therapy. For example, an older patient with a long history of passive-dependent behavior and depression emotionally survived a rehabilitation hospitalization by using one or more staff as confidants as she had done with various people in the past (e.g., therapist, maid, son). In this case, the therapist supported this coping strategy by allowing a similar relationship in psychotherapy as well as informing team members of the potential for their filling such a need.

A counseling approach accesses the adaptive capacities of the patient through explanatory, didactic techniques which provide information, skill-building, and intellectual understanding of chronic illness and disability. A counseling intervention is often helpful with the older adult who has sufficient emotional maturity to independently handle the stress of hospitalization and readily identifies with an active coping position. These elders have the emotional energy to anticipate their life with a new disability and can value counseling to prevent psychosocial complications. Such an approach appeals to the hardiness (the *survivor* persona) that can be accessed in the life experience of the older adult and the capacity for life-long learning from new experiences, such as a disability. Consider the case of a 70-year-old woman, an active school administrator, who sustained a stroke. Valuing education at any age, she benefited from a counseling approach to psychotherapeutic intervention. This form of therapy gratified her coping strategy of curiosity about the stroke, its cause and effects, possible future complications, and how she would relate to others with her new, visibly disabled, status.

An exploratory, insight-oriented approach allows the patient a safe interpersonal environment within which to examine long-standing conflicts, perhaps stirred by the onset of illness and disability, and attempt personal change. For the older adult, unresolved feelings regarding loss, dependence, and death and dying may predominate. In addition, long-standing interpersonal conflicts with spouse or children who are now drawn into caregiving negotiations may be an issue. An insight-oriented approach is best taken with the cognitively intact, psychologically-minded elder (perhaps someone with prior experience in long-term psychotherapy) who can rapidly develop a therapeutic relationship and access and tolerate feelings in the course of psychotherapy. Sifneos (1987) and Kahana (1987) also include as criteria for this form of treatment the need for definition and limitation of the problem area as well as the patient's future orientation and capacity for interest and enjoyment. Short-term insight-oriented therapy challenges the notion that the older adult is incapable of or unlikely to appreciate "talk" therapy as helpful. Therapy with a 65-year-old male confronting progressive deterioration with lung disease serves as an example of this type of intervention. This well-educated professional man had previously engaged in long-term psychotherapy as a young adult. Short-term insight-oriented psychotherapy now helped him address problems of anger and depression over his anticipated retirement and increasing dependence on a younger, more physically fit, spouse.

The above discussion illustrates a range of approaches which may be considered within a time-limited context. Use of these approaches will vary and blend depending upon such factors as the therapist's theoretical orientation, the focus of therapy, and the characteristics of the older patient. It is possible that in the course of short-term contact, the therapist will be simultaneously supporting existing defenses, assisting in the development of new coping skills, and facilitating insight into the older adult's psychological functioning. Short-term intervention might also be conceived as primarily a way to stabilize the patient, clarify the problem, and convince the older patient of the efficacy of psychotherapy so that referral for longer-term, outpatient therapy will be accepted.

Long-Term Therapy

Traditionally, long-term psychotherapy has been defined as intensive, consistent treatment over an extended period for the purpose of pervasive personal change. Treating professionals have argued against the utility and ability of the older adult to engage in such treatment; more recent opinions positively assert the older adult's capability for self-examination and change (Butler and Lewis 1982). The approaches utilized in long-term therapy may vary as in a short-term format with similar criteria for patient eligibility. The obvious exception is treatment length which allows the patient and therapist the benefit of a relationship of greater depth and endurance as they share the patient's ongoing life experiences.

Within the context of rehabilitation, long-term therapy is usually conducted on an outpatient basis or extends to outpatient from a therapy relationship begun during an inpatient stay. Unlike traditionally defined long-term treatment, extended therapy with older adults in the rehabilitation setting may assume a pattern of sporadic intensity. Over the course of years, the therapist may become identified as a trusted emotional resource by whom the older patient feels known. As such, the therapist may be available in person or via telephone for short periods of treatment since the long-term relationship had been established over time. It might be argued by some that such an arrangement represents a dilution of the psychotherapy and that the therapist merely becomes a person upon whom the older adult (who perhaps has no one else) can depend. However, the impact that this type of intervention may have upon the older adult should not be underestimated. Butler and Lewis (1982) speak of the myth that termination is necessary in work with older adults, stressing the importance of continuity and accessibility of care. They note that work with the older person may require ongoing support until termination by death. Within the context of aging and disability, such a format of intermittent contact with underlying continuity may represent a distinct difference in long-term psychotherapy with older individuals.

SPECIAL ISSUES IN TREATING THE OLDER ADULT

Butler and Lewis (1982) succinctly discuss obstacles to mental health treatment of the older adult. Ageism, countertransference, older adults' lack of ease with mental health treatment, financial and bureaucratic blocks, and professional elements of discrimination all stand in the way of effectively providing mental health services to the older rehabilitation population.

Professionals in the mental health field, immersed in a culture of psychology, are prone to forget the stigma still attached by many in our culture to mental health services. The stigma is more likely to be found in the older cohort, since the idea of psychological treatment has had less benign meanings during this group's life span. Grunes (1987, 33) states that, "prejudice against treatment often exists in both patients and therapists." He describes the tendency of the older patient to view the psychotherapist as intrusive, bent on exposing the patient's psychopathology. To meet a mental health professional may mean acknowledging feelings of fear and anxiety of which the older patient is ashamed. The particular transference and countertransference issues associated with the pairing of older patients and younger therapists are further elaborated in Chapter 10.

Unfortunately, mental health professionals are not free of the tendency to stigmatize the older psychotherapy patient. Therapists may hold conscious or unconscious biases about the efficacy of any meaningful treatment for older adults. Pollock (1981) and others have discussed the sustaining power of the belief that the psyches of people in the later portion of their lives are too rigid to change. In more mundane terms, therapists talk about there being too much past material to delve into and thereby relieve themselves of the task of fully engaging with the older patient. Therapists who doubt their ability to be of help will be of little help and will overlook the potential for substantive psychological treatment of older adults. Erikson, Erikson, and Kivnick (1986) have underscored the vast psychological resources that are in fact available in the last part of the life cycle. These resources are available to the rehabilitation team that is open to finding them in their older patients.

Developing a Therapeutic Alliance

How then are the above issues manifested in the unique rehabilitation setting? For one, there is usually no expectation on the part of the older rehabilitation patient that a mental health professional will be a part of the team treating him. The initial approach of the mental health professional is likely to trigger the fear that the patient is unique, problematic, crazy, and so on. Therefore, the mental health professional must frame his involvement with the patient as routine and/ or regular. Where the team's mental health professional does see each patient on the unit, this regularity should be conveyed (sometimes repeatedly) to the patient so that the fear that he has been singled out can be alleviated.

In settings where psychological intervention is not routinely prescribed or when routinization is not a sufficient palliative, the mental health professional may need to be more creative in framing his participation in order to dispel the fears of the older patient. Where the cause of the patient's hospitalization is directly related to brain injury (e.g., stroke or head injury) and the therapist is a psychologist, he can establish himself as a specialist in assessing and treating cognitive functioning. Similarly, the team social worker may establish his expertise via his command of community resources. Terminology that may be less charged for the older patient may be employed to establish an alliance. For example, the mental health professional may talk about "consulting" with the older patient rather than psychotherapy. Identifying oneself as a resource for coping with the exigencies of hospitalization, an inherently stressful event, may also help in developing a working relationship. Further, an appeal to collaborate in helping family members with their anxieties and worries about the patient may be another avenue toward establishing a therapeutic alliance with the older patient. The older patient may be more comfortable participating in assisting others than in being on the receiving end of help.

Whatever method is used to alleviate the stigma attached to mental health services by this cohort, it is crucial for the mental health professional to keep in mind that the older patient can benefit and may want his services as readily as the younger patient. The mental health professional must not accept at face value protests from the older patient such as being too old, unable, or unwilling to participate in treatment. It is the role of the therapist, not of the patient, to find the means for an accommodation.

The mental health professional is the one interdisciplinary team member who may approach patients and ask them to tell the story leading to their hospitalization from their own points of view. Frequently, other team members are more restricted to outlining deficits and potentials and conveying them to the patient. While, more often than not, mental health professionals will need to assess and convey information based on what they observe, they should also be interested in the phenomenology of the patient's condition. Unlike others who may first gather a highly factual history from the patient or talk to collateral informants (e.g., family), mental health professionals should speak with patients initially to obtain their perceptions and begin to develop a therapeutic alliance. This first caveat must be observed no matter how severely impaired the patient is. Such an approach will convey an attitude of respect and alliance that increases the chances of the older patient reciprocating and making use of the rehabilitation program. It is important to remember that the older patient will have had a number of experiences with being brought to the hospital or emergency room by others and being spoken for by others.

Therapy Format

Within a rehabilitation setting where psychological services are an adjunct to the core physical therapies, mental health treatment should be conceived in a broad perspective to include intervention in varying forms. Particularly in an inpatient setting, an emotionally *teachable moment* may occur in a verbal exchange during the patient's breakfast, through another patient's modeling of an appropriate coping response, or working conjointly with a physical therapist during an exercise program. Expanding one's idea of therapy beyond the traditionally timed session in a private office is essential to the work of the mental health professional in rehabilitation. The range of needs and impairments necessitates a loosening of the formal structure of psychotherapy. This is particularly relevant to work with the disabled older adult who will appreciate interventions on a practical, here and now level. The fact that the setting in question is one of rehabilitation, and not exclusively mental health, will not be lost on the patients. They are engaging in rehabilitation therapies for such reasons as to regain use of their legs, improve their speech, or get better in general.

Knight (1986) notes that initial therapy sessions with older clients should focus on the appropriateness of psychotherapy versus other interventions with emotionally therapeutic value. The rehabilitation setting, which affords team members many different opportunities to interact with the patient under different circumstances, is well suited to this assessment of the intervention(s) of choice. The preference many older rehabilitation patients have for brief and nonthreatening assessments is also easily accommodated in the rehabilitation milieu.

Mental health professionals are best equipped to function in the rehabilitation setting if they think of themselves as offering a range of psychological services, only one of which may be psychotherapy. The interdisciplinary team approach offers opportunities and demands a variety of collaborative approaches such as patient observation, staff consultation, conjoint sessions with other nonmental health therapists, and family meetings. Psychotherapeutic intervention in the rehabilitation setting is almost always provided not as a primary treatment but as one aspect of comprehensive rehabilitation. Often, it is intended to increase the efficacy of the other therapies by supplying the emotional strength to work for physical recovery. While some of the older patients that the mental health professional will see may become psychotherapy patients, the vast majority remain *rehabilitation* patients.

Use of Reminiscence/Life Review

It is of great importance for the mental health professional to keep in mind that the older rehabilitation patient is most likely well-adapted but in a period of great stress. The loss of continuity with the preinjury self is often at the core of psychological difficulties in the older rehabilitation patient. The injury that brought the older patient to the rehabilitation setting may in fact lead to an entirely new, less satisfying "life structure" (Levinson et al. 1978). The use of special psychotherapy techniques may therefore be especially indicated; in particular, techniques that seek to restore a continuous sense of connection with the preinjury self may be needed.

One method of psychotherapeutic intervention increasingly considered of great utility in this setting is that of life review/reminiscence (Butler 1963). Grunes (1981) discusses the common error of shifting from a psychological to an organic view of personality once significant motoric or cognitive impairments are noted in a patient. The typical older rehabilitation patient almost always has suffered some type of brain-based or motoric impairment. Once such an organic diagnosis is made, psychotherapeutic interventions are invariably written off. Ironically, Grunes tells us, it is organically impaired older patients who may be most in need of a psychological link with their past selves.

It is easy to understand why evaluation of past memories may serve the older rehabilitation patient. Evocation of a meaningful, substantive, more pleasant past is preferable to the now damaged present. Of even greater significance psychologically is the fact that memories inform patients that they were not always the way they are now. Rehabilitation staff will likely take for granted that patients retain their former sense of self when this is in fact not the case. Memory deficit, depression, and an acute focus on rehabilitation are only some of the reasons that a profound rupture with the past self may occur.

Reminiscence and life review are useful ways of reconnecting with an older patient's past. While the therapist must, of course, be very present- and future-oriented with older rehabilitation patients, it is the past which holds the patient's potential assets and strengths. These assets are often overlooked by a rehabilitation team eager to forge ahead. The following case examples illustrate the usefulness of this type of intervention in working with the older adult.

> Father B. was a 64-year-old Catholic priest admitted to a rehabilitation hospital subsequent to a left hemisphere stroke whose main effects were sensorimotor. His church superiors were eager for him to make a decision about whether he would retire or resume work and also pressed the rehabilitation staff for "definitive" information about his post-stroke capabilities. Meanwhile, Father B. stayed very marginal to the rehabilitation program and ruminated endlessly about his post-hospital options. He made little progress and the staff became eager to discharge him quickly to a retirement home. Father B.'s psychotherapist was able to discern an underlying depression linked to a rupture in the patient's sense of continuity. He had come to view himself only as a "discharge plan" and not the active priest he had been. The psychotherapist began having long chats with Father B. involving various life and philosophical issues just as Father B. had himself done with his parishioners in the past. These discussions served the psychotherapeutic end of reconnecting Father B. with his prestroke self. He gradually became more eager to engage in some physical "exercise" (as he called the physical therapies) and "not spend all day talking." He eventually made enough progress to go to a church retirement home where he counseled older, less able clergy.

In this case, the psychotherapist served as a linking object with the patient's past. Once the link was reestablished, the patient's previously adaptive personality was able to resume its self-direction without further intervention.

> Mrs. F. was a 79-year-old widowed female admitted to a rehabilitation setting subsequent to a hip fracture. She antagonized both staff and

fellow patients by bossing them around and acting inappropriately parental to all. Mrs. F.'s psychotherapist, who was willing to sit and listen to the patient's suggestions for improving her life, soon discovered that this patient's identity had centered around her roles as wife and mother. The hip fracture led to a strong fear that she would now have to assume a dependent role and lose her matriarchal position in the family. Mrs. F.'s bewilderment over how to negotiate her present status had led her to withdraw from her own family and invest inappropriately in the hospital population. The therapist initiated increased contact between her and her family. Despite her dependent physical status, Mrs. F. was able to talk, listen, and offer advice as always. She became more invested in her own rehabilitation program, viewing the resumption of the strong link with her own family as an incentive for rehabilitation and discharge.

Through careful processing of the patient's life history, the psychotherapist in this situation came to understand and respect this patient's defenses. The therapist then worked to restore a broken family link with this patient. In this case, other people were available as strengthening figures. The therapist had to understand the nature of the patient's family system and assist in its reorganization.

DEVELOPMENTAL HISTORY AND TREATMENT: THE HARDY VERSUS FRAIL ELDER

Living to old age does not automatically guarantee adaptation and contentment. The older adult brings an extensive developmental history to these later years. This unique life history impacts upon how well he makes use of rehabilitation and adjusts to new physical limitations. The mental health professional can render a vital service to other therapists on the rehabilitation treatment team by providing an understanding of the older adult's premorbid adjustment and its therapeutic implications. To this end, the mental health professional must distinguish between the older adult who has made a reasonable late life adaptation versus the emotionally dysfunctional older adult. Life span/developmental theorists (e.g., Erikson 1950; Erikson et al. 1986; Havighurst 1974; Levinson et al. 1978) emphasize critical tasks or conflicts that occur throughout a lifetime, and their enduring influence when they remain incompletely resolved. The well adjusted, *emotionally hardy* elder has gained by life experience, appreciating achievements and surviving losses. In contrast, the poorly adapted, *emotionally frail* elder has failed to fully mature and is ill-prepared for the challenges of later life. Such a tenuous adaptation to life may be overturned by a disabling injury.

The Emotionally Hardy Elder

The majority of literature on psychotherapy with older adults sees this population as having suffered losses and in need of external support (e.g., Fry 1986). Overlooked, however, is the fact that physical loss and disability become somewhat expected in this phase of the life cycle and that most older adults cope quite well in the face of physical insults. Their accumulated life experience will usually provide strengths to cope with the crisis of disability. In fact, many older adults successfully invoke the belief of survivorship as a means of coping with the inevitable loss and incapacitations that come with aging.

As stated earlier, most of the older patients that the rehabilitation mental health professional will encounter will be psychologically normal. The mental health professional should help convey the understanding that, while many older patients seem initially unmotivated, depressed, and so on, these are normal stress reactions in response to illness, hospitalization, and medication. To consider aging as psychopathology (an ageistic notion) is destructive for all parties concerned. The hardiness of the typical older adult, accrued from a wealth of life experience, must be tapped to facilitate successful rehabilitation. The normal grieving reaction in response to physical disability must be allowed to take place without labeling it as pathological.

Berezin (1987) and Pollock (1987) point out that despite common beliefs to the contrary, older adults, especially the old-old, do not fear death. They do fear disability, pain, and dependency—the very conditions that exist during the rehabilitation stay. For the majority of patients, an approach that accesses old strengths through explanatory, didactic techniques and intellectual understanding of chronic illness and disability will suffice. (See the short-term counseling approach described earlier.) Older patients will naturally attempt to find a new equilibrium, given the normative losses of the latter part of life. The cases of Father B. and Mrs. F. were examples of psychologically healthy patients who were put back on track through the use of reminiscence/life review, requiring only the addition of this therapy to resume strong rehabilitative efforts.

The Emotionally Frail Elder

The patient with pre-existing psychological problems, though in the minority, will draw a disproportionate amount of energy from the treatment team. The mental health professional can help other team members by ensuring that they deal with this type of patient more selectively. This older patient's pre-existing vulnerabilities may lead to difficulty in making use of the rehabilitation setting. For the patient who is not accessible psychologically, management of their psychopathology may be necessary through more supportive techniques. Rehabilitation mental health professionals are typically able to work only within a short-term psychotherapy framework. Therefore, they must honor patients' existing defenses and set realistic goals with them within this context. Helping all interested parties (i.e., staff, family, and patient) determine realistic goals, given the patient's state of mind, is a vital contribution made by the mental health professional. In select instances, short-term, supportive therapy is not sufficient for the premorbidly dysfunctional elder to move past a psychological barrier. In such cases, it may be necessary for the rehabilitation goals to be kept modest (i.e., below the patient's potential) but sufficient for discharge, allowing time and a referral for longer-term psychotherapy to take precedence. Hopefully, the older patient will reinvest sufficient energies in rehabilitation therapies at a later date when emotionally restabilized. The following case illustrates this point.

> Mr. S. was an 81-year-old lawyer admitted to a rehabilitation hospital after a stroke that ended any possibility of his resuming work. Mr. S. had continued his law practice until the day of his stroke. The mental health professionals treating him were unable to affect the profound depression that kept him from engaging in the rehabilitation program. His history indicated that he had grown up with a weak and distant father and domineering mother. A life-long adaptation whereby he functioned in a strong, stereotypically masculine role ended with his stroke. He was overcome with the fear that he was now like his weak father and at the mercy of his mother. This patient's personality had not allowed him to retire or slow down with age. To do so would have meant becoming weak and vulnerable like his father. The finality of the stroke ended the viability of his defensive system. The mental health professional in this case recommended discharge and arranged for intensive psychotherapy. The patient began in-depth psychological treatment at the rehabilitation hospital which continued on an outpatient basis. His depression ameliorated although the future of physical rehabilitation efforts remained unclear after one year. The mental health professionals were instrumental in helping staff and family accept that psychological treatment needed to take precedence in this case.

GROUP THERAPY

Group therapy is another form of treatment often employed with older adults in a rehabilitation setting. Group discussions often occur spontaneously among patients on a rehabilitation unit. Intentionally structuring group psychotherapy sessions captures some of this peer contact and directs it in a therapeutic fashion. Butler and Lewis (1982) report that the use of groups with elders may be underestimated due to their often informal structure and the lack of their scientific investigation. In fact, the use of groups with older adults may have been an outgrowth of the bias that they were not worth the effort of intensive individual therapy. Groups have been used with older adults for purposes of resocialization, reality orientation, emotional release, life review, as well as increasing self-esteem and motivation (Busse and Pfeiffer 1977; Lazarus and Weinberg 1980). As Leszcz (1987) points out, group therapy with older adults provides an opportunity for genuine relating to peers at a time of depletion of object relationships. It provides an opportunity for emotional intimacy and adaptive role modeling among members. The format of group therapy can also provide other unique advantages in treating older adults. Attendance at a discussion group with other members of similar experiences can dilute the older adult's fear of being perceived as crazy or the shame of needing emotional help. A group of age peers can also compensate for the therapist's inexperience with certain eras or life events, thus helping to bridge the generation gap.

Unique Technical Features

While in most ways group therapy with older adults is similar to group therapy with adults in general, there are some unique technical features to be considered. Group therapy with older adults should emphasize individual participation, active leadership, limitation of interpersonal conflict, and flexibility in content. Busse and Pfeiffer (1977) place an emphasis on group participation with enjoyment of the actual group exchange being a goal itself, rather than making the group process paramount.

Effective leadership is more often recommended to be active, supportive, and flexible (Leszcz 1987; Leszcz et al. 1985), with the therapist using a more engaging, self-disclosive style. Structure is advocated in the form of group exercises or "go-rounds" in order to more deliberately draw in quiet, withdrawn members. Leszcz (1987) and Leszcz and associates (1985) stress the importance of limiting the amount of negativism expressed in a group of older adults. Considering particularly the goal of supportive socialization, they advocate optimizing the chance of a positive group experience for the members by minimizing regression, supporting defenses with practical, adaptive value, and carefully balancing the amount of conflict within the group.

Finally, Ingersoll and Silverman (1978) advocate a flexible format in therapy groups for older adults, integrating contemporary issues and memories of life history. Contrary to traditional group psychotherapy technique, where great value is placed upon the dynamics of immediate interactions, group therapy with elders supports the benefit of content, specifically the review of past life experiences.

Group Therapy in Rehabilitation

In a rehabilitation setting, group intervention with older adults is largely viewed as a useful means of treatment, although its effectiveness has not been demonstrated in a rigorous fashion (Kemp 1986). The advantages of age segregated groups versus age integrated groups are not often addressed, but age integration appears to be more the norm. Most groups appear to be conceived for purposes that may only secondarily result in age segregation (e.g., by diagnosis).

Groups that are designed with the intention of addressing emotional issues range from very broadly focused discussion groups (Cordiner and Wilson 1982; Rosin 1975) to much more specifically structured groups organized around diagnoses, such as stroke (Bucher et al. 1984; D'Afflitti and Weitz 1974; Oradei and Waite 1974; Pierce and Salter 1988; Singler 1975). In a more innovative approach, Evans and associates (1986) reports on the use of group therapy via a telephone conference call, employing cognitive and problem-solving strategies for more isolated, disabled elders.

The most frequent content of the group discussions involves illness related information; attitude adjustment to disability; interpersonal issues with other patients or treating staff; reactions to the hospital setting; and age related issues, such as death and dying or negotiating increasing dependency. Benefits most frequently cited include increased emotional expression, particularly associated with the physical disability, along with validation of the universality of such feelings, both positive and negative. Decreased isolation and development of a support system (whether transitional or enduring) are also especially noted as beneficial in groups with older adults. Finally, release of feelings regarding institutionalization and concomitant increase in participating staff's empathy are also frequently described.

The optimal format for a group intervention with older adults varies by situation and purpose, even under the more specialized condition of physical rehabilitation. However, several critical variables are worthy of consideration. These include characteristics of the group leaders, patient eligibility and recruitment, group structure, and evaluation of the group's effectiveness.

Group Leaders

Consistent group cotherapists are most frequently recommended whenever possible. Most clinicians espouse the therapeutic merit of a male/female couple for balance and parental transference value. Larger, more variable numbers of group leaders are considered countertherapeutic (Cordiner and Wilson 1982;

Oradei and Waite 1974). In instances where the group is led by rehabilitation staff who serve other functions for the patient (e.g., physician, nurse, social worker, psychologist, therapeutic recreation specialist), the impact of the multiple roles on the character of the group should be considered (e.g., Rosin 1975). The interdisciplinary team approach in rehabilitation offers opportunities for groups to be run by leaders not specifically trained in mental health areas. When none of the group facilitators have a mental health background, it is advisable for them to have a consultant knowledgeable in group behavior (Pierce and Salter 1988).

Eligibility and Recruitment

Given the emphasis on socializing and ego-strengthening in groups of older adults, homogeneity of members is most often recommended to promote cohesiveness (Yalom 1975). Busse and Pfeiffer (1977) indicate that group members should have similar levels of social and problem-solving skills. Age segregation appears to be less strongly advocated. For example, Butler and Lewis (1982, 331–2) report the benefits of broad integration of age groups in a "life-crisis" group therapy experience. Studies also suggest the value of adequate initial preparation in assuring successful integration of members into the group (Bucher et al. 1984; Yalom 1975).

Group Structure

In a hospital setting, such factors as size, frequency and length of meetings are often not fully under the control of the group designers. What may be most important is to realize that the ultimate configuration of the group will dictate its purpose. For example, participation in a group of unlimited size, meeting monthly, fills a different need than time-limited participation in a small group meeting twice weekly. The degree of structure imposed by the group leaders is often predicated upon the length of participation and cohesion of the group membership. If the format of the group promotes longevity and cohesiveness, imposition of structure by group leaders may be less necessary. Cohesiveness and ensuing intimacy of participants promotes interpersonal risk taking and greater depth of expression of feeling.

Whether the group is closed or open to new members will influence the level of intimacy and the importance of group leaders imposing structure on discussion. Most groups in a medical hospital setting (where patient flow is a consideration) are of necessity continuously open to new members. Length of participation may also be dependent upon length of hospital stay. Singler (1975) suggests closing the group for a limited number of sessions, allowing new members to enter at established intervals only. When the source of patients permits such a strategy, the group may experience greater continuity and depth of discussion.

Evaluation

Most groups of this nature have been evaluated through cataloguing clinical observations and by subjective evaluation of the group's helpfulness to participants. Research design is often poorly controlled for validity threats such as the influence of other forms of treatment, patients' desire to please, and so on. While most studies present some evidence of the value of group intervention, the mechanisms of effectiveness have not been rigorously elucidated. For instance, do the groups simply provide a forum for support during hospitalization, decreasing anxiety and isolation, or are their effects more far-reaching? Greater sophistication is now needed in isolating the critical variables of a group's effectiveness for the disabled older adult. For example, contrasting instrumental versus affective knowledge may be an important source of information about outcome. While members may profess greater knowledge of their disability as a result of participation in a structured group (where information delivery has been a goal), is this knowledge base a reality or an anxiety-reducing illusion? Perhaps the content is much less critical than the process of empathic awareness and interpersonal contact.

Clinical Application: The Stroke Group

A typical group treatment for stroke patients serves as an illustration of the variables described above. Due to the increased frequency of stroke with age (Garrison et al. 1988), the majority of participants in this type of group will be middle to old aged. The design of this particular group, however, is age-integrated, allowing for a full range of life experience.

> The group is co-led by a psychologist and social worker and meets twice weekly for the duration of a patient's hospital stay. Patients capable of adequate communication who are not severely disruptive due to confusion or disinhibition are eligible, but participation is voluntary to increase the value of involvement. The group is continually open to new members to replace patients leaving as they are discharged from the hospital. The format is one of structured discussion of various topics related to stroke, disability, and hospitalization. Despite the structure of the discussion, the group leaders remain sufficiently flexible to allow digression to such areas as personal reminiscence or criticism of hospital policies. Education, guided discussion, emotional expression, and peer support are the major therapeutic strategies employed. An optimistic tone is deliberately fostered in the group, with support of adaptive defenses and pacing of intimacy and confrontation. It is described as a "stroke discussion group" to circumvent the older adult's negative perception of psychotherapy. The style of the group leaders is

active and didactic with a problem-solving, preventative approach. The goal of the group is to stimulate the patients' problem-solving capacities, to re-establish a sense of control, and actively cope with disability.

In this illustration, the apparent superficial level of interaction promoted in the group belies a forum for deeper emotional expression with frequent validation and support of feelings, as well as modeling of adaptive responses. Using this format, subgroups of enduring support that carry on beyond their hospitalization are frequently observed to develop among patients. Participants will spontaneously bring their experiences of accomplishment and failure back to the group for recounting and validation. Patients congratulate one another on progress toward recovery and offer consolation and encouragement when an obstacle is encountered (e.g., frequently revealed when recounting the experience of a visit home). Discussion of the hospital experience also affords the group leaders an empathic awareness of the patients' position as older adults who find themselves in a subculture of rehabilitation which can be both threatening and insulting to them.

Group treatment, while not a complete substitute for individual therapy, should be considered a viable means of treatment for older adults. The preceding discussion and clinical application illustrate the use and problems of groups which include older adults in a rehabilitation setting. Older adults can be valuable members of either age-integrated or age-segregated groups with expressed psychotherapeutic purpose. Sharing their life experience can be mutually satisfying to themselves as well as other members, while participation can help reestablish lost social roles of parent/teacher or friend/intimate. Special benefits are evident for the disabled older adult, although the identification of critical factors of format and effectiveness are an area still open for research and greater understanding.

CONCLUSION

This chapter has attempted to demonstrate the crucial role psychotherapeutic intervention can play in treating the older rehabilitation patient. Mental health professionals in rehabilitation must remain open to older adults as viable therapy candidates and be flexible in their interventions. A continuum of treatment has been described as applicable to elders in a rehabilitation setting—from brief, crisis intervention to longer term therapy. In addition, it is the responsibility of the mental health professional to assist the older patient in bypassing psychological obstacles to effective rehabilitation treatment. As discussed, these obstacles may take psychosocial, intrapsychic, or interpersonal forms. An accurate determination of the level of hardiness of the elder patient aids in identifying which obstacles are most crucial to address. Finally, the particular benefits and unique technical aspects of a group psychotherapy approach for the older rehabilitation patient were discussed. Group interventions, whether age-integrated or segregated, are of value in diminishing the isolation often experienced by the older patient in an institutional setting.

While the importance of psychotherapy as part of rehabilitation treatment should be stressed, it is most appropriately viewed as adjunctive and catalytic. Staff and patients will almost always view psychotherapy in the rehabilitation setting in this way, and the mental health professional will have the greatest positive impact by staying in synch with this expectation. Older adults may require special considerations regarding their needs and approach to psychotherapy, but they should not be exempted from this aspect of comprehensive rehabilitation.

REFERENCES

Berezin, M.A. 1987. Reflections on psychotherapy with the elderly. In *Treating the Elderly with Psychotherapy: The Scope for Change in Later Life*, edited by J. Sadavoy and M. Leszcz, 45–63. New Haven, Conn.: International Universities Press.

Bucher J., E. Smith, and C. Gillespie. 1984. Short-term group therapy for stroke patients in a rehabilitation centre. *British Journal of Medical Psychology* 57: 283–90.

Busse, E.W., and E. Pfeiffer. 1977. *Behavior and Adaptation in Late Life*, 2d ed. Boston: Little, Brown and Co.

Butler, R.N. 1963. The life review: An interpretation of reminiscence in the aged. *Psychiatry* 26: 65–76.

Butler, R.N., and M.I. Lewis. 1982. *Aging and Mental Health: Positive Psychosocial and Biomedical Approaches*, 3d ed. St. Louis: C.V. Mosby Co.

Cordiner, C.M., and L.A. Wilson. 1982. Group psychotherapy for hospital patients with chronic physical illness. *Health Bulletin* 40: 16–19.

D'Afflitti, J.G., and G.W. Weitz. 1974. Rehabilitating the stroke patient through patient-family groups. *International Journal of Group Psychotherapy* 25: 323–32.

Erikson, E.H. 1950. *Childhood and Society*. New York: W.W. Norton and Co.

Erikson, E.H., J.M. Erikson, and H.Q. Kivnick. 1986. *Vital Involvement in Old Age*. New York: W.W. Norton and Co.

Evans, R.L., K.M. Smith, W.S. Werkhoven, et al. 1986. Cognitive telephone group therapy with physically disabled elderly persons. *The Gerontologist* 26: 8–11.

Fry, P.S. 1986. *Depression, Stress, and Adaptations in the Elderly: Psychological Assessment and Intervention*. Gaithersburg, Md.: Aspen Publishers.

Garrison, S.J., L.A., Rolak, R.R. Dodaro, et al. 1988. Rehabilitation of the stroke patient. In *Rehabilitation Medicine: Principles and Practice*, edited by J.A. DeLisa, 565–84. Philadelphia: J.B. Lippincott.

Goldfarb, A.I., and J. Sheps. 1954. Psychotherapy of the aged: III. Brief therapy of interrelated psychological and somatic disorders. *Psychosomatic Medicine* 16: 209–19.

Grunes, J.M. (1981). Reminiscences, regression and empathy: A psychotherapeutic approach to the impaired elderly. In *The Course of Life: Psychoanalytic Contributions Toward Understanding Personality Development*, vol. 3, edited by S.I. Greenspan and G.H. Pollock, 545–48. Washington, D.C.: National Institute of Mental Health.

Grunes, J.M. 1984. Brief psychotherapy with the aged: A clinical approach. In *Geriatric Mental Health*, edited by J.P. Abrahams and V.J. Crooks, 97–107. Orlando, Fla.: Grune and Stratton.

Grunes, J.M. 1987. The aged in psychotherapy: Psychodynamic contributions to the treatment process. In *Treating the Elderly with Psychotherapy: The Scope for Change in Later Life*, edited by J. Sadavoy and M. Leszcz, 31–44. New Haven, Conn.: International Universities Press.

Havighurst, R.J. 1974. *Developmental Tasks and Education*, 3d ed. New York: David McKay Co.

Ingersoll, B., and A. Silverman. 1978. Comparative group psychotherapy for the aged. *The Gerontologist* 18: 201–6.

Kahana, R.J. 1987. Geriatric psychotherapy: Beyond crisis management. In *Treating the Elderly with Psychotherapy: The Scope for Change in Later Life*, edited by J. Sadavoy and M. Leszcz, 233–63. New Haven, Conn.: International Universities Press.

Kemp, B. 1986. Psychosocial and mental health issues in rehabilitation of older persons. In *Aging and Rehabilitation: Advances in the State of the Art*, edited by S.J. Brody and G.E. Ruff, 122–58. New York: Springer Publishing Co.

Knight, B. 1986. *Psychotherapy with Older Adults*. Beverly Hills, Calif.: Sage.

Lazarus, L.W., and M.S. Groves. 1987. Brief psychotherapy with the elderly: A study of process and outcome. In *Treating the Elderly with Psychotherapy: The Scope for Change in Later Life*, edited by J. Sadavoy and M. Leszcz, 265–93. New Haven, Conn.: International Universities Press.

Lazarus, L.W., and J. Weinberg. 1980. Treatment in the ambulatory care setting. In *Handbook of Geriatric Psychiatry*, edited by E.W. Busse and D.G. Blazer, 427–52. New York: Van Nostrand Reinhold Co.

Leszcz, M. 1987. Group psychotherapy with the elderly. In *Treating the Elderly with Psychotherapy: The Scope for Change in Later Life*, edited by J. Sadavoy and M. Leszcz, 325–49. New Haven, Conn.: International Universities Press.

Leszcz, M., E. Feigenbaum, J. Sadavoy, et al. 1985. A men's group: Psychotherapy of elderly men. *International Journal of Group Psychotherapy* 35: 177–96.

Levinson, D.J., C.N. Darrow, E.B. Klein, et al. 1978. *The Seasons of a Man's Life*. New York: Ballantine.

Oradei, D.M., and N.S. Waite. 1974. Group psychotherapy with stroke patients during the immediate recovery phase. *American Journal of Orthopsychiatry* 44: 386–95.

Pierce, L.O., and J.P. Salter. 1988. Stroke support group: A reality. *Rehabilitation Nursing* 13: 189–90, 197.

Pollock, G. 1981. Aging or aged: Development or pathology. In *The Course of Life: Psychoanalytic Contributions Toward Understanding Personality Development*, vol. 3, edited by S.I. Greenspan and G.H. Pollock, 549–85. Washington, D.C.: National Institute of Mental Health.

Pollock, G.H. 1987. The mourning–liberation process: Ideas on the inner life of the older adult. In *Treating the Elderly with Psychotherapy: The Scope for Change in Later Life*, edited by J. Sadavoy and M. Leszcz, 3–29. New Haven, Conn.: International Universities Press.

Rechtschaffen, A. 1959. Psychotherapy with geriatric patients: A review of the literature. *Journal of Gerontology* 14: 73–84.

Rosin, A.J. 1975. Group discussions: A therapeutic tool in a chronic diseases hospital. *Geriatrics* 30: 45–8.

Sadavoy, J., and M. Leszcz, eds. 1987. *Treating the Elderly with Psychotherapy: The Scope for Change in Later Life*. New Haven, Conn.: International Universities Press.

Sifneos, P.E. 1987. *Short-term Dynamic Psychotherapy: Evaluation and Technique*, 2d ed. New York: Plenum Medical Book Co.

Singler, J.R. 1975. Group work with hospitalized stroke patients. *Social Casework* 56: 348–54.

Yalom, I.D. 1975. *The Theory and Practice of Group Psychotherapy*, 2d ed. New York, Basic Books.

Chapter 12

The Caregiving Family for the Disabled Older Adult

Rebecca Brashler and *Robert J. Hartke*

An understanding of the experience of disability for older adults would be incomplete without consideration of those significant others who assume a helping role for them—family caregivers. Current societal trends provide evidence of the difficult task facing caregivers: increasing longevity and chronic disability, coupled with increasingly scarce resources for support. The demand is simply to do more with less. And families, for the most part, make themselves available for the challenge. It is the job of the rehabilitation professional to prepare and support them in their efforts to provide responsible, continuing care for their disabled elder members.

The majority of daily care for frail older adults is provided by family with little support from formal systems (Pratt and Kethley 1988). Pilisuk and Parks (1988) estimate that 80 percent of care for elders is provided by families, with fewer than 10 percent using any formal support services. Brody (1985) further estimates that well over five million people are involved in parent care at any given time. Certainly, the myth of families abandoning their frail elders has been proven untrue over and over again (Shanas 1979; Brody 1985). In fact, caregivers often need help in clarifying how much they can realistically expect of themselves, given the various competing demands on their time.

This chapter focuses on the *caregiving family* of the disabled older adult. The intent is to define family quite broadly, beyond the bounds of blood and marriage, as caregivers can range widely in their relationship with and function toward an older adult. Likewise, caregiving itself is considered quite broadly to include delivery of a simple, discrete service (e.g., friendly visits for emotional support) as well as comprehensive care (e.g., meeting daily needs and coordination of formal care systems).

This chapter will explore the work of a rehabilitation team in helping families develop and sustain caregiving for their elder members. While the focus of the chapter is on the role and stressors of the family during inpatient rehabilitation, it is important to acknowledge that these caregivers have likely provided some level of assistance to their elder member leading up to a disabling event and will continue (and intensify) their efforts postdischarge. Their problems and stress precede and will succeed the time of hospitalization. The rehabilitation team encounters them at a crossroads where serious disability has been introduced. This chapter will cover how caregiving roles are defined; identify the typical caregivers of older adults and their unique problems; discuss how care providers can be assisted in the discharge planning process; and provide a review of interventions for caregiver stress management. The chapter concludes with a section devoted to the role of the rehabilitation professional in counseling families who become surrogate decision makers for their elder members. The role of families in rehabilitation, and even specifically as caregivers for older adults, is an extensive field of study; therefore, this chapter can only be a selected review and commentary. Specifically excluded is a more broadly focused discussion of family assessment and treatment addressed elsewhere (e.g., Bray 1987; Power et al. 1988; Smith and Messikomer 1988; Versluys 1980) as well as consideration of dysfunctional families as they meet the crisis of disability in their elders (e.g., Corgiat 1990).

DEFINING THE CAREGIVING ROLE

The gerontology literature is replete with research on caregivers of older adults, including identification of characteristics of these caregivers and the types of roles they fulfill. Not surprisingly, family members, particularly spouses and adult children, usually assume the role of caregiver to dependent elders. (For a review of the literature see Horowitz and Shindelman 1983; Horowitz 1985). The value of including family members in the rehabilitation process becomes self-evident, given this information, for it will be these relatives who will implement long-term rehabilitation goals and facilitate improved functioning after discharge from the hospital (Brody 1986).

Determining a family's constellation and the quality of its bonds is critical for identifying caretakers of older members and their various roles. The following case illustrates one family's efforts at planning for the care of an older member:

> Mr. P., a 75-year-old retired widower with failing vision, was admitted to rehabilitation following a hip fracture. He has three adult children: two daughters living nearby and one son living out of state. He also has a close friend/neighbor with whom he spent much of his free time. During the initial interview with the social worker, Mr. P. was accompanied by his friend who had made a commitment to visit each day after therapy in order to keep Mr. P. company and help fill his leisure

hours. This friend was clearly uncomfortable accompanying the patient to therapy or assuming any formal involvement in the rehabilitation process. The patient's oldest daughter had three young children at home and would not be readily available during the day. However, she was preparing to have Mr. P. live with her temporarily after discharge. She was comfortable providing unskilled personal care and was planning to come to the hospital prior to discharge to learn the patient's care. The patient's younger daughter, a registered nurse, was expecting her first child within two weeks and was on strict bed rest because of medical complications. She was unable to assist with Mr. P.'s rehabilitation, but called her father each evening to provide emotional support and to help explain various medical procedures, medications, hospital rules, and so on. The patient's son had visited during the acute hospitalization, but would not be able to return in the near future. He did, however, agree to take responsibility for the management of the patient's finances and medical bills, a task which had become increasingly burdensome to Mr. P.

This well-functioning family was able to meet most of Mr. P.'s needs by dividing the caregiving responsibility into specific tasks and clearly defining each member's limitations. Each task was then assigned to the most appropriate family member. The one need unmet by the family was skilled nursing care for wound dressings. A formal community support (i.e., a visiting nurse from a home health agency) was identified to perform this task.

This case also illustrates the important distinction between *caregivers* and *decision makers* within the family system of a disabled elder. Although Mr. P.'s children were willing and able to provide for him, they left him the all-important role of *primary decision maker*. No task was assigned to anyone unless the patient felt comfortable relinquishing that responsibility and agreed with the designated caregiver. In short, Mr. P. remained the coordinator of his care. He decided which rehabilitation unit to enter; he sanctioned the plan to live with his daughter temporarily; and ultimately he would determine when he was ready to return to his own home. Often in the rush for relatives to show their concern and assume caregiver roles, they neglect to consider patients' preserved ability to direct their own care. It is crucial that the rehabilitation team share with families their assessments regarding patients' cognitive/emotional status to insure that the patients remain part of the decision-making process whenever possible (see Chapters 5 and 6). By helping to define a patient's need for care, the common pitfalls of fostering dependence and infantilization of older adults can be avoided. Finally, this family illustrates the preference of older adults to have caregiving be a shared responsibility distributed across family members (Mathews 1987; Tennstedt et al. 1989). Multiple caregivers minimize the burden placed on any single individual, foster family unity, and increase the patient's sense of security.

Helping family members define their strengths and limitations is also critical when identifying potential caregivers and their role or roles. Many loving relatives respond with an enthusiastic, "we'll do whatever is necessary," when first learning of an elder's illness or disability. The sentiment is genuine but fails to consider the realities of conflicting responsibilities, limited resources, physical stress, and emotional barriers. Moore (1987) speaks of a "capacity to care curve" illustrating that family well-being is jeopardized if caregiving demands exceed a threshold unique to that system. During the course of rehabilitation, family members must experience caregiving tasks and define their own capacity to care. Families may have great difficulty assessing or admitting their limitations and may need time to rehearse various caregiving tasks before settling on an appropriate role. The rehabilitation team should acknowledge every family's unique capacity and remain reassuring and nonjudgmental as family members explore their roles of support for the older patient.

While some families initially respond by overestimating their capacity, others may be so overwhelmed by the patient's disability that they feel incapable of playing any caregiving role. These relatives need help in analyzing the patient's dependency needs into discrete tasks. They also need reminders of their skills and strengths as well as permission to start small in their efforts to help. Assisting them in viewing the provision of emotional support via family visits as a crucial caregiving task may help them realize that they have already assumed a major role. Also, by reminding family members that they will provide coordination, whether they perform hands-on care or delegate tasks to others, keeps them engaged and identified as important members of the team.

In addition to assessing a family's psychosocial resources, it is important to explore their financial assets and the availability of programs to assist them in their community. Disability and chronic illness result in tremendous financial strain, especially for older patients who are often already on fixed incomes. Further, society has yet to make comprehensive entitlements and agencies available to assist this growing segment of the population. Many older adults mistakenly believe that Medicare will cover the cost of all necessary care, and they feel shocked and abandoned to learn of the substantial gaps in this insurance (most notably, non-skilled nursing home care, prescription medications, home modifications, nonemergency medical transportation, custodial or full-time skilled nursing care in the home, and some types of durable and disposable medical supplies) (*The Medicare Handbook* 1989). Those who feel protected by Medi-Gap supplemental insurance policies are often unprepared for the complex labyrinth of paper work associated with filing a claim and never receive the benefits to which they are entitled. State, local, and private programs designed to help older adults in their homes vary widely from one community to the next. The many services that do exist often have restrictions regarding eligibility, with financial means tests, sliding scale fees, uneven staffing, and complex application or waiting list procedures. There is no umbrella agency to centrally administer programs for older adults, and, therefore, families need assistance in locating and securing those services that will enable them to fulfill their goals as caregivers (Lawton et al. 1990).

TYPES OF CAREGIVERS AND THEIR DIFFICULTIES

The Aged Spouse As Caregiver

While gerontologists and ethicists hotly debate how much responsibility adult children should assume for their aging parents (Callahan 1985), it is generally assumed that older spouses will care for each other. In fact, older persons look to spouses first when identifying surrogate decision makers or caregivers (Brody 1986; High 1988), and older husbands and wives go to great lengths to care for each other. (For a review of the literature see Young and Kahana 1989). Wedding vows include the phrase "in sickness and in health" and caregiving is thought to be a "normative expectation" of marriage (Troll et al. 1979).

Probably the most significant characteristic of aged spouse caregivers is their own vulnerable medical condition. They are likely to have one or more age-related infirmities or chronic illnesses themselves (Brody 1986). Reductions in endurance and strength have major implications for assisting with physical care and 24-hour supervision. Should the caregiving spouse have age-related cognitive deficits, the picture becomes even more complex. These factors often prompt the rehabilitation team to suggest that the patient's spouse also undergo a geriatric assessment.

In some cases, the hospitalization of one member of a frail older couple can actually place the spouse in jeopardy:

> Mr. and Mrs. S. were both in their late seventies and had been married for more than fifty years. They seemed to be adjusting well to normal aging challenges, such as retirement, loss of peers, decreased mobility, and minor infirmities. As their contacts in the community dwindled, they had become increasingly dependent upon each other for emotional support and assistance with daily tasks. When Mr. S. was suddenly hospitalized with a stroke, the hospital staff gradually noticed that Mrs. S. was having great difficulty managing at home alone. She arrived at the hospital looking disheveled and exhausted. She was not eating adequately and not taking her antihypertensive medication. Mrs. S. also had repeated problems finding her husband's room when

entering the unit and was seemingly unable to process much information regarding her husband's condition.

It became clear to the treatment team that Mrs. S. would be unable to assume
sole responsibility for the care of her husband and, in fact, needed some care
herself. This couple's children, friends, and family physician were all surprised
to learn of Mrs. S.'s difficulties, since none of her deficits had been apparent
prior to her husband's stroke. In fact, she always appeared to be the more outgoing and social member of the couple. Like many older couples, Mr. and Mrs. S.
had gradually learned to compensate for each other's limitations enabling them
to function well as a dyad, although each would have had difficulty living alone.

When a spouse becomes hospitalized or disabled, the intact caregiving partner
must also cope with a basic loss of companionship. The disability and ensuing
loss of function usually causes alteration in interpersonal relationships (social or
intimate). While adult children who assume the challenge of caregiving often
still have intact generational supports (i.e., spouses, friends, etc.), older spouses
with diminishing peer relationships sustain a partial loss of the single most important person in their lives. It has been shown that having a spouse contributes
to healthy adjustment to aging, and any disruption in a relationship that may
have endured many decades will be devastating for both partners (Weishaus
1979).

The assumption of new roles is inherent to the adjustment process for
caregivers. In a rehabilitation setting, the older caregiver may be asked to learn
new skills associated with the physical care of a spouse including tasks requiring
an uncomfortable level of intimacy (such as toileting and bathing). Apart from
actual physical care, the spouse may need to undertake household or maintenance jobs formerly performed by the patient, such as homemaking, financial
management, provision of transportation, and coordination of social contacts. Finally, the caregiver may have to assume unfamiliar interpersonal roles within the
family. A formerly passive spouse may need to make major decisions regarding
discharge plans or medical intervention. Or an emotionally dependent spouse
may be called upon to provide encouragement and support to a depressed patient. There is no evidence to support the theory that cognitively intact older
spouses are less capable of assuming new roles than are younger caregivers.
However, given the disruption of functional and emotional homeostasis within
the marriage triggered by disability, the added stress of role adaptations may
seem intolerable.

Adult Children As Caregivers

Currently, adult children are providing more care to their parents for longer
periods of time than ever before (Brody 1985). Rehabilitation professionals en-

list and encourage the aid of adult children, often giving little thought to what motivates them to help their parents. In examining the motivation of adult children to care for their parents, gerontologists often speak of *filial maturity* (a concept generally attributed to Blenkner 1965). Filial maturity is defined as a developmental stage of adulthood when parents can no longer be viewed as protectors or guardians but may in fact require assistance themselves. Treas (1979) elaborates on this concept by stating that it implies a deeply ingrained sense of responsibility to help older generations. Filial maturity (and the responsibility it implies) seems to minimize the importance of strong bonds of affection and genuine concern as motivating forces for most adult children to care for their aged parents. In fact, research indicates that strong affective bonds are not a prerequisite for adult children to assume caregiving roles (Horowitz and Shindelman 1983). Other drives have also been invoked to explain caregiver motivation in this group, such as guilt (Hirschfield and Dennis 1979), as well as an adult child's ongoing efforts to gain parental approval (Silverstone and Hyman 1976).

Regardless of their motivation, adult children shoulder unique burdens. When becoming caregivers to a disabled parent, the stress of competing responsibilities felt by the middle or "sandwich" generation is particularly poignant. They struggle to find time for caregiving when already balancing work responsibilities with child care, a commitment to marital relationships, and a need for privacy and social outlets. Rehabilitation staff must avoid adding to their stress by rigidly dictating or structuring the involvement of overextended adult children. For example, providing evening and weekend times for education and counseling can be enormously helpful. A generous visitation policy for adults and children will also encourage participation as will simply acknowledging the pressures felt by these caregivers.

Similar to spouses, adult children are often asked to assume unfamiliar roles when a parent becomes ill or disabled. It is overly simplistic to view this in terms of a role reversal. Would the older patient truly become a child, both physically and emotionally, the adult child might have little difficulty taking on the role of the parent. But as Brody (1979, 274) points out:

> The dependent elderly who refill their aging children's 'empty nests' physically or in terms of psychological/emotional needs do not become children to their children, and the children do not become parents to their parent(s). Half a century or more of adulthood and of a parent-child relationship cannot be erased or disregarded.

An adult son learning to catheterize or bathe his mother does not view her as a child but must struggle to fit this unfamiliar and very possibly uncomfortable new interaction into their previously defined relationship. Once again the identified caregivers must evaluate the limits of their new role and their ability to function so differently.

Along with dramatic role changes, an elder's disability forces adult children to examine issues of aging and mortality. A sudden decline in physical or mental status, a near-death experience, and the onset of dependency are all reminders that our older relatives will not live forever and that often the aging process is painful. Children may need to carefully assess their own attitudes about older adulthood and how they feel about their own aging. Silverstone and Hyman (1976, 27) note:

> People who have a generally positive attitude toward old age . . . are more likely to be able to reach out to their elderly parents with concern, compassion and constructive support. If old age appears as a time to be dreaded, . . . then our parents' decline may seem very threatening. Their aging seems to toll the bell for our own aging and our inevitable death.

While increased contacts with parents force adult children to look ahead for themselves, they can simultaneously evoke strong feelings and conflicts from the past. Often adult children in caregiving roles will reminisce about their childhood and reassess their parents' parenting efforts. This may surface in a positive way with the rationale of repaying parents for all their years of support. This notion of reciprocity appears to be a crucial factor in caregiving, with adult children providing greater assistance the more they believe they were assisted in the past (Horowitz and Shindelman 1983). However, not all adults will harbor fond memories of their childhood. Those adult children who feel they received little support, poor, or even abusive parenting will understandably be more conflicted about providing care to their parents.

When there is only one adult child available, the adult child may feel particularly stressed. With no siblings to share the burden, an only child may be called upon to care for two parents and may more urgently need to identify community supports for assistance. On the other hand, sharing caregiving with siblings, while inherently easier, carries its own problems. Just as childhood experiences and the adequacy of parenting are reviewed, so are sibling rivalries and conflicts, which can serve to complicate effective caregiving. Often one child (usually female) emerges as the major caregiver with other family members assuming secondary roles. Dividing responsibilities equally or fairly can be troublesome especially if some siblings reside out of town. The geographically distant siblings may feel guilty for being absent and simultaneously resent the fact that they are not included in decision making. However, research validates the "persistence and durability of emotional bonds between parents and their children despite geographic distance" (Schoonover et al. 1988, 489), even though the distance may influence the type or style of social contacts (Dewitt et al. 1988). It would seem productive, then, for the rehabilitation team to reach out to distant children and facilitate whatever assistance they can provide in order to maximize the patient's support network.

Others As Caregivers

In the absence of spouse and adult child caregivers, older adults look to other relatives for assistance; those without extended family will turn to friends or neighbors (Shanas 1979). The commitment of these alternate caregivers and the assistance they can offer may, however, be qualitatively and quantitatively different from that of nuclear family members. Siblings of the older person often have their own age-related medical problems and may have responsibilities within their immediate families that conflict with caregiving. Nieces, nephews, and relatives of the younger generation may substitute for adult children, but frequently are not bound by the same sense of filial responsibility. Cantor (1979) noted that the assistance of neighbors and friends during illness is usually short-term, provided in response to emergencies, and available only when other caregivers are not found.

Our society has also seen a dramatic increase in remarriages late in life as well as older adults who choose to share a household outside of marriage (Peterson 1979). There can be confusion in these older blended families around caregiving responsibilities with intergenerational conflicts as strong as those found in stepfamilies with school-aged children. Chronically ill older people without families but with ample financial resources also may engage paid attendants or nurses as their caregivers. There is little in the literature about this unique group of caregivers in spite of the fact that many rehabilitation professionals are instrumental in finding attendants for their patients.

Finally, there are many atypical caregivers who are as committed and competent as those listed above. Older patients without any relatives, those in communal living situations, those with different sexual orientation, and so on, resolve caregiving needs in unique ways. Various minorities and ethnic groups have also developed specific caregiving patterns congruent with their heritage. Certainly, caregiving standards will evolve over time, along with ever-shifting social values and changing demographics. It will be important for rehabilitation professionals to be informed of and remain sensitive to the diversity in types of care providers, as well as cultural trends, to be most effective in guiding families in their caregiving efforts.

CAREGIVERS AND THE DISCHARGE PLANNING PROCESS

Helping patients and their caregivers achieve maximal independent functioning in the community is a primary goal of rehabilitation, and this necessitates a clear focus on discharge planning. With decreasing lengths of stay, the rehabilitation team has less time to prepare for discharge and must start planning for community re-entry while still completing initial assessments. In fact, the *Accreditation Manual for Hospitals* (1989, 206) mandates that "discharge planning [be] addressed as part of goal setting early in the rehabilitation process."

Although the team may appreciate the need to address discharge issues immediately, patients and their caregivers are often emotionally and physically unprepared to join in these early efforts. They may still be focused on the crisis of survival following the patient's sudden onset of disability. Unfortunately, decisions regarding post-hospital care are usually made under these less than ideal circumstances. This pressure placed on caregivers to arrange timely discharges can further disrupt their normal patterns of problem solving (Coulton et al. 1989).

In addition to the immobility produced by crisis reactions, many patients and their families arrive at rehabilitation settings with extraordinarily high expectations for recovery. They are, therefore, unprepared to discuss discharge plans until the patient has achieved a nearly complete recovery, a goal that may or may not be realistic. While working to accept the patient's limitations, older adults and their caregivers also grieve the losses sustained. Older patients mourn the lost dream of enjoying retirement in good health and remaining independent in their golden years. They may also have realistic fears regarding the financial hardships that accompany chronic illness and worries about the burden of patient care. In spite of these barriers, most patients and families are able to engage in the planning process, once provided with information, support, and encouragement. Repeatedly communicating the team's belief in their right to self-determination should help engage patients' caregivers earlier in their admissions.

There are a variety of discharge plans possible for the older adult and caregiver depending upon the extent of disability and the resources available. Each presents specific challenges to the patient, family, and the treating professionals as described below.

Discharge to Patient's Home without Assistance

Some older patients will indeed achieve a full or nearly full recovery through rehabilitation. Fractured hips heal and patients regain strength after cardiac arrests and mild strokes. It is important, however, for the team and caregivers not to minimize the anxiety created by discharge for patients returning to their former living arrangements. Hospitalization in and of itself instills feelings of vulnerability. Around-the-clock care and hospital-imposed restrictions promote the message that patients need protection. Kubie (1944) spoke about recovering from the "lure of hospital care" as a necessary step toward independence. Rehabilitation teams should facilitate patients' adjustment to discharge by gradually increasing their independence and control in the hospital prior to sending them home. Allowing patients to administer their own medication, eat in the public hospital cafeteria, and experiment with trips outside, particularly to home, will increase self-confidence and decrease fears of re-entry.

Concerns regarding future medical problems often go unarticulated yet contribute to discharge anxiety. Fears of another fall, the likelihood of a second stroke, and the risk of future heart attacks should be addressed whether or not the patient or caregiver can clearly verbalize them. Patients and family members need information about follow-up plans and reassurance that discharge does not mean abandonment by the rehabilitation team. A specific appointment for medical rechecks and a list of emergency phone numbers will convey the staff's ongoing concern for departing patients and their families. Conducting a therapeutic home visit during which select members of the treatment team accompany patients to their homes to assess the environment for accessibility, safety, and maximizing function is another strategy for decreasing discharge anxiety. Having patients experience their revised mobility skills in their home environments and solve tactical problems with the therapists *in vivo* can be tremendously reassuring. In some instances (particularly when a family is viewed to be at risk for complications), a phone call in the first few days after discharge will yield valuable information about initial home adjustment.

Discharge to Patient's Home with Outside Assistance

If outside assistance will be needed to facilitate a home discharge, patients and caregivers must first be made aware of their eligibility for supportive home care. Available services, their costs, and their limitations are generally unknown to patients prior to onset of a disability. Some older patients need to overcome a reluctance to accept community services, particularly if the help is viewed as charity or if its necessity is questioned. Others will struggle with the loss of privacy and invasion of space created by having professionals, or even relatives, in their home on a daily basis. Many will hesitate to hire outside assistance if it means using money previously earmarked for heirs, retirement activities, or emergencies.

In addition to adapting to the idea of outside help, patients need instruction in how to coordinate their home-care plan. Due to scarcity and lack of coordination of services for older adults, a complex discharge plan might involve several different agencies: a home health service for skilled care, a local department on aging for custodial assistance, a transportation setup, and a meals on wheels program are a few examples. Monitoring each component of such a plan takes time as well as consumer advocacy skills. It is important to designate a particular caregiver or relative to coordinate a complex home plan if this task is too overwhelming for the older patient. *Case management programs* for older patients are emerging in some locales to help patients cope with the complexities of home-care services. They combine assistance in coordinating medical and community help with supportive counseling to aid in the adjustment to disability and the hospital discharge.

Learning to get along with a caregiver is another crucial skill necessary for viable home-care plans. A patient who was chronically dissatisfied with nursing care while hospitalized, who failed to establish good working relationships with rehabilitation staff, and who was viewed as demanding or critical is at high risk for major difficulties with outside help at home. Whether the caregiver will be a professional or a relative, rehabilitation teams rarely think about teaching patients to be good employers. There are a multiplicity of factors which are important but often ignored in patient/professional caregiver relationships, such as racial, socioeconomic, and generational differences. Yet, it is a disservice to send patients home without instructions on how to keep their caregivers engaged and satisfied.

At times, professionals who are unfamiliar with available resources, eligibility requirements for assistance, or a particular patient's financial situation, make impossible recommendations about home care, inadvertently creating confusion and adding to discharge anxiety. Insisting on around-the-clock home care when this is obviously unaffordable or unavailable can undermine a posthospital plan. While advocating for more resources in the future, patients, caregivers, and staff have to accept the limitations in services for older adults in the present and work together as a team to make imperfect plans successful.

Discharge to a Relative's Home

The rehabilitation team may view a discharge to a relative's home as ideal for many older patients. Such a plan often simultaneously solves the problem of coordinating complex home-care plans, while providing around-the-clock supervision, preventing premature institutionalization, and reaffirming staff's beliefs in filial responsibility. However, the patient may be more hesitant to embrace the plan. Although living with relatives is generally preferred to institutionalization, most older patients would rather remain in their own homes (Silverstone and Hyman 1976; Stoller 1985). Many older patients mourn the loss of their homes, which are symbols of their independence and hold treasured memories of earlier times. Loss of home also usually involves loss of personal items that cannot fit into the space being provided within a relative's house. Due to hospitalization and illness, the move often takes place without the patient's involvement, furthering the sense of dependence and separation. Relocating also disrupts social contacts and friendships for elders who have already been experiencing gradually constricting support networks. All of these factors contribute to ambivalent feelings in the older patient when faced with joining a relative's household.

The family members, usually adult children, who prepare to have the patient in their homes also face major adjustments. A decision to form a multigenerational household is not the end of discharge planning, but should stimulate many of the same discussions as a discharge to the patient's home. Who will provide care? Will outside assistance be necessary? How will the patient manage with the caregiver? The feelings of any children in the household may inadvertently be ignored, as may the opinions of the adult child's spouse. These family members should be included in the decision-making and planning process during rehabilitation to insure the success of the combined household.

Discharge to a Nursing Home

The most painful discharge plan usually involves a transfer to a nursing home. Since the overriding goal of discharge planning is placement in the *least* restrictive environment, nursing home placement is often viewed as the culmination of a series of failures. These include failure of the patient to progress, failure of the family to provide the needed care, failure of the rehabilitation team to make the patient well, and failure of society to provide more acceptable solutions. Amidst these feelings of disappointment and broken promises, run all of the misconceptions, myths, and negative images of nursing homes. Silverstone and Hyman (1976, 202) point out that

> . . . the very term nursing home conjures up a series of unhappy, even terrifying images in the minds of old and young alike. The words suggest coldness, impersonality, and regimentation at best—at worst, neglect, mistreatment, cruelty, and loneliness.

Furthermore, a commonly held belief is that patients become so demoralized by nursing home placement and substandard care that they give up and die.

Too frequently, rehabilitation teams become less involved with the patient once a decision for nursing home placement is made. This may reflect the professionals' sense of failure or their own aversion to institutionalization. Such withdrawal is particularly unfortunate because it comes at a time when patients and families need even greater support. Also, it subtly reinforces the notion that nursing home placement is offensive and leads to abandonment. The rehabilitation team instead should mobilize to help patients and relatives cope with the transition by preparing them for the nursing home setting and dispelling some of the myths surrounding placement. It is helpful for the treatment team to be aware that research indicates nursing home placement does not imply or cause family breakdown (Bowers 1988). Also, families should know that placement can relieve them of the burden of daily physical care, free them to enjoy the patient's company and allow them to concentrate on providing emotional support (Smith and Bengtson 1979). Placement may also relieve the older person from the chore of maintaining a home and provide an alternative to the social isolation of living alone.

While dispelling myths, the rehabilitation team should remain realistic about the potential problems of nursing home care. Informing families about nursing home residents' rights and building skills for assertive resident advocacy can be invaluable. Further, the staff can stress the continuing need for family members to learn patient care so they can monitor the nursing home personnel. Teaching therapy techniques to families relays the hopeful message that the functional level achieved during rehabilitation can be maintained even if further therapy is not offered at the nursing home. Planning therapeutic passes out of the hospital to the family's home in anticipation of visits outside the extended care center can also provide enormous reassurance and maximize the patient's access to the community in the future. Above all, the involved family members should still be considered caregivers since they will in all likelihood remain involved and continue to play a vital role in the patient's well-being.

MANAGING THE STRESS OF CAREGIVING

It has long been acknowledged that professions which emphasize caregiving (e.g., medical fields, social services, etc.) are inherently stressful and lead to burnout. However, the stress of everyday caregiving to a life partner or relative is often less well appreciated and treated. The descriptor *informal* is frequently used to characterize the care provided by a family, and, unfortunately, it not only implies that such caregiving is easy and automatic, but that the commitment of the relationship somehow compensates for any stress it might generate. This is obviously untrue and rehabilitation professionals are faced with the challenge of understanding and ameliorating the unique aspects of caregiving stress among family members. In the elder population, the increase of chronic illness and long-term care along with families' desire and need to provide assistance gives this area even greater salience.

The impact of caregiving can be quite diverse since the factors involved in the caregiving situation are multifaceted. Care providers are a heterogeneous group as are the disabled loved ones whom they assist. Resources available to buffer the caregiving tasks vary as well. Ultimately, the experience of stress or burden is a subjective appraisal of these many variables by the caregiver (Poulshock and Deimling 1984). These multiple factors and perceptions affirm how individualized the caregiving experience can be.

Caregiving stress can be manifested in a variety of symptoms (Gallagher 1985; Pilisuk and Parks 1988; Schmall and Pratt 1989). Most frequently noted and worrisome are symptoms of anxiety and depression. Caregivers are faced with numerous fears and losses. Among these are fear for their own resources and further impairment in the care recipient, as well as loss of prior roles and expectations. Caregiving for an older adult has also been described as including an inherent grieving process, complicated by lack of finality as the care receiver continues to live in a compromised manner. Gallagher and associates (1989) report nearly a 40 percent prevalence rate of clinical depression in a sample of caregivers, and Stommel and associates (1990) provide evidence that depression significantly affects a caregiver's perception of burden. Aside from depression, ambivalent feelings of guilt, anger, and resentment can surface in the caregiver. Stressed caregivers often report both physical and emotional exhaustion.

Conflict within the family system may also be a manifestation of caregiver stress. Friction between care provider and receiver, role conflict due to competing obligations, or conflict with uninvolved family can occur. Finally, social constriction or isolation may result from caregiving. Care providers frequently intensify their stress by sacrificing leisure time and withdrawing from social occasions to fulfill care demands.

The type of impairment of the disabled older adult is also a significant factor in the experience of caregiver stress. Poulshock and Deimling (1984) note that the burden experienced in caring for a physically impaired elder is qualitatively different from the burden in care of a mentally impaired elder. Houlihan (1987) and Silliman and Sternberg (1988) review and compare these caregiving situations and conclude that greater caregiver burden is experienced when the care receiver is mentally impaired. It follows that more stress is also placed upon the caregiver when the older care receiver is both physically and mentally impaired. Caregiving in the instance of mental impairment is tremendously time consuming as well as labor intensive, due to the need for continuous supervision of the disabled elder. Along with completing physically demanding care tasks, the caregiver is faced with solving complex, amorphous behavioral and cognitive problems which are less frequently resolved with complete, enduring success. Due to personality changes and decreased social skills, the care receiver may be unable to emotionally reciprocate, may become uncooperative, and in fact, could be combative and appear as a stranger to the caregiver. Finally, in the case of a progressive dementia, the lack of reinforcement for caregiving efforts is intensified by the elder's continuing, unpredictable decline.

This review of symptoms of distress in the caregiver and family clearly substantiates the potential for overwhelming stress reactions which lead to caregiver incapacitation and at times unnecessary institutionalization of the disabled elder. Rehabilitation professionals should approach caregiver stress in a remedial as well as a preventative way. Evidence of the symptoms noted above, elder abuse, request for placement of the elder patient, or direct reports of distress from family members should prompt the rehabilitation staff to evaluate and treat caregiver stress as part of their comprehensive care plan. However, some counseling on the stress of caregiving and how to cope with it should be conducted preventatively for all family members when they become caregivers for a disabled elder member.

Caregiver Stress during Hospitalization

Even when a caregiver is not directly assisting the older patient, the stress of caregiving can be present. For example, Schmall and Pratt (1989) note that nursing home placement of a disabled elder does not eliminate feelings of stress for the caregiver, but rather redefines them. Similarly, while a disabled older adult is hospitalized for rehabilitation, stressors are present for the identified caregiver. Tasks of visiting and providing emotional support, planning and coordinating, as well as handling the caregiver's own emotional reaction can be taxing (e.g., Power et al. 1988). The emotional position and stresses experienced by caregivers at this point are significantly dependent upon the recency and longevity of their caregiving role. If the rehabilitation stay follows an acute hospitalization in which a disabling illness has just been diagnosed (e.g., stroke), caregivers may be newly identifying their roles, acutely reacting to the dependence of the disabled loved one, and anticipating the work of providing care after discharge. In contrast, if the rehabilitation stay comes in the midst of a chronic disability where caregiving patterns are already established, caregivers are coping with different tasks—perhaps the fatigue of sustained caregiving responsibilities, or the stress of considering a new discharge placement.

Caregiver fatigue is often a prominent stressor continuing throughout a rehabilitation hospitalization, regardless of the duration of disability. Caregivers who have coped with a disabled elder in the community for some time may use a hospitalization as a partial respite. This is often adaptive and absence of the caregiver during the hospital stay should not be misinterpreted as abandonment of the patient. Caregivers who are experiencing a new onset of disability and have yet to assume full responsibility for patient management may be entering a rehabilitation phase of hospitalization after an exhausting acute care period where vigilance and personal support of the patient were quite high. In this instance, strategies for stress management may focus on helping caregivers retreat to a position of less intensity and begin to concentrate on their own needs. This may involve counseling them to return to daily routines in at least a modified form or inquiring into the status of basic personal needs, such as getting adequate rest and nutrition (especially important for the older caregiver). Other practical issues may also be appropriately addressed, such as temporarily delegating responsibilities within the family to ease the work of the caregiver. In the instance of an older caregiver, simply facilitating safe, effective transportation to and from the hospital for visits and staff consultation can be significant.

These types of interventions help to re-establish a sense of normalcy and competence within the family (Power 1988).

Helping the caregiver achieve an appropriate balance of involvement with the
disabled elder is central to stress management and can begin during the inpatient
rehabilitation stay. While the elder is hospitalized, this balance of involvement
will be demonstrated by how readily the caregiver can engage to learn care tasks
and support the patient, yet also disengage and delegate responsibilities in order
to meet personal needs. Seeing how this difficult balance is negotiated provides
an opportunity for the rehabilitation team to work with the caregiver to anticipate problems and plan for long-term management. This is particularly relevant
in the care of older adults whose needs will invariably increase with time.

Sometimes caregivers will be reluctant to focus on their own stress. Their
value system may dictate against seeking outside help for emotional issues, or
attention to themselves may feel irrelevant or misplaced away from the patient.
A persistent effort may be required to engage the caregiver in a credible, supportive relationship and demonstrate the importance of outside support to their
long-term effectiveness.

It is critical for the rehabilitation team to be sensitive to the caregivers' perspective and appreciate the dilemmas facing them. Most often, a family enters
rehabilitation treatment in a highly selfless mode, very motivated to help their
disabled elder. They are then asked to refocus on themselves for the sake of
managing stress, perhaps before they have emotionally understood the long-term
nature of their situation and the ramifications of failing to do so. The treatment
team needs to understand this dilemma and the potential for caregivers to experience double messages in the process of planning and handling their stress.
Learning the many necessary care tasks can ultimately be experienced as, "Do
all of this, but remember your limits and don't forget to meet your own needs
too." Being aware of contradictory messages and discerning the individual
caregiver's needs are important tasks for team members in helping to predict and
manage the stress of care provision. Supportive repetition of the simple fact that
everyone has limited time and energy can be helpful when caregivers' unrealistic expectations of themselves surface. Finally, it is important to relate the
caregiver's receiving or accepting of help directly to the well-being of the disabled elder. Employing the advice, "You will only be helpful to your loved one
in as much as you help yourself," will draw upon the caregivers' motivation to
do the best they can for the elder family member by also managing their own
needs.

Forms of Stress Management for Caregivers

A number of intervention formats have been applied to support caregivers of
disabled older adults. Many of these interventions developed out of the need to

help caregivers of demented elders, and, as the need has escalated, research has significantly lagged behind their use. The critical parameters and overall effectiveness of treatments as well as their differential use are only now being fully explored and evaluated. Considering these limitations, the following discussion will review individual, family, group, and respite interventions (also see Gatz et al. 1990).

Individual/Family Intervention

One-to-one psychotherapy with the stressed caregiver allows for personally tailored intervention and maximal attention to the individual during each session. Zarit and associates (1983) promote the value of individual intervention when caregivers first seek help, stressing that they are most needy at this point. They further advocate use of family meetings during the course of individual therapy to broaden the base of support for the caregiver and facilitate some distribution of care tasks. Schmall and Pratt (1989) also support the importance of family sessions and further discuss the advantages of involving the disabled elder. Gallagher (1985) describes the efficacy of individual treatment with caregivers when depression is a prominent feature of the stress reaction.

A variety of theoretical approaches have been employed in individual therapy for caregivers, ranging from more cognitive behavioral and skill building approaches to more dynamic, emotionally expressive formats. Most reports describe short-term intervention. Techniques utilized with group interventions have been used in individual therapy as well, emphasizing the need for support, education, and skill building.

Therapeutic work for management of caregiver stress which emphasizes the efficacy of emotional expression to resolve ambivalent feelings and facilitate grief has been largely conducted on an individual basis. An individual format may be more readily conducive to this potentially intense type of therapeutic interaction. Schmidt and associates (1988) compared an individual approach involving support and problem solving to one of support, problem solving, and expressive work (facilitating exploration of anger and grief) in treating caregivers of demented older adults. They found the addition of the expressive therapy component to be superior but qualified their results as preliminary and questioned the advisability of the indiscriminate use of this technique for any caregiver or stress-related problem.

Group Intervention

Professionally led and self-help groups are frequently used in stress management for caregivers. Group interventions are uniquely effective in their ability to normalize caregiver reactions and provide social support and peer level advice (Schmall and Pratt 1989). They may also be used as a vehicle for sensitizing caregivers to general aging issues and counteracting stereotypic attitudes through the use of discussion, media presentations, and experiential exercises. A diversity of formats can be employed in these groups, although most are fairly structured and take a supportive, educational approach. In a review of group interventions, Toseland and Rossiter (1989) describe several recurrent themes in group discussion: information about caregiving and home care skills, developing a support system in and out of the group, the emotional impact of caregiving and self-care, and difficult interpersonal problems. Occasionally, groups are employed to teach specific stress and behavior management principles, such as assertion and relaxation training and coaching in strategies for problem behavior.

Some group formats are designed to combine both structured and unstructured time, beginning each session with a didactic presentation, followed by a break for socializing, and reconvening the group for unstructured discussion intended to facilitate emotional exploration and support (Houlihan 1987). Schmall and Pratt (1989) highlight a number of parameters which may be of therapeutic significance in successful group intervention such as, group leadership (peer versus professional), group composition (homogenous versus heterogeneous), format (discussed above), length, and other eligibility criteria for participants. While caregiver support groups are universally applauded for their efforts and favorably evaluated by participants, their impact upon more objective indices of caregiver burden/stress has yet to be conclusively substantiated (Toseland and Rossiter 1989; Zarit and Toseland 1989).

Respite Intervention

Respite is broadly defined as temporary transfer of responsibility for the disabled elder to an alternate caregiver or caregiving system in order to relieve the stress of the primary caretaker. Respite interventions run a wide gamut of services. Schmall and Pratt (1989) organize the variations in respite care by characteristics of in-home or out-of-home, short- or long-term, emergency or planned, and professional or volunteer. This full spectrum conceptualization covers commonly offered options of attendant or day care as well as less frequently available total respite in which the disabled elder is temporarily housed in an extended care facility. Gallagher (1985) notes that preliminary evidence suggests the efficacy of the concept of respite, but it is questionable whether it can be said to delay institutionalization of an older disabled person. In addition, effectively matching characteristics of caregivers and disabled older adults with beneficial forms of respite is not fully understood. For example, Burdz, Eaton and Bond (1988) found a two-week nursing home respite to be beneficial for both demented and nondemented elders and their caregivers, despite their initial hypothesis that the demented patients would not tolerate the temporary relocation very well. However, not all members of the respite group reported positive consequences and the authors caution against its indiscriminate use in cases of demented elder care.

The expense and limited availability of a full range of respite services are primary obstacles to this form of caregiver stress management. Initial research suggests fears of excessive public financial burden and overutilization by caregivers are unwarranted. Lawton and associates (1989a) did not find caregivers to excessively depend upon respite service when it was made available, nor did its use decrease care provision by the family's informal support network. Schmall and Pratt (1989) emphasize the need to begin to use respite earlier in treatment of caregiver stress as a more preventative rather than remedial measure. It is often a resource of last resort, becoming too little, too late. Caregivers are frequently resistant to its use, interpreting such services as intrusive or implying failure of their ability to cope (Dell Orto 1988; Montgomery and Borgatta 1989; Schmall and Pratt 1989). Along with advocating increased availability of options for respite, rehabilitation professionals must educate caregivers to their effective use as viable treatment options for their stress (Lawton et al. 1989b).

Differential Use of Interventions for Caregiver Stress Management

The interventions described above to help manage caregiver stress are receiving qualified, preliminary support as beneficial in the short-term, although research is often more impressionistic than rigorous. But discriminating when and with whom they are effectively used remains even more a clinical art than science. More research is required to delineate the therapeutic mechanisms of each form of intervention, who benefits from their use, and at what point in the caregiving process (Gallagher 1985).

A number of initial hypotheses have been suggested to begin this research and aid the clinician currently faced with differential prescription. For example, Houlihan (1987) concludes that caregivers of frail older adults primarily need relief from the actual burden of care tasks, while caregivers of demented older persons require additional support to meet their emotional needs and manage the elder's disordered behavior. Regarding the importance of caregiver characteristics in dictating intervention, research suggests that women (the more frequent caregiver) report more caregiver stress than men, particularly among younger, adult child caregivers (Barusch and Spaid 1989; Krause and Markides 1987; Young and Kahana 1989).

In reference to timing of interventions, Gallagher (1985) hypothesizes the need to focus on enhancing coping skills in initial stages of caregiving and on facilitating expression of grief as caregiving proceeds to the latter stages of a progressively debilitating illness (such as dementia). Similarly, Toseland and associates (1989) hypothesize about the merit of providing caregivers with educative, structured group intervention at first, followed by a variety of optional treatments (booster sessions, individual, group, or family) for those who wish to explore caregiving issues in greater depth. Zarit and his colleagues (1983, 1987) in their work with the caregivers of dementia patients suggest a series of limited individual sessions initially, including a family meeting, followed by use of a support group for ongoing stress management. This approach follows the principle discussed by others (Clark and Rakowski 1983; Haley et al. 1987; Steinberg et al. 1989) that, particularly for a disability as encompassing as dementia, an isolated intervention is of limited power and should be embedded in a multifaceted program.

These conclusions must be viewed as preliminary and suggestive. There are a myriad of potential variables yet to be considered in more fully discriminating effective interventions for caregiver stress, such as shared versus separate living arrangements (Deimling et al. 1989), the psychological stage of caregiving, as well as other caregiver characteristics (Clark and Rakowski 1983). The future will, hopefully, bring a richer, clearer understanding of how caregivers can be helped to optimize their ability to care for their loved ones and manage the inevitable stress that it entails.

CAREGIVERS AS SURROGATE DECISION MAKERS

Often professionals in a rehabilitation setting find themselves discussing issues with legal/ethical implications as older patients or their families emotionally react to a disability, decide upon treatments, or plan for the future. The physician's interaction with the patient and family is important for critical information exchange in medical decision making regarding risk, prognosis, and so on, but allied treating staff can often serve the function of a secondary processing agent. Families and patients may perceive other members of the treatment team as more available and less threatening as they weigh alternatives or attempt to plan for an uncertain future. Such issues as advance directives and guardianship arise with increasing frequency as the patient population in the rehabilitation setting changes. Older and more severely disabled patients are admitted for rehabilitation in growing numbers, and questions of personal autonomy, level of supervision, and quality of life are more frequently asked. Thus, it is imperative that members of the rehabilitation team acquaint themselves with general legal concepts and broad ethical principles so that they may effectively support older patients and their families as they make important medical care decisions (e.g., Brown 1989).

The following discussion comments on some legal directives and underlying emotional/ethical issues regarding control and decision making as they apply to the rehabilitation setting. This review is intended to raise rehabilitation professionals' awareness and facilitate their interaction with older adults and their families. Exhibit 12-1 provides definitions of five medical/legal transactions which frequently arise within the rehabilitation setting. These include mechanisms for providing advance directives and appointing a surrogate decision maker. The concepts are defined in rather broad terms because their details are currently being refined through precedent-setting court cases and legislation governing each can vary from state to state.

Guardianship

Power of attorney and guardianship are perhaps more frequently encountered and commonly understood than other decision-making issues. Iris (1988) provides a thorough review of the decision-making process for guardianship and older adults, describing the roles of the family, attorneys, doctors, and the court. In the rehabilitation setting, the concept of and need for guardianship often arises when counseling the older patient's family regarding long-term treatment and management plans.

Guardianship becomes most pertinent when there are no family or friends to assume the role or when older, incompetent patients resist treatment and the need for supervision necessary for their well-being. In such cases, treating professionals may also be dealing more directly with the elders, absorbing their feelings of anger at having personal autonomy compromised or fears that others will abuse such power over them. A determination of incompetence does not eliminate the need to process such emotional reactions with older patients and promote their best possible understanding and acceptance of the guardianship concept.

Finally, it is also important to recognize that many families and their elder members arrive at *natural guardianship* arrangements that do not require outside legal sanction. These are the family units where trust and role flexibility have allowed for the implicit transfer of responsibilities for care and protection from parent to child, aunt to nephew, sibling to sibling, and so on. Such a process is adaptive and clearly preferred (President's Commission 1982), and it is primarily in its breakdown that external structuring is imposed.

Surrogate Decision Making

Contemporary standards for use of advance directives and surrogate decision making are influenced by the prevailing opinions of the current older generation. In brief, today's elders largely believe in the responsibility of family members to look out for one another. Older adults perceive their families as duty-bound by

Exhibit 12-1 Medical/Legal Transactions

Do Not Resuscitate (DNR)

An advance medical directive written by a patient's physician stating that resuscitation will not be attempted in the event of cardiac arrest considering the unlikely probability of a positive outcome and the trauma of the procedure. DNR orders arose from the concern that resuscitation procedures were being too frequently used with questionable benefit to the overall well-being of patients.

Power of Attorney

A document in which one individual ("the principal") empowers another ("the agent") to act in his place under specific circumstances. A power of attorney can be limited or broad in its scope and can be revoked by the principal at any time.

Guardianship*

When an individual is judged to be incompetent, a guardian is appointed by a court of law. The legal process confers upon the guardian the right and authority to make a range of decisions for a ward (the incompetent patient). Guardianships can be limited to decisions regarding estate (such as financial matters) or can include decisions regarding the person (such as living arrangements and health care). In addition, special guardianship arrangements can be fashioned by the court to meet the specific needs of the ward.

Living Will

An advance written directive in which an individual may indicate a preference for no extraordinary life sustaining procedures which serve only to artificially prolong the dying process should death be certain and imminent. Living wills have various conditions which must be satisfied in order for the directive to have legal effect. Perhaps their greatest value has been as a stimulus for discussion between patient and practitioners about decisions to forego life-sustaining treatment.

Durable Power of Attorney

An advance proxy directive in which an agent is specified to act (i.e., make decisions) on one's behalf. A durable power of attorney can be specified for a variety of decisions, including health care matters. A durable power of attorney for health care is considered more flexible and powerful than a living will since a decision maker rather than specific decisions are designated. It can be tailored to the unique needs and circumstances of the individual and can be used for a broader range of health care decisions than only those pertaining to imminent death.

*In some states, the term *conservatorship* is used in place of guardianship. Conservatorship may or may not confer the same powers as guardianship; local legislation should be reviewed for specific distinctions.

Sources: Baker and Finkel 1988; Dejowski 1987; Mishkin 1987; President's Commission 1983; Storto 1989.

tradition to become decision makers for them in the event of incapacitation. Such a perception of responsibility appears to apply regardless of level of intimacy, affection, or even knowledge of preferences. High (1988, 1990) and High and Turner (1987) offer evidence of such beliefs in their study of older adults' views on surrogate decision making. They conclude that elders have an implicit hierarchy of preferred substitute decision makers, starting with spouses and children and ending with outside professionals (i.e., doctors, lawyers). Further, they found that older adults prefer less formal arrangements for appointing surrogate decision makers, tacit understandings with them regarding their choices, and congregate decision making among family members.

These preferences are both informative and perplexing as they present the rehabilitation professional with several possible dilemmas. The treatment team may be faced with poorly prepared families, variously informed as to their elder member's true wishes, who must come to agreement as a group. Not only is this traumatic and time-consuming, but it may also be highly conflictual, depending upon the emotional health of the family. Nevertheless, rehabilitation professionals need to be sensitive to the subtle, complex dynamics of the older person's view of advance directives and family involvement. Premature or poorly prepared presentation of formalized directives and documents can be misinterpreted as usurping family autonomy.

The reports of the President's Commission for the Study of Ethical Problems in Medicine and Biomedical and Behavioral Research (1982, 1983) attest to the prevailing opinion that the family is critically important to the process of informed consent and surrogate decision making in medical settings. Informed consent is ideally viewed as an active, shared decision-making process between patient and practitioner that can be improved by the involvement of interested family members to promote accuracy of information, help desensitize the patient to threatening material, and facilitate decision making. In cases of patient incapacitation and need for surrogate decision making, the Commission also designates the family as a viable autonomous social unit with decision-making powers for its members. However, *family* is broadly defined to include intimate friends, and exception is taken to the family's pre-eminence if their desires are suspected to conflict with patients' values or fail to promote their well-being.

Two standards for surrogate decision making are delineated by the Commission: the standard of *substituted judgment* and the standard of *best interests*. Substituted judgment attempts to duplicate the choices that the patient would make if competent. Legally and ethically, this standard imposes some restrictions upon the proxy decision maker and can only be followed if there is prior knowledge of the patient's values, life goals, and desires, communicated verbally or in writing. Although the ideal standard, the ability of a proxy (particularly a person not necessarily chosen by the patient) to accurately reproduce the desires of the incapacitated patient is not fully substantiated (e.g., Zweibel and

Cassel 1989). However, recent research suggests that accuracy may be enhanced by careful wording of the decision for the proxy (e.g., how would the impaired elder make this decision if that were possible?) (Tomlinson et al. 1990).

The best interests standard serves as an alternative when substituted judgment is not possible. This standard refers to decisions made on the basis of promoting the welfare of the average person (by usual social norms), taking into account relief of suffering, preservation and restoration of functioning, and quality and extent of life sustained. The Commission recommends that proxy decisions be made on the basis of substituted judgment whenever possible and that when incompetent patients are able to communicate, their participation in decisions should still be encouraged despite the fact that their wishes may be overridden. It is important for rehabilitation professionals to be cognizant of these recommendations and standards when guiding a family through the process of surrogate decision making. Ethical principles of autonomy and fairness can thus be respected.

Resolving questions of informed consent and substitute decision making are difficult and often highly emotionally charged. Knowledge of ethical principles (Lo 1990) and legal options can assist a treatment team in accurately clarifying conflicts over decision making among patient, family, and staff, rather than simply explaining them away as poor motivation, resistance, or even incompetence. Guidelines proposed to deal with ethical dilemmas highlight the chronic tension that exists between individual autonomy and medical beneficence, and clinicians are often faced with the difficult task of negotiating these troubled waters with patients and families. In actuality, many such questions are resolved by accurate, empathic communication and accommodation in order to find a comfortable, common ground for patient, family, and treatment team. This is no small matter in the rehabilitation setting, given the anxiety raised by these questions and the diversity of opinions voiced in an interdisciplinary team. Nevertheless, the preferred path to resolution is within the confines of interpersonal relationships (be they patient/practitioner or family/practitioner) where the risk of objectification of the patient can be minimized (Jecker 1990).

CONCLUSION

The families of disabled older adults present themselves at the rehabilitation setting with varying degrees of understanding of potential caregiving roles, the resources available to them, and the stress of providing ongoing assistance. Their emotional reactions to disability and caregiving are individualized and must be discerned and worked through in order to make critical decisions and provide a viable discharge plan for their elder members. Caregivers are vital members of the rehabilitation team. They are, in essence, the patient behind the patient who the rehabilitation team must include in their efforts. Data continue to substantiate that most care of older adults is informal and centered in the family. Resources to assist caregivers are scarce and advocacy for public subsidy in the future is necessary. With appropriate help from rehabilitation professionals and linkages within the community, caregivers can assume their roles appropriately and assist disabled older adults to live with respect and comfort.

REFERENCES

Accreditation Manual for Hospitals. 1989. Chicago: Joint Commission on Accreditation of Health Care Organizations.

Baker, F.M., and S.I. Finkel. 1988. Legal issues in geriatric psychiatry. In *Essentials of Geriatric Psychiatry: A Guide for Health Professionals*, edited by L.W. Lazarus, 214–29. New York: Springer Publishing Co.

Barusch, A.S., and W.M. Spaid. 1989. Gender differences in caregiving: Why do wives report greater burden? *The Gerontologist* 29: 667–76.

Blenkner, M. 1965. Social work and family relationships in later life. In *Social Structure and the Family: Gerontological Relations*, edited by E. Shanas and G. Strieb. Englewood Cliffs, N.J.: Prentice Hall.

Bowers, J.B. 1988. Family perceptions of care in a nursing home. *The Gerontologist* 28: 361–8.

Bray, G.P. 1987. Family adaptation to chronic illness. In *Rehabilitation Psychology Desk Reference*, edited by B. Caplan, 171–83. Gaithersburg, Md.: Aspen Publishers.

Brody, E.M. 1986. Informal support systems in the rehabilitation of the disabled elderly. In *Aging and Rehabilitation: Advances in the State of the Art*, edited by S.J. Brody and G.E. Ruff, 87–103. New York: Springer Publishing Co.

Brody, E.M. 1985. Parent care as a normative family stress. *The Gerontologist* 25: 19–29.

Brody, E.M. 1979. Aging parents and aging children. In *Aging Parents*, edited by P.K. Ragan, 267–87. Los Angeles, Calif.: University of Southern California Press.

Brown, R.N. 1989. *The Rights of Older Persons*, 2nd ed. Carbondale, Ill.: Southern Illinois University Press.

Burdz, M.P., W.O. Eaton, and J.B. Bond. 1988. Effect of respite care on dementia and nondementia patients and their caregivers. *Psychology and Aging* 3: 38–42.

Callahan, D. 1985. What do children owe elderly parents? *The Hastings Center Report* 15: 32–7.

Cantor, M.H. 1979. Neighbors and friends. *Research on Aging* 1: 434–63.

Clark, N.M., and W. Rakowski. 1983. Family caregivers of older adults: Improving helping skills. *The Gerontologist* 23: 637–42.

Corgiat, M.D. 1990. Assessment and treatment of disabled families in geriatric rehabilitation. In *Geriatric Rehabilitation*, edited by B. Kemp, K. Brummel-Smith, and J.W. Ramsdell, 307–24. Boston: Little, Brown and Co.

Coulton, C.J., R.E. Dunkle, M. Haug, et al. 1989. Locus of control and decision-making for posthospital care. *The Gerontologist* 29: 627–32.

Deimling, G.T., D.M. Bass, A.L. Townsend, et al. 1989. Care-related stress: A comparison of spouse and adult-child caregivers in shared and separate households. *Journal of Aging and Health* 1: 67–82.

Dejowski, E. 1987. Financial planning. In *The Encyclopedia of Aging*, edited by G.L. Maddox, 257. New York: Springer Publishing Co.

Dell Orto, A.E. 1988. Respite care: A vehicle for hope, the buffer against desperation. In *Family Interventions Throughout Chronic Illness and Disability*, edited by P.W. Power, A.E. Dell Orto, and M.B. Gibbons, 265–84. New York: Springer Publishing Co.

Dewitt, D.J., A.V. Wister, and T.K. Burch. 1988. Physical distance and social contact between elders and their adult children. *Research on Aging* 10: 56–80.

Gallagher, D.E. 1985. Intervention strategies to assist caregivers of frail elders: Current research status and future research directions. In *Annual Review of Gerontology and Geriatrics*, vol. 5, edited by C. Eisdorfer, 249–82. New York: Springer Publishing Co.

Gallagher, D., J. Rose, P. Rivera, et al. 1989. Prevalence of depression in family caregivers. *The Gerontologist* 29: 449–56.

Gatz, M., V.L. Bengtson, and M.J. Blum. 1990. Caregiving families. In *Handbook of The Psychology of Aging*, 3d ed, edited by J.E. Birren and K.W. Schaie, 404–26. New York: Academic Press.

Haley, W.E., S.L. Brown, and E.G. Levine. 1987. Experimental evaluation of the effectiveness of group intervention for dementia caregivers. *The Gerontologist* 27: 376–82.

High, D.M. 1990. Who will make health care decisions for me when I can't? *Journal of Aging and Health* 2: 291–309.

High, D.M. 1988. All in the family: Extended autonomy and expectations in surrogate health care decision-making. *The Gerontologist* 28, Suppl.: 46–51.

High, D.M., and H.B. Turner. 1987. Surrogate decision-making: The elderly's familial expectations. *Theoretical Medicine* 8: 303–20.

Hirschfield, I.S., and H. Dennis. 1979. Perspectives. In *Aging Parents*, edited by P.K. Ragan, 1–10. Los Angeles, Calif.: University of Southern California Press.

Horowitz, A. 1985. Family caregiving to the frail elderly. In *Annual Review of Gerontology and Geriatrics*, vol. 5, edited by C. Eisdorfer, M.P. Lawton, and G.L. Maddox, 194–246. New York: Springer Publishing Co.

Horowitz, A., and L.W. Shindelman. 1983. Reciprocity and affection: Past influences on current care. *Journal of Gerontological Social Work* 5: 5–20.

Houlihan, J.P. 1987. Families caring for frail and demented elderly: A review of selected findings. *Family Systems Medicine* 5: 344–56.

Iris, M.A. 1988. Guardianship and the elderly: A multiperspective view of the decisionmaking process. *The Gerontologist* 28, Suppl.: 39–45.

Jecker, N.S. 1990. The role of intimate others in medical decision making. *The Gerontologist* 30: 65–71.

Krause, N., and K. Markides. 1987. Illness of spouse and psychological well-being in older adults. *Comprehensive Gerontology Bulletin* 1: 105–8.

Kubie, L.S. 1944. Motivation of rehabilitation. Proceedings of the conference of the Committee on Public Health Relations of the New York Academy of Medicine.

Lawton, M.P., E.M. Brody, and A.R. Saperstein. 1990. Social, behavioral, and environmental issues. In *Aging and Rehabilitation II: The State of the Practice*, edited by S.J. Brody and L.G. Pawlson, 133–149. New York: Springer Publishing Co.

Lawton, M.P., E.M. Brody, and A.R. Saperstein. 1989a. A controlled study of respite service for caregivers of Alzheimer's patients. *The Gerontologist* 29: 8–16.

Lawton, M.P., E.M. Brody, A. Saperstein, et al. 1989b. Respite services for caregivers: Research findings for service planning. *Home Health Care Services Quarterly* 10: 5–32.

Lo, B. 1990. Ethical issues in rehabilitation. In *Geriatric Rehabilitation*, edited by B. Kemp, K. Brummel-Smith, and J.W. Ramsdell, 405–16. Boston: Little, Brown and Co.

Mathews, S.H. 1987. Provision of care to old parents: Division of responsibility among adult children. *Research on Aging* 9: 45–60.

The Medicare Handbook. 1989. Publication no. HCFA 10050. Baltimore: U.S. Department of Health and Human Services.

Mishkin, B. 1987. Living wills and other directives for health care. In *The Encyclopedia of Aging*, edited by G.L. Maddox, 405–6. New York: Springer Publishing Co.

Montgomery, R.J.V., and E.F. Borgatta. 1989. The effects of alternative support strategies on family caregiving. *The Gerontologist* 29: 457–64.

Moore, S.T. 1987. The capacity to care: A family focused approach to social work practice with the disabled elderly. In *Gerontological Social Work with Families: A Guide to Practice Issues and Service Delivery*, edited by R. Dobrof, 79–97. New York: Hayworth Press.

Peterson, J.A. 1979. The relationships of middle-aged children and their parents. In *Aging Parents*, edited by P.K. Ragan, 27–36. Los Angeles, Calif.: University of Southern California Press.

Pilisuk, M., and S.H. Parks. 1988. Caregiving: Where families need help. *Social Work* 33: 436–40.

Poulshock, S.W., and G.T. Deimling. 1984. Families caring for elders in residence: Issues in the measurement of burden. *Journal of Gerontology* 39: 230–9.

Power, P.W. 1988. An intervention model for families of the disabled. In *Family Interventions Throughout Chronic Illness and Disability*, edited by P.W. Power, A.E. Dell Orto, and M.B. Gibbons, 24–43. New York: Springer Publishing Co.

Power, P.W., A.E. Dell Orto, and M.B. Gibbons, eds. 1988. *Family Interventions Throughout Chronic Illness and Disability*. New York: Springer Publishing Co.

Pratt, C.C., and A.J. Kethley. 1988. Aging and family caregiving in the future: Implications for education and policy. *Educational Gerontology* 14: 567–76.

President's Commission for the Study of Ethical Problems in Medicine and Biomedical and Behavioral Research. 1983. *Deciding to Forego Life-Sustaining Treatment*. Washington, D.C.: Government Printing Office.

President's Commission for the Study of Ethical Problems in Medicine and Biomedical and Behavioral Research. 1982. *Making Health Care Decisions*. Washington, D.C.: Government Printing Office.

Schmall, V.L., and C.C. Pratt. 1989. Family caregiving and aging: Strategies for support. *Journal of Psychotherapy and The Family* 5: 71–87.

Schmidt, G.L., M.J. Bonjean, A.C. Widem, et al. 1988. Brief psychotherapy for caregivers of demented relatives: Comparison of two therapeutic strategies. *Clinical Gerontologist* 7: 109–25.

Schoonover, C.B., E.M. Brody, C. Hoffman, et al. 1988. Parent care and geographically distant children. *Research on Aging* 10: 472–92.

Shanas, E. 1979. Social myth as hypothesis: The case of the family relations of older people. *The Gerontologist* 19: 3–9.

Silliman, R.A., and J. Sternberg. 1988. Family caregiving: Impact of patient functioning and underlying causes of dependency. *The Gerontologist* 28: 377–82.

Silverstone, B., and H.K. Hyman. 1976. *You and Your Aging Parent*. New York: Pantheon Books.

Smith, K.F., and V.L. Bengtson. 1979. Positive consequences of institutionalization: Solidarity between elderly parents and their middle-aged children. *The Gerontologist* 19: 166–74.

Smith, V.J., and C.M. Messikomer. 1988. A role for the family in geriatric rehabilitation. *Topics in Geriatric Rehabilitation* 4: 8–15.

Steinberg, G., E. Shulman, M. Mittelman, et al. 1989. *Alzheimer's Disease Caregiver Well-Being, A Treatment Strategy*. Poster presented at the 42nd meeting of the Gerontological Society of America, Minneapolis, Minn.

Stoller, E.P. 1985. Elder-caregiver relationships in shared households. *Research on Aging* 7: 175–93.

Stommel, M., C.W. Given, and B. Given. 1990. Depression as an overriding variable explaining caregiver burdens. *Journal of Aging and Health* 2: 81–102.

Storto, D. 1989. Personal communication.

Tennstedt, S.L., J.B. McKinlay, and L.M. Sullivan. 1989. Informal care for frail elders: The role of secondary caregivers. *The Gerontologist* 29: 677–83.

Tomlinson, T., K. Howe, M. Notman, et al. 1990. An empirical study of proxy consent for elderly persons. *The Gerontologist* 30: 54–64.

Toseland, R.W., and C.M. Rossiter. 1989. Group interventions to support family caregivers: A review and analysis. *The Gerontologist* 29: 438–48.

Toseland, R.W., C.M. Rossiter, and M.S. Labrecque. 1989. The effectiveness of peer-led and professionally-led groups to support family caregivers. *The Gerontologist* 29: 465–71.

Treas, J. 1979. Intergenerational families and social change. In *Aging Parents*, edited by P.K. Ragan, 58–65. Los Angeles, Calif.: University of Southern California Press.

Troll, L., S. Miller, and R. Atchley. 1979. *Families in Later Life*. Belmont, Calif.: Wadsworth.

Versluys, H.P. 1980. Physical rehabilitation and family dynamics. *Rehabilitation Literature* 41: 58–65.

Weishaus, S. 1979. Aging is a family affair. In *Aging Parents*, edited by P.K. Ragan, 154–74. Los Angeles, Calif.: University of Southern California Press.

Young, R.F., and E. Kahana. 1989. Specifying caregiver outcomes: Gender and relationship aspects of caregiving strain. *The Gerontologist* 29: 660–6.

Zarit, S.H., and R.W. Toseland. 1989. Current and future direction in family caregiving research. *The Gerontologist* 29: 481–3.

Zarit, S.H., C.R. Anthony, and M. Boutselis. 1987. Interventions with care givers of dementia patients: Comparison of two approaches. *Psychology and Aging* 2: 225–32.

Zarit, S.H., N.K. Orr, and J.M. Zarit. 1983. *Working with Families of Dementia Victims: A Treatment Manual*, vol. 4, Washington, D.C.: Department of Health and Human Services U.S. Government Printing Office.

Zweibel, N.R., and C.K. Cassel. 1989. Treatment choices at the end of life: A comparison of decisions by older patients and their physician-selected proxies. *The Gerontologist* 29: 615–21.

Index